VENICE

This book is a sweeping historical portrait of the floating city of Venice from its foundations to the present day. Joanne M. Ferraro considers Venice's unique construction within an amphibious environment and identifies the Asian, European, and North African exchange networks that made it a vibrant and ethnically diverse Mediterranean cultural center. Incorporating recent scholarly insights, the author discusses key themes related to the city's social, cultural, religious, and environmental history, as well as its politics and economy. A refuge and a pilgrim stop; an international emporium and center of manufacture; a mecca of spectacle, theater, music, gambling, and sexual experimentation, and an artistic and architectural marvel, Venice's allure springs eternal in every phase of the city's fascinating history.

Joanne M. Ferraro is professor and chair of the Department of History at San Diego State University. She is the author of *Family and Public Life in Brescia, 1580–1650: The Foundations of Power in the Venetian State* (Cambridge University Press, 1993); *Marriage Wars in Late Renaissance Venice* (2001), which was named best book by the Society for the Study of Early Modern Women and was awarded the Helen and Howard R. Marraro Prize in Italian History; and *Nefarious Crimes, Contested Justice: Illicit Sex and Infanticide in the Republic of Venice, 1557–1789* (2008).

VENICE

History of the Floating City

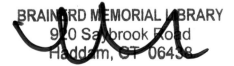

JOANNE M. FERRARO
San Diego State University

CAMBRIDGE
UNIVERSITY PRESS

CAMBRIDGE UNIVERSITY PRESS
Cambridge, New York, Melbourne, Madrid, Cape Town,
Singapore, São Paulo, Delhi, Mexico City

Cambridge University Press
32 Avenue of the Americas, New York, NY 10013-2473, USA

www.cambridge.org
Information on this title: www.cambridge.org/9780521883597

First published 2012

Printed in the United States of America

A catalog record for this publication is available from the British Library.

Library of Congress Cataloging in Publication data
Ferraro, Joanne Marie, 1951–
Venice : history of the floating city / Joanne M. Ferraro.
p.   cm.
Includes bibliographical references and index.
ISBN 978-0-521-88359-7 (hardback)
1.   Venice (Italy) – History.   I. Title.
DG676.F47   2012
945'.311–dc23   2012007348

ISBN 978-0-521-88359-7 Hardback

For Elsa Dalla Venezia

CONTENTS

List of Plates   *page* ix

List of Illustrations   xi

List of Maps   xiii

Acknowledgments   xv

Preface   xvii

Chronology of Historical Events   xxiii

1   Reconstructing the Floating City   1

2   The Riches of Asia, Europe, and North Africa   29

3   A Pride of Lions   51

4   Identities and Modes of Socialization   75

5   Material Life   106

6   City of Myth   125

7   The Serenissima's Wayward Subjects   151

8   The Baroque Stage   174

9   Epilogue: The Tides of Change   201

Appendix I. Approximate Population of Venice during the Republic   215

Appendix II. Population of the Historic Center of Venice, 1871–2010   216

Glossary   217

Notes   225

Bibliography   231

Index   241

PLATES

Plates follow page xxxii.

    I Mosaics (1280). Porta di Sant'Alipio, Basilica San Marco

   II Apse, Santa Maria Donato. Murano

  III Ca' Farsetti

  IV Aerial View of Basilica Domes and Palazzo

   V Lunette with the Four Evangelists over the Porta di Sant' Alipio, Basilica San Marco

  VI The Palazzo Ducale

 VII Church of San Giovanni e Paolo and the Scuola di San Marco

VIII Fondaco dei Tedeschi

  IX Street Signs Indicating the Old and New Ghettos; Tall Building in the Ghetto Nuovo

   X Italian Synagogue (Schola Italiana) in the Ghetto Nuovo

  XI Ca' D'Oro

 XII Ca' Loredan, Now Palazzo Vendramin-Calergi

XIII The Mint and the Library of Saint Mark's on the Piazzetta San Marco

XIV Church of San Giorgio Maggiore

 XV Church of Santa Maria della Salute and Southwest End of Piazza San Marco, Renovated under Napoleon

XVI Aerial Photo of Venice, 2011

ILLUSTRATIONS

1   San Giacometto di Rialto   *page* 7
2   *Joseph Gathering Up All the Food*, Byzantine mosaic,
    thirteenth century CE   13
3   Sixth-century columns from Acre. South side of
    Basilica San Marco   14
4   Replica of the Four Tetrarchs   14
5   The Horses of Saint Mark's Basilica   15
6   The Porta della Carta   17
7   Jacopo de' Barbari (c. 1460/70–c. 1516). *The Arsenal.*
    Detail of *The Map of Venice*   18
8   Ca' Loredan   22
9   Salizzada San Lio   23
10 Church of Santa Maria Gloriosa dei Frari   25
11 Jacopo Robusti Tintoretto (1518–94). *The Conquest of*
    Constantinople in 1204. Episode of the Fourth Crusade   30
12 Aerial view of the Rialto Bridge   39
13 Giovanni Bellini (1430–1516). *The Doge Leonardo Loredan*, 1501–4   52
14 Leandro Bassano (1557–1622). *The Virgin in Glory and*
    Portraits of Three Avogadori   57
15 The structure of government   64
16 Gentile Bellini (1429–1507). *Procession in Piazza San Marco*   76
17 The Plague Doctor's Dress, on Calle del Paradiso   77
18 Scuola di San Giorgio degli Schiavoni   85
19 Jacopo Robusti Tintoretto (1518–94). *Fellows of a Confraternity*   87
20 Joseph Heintz the Younger (1600–78). *Bull Hunt in Campo*
    San Polo   89
21 Gabriele Bella (fl.1700–50). *Combat Scene on the Ponte dei Pugni*
    (Bridge of the Fists)   96
22 Pietro Longhi (1702–85). *Carnival Scene in Venice*   98
23 Andrea Palladio (1508–80). Villa Barbaro, Maser, Italy   107

24 Pietro Longhi (1702–85). *The Pharmacist*   114
25 Titian (Tiziano Vecellio) (c. 1488–1576). *Portrait of a Woman
    Known as La Bella*   119
26 Bonifacio de' Pitati (1487–1553). *Apparition of God the Father*   126
27 Vittore Carpaccio (1455–1525). *The Lion of Saint Mark*   129
28 Gentile Bellini (1429–1507). *The Miracle of the Holy Cross*   130
29 Gentile Bellini (1429–1507). *Saint Mark Preaching in Alexandria* 131
30 Paolo Veronese (1528–88). *Venice Receiving the Ducal Horn*   133
31 Paolo Veronese (1528–88). *Allegory of Justice
    before Venice Enthroned*   134
32 The two Giustiniani Palaces and Ca' Foscari   136
33 Palazzo Grimani, San Luca   138
34 Church of the Redentore   141
35 Joseph Heintz the Younger (1600–78). *The Procession
    on Redemption Day*, Detail   146
36 Paolo Veronese (1528–88). *Feast in the House of Levi*   152
37 Giovanni Antonio Guardi (1698–1760). *The Parlor of the
    Nuns at San Zaccaria*   163
38 Francesco Guardi (1712–93). *The Feast of Maundy
    Thursday in Venice*   175
39 Gabriele Bella (fl.1700–50). *Old Fair of the "Sensa"*   188
40 Pietro Longhi (1702–85). *Il Ridotto* (Theater Lounge)   194
41 Bedroom from the Sagredo Palace, Venice, c. 1718   197
42 Salon with frescoes by Tiepolo (1753). Venice, Palazzo Labia   199
43 Giuseppe Borsato (1771–1849). *Napoleon Bonaparte's
    Arrival in Venice in 1807*   202
44 Claude Monet (1840–1926). *Palazzo Dario,* Venice, 1908   209
45 "The Last Train," by Arbit Blatas (1908–99), 1993. Monument
    Commemorating the Fiftieth Anniversary of the
    Deportation of the Jews from the Venetian Ghetto   212

MAPS

1	Venice (twenty-first century)	*page* 6
2	Major Trade Routes. Europe, North Africa, Asia	32
3	Greek Locales at Times under Venice	34
4	Trade Routes of Greater Asia	36
5	The Mainland Empire after 1426	62

ACKNOWLEDGMENTS

I first came under Venice's enchanting spell as a UCLA international student at the University of Padua in 1971–2. Six years later, in 1978, I returned to research my PhD thesis, and ever since the city has been my home away from my U.S. home. There are, thus, a lifetime of people to acknowledge as sources of support and inspiration for this book. First on the list is the international community of scholars whose work is cited here and with whom I have had the pleasure of exchanging ideas. Their output is important testimony to Venice's eternal allure and scholarly significance. The staff in Venice's archives and libraries also deserve special acknowledgment for the work they do in historical preservation and assisting scholars. The Gladys Krieble Delmas Foundation, the National Endowment for the Humanities, and the American Council of Learned Societies have all generously supported my various Venetian research projects over the years, endeavors that gave me the insight to produce the present work. Guido Ruggiero continues to be a valuable mentor and friend. Many others have also furnished excellent scholarly advice and friendship in Venice, including Patricia Fortini Brown, Stanley Chojnacki, Tracy Cooper, Laura Giannetti, John Jeffries Martin, Edward Muir, and Predrag Prtenjača. At home, my sisters Sadie Feliciano and Ann Maimone and my friends Edith Benkov, Jeanne Dunn, Elyse Katz Flier, Linda Holler, Ron and Ada King, Fred Kolkkhorst, Howard and Carol Kushner, Nancy Marlin, the late Alice Goldfarb Marquis, Barbara Rosen, Rosalie Schwartz, and Melody and Mark Singer offered me warm encouragement, while Ross Dunn furnished valuable perspectives on world history and Laurie Baron, Marilyn J. Boxer, and Paula DeVos kindly reviewed parts of the manuscript. I must thank my editor Beatrice Rehl for inviting me to write this book and helping me to stay the course through the various stages of review and production. Hamlet, my Renaissance cat, as always typed in a few incomprehensible symbols with his intrusive paws. Finally, it is to Elsa Dalla Venezia, nonagenarian Veneziana whose home in Venice over the last thirty-three years has been my home, that I dedicate this book.

PREFACE

The only way to care for Venice as she deserves it is to give her a chance to touch you often – to linger and remain and return

Henry James[1]

Perhaps no city in the world holds the allure of Venice, with its endless maze of narrow alleys and waterways. An obligatory stop on the Grand Tour, the love of John Ruskin, Henry James, Mary McCarthy, and other celebrated writers, droves of artists, scholars, and tourists continue to explore its *calli* and *campi* year after year. The floating city brings sighs of utter astonishment as sky and sea paint the landscape, changing the palette in rhythm with breaking light. Domes, rooftops, and towers glint and glaze in the summer, retreating mysteriously like ghostlike forms during the dark and misty winter. All the while the water mirrors the atmosphere, yielding tantalizing glimpses of Byzantine, Islamic, and Gothic styles.

Over the ages, Venice has been a beacon of hope for many: to the original island settlers, it augured refuge; to Crusading adventurers, it was a pilgrim stop and a place to book passage to the Holy Land; to laborers, it promised employment opportunities; to pleasure seekers, it offered spectacle, gambling, and sexual experimentation; to gentlemen on the Grand Tour, it was a finishing school to study the Venetian constitution, view monumental art, and savor Baroque music; to expatriates, it provided new ways of life; to scholars, it became a place to preserve or reinterpret the past; to artists, writers, and composers, it offered a source of inspiration and a place to seek solace and consolation. Now the floating labyrinth is one of the most visited cities in the world, luring tourists with its artistic patrimony, film festivals, Carnival celebrations, and avant-garde art expositions.

Venice's history and culture are filled with worldly connections. Its medieval origins were tied to the Byzantine Empire, which carried a rich

Greco-Roman legacy; to the broader cultural and economic life of the Mediterranean basin; and to such far-off places as India and China. The city's material and cultural development paralleled that of commerce, following a southeast axis. From their Adriatic hub, the Venetians routed ships southward, with obligatory stops at ports along the east Adriatic Coast, a stretch of gulf that harbored Slavic peoples but whose language of commerce and material culture remained Italic, if not Venetian, and Christian. The cogs and galleys passed the strategic island of Corfu, which guarded the entrance to the Adriatic Sea, and reaching Modone turned in any number of directions – toward Alexandria on the North African Coast, or Acre in the Levant, or northeast along the Greek Archipelago and up to Constantinople, which was first a great Byzantine capital and after 1453 a metropolis of the Ottoman Empire. Alexandria, Acre, and Constantinople were depositories for Venetian cargo as well as supply regions for the goods that arrived via horse, mule, camel, and wagon from India, Persia, and China. Venetians also planted colonies of landowners, farmers, and merchants on some of the islands along their sea routes. These settlements served as strategic stepping-stones for the convoys making their way to the major trade termini, but they also supplied food and merchandise to the Rialto emporium. Through the trade and transport businesses, as well as colonization, Venice thus became a principal force, like Genoa, Alexandria, and Constantinople, endowing the Mediterranean world with common cultural components. Moreover, it carried the Mediterranean's material culture to its northern European trading posts, both by land and by sea, and brought back to Venice transalpine ways of life. The travelers who returned to the lagoon from Asia, Europe, and North Africa, together with the city's immigrant groups, helped shape Venice's civilization in important ways.

With roots firmly planted in Byzantium and the Islamic world, at the start of the fifteenth century the Venetians also discovered the cultural idioms of northern and central Italy. The establishment of a territorial state in northeast Italy heightened Venetian awareness of Latin civilization, infusing the arts, humanities, and material life with new cultural energies. The Venetian Renaissance arrived much later than that of Tyrrhenian Italy but nonetheless made a lasting impact both on the urban fabric and upon European civilization. The acquisition of the mainland territories to Venice's west included one of Europe's greatest universities at Padua, where science and medicine were developing in leaps and bounds.

Although Venetian power in the Mediterranean waned after 1625, its importance as a port and emporium bringing in goods from around the world remained intact, and its material culture continued to absorb the aesthetics of worldly encounters. Moreover, the city experienced an efflorescence in music, theater, and painting, becoming one of Europe's most important cultural capitals. The Venetians thus exhibited a remarkable capacity to adapt to contingent circumstances by making their city a virtual Baroque theater of entertainment. At the same time they continued to refashion their own history and civic identity through the visual arts and an elaborate public pageantry.

It was primarily the constitutional hereditary elite that gave continuity to the city's history by reiterating its myths and triumphs both visually and in print in the midst of broader transformations. The aristocratic regime that ruled the Republic for several centuries held tenaciously to a distinctly Catholic orientation, albeit to a Venetian rather than Roman church. While Venice was home to Jews, Muslims, Orthodox Christians, and Protestants, the Venetian ruling class discouraged intermarriage between Roman Catholics and non-Christians as rigidly as it did interclass unions. Moreover, patricians officially upheld Catholic prescriptive literature, with its emphasis on female virginity and chastity, and its strict definitions of legitimacy, structures that sustained the secular model of family estate management. Yet this continuity at the top, which was indelibly imprinted in the city's iconology and repeated regularly on feast days and during public celebrations, was not immune to ruptures. People found ways to breach boundaries, transgressing the Republic's laws to live out their own lives.

★ ★ ★

THE PRESENT WORK AIMS TO CAPTURE A BROAD RANGE OF THE scholarly literature that has emerged since Frederick Lane's *Venice: A Maritime History*, still a pivotal work for Venetian studies. The vast body of interdisciplinary scholarship on this remarkable city has continued to explode in the decades following Lane's 1973 opus, yet another testament to Venice's endless allure. From this impressive output, I have chosen to emphasize four themes that are timely and important in the postmodern age: the construction and evolution of identities; the multiculturalism of material life; social hierarchy; and gender as a cultural construction. The first theme, identities, is explored in terms of both Venetian insularity and new encounters created by networks of trade and immigration. On the one hand, the floating city, detached from the mainland until the nineteenth century, developed definitions of self rooted in local family and corporate traditions, in devotion to the Venetian ruling class, in civic life and neighborhood community, in Christian traditions and piety, and in performance, through mythmaking, the creation of visual imagery, processions, theater, and music. On the other, contact with peoples and goods from many different parts of the world also helped shape both individual and collective identities. Moreover, family, corporate, and civic self-fashioning was not fixed in time but rather evolved in response to changing circumstances. The second theme, multiculturalism, portrays medieval and early modern Venice as a mirror of the Mediterranean world, where Hebrew, Spanish, Ottoman Turkish, Portuguese, Greek, German, and many Italian dialects including Venetian were spoken. New foods, raw materials, and finished products that reached the city from exotic places allowed for a variety of modes of familial and corporate self-representation. The third theme, social hierarchy, underlay Venice's purported social and political cohesion and supported the aristocratic state's myth of enduring stability. It was sustained by law and a variety of cultural forms, including models of marriage, Catholic prescriptive literature, housing, dress, and performance. Class distinctions assumed increasingly sharper boundaries, but not without the anomalies that exposed the fragility of certain secular ideals and restrictions, like arranged marriage and estate planning, the forced enclosure of aristocratic women and some men into religious institutions, and the sexual demands of the body. There was also a lack of consensus over Catholic orthodoxy, evident in cases of heresy, feigned sanctity, and magic. That Venice was one of the greatest printing capitals in Europe from the late fifteenth century brought the underlying forms of resistance into the discursive arena of learned men and a small group of women writers in academies and salons. The fourth theme, gender as a cultural construction, underlines the fragility of secular and ecclesiastical prescriptions designed to sustain patriarchy and hierarchy. Assumptions about the nature of women kept them out of politics and formal education, and for enclosed nuns out of society in general, but there were defiant groups of females that resisted patriarchy, claiming power and finding outlets for self-expression on the fringes as folk healers, midwives, witches, innkeepers, and courtesans. Their transgressions, which implicitly involved men as well, come to us through Venice's numerous tribunals of repression, exposing the rifts and fissures of a Republic that shrewdly persisted in portraying itself as "Most Serene."

The focus of this history remains the Republic of Venice, while only brief attention is given to the modern period. Napoleon's armies swept away the ironies of the Republic with its fall in 1797, but others replaced them, as historians of the modern period have ably attested. The city underwent an extended period of decline under French and Austrian occupation during the nineteenth century. Artists and writers mourned the Republic's ghostly forms as pavements and structures cracked and crumbled. The city became a metaphor for death but also a cause célèbre for advocates of renovation.

Modernity perforce propelled Venice into the mechanized world of the twentieth century, steamboats and electricity replacing gondoliers and lanterns, motorways and railroad tracks linking the islands of the lagoon to land. But the city itself did not undergo industrialization, instead harkening back to its tradition of tourism, with the legacy of the Republic its central draw. The choice ushered in a new wave of cultural development during the twentieth century, oriented toward attracting visitors. Only temporarily interrupted by two world wars, the tourist magnet remained on an inexorable trajectory, receiving busloads and boatloads of curious visitors. The weight of tourism on Venice's sinking foundations, together with environmental pollution and flooding, remain in the twenty-first century a cause of international concern. The sea, once the key to Venetian independence, a cushion against uninvited marauders, the principal element shaping an enchantingly unique urban morphology, has now become a source of peril, invading *calli* and *campi*, drowning buildings, holding inhabitants hostage in their homes, and eroding foundations. Let us hope the tides change, for Venice is a truly remarkable city, one that has won the admiration of the world.

CHRONOLOGY OF HISTORICAL EVENTS

307–37	Reign of Constantine, Roman Emperor
330	Transfer of the capital of the Roman Empire to Constantinople
401	Barbarian invasions in western Europe
421	Legendary foundation of Venice
493–553	Ostrogoth kings rule northern Italy
537	Cassiodorus's letter to the lagoon dwellers
554	Byzantine Emperor Justinian rules peninsula at Ravenna
568	Lombard invasions of Italy; mainlanders flee to the lagoon
697	Election of first doge
727–8	Italy revolts against Byzantium
751	The Lombards occupy Ravenna
773–4	Charlemagne conquers the north Italian Lombard kingdom
800	Charlemagne crowned Holy Roman Emperor in Rome
828–9	Relics of St. Mark brought to Venice
900s	Development of hydraulic energy; development of the *commenda* (business partnerships)
962	Otto I, king of Germany, invades Italy; crowned Holy Roman Emperor in Rome
1000	Pietro II Orseolo doge; Venetians defeat the Normans in southern Italy
1075	Seljuk Turks conquer Jerusalem
1082	Golden Bull of Byzantine emperor; Venice acquires trading privileges in return for naval aid against the Normans
1096–1109	The First Crusade
c. 1100	Spinning wheel in Europe (c. 1000 in China)
1118–30	Domenico Michiel doge; naval triumphs at Ascalon and in Aegean
1154–76	Wars between Barbarossa and the northern Italian communes

1176	Northern Italian communes form the Lombard League; win independence from Fredrick I
1177	Peace of Venice
c. 1200	Manufacture of paper (from China)
1204	Fourth Crusade; Sack of Constantinople; Partition of Byzantine Empire under Doge Enrico Dandolo
1205	Bronze horses arrive from Constantinople
1207	Annexation of Corfu, Modone, and Corone
1211	First colonization of Crete
1253–68	First Genoese War under Ranieri Zeno doge; Fort of Marcamò constructed on the Po
1259	Loss of Constantinople
1268–75	The Polo brothers travel to China
1278	Earthquake
1285	Earthquake
1289	Second War with Genoa
1297	First Closing of the Great Council, under Pietro Gradenigo doge
c. 1300	Development of the compass (from Arabs) replaces needle-and-bowl; first clocks; first firearms (from China)
1309–77	Papacy transferred to Avignon
1310	Tiepolo-Querini conspiracy
1323	Great Council membership becomes hereditary
1343–54	Third Genoese War; Dalmatia lost
1347	Earthquake
1347–9	Black Death
1355	Doge Marin Faliero decapitated; peace with Genoa
1362	Petrarch visits Venice; donates books for a library in San Marco
1378–81	War of Chioggia; Venice in the Mediterranean
1382	Plague
1395	Jews barred from residency
1400s	Full-rigged ship developed; artillery
1400	Plague
1403	Peace with Suleiman
1404–5	Acquisition of Verona, Vicenza, Rovigo, Treviso, Feltre, Belluno, Padua
1409	Acquisition of Zara, Scutari, Durazzo, Valona, Corfu
1414–18	End of Papacy's Great Schism

1420	Acquisition of Udine and Friuli under Doge Tommaso Mocenigo
1425–54	War with the Visconti; annexation of Peschiera, Brescia, and Bergamo under Doge Francesco Foscari
1431	The lagoon freezes
1451	Creation of the Patriarcate
1453	Fall of Constantinople to Mehmed II; Constantinople becomes Istanbul
1454	Treaty with the Ottoman Turks; Peace of Lodi among Italian states
c. 1455	Gutenberg Bible, first printed book in Europe
1468	Cardinal Bessarion donates his library to Venice
1469	Movable print established in Venice; plague
1469–80	54 printing shops established: 16 were German; 21 Italian; 6 French or Flemish; others unknown
1470–9	War with the Ottoman Turks; fall of Negroponte
1479	Treaty with Sultan Mehmed II rejuvenates Aegean commerce
1481–4	League against Venice: Milan, Florence, Mantua, Aragon, the Papacy
1488	Bartolomeo Diaz reaches the Cape of Good Hope
1489	Caterina Corner, Queen of Cyprus, donates the island to the Republic
1492	Columbus discovers America
1493	Aldo Manutius establishes a print shop in Venice
1494	Charles VIII attempts to conquer the kingdom of Naples; beginning of the Italian Wars
1498	Vasco da Gama circumnavigates Africa and reaches India via the sea
1499–1500	Venice loses Lepanto, Modone, and Corone to the Ottoman Turks
1499–1517	Portuguese discover sea route to India; competition for spices
1503	Peace with Ottoman Turks
1508–17	Wars of League of Cambrai
1509	Venice defeated by pope, emperor, France, Spain at Agnadello
1516	The Jewish ghetto established
1517	Venice regains Italian mainland possessions; Martin Luther advocates Church reform

1519	Charles V crowned Holy Roman Emperor
1520	Martin Luther's works are confiscated in Venice
1527	Sack of Rome by Imperial troops
1528	Paracelsus writes a modern manual of surgery
1530	Venice does not recognize Charles V's jurisdictions
1537	Jacopo Sansovino designs St. Mark's Library
1537–40	War with Ottoman Turks
1539	Famine; Ignatius of Loyola's Society of Jesus receives papal approval
1542	Roman Inquisition created
1543	Andreas Vesalius founds the modern study of anatomy with *De Humani Corporis Fabrica*
1545–63	Council of Trent; start of Catholic Reform and Counter-Reformation
1549–91	Veronica Franco, poet and courtesan
c. 1550	Casting of iron guns
1556	Abdication of Charles V; Italy ceded to Spain; office of Provveditori ai beni inculti established to oversee agriculture
1559	Treaty of Cateau-Cambresis; France renounces claims to Italy
1564	Tintoretto paints at San Rocco
1571	Victory of Venice and the Papacy over the Ottoman Turks at Lepanto, but Venice loses Cyprus
1574	Henry III of France visits Venice
1575–7	Plague; building of Church Il Redentore
1582–1630	The Young Party (*Giovani*) are in power; Council of Ten's powers limited
1588	Building of Procuratie Nuove by Vincenzo Scamozzi
1591	Famine
1602	Polar temperatures freeze the canals
1606–12	Papal Interdict defied under Leonardo Donà doge
1607	Vittorio Zonca (Padua) designs water-powered machine for throwing silk
1608	Cold winter
1609	Calvinists in Venice
1610	Galileo Galilei publishes *The Starry Messenger*
1615–17	War with Austria at Gradisca; removal of Uskoks
1618	Spanish plot to take Adriatic and Venice
1618–48	The Thirty Years' War in Europe

1619	Unauthorized edition of Paolo Sarpi's *History of the Council of Trent* published in London
1628	Powers of Ten challenged
1629	Famine
1630	War of Mantuan Succession under Nicolò Contarini doge; League with the Papacy, France, and Mantua against Spain
1630–1	Plague
1631	Baldassare Longhena designs Church of Santa Maria della Salute; papal condemnation of Galileo Galilei for favoring the Copernican view of the universe
1637	First public opera house in Venice
1643	First performance of Monteverdi's *L'incoronazione di Poppea* in Venice
1645–68	War with Candia
1677–82	Punta della Dogana constructed
1684–98	First War of the Morea
1687	Venice bombs the Parthenon
1699	Peace of Carlowitz
1700–12	War of the Spanish Succession
1706–7	Austria conquers Milan and the Kingdom of Naples
1709	Icy temperatures in Venice
1714–18	Second War of Morea
1720	Caffè Florian opens
1776	Independence of the United States
1789	The French Revolution
1796	Austrian and French invasions
1797	12 May: Great Council abdicates; Napoleon takes Venice; 17 October: Treaty of Campo Formio; Venice ceded to Austria
1798	18 January: Austrian troupes enter Venice
1802	Napoleon Bonaparte becomes president of the Italian Republic
1804–5	Napoleon crowned Emperor and King of Italy
1814–15	Fall of Napoleon in Italy
1825	First performance of Rossini's *Semiramide* in Venice
1846–7	Famine in Europe
1848	Revolution in Europe and in Venice under Daniele Manin and T. Niccolò Tommaseo
1851	First performance of Giuseppe Verdi's *Rigoletto* in Venice
1861	Proclamation of the Kingdom of Italy

1870	Rome becomes capital of Italy
1915–18	Italy participates in World War I on the side of the Allies
1922–43	Establishment of Fascist regime in Italy under Benito Mussolini
1938	Fascist racial laws deprive Jews of civil rights in Italy
1940–3	Italy in World War II as an Axis power; joined the Allies in 1943
1943–4	Nazi deportation of Italian Jews, with roundups in Venice
1943–5	German occupation of Venice
1946	Kingdom of Italy falls
1969	Proclamation of the First Italian Republic

Architecture, Art, Literature, and Music[2]

600s	Cathedral at Torcello; Church of Santi Maria e Donato, Murano
775	Church of San Pietro di Castello
800s	San Giacometto at Rialto
829	Basilica San Marco begun
1100s	Ca' Loredan, Ca' Farsetti
13th century	Churches of Santi Giovanni e Paolo; Santa Maria Gloriosa dei Frari
1340	South wing of Doge's Palace and Great Council Hall begun
1345	*Pala d'Oro*
14th–15th centuries	Scuola Vecchia della Misericordia, Doge's Palace
1421–43	Ca' D'Oro
1424	West wing of Doge's Palace
1430s–60s	Jacopo Bellini, painter
c.1435–1516	Giovanni Bellini, painter
1437	Scuola of San Marco
1438–43	Porta della Carta, Bon family
1438–89	Arco Foscari, Bon family; Antonio Rizzo; Antonio Bregno, sculptors
1444–1500	Church of San Zaccaria
1449–1515	Aldo Manutius, printer
1452	Ca' Foscari begun; Palazzo Loredan
1454–1512	Scuola of San Giovanni Evangelista
1460	Porta Magna of the Arsenale
1466	Antonio Vivarini, painter

1469–78	Church of San Michele in Isola, Mauro Codussi, architect
1474–1516	Gentile and Giovanni Bellini, painters at Doge's Palace
1480	Scuola San Giorgio degli Schiavoni (Dalmatians) begun
1481–8	Andrea Verrocchio and Alessandro Leopardi, artists; equestrian monument of Bartolomeo Colleoni
1481–94	Santa Maria dei Miracoli church, Pietro Lombardo, architect
1483–98	East wing of Doge's Palace, Antonio Rizzo, architect
1485–93	Scala dei Giganti, Doge's Palace, Antonio Rizzo, architect
1485–95	Scuola Grande of San Marco
c.1485–1576	Titian (Tiziano Vecellio), painter
1487–95	Façade, Scuola Grande di San Marco; Entry, San Giovanni Evangelista
1490	Palazzo Corner Spinelli, Mauro Codussi, architect
1492–1510	Gentile Bellini paints *Miracle of the Holy Cross*
1495–1500	Vittore Carpaccio paints *Legend of St. Ursula*
1496–1506	Clock Tower, Mauro Codussi and Pietro Lombardo, architects
1498	Scuola of San Nicolò (Greek)
1500–32	Procuratie Vecchie
1500	Palazzo Grimani; Jacopo de'Barbari, woodcut view of Venice
1502–7	Vittore Carpaccio paints the lives of Sts. George, Tryphon, Jerome in the Scuola San Giorgio degli Schiavoni
1504	Alessandro Leopardi, bronze flagpole bases, San Marco
1505	Giovanni Bellini paints the San Zaccaria Altarpiece
1505–8	Fondaco dei Tedeschi
1506	Albrecht Durer, Lorenzo Lotto, Giorgione, painters
1508–9	Sebastiano del Piombo, painter
1508–80	Andrea Palladio, architect
1515–60	Scuola Grande di San Rocco
1516	Ghetto Nuovo
1518–94	Jacopo (Robusti) Tintoretto, painter
1527	Ospedaletto, shelter for the old and indigent
1528–88	Paolo Veronese, painter
1532–61	Palazzo Corner, Jacopo Sansovino, architect
1535–83	Scuola Grande of the Misericordia, begun by Sansovino, architect
1536–45	Palazzo Dolfin, Jacopo Sansovino, architect
1537–66	Roman *renovatio*: Loggetta, Library of St. Mark's, the Mint; Jacopo Sansovino, architect
1539–61	Church of San Giorgio dei Greci

1540	Bonifazio de'Pitati paints *God the Father above Piazza San Marco*
1550s	Paris Bordone, painter
1552	Church of the Mendicanti, Vincenzo Scamozzi, architect; façade 1673, Giuseppe Sardi, architect
1555–6	Fabbriche Nuove of Rialto, Jacopo Sansovino, architect
1560s	Paolo Veronese, Jacopo Tintoretto, Titian, painters
1560–3	Refectory of San Giorgio Maggiore, Andrea Palladio, architect
1563–1614	Prisons, Antonio da Ponte and Antonio Contin, architects
1564	Tintoretto paints the interior of the Scuola of San Rocco
1565	Ospedale degli Incurabili, Jacopo Sansovino, architect
1577	Fire incinerates Great Council hall; Antonio da Ponte rebuilds it
1577–92	Church of Il Redentore, Andrea Palladio, architect
1579	Church of San Giorgio Maggiore, Andrea Palladio, architect
1579–	Construction begins on the Scuola Grande of San Teodoro
1579–91	Rope Works of the Tana remodeled, Antonio da Ponte, architect
1579–1620	Paolo Veronese, Jacopo and Domenico Tintoretto, Francesco Bassano, Jacopo Palma il Giovane paint for the Doge's Palace
1582–6	Church and Hospice of the Zitelle, Andrea Palladio and Giacomo Bozzetto, architects
1586–1616	Procuratie Nuove, Vincenzo Scamozzi, architect
1588–91	Rialto Bridge in stone, Antonio da Ponte, architect
1595–1600	Bridge of Sighs, (Antonio Abbondi) Scarpagnino, architect
1601–49	Church of San Lazzaro dei Mendicanti, Vincenzo Scamozzi and Giuseppe Sardi, architects
1627–63	Scuola Grande of the Carmini, Baldassare Longhena, architect
1630	Palazzo Widmann-Rezzonico, Baldassare Longhena, architect
1631–81	Church of Santa Maria della Salute, Baldassare Longhena, architect
1638–1700	Scuola Levantina at the Ghetto Vecchio
1641–71	Library at San Giorgio Maggiore, Baldassare Longhena, architect
1642	Monteverdi composes the opera *L'incoronazione di Poppea*
1652–82	Ca' Pesaro, Baldassare Longhena and Gian Antonio Gaspari, architects
1660	Scuola Ponentina at the Ghetto Vecchio, attributed to Baldassare Longhena, architect

1660–89	Church of the Scalzi (barefoot), Baldassare Longhena and Giuseppe Sardi, architects
1667–74	Ospedaletto and Church of Santa Maria dei Derelitti, Baldassare Longhena and Giuseppe Sardi, architects
1667–82	Ca' Rezzonico, Baldassare Longhena and Giorgio Massari, architects
1668	Church of San Moisè, Alessandro Tremignon, architect
1675–82	Church of Santa Croce degli Armeni
1677	Malibran Theater, Grimani family
1677–8	Dogana da Mar, Giuseppe Benoni, architect
1678–80	Scuola of San Nicolò dei Greci, Baldassare Longhena, architect
1678–83	Church of Santa Maria del Giglio, Giuseppe Sardi, architect
1700	Palazzo Labia, Alessandro Tremignon and Andrea Cominelli, architects
1715–28	Church of the Gesuiti, Domenico Rossi, architect
1724–7	Ca' Corner della Regina, Domenico Rossi, architect
1726–36	Church of the Gesuati, Giorgio Massari, architect
1734–59	Church and Hospital of San Servolo, Tommaso Temanza and Giovanni Scalfarotto, architects
1744–60	Church of the Pietà, Giorgio Massari, architect
1748	Palazzo Venier dei Leoni (Peggy Guggenheim Foundation), Lorenzo Boschetti, architect
1748–72	Palazzo Grassi, Giorgio Massari, architect
1786–1928	Tobacco Factory
1790	La Fenice Theater, Antonio Selva, architect
1807	Cemetery of San Michele, Antonio Selva, architect
1807–11	Galleria and Accademia delle Belle Arti, Antonio Selva, architect
1810	Napoleonic Gardens, Antonio Selva, architect
1810–15	Napoleonic Wing, Giovanni Antonio Antolini; Giuseppe Soli; Lorenzo Santi, architects
	Dockyards of the Free Port at San Giorgio, Giuseppe Mezzani; Romeo Venturelli, architects
1830	Salt Warehouse, Alvise Pigazzi, architect
1836–50	Patriarch's Palace, Lorenzo Santi, architect
1840s	Iron bridges at Accademia and the Scalzi
1846	Construction of a railway linking Venice and Milan
1855–67	Hotel Londra, Carlo Ruffini, Giovanni Fuin, architects
1858	Caffè Florian, Lodovico Cadorin, architect

1869	Federico Berchet rebuilds Fondaco dei Turchi
1878–1947	Vittorio Zecchin, Muranese painter
1883	Richard Wagner dies in Venice at Palazzo Vendramin-Calergi
1883–1911	Cotton Mill at Santa Marta
1887	Site of the Biennale, Giardini at Castello
1895	Pavilions of the Biennale
1897–1920	Mulino Stucky at Giudecca, Ernest Wullekopf architect
1898–1908	Hotel Excelsior at Lido, Giovanni Sardi, architect
1905–9	Hotel des Baines at Lido, Francesco Marsich, architect
1906	Villa Monplaisir at Lido, Guido Sullam, architect
1907	Fish Market at Rialto, Cesare Laurenti and Domenico Rupolo, architects
1908	Ezra Loomis Pound publishes poems *A Lume Spento*
1909–20	Brewery at Giudecca
1913–27	Marcel Proust writes *À la recherche du temps perdu*
1922–3	Heliotherapic Hospital at Lido, Duilio Torres, architect
1924–7	Public Housing at Sant'Elena, Paolo Bertanza and other architects
1926–7	House of the Pharmacist at Lido, Brenno del Giudice, architect
1930–3	Ponte della Libertà
1931–4	INA Parking Garage at Piazzale Roma, Eugenio Miozzi, architect
1932	Accademia Bridge, Eugenio Miozzi, architect
1934	Airport for passengers at the Lido
1937–52	Palazzo del Cinema, Lido, Luigi Quagliata and Angelo Scattolin, architects
1952–5	Railway Station
1958–67	UBA CASA Development at Sacca Fisola, Ufficio Tecnico IACP
1961–3	Querini-Stampaglia Foundation, Carlo Scarpa, architect
1980	Peggy Guggenheim Museum and Solomon Guggenheim Foundation
1980–6	IACP Complex at the Giudecca, Gino Valle, architect
1982–9	Residential Complex at Sacca Fisola, Iginio Cappai, Pietro Mainardis, Valeriano Pastor, architects
1987–90	Public Housing at the Sacca San Girolamo, Franco Bortoluzzi, architect

Plate I. Mosaics, Porta di Sant' Alipio, Basilica San Marco, 1280. Location: Venice, Italy. Photo credit: J. M. Ferraro. The mosaics illustrate the transport of St. Mark's body and offer the first pictorial reproduction of the Basilica.

Plate II. Apse of Santi Maria e Donato, seventh–twelfth century. Location: Murano, Italy. Photo credit: J. M. Ferraro.

Plate III. Ca' Farsetti, early thirteenth century. Location: Venice, Italy. Photo credit: J. M. Ferraro.

Plate IV. Aerial view of Venice with Basilica San Marco Domes and Palazzo Ducale. Location: Venice, Italy. Photo credit: J. M. Ferraro.

Plate V. Lunette with the Four Evangelists over the Porta di Sant'Alipio, fourteenth century. Location: Basilica San Marco, Venice, Italy. Photo credit: J. M. Ferraro.

Plate VI. The Palazzo Ducale, south wing begun 1341; Piazzetta façade begun 1424. Location: Venice, Italy. Photo credit: J. M. Ferraro.

Plate VII. Church of San Giovanni e Paolo (large brick structure), begun 1333. The white, Renaissance-style building to its left is the former Scuola of San Marco, rebuilt after 1485. Begun by Pietro Lombardo and Giovanni Buora, it was completed by Mauro Codussi, 1490–5. The Cemetery of San Michele is behind the Scuola (now a hospital), and the island of Murano is in the background. Location: Venice, Italy. Photo credit: J. M. Ferraro.

Plate VIII. Fondaco dei Tedeschi, first built 1228; rebuilt 1506–8. The Central Post Office since 1870. Location: Venice, Italy. Photo Credit: J. M. Ferraro.

Plate IX. Street Signs for the Old and New Ghetti; tall building in the Ghetto Nuovo. Photo Credit: J. M. Ferraro

Plate X. Italian Synagogue (Schola Italiana) in the Ghetto Nuovo, 1575. Location: Venice, Italy. Photo Credit: J. M. Ferraro.

Plate XI. Ca' D'Oro, begun 1421. Location: Venice, Italy. Photo Credit: J. M. Ferraro.

Plate XII. Ca' Loredan, by Mauro Codussi, c. 1502; now Palazzo Vendramin-Calergi. Location: Venice, Italy. Photo Credit: J. M. Ferraro.

Plate XIII. The Piazzetta San Marco. On far left: The Mint, by Jacopo Sansovino, begun 1536. Left of the Piazzetta: The Library of Saint Mark's, by Jacopo Sansovino, begun 1537. Vincenzo Scamozzi completed the south end of the Library between 1588 and 1591. Location: Venice, Italy. Photo Credit. J. M. Ferraro.

Plate XIV. San Giorgio Maggiore, by Andrea Palladio, begun 1566; façade constructed 1607–11. The Lido is in the background. Location: Venice, Italy. Photo Credit: J. M. Ferraro.

Plate XV. Church of Santa Maria della Salute (left), by Baldassare Longhena (1596–1682), begun 1631. Right foreground features the southwest end of Piazza San Marco, renovated under Napoleon. Location: Venice, Italy. Photo Credit: J. M. Ferraro.

Plate XVI. Venice, 2011. Backdrop: Marghera's Smokestacks and Cruise Ships. Photo Credit: J. M. Ferraro.

RECONSTRUCTING THE FLOATING CITY

The most august city of Venice is today the one home of liberty, peace, and justice, the one refuge of honorable men, haven for those who, battered on all sides by the storms of tyranny and war, seek to live in tranquility.

Petrarch, 1364[1]

1. Foundation Myths

Myths have always been a creative means of fostering civic pride and projecting civic identity. The story of Venice's birth inspired mythmaking from its very beginnings. Some two hundred years after the Roman Empire had separated into eastern (Byzantine) and western (European) spheres, Cassiodorus (537–38), a Roman official stationed in the Byzantine capital of Ravenna, constructed an ideal template of the boat peoples on the Venetian lagoon. His description of a humble fishing population far removed from the official centers of political power inspired learned writers nearly a thousand years later to create a lasting image of a free people bathing in peace and prosperity. In the fifteenth and sixteenth centuries, an age when intellectuals emulated Greek and Roman ideals, humanist writers generously elaborated on Venetian origins. Among the most popular stories was the one linking Venetians with the free-spirited, noble warriors of Troy, who reputedly fathered the inhabitants of *Venetia*, the present-day Veneto, Friuli, and Trentino regions. Some mythmakers endowed the mainland peoples that colonized the lagoon with Gallic bloodlines, while still others situated both Trojans and Gauls in Venetia in order to infuse Venetians with the noble ancestry of classical antiquity, the most coveted of genealogies in Renaissance elite circles.

Indeed, the Romans had founded colonies throughout mainland Venetia, the Adriatic littoral, and the lagoon by the first century of the Common Era.

But the city of Venice itself could not truthfully lay claim to Roman origins, as humanist writers and architects continued to insist throughout the Renaissance, when other major Italian cities were vaunting their genuine links with classical antiquity. Jacopo Sansovino's Loggetta (1537–66) at the foot of the bell tower is a tribute to the city's penchant for mythmaking: the iconography placed Venetians on the same level with the deities of antiquity. A century before the classical structure went up, writers were fabricating Roman associations. Venice, asserted Bernardo Giustiniani (1408–89) was the heir to a justly punished Rome; its earliest settlers, unlike the Romans, had successfully escaped the ravages of Attila the Hun. Another famous humanist, Francesco Sansovino (1521–86), borrowed a fourteenth-century myth from the neighboring city of Padua: that Venice's birthday was on the feast day of the Annunciation in 421 CE. The exact date, March 25, was the same day Rome was founded, the Christian era began, and nature habitually awakens from winter slumber. Thus folklore and civic pride blended over the centuries to produce the mythical foundations of a Roman and Christian past, values that sustained the power and imagination of Venetian rulers, writers, and visual artists.

The classical mythmaking of the fifteenth and sixteenth centuries corresponded with Venetian involvement in the period's Peninsular conflicts, a period of economic competition and political strife that necessitated building a larger territorial power base. As Venetians joined in rivalry with other nascent Italian regional states, they became aware of their unique origins, as the only Italian city without a classical past. Imbued with a sense of their specialness, they invented one. It was only one of many myths the peoples on the lagoon would go on to fabricate, in tandem with their construction of a floating city.

2. Real Beginnings: The Flight to the Lagoon

Venetian origins really belong to the sixth-century fishing peoples who put together fragile huts raised on stilts above mud flats, amid the silt from the rivers, reeds, swamps, and salt marshes of the lagoon. Venetia's refugees, preferring the boggy terrain of the lagoon and the littoral to the aggressive Lombard tribes that were colonizing northern Italy, scattered along the mud flats and salt marshes of Caorle, Jesolo, Torcello, Chioggia, Malamocco, and Rivo Alto. They dispersed as far north as Aquileia and Grado and as far south as Chioggia, stoically conquering the harsh amphibious environment that stood between the open Adriatic Sea and some thirty-one miles of coastline. It was filled with clay and sand bands carried down by the river currents of the Po Delta and shaped by marine tides. The migrants settled on raised, wet, salt flats amid carpets of algae, rush beds, river estuaries, and wild fowl and a variety of other fauna. Nothing was fixed in time or place. When their marginal plots of land receded, in rhythm with the tides and floods of the lagoon's brackish waters, they toiled to consolidate the ground with mats made of reeds and dry soil. There was no firm shoreline separating land and sea, only the slippery mud and fluid margins that made settlement so precarious. The groups around mainland Treviso, Indo-Europeans who harkened back to pre-Roman times, founded Venice's earliest settlements, Rivo Alto (which signified "high bank" and was the future Rialto) and Malamocco, on the central sand bar generically named Lido (see Plate XIV). They were joined by the elite lines from the imperial administration and military hierarchy that had peopled Oderzo, Altino, Padova, and Aquileia, as well as clerics, carpenters, ironworkers, and glassmakers. All of these peoples carried with them centuries of tradition linked to the Etruscans, the Greeks, and Mediterranean culture in general, including burial rites, metalwork and jewelry, and textile handicrafts. Transalpine Gauls and Celts had also crossed their paths via the old Roman roads and canals, leaving traces of their cultures. In the sixth century, boatmen and barge men took advantage of the Roman waterworks that had rendered the lagoon more navigable, including land reclamation and deforestation. They navigated around the littoral islands and up and down the rivers that connected the lagoon to the mainland, earning their living from transport, and from fish and salt, which they traded for timber to construct boats and later merchant galleys.

Although Venetian chroniclers proudly claimed the city was independent at birth, the island archipelago, situated in a strip of central and northeast Italy called the Exarchate of Ravenna, was linked politically as well as culturally to Byzantium, then a flourishing commercial power on the Black Sea. The most enduring material evidence of this lies with the seventh-century Veneto-Byzantine churches of Torcello and Murano (Plate II), which had counterparts in Ravenna and Grado as well as original templates in Rome and Constantinople. They had a simple basilical plan based on Roman models that was typical of early Christian churches. As followers of Latin Christianity, the inhabitants of these two islands, called *venetica* to distinguish them from the Lombard inhabitants of mainland Venetia, revived Roman and early Christian traditions, but they also adapted the Byzantine idiom of patterned brick exteriors and still-life interiors of two-dimensional gold mosaics, an ancient technique from the Greco-Latin era. Both the cathedral of Santa Maria Assunta on Torcello and Santi Maria e Donato of Murano were centers of Marian devotion. Their parishioners thrived on agriculture as well as glass manufacture deriving from the techniques of late antiquity.

Yet Byzantine cultural representation and religious symbolism did not mask the virtual reality that the eastern emperors lacked the resources to rule their western margins, a limitation that afforded Venetians the liberty to develop separately. Initially the exarch appointed a master of soldiers to rule over the littoral, but by 730 the inhabitants elected a doge (dialect for duke) as their leader and became, with the Adriatic city of Ravenna, one of two Italian settlements retaining political affiliation with Roman Byzantium. The link was important, for it offered lucrative trading privileges and tax exemptions with the eastern sphere of the Roman Empire, as well as some measure of protection, for several centuries.

Venetian independence developed in tandem with the gradual disintegration of Byzantium but also as a result of the failings of other powers. When in 750 the Lombards seized the Exarchate, the doge gained independence, reigning over the islands and the lidi with unlimited powers. By 810, Charlemagne, the self-proclaimed heir to the (western) Roman Empire, had absorbed the Lombards of Venetia into his own kingdom and began to set his sights on Venice. In this instance the Byzantine fleet came to the defense of the peoples on the lagoon. When Charlemagne's son, Pepin, sacked Malamocco on the Lido that year, the islanders transferred their political capital to the cluster of islands around Rivoalto in the center of the lagoon. Gradually the Franks retreated, and Venice achieved semiautonomy, establishing the center of government (*dogado* in Venetian) on the island of Rialto. In 827 the Venetian *ducato* came under the religious authority of Aquileia, which temporarily became a sort of mother city for the Christian polity. Centuries later, the city's blacksmiths would celebrate Venice's victory over Aquileia's patriarch during Lenten season by butchering pigs on the Fat Thursday of Carnival, but some vestiges of Aquileia's tenure remained, such as the Friulan liturgical rite in the ducal Basilica of San Marco. In 828 the Venetians replaced their patron saint, Theodore, with Saint Mark the Evangelist, whose body they pirated from Alexandria. (Plate I). Saint Mark's symbol, the lion, became synonymous with Venice's expanding dominion, and his body became an essential relic for the city's protection, to sanction the established political order and to foster civic loyalty.

3. Engineering the Island Parishes

The construction of the floating city was a remarkable technological feat, an essential part of the city's eternal allure. The principal challenge of the early settlers on high banks such as Rialto was to subjugate the sea and create dry land masses. Plot by plot, workers, largely from the noble houses and principal religious orders, drained and consolidated the soil, bringing in dirt, gravel, and even trash, where once there had been water. Early construction workers excavated canals, using mud to raise the level of land. The city then expanded with the addition of new landfills around its edges. (Map 1).

Rialto and San Marco were certainly the most important settlements, but they were not the oldest. The fisherman colonies around San Angelo Raffaele and San Niccolò dei Mendicoli, in the district of Dorsoduro on Venice's southern flank, reputedly originated in the seventh century. San Pietro di Castello, a tiny island at the tail of the Venetian "fish," east of San Marco, also preceded Rialto. It was founded as early as 764, and became the seat of the Venetian episcopate in 775. Principally, however, it was the central zone of the city, San Marco and Rialto, that grew first. Churches were built in both parishes in the ninth century based on the classical prototype of the Greek cross. Rialto's San Giacometto (Fig. 1), with the clock tower on its façade, was the oldest, but the Basilica at San Marco, the chapel of the doge, was the city's principal church. Residents in the eastern section of Santa Croce, on the northwest side of Venice, also built churches in the ninth and tenth centuries, including San Giacomo, San Simeone Grande, and Santa Maria Mater Domini. The northwest district, Cannaregio, began development slightly later, with Santa Fosca in the tenth century and San Marcuola in the eleventh century, and it was slower to fill. It was still a peripheral area in the fifteenth century, largely housing the crafts industries.

The Christian church defined Venice's topographical divisions from the outset. Each island corresponded with a parish. In 812 there were little more than a dozen island parishes around Rialto. In the following two centuries, the churches acquired *campi*, literally drained and consolidated fields, each with a residential development along transverse streets. By the tenth century there were seventeen parishes located east and west of the river mouth that formed the Grand Canal. Their configuration, with seven situated on the left bank between San Bartolomeo and San Marco, and ten on the right bank, formed a U-shaped canal (*rio*). The four major churches abutting the canal, San Giovanni Degolà, San Giacomo del Orio, Sant'Agostin, and San Polo, became central axes of communication via water.

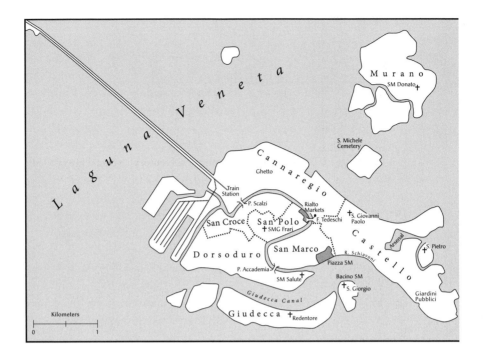

By 1100 the Venetians had constructed almost seventy island parishes, whose overall form continued to evolve as tidal waters deposited silt. Builders made great efforts to ensure that the natural flow of the tides was not disrupted, as the canals and the tides served as their sewage system. Moreover, water was their most vital form of transporting goods and materials. Parish borders acquired firmer lines. The areas between San Marco and San Samuele and between Santa Maria Formosa and Sant'Apostoli teemed with new residents, such that the city was propelled to expand further by adding new landfills to its periphery. Ultimately, Venice resembled not just a fish but a Byzantine mosaic, with canals separating irregular and multishaped plots of land that had been drained and reclaimed. Its asymmetrical shape was the product of silt deposits continually sculpted by the ebb and flow of the tides.

While church building gave physical form to neighborhoods, social organization was by no means the purview of the religious hierarchy. On the contrary, it was the elite families that dominated the island parishes in the early centuries of the city's formation, families such as the Participazi at the Rialto and the Orio and Gradenigo at San Giovanni Elemosinario. The islands were in essence family estates, clustered in blocks, with enclosed courtyards cut off

Map 1. Venice (twenty-first century). Map by Harry D. Johnson, Department of Geography, San Diego State University.

Figure 1. San Giacometto di Rialto. Restored in the eleventh and seventeenth centuries. Location: Venice, Italy. Photo credit: J. M. Ferraro.

from pedestrian traffic. The clients and retainers of the most powerful dynasts domiciled near these stately dwellings, while the humbler folk lived behind them, on traverse streets.

Each parish exhibited unique characteristics but also belonged to an integrated network. The community chose its own patron saint, staged its own festivals, congregated around its own market center, constructed its own bell tower, and developed its own customs. Each colony was an island, separated by canals and basins and navigable only by watercraft. Every island had a central square with a church usually facing a canal; a wharf nearby to bring in goods and fuel; the opulent homes of the church's richest donors lining the perimeters of the square; and the more modest dwellings of ordinary people occupying the narrower alleys behind them.

The parish accommodated two main forms of transportation, watercraft and foot traffic. (There were only a few horses in Venice.) Wealthy households owned private gondolas for their own transportation and small flat-bottomed boats for carrying supplies. Among the watercraft serving the lagoon were the small, wooden fishing vessel named *sanpierota*; the larger, sailed *topo* for big-scale fishing; and the low-lying *sandalo da s'ciopo*, used in shallow waters to hunt duck and other game. While only the wealthy could afford private *gondolas* with rowers, the city did provide public transportation by *traghetto*, a gondola propelled by two oarsmen that normally crossed the Grand Canal or taxied merchants to and from the mainland.

THE GONDOLA

The crafting of the 280-piece *gondola* was complex. The frame was made of oak planks that were first bathed, then gradually warped over heat and then given several coats of paint. (It was only after 1633 that *gondole* were painted black, in a measure by the Venetian government to restrain excessive ostentation.) The shape of the rowlock, carved from a block of walnut or cherry, and the hull, were adjusted to accommodate the size of a gondolier. One side of the gondola was broader than the other so that it heeled and yawed to starboard. The gondolier controlled its direction by standing at the stern with one leg forward and guiding his oar. The oar was carved from a single block of beech, with a ribbed blade and a round, smooth surface where the propeller joins the notch in the rowlock. The floating surface was very small, measuring approximately thirty-six feet in length by five feet in width. The prow was decorated in iron, in the shape of a doge's hat and representing the six Venetian districts. The place where gondolas are made and repaired is called a *squero*. One of the most picturesque gondola yards in Venice today is at San Trovaso, built in the seventeenth century.[2]

Walking was the other alternative to boating. The pedestrian's perspective of the developing city emerged during the twelfth century, as each island established a network of earthen footpaths, generally running at right angles to the canals. Larger thoroughfares (*calli*) traversed the footpaths, interrupted at intervals by large (*campi*) and small (*campielli*) open spaces. Over time, these pedestrian walkways formed a dense maze of asymmetrical routes. Bargemen ferried commuters across the canals dividing one island from another, but people also traveled on foot across crude wooden bridges; these were built of planks atop pilings or lashed-together boat hulls that were set at odd angles to link these floating parish communities. Among the early pedestrian hubs were San Giacomo and San Bartolomeo, on the right and left banks of Rialto, respectively.

The evolution of footpaths, with bridges connecting the once isolated islands, developed a new sense of community, as did the evolution of guilds after 1150. Street names recognized vocational activities as well as ethnicities in addition to the preeminence of noble families and ecclesiastical orders. Each guild or craft had a *ruga*, the term used to designate a pathway with a row of market stalls and workshops. Milk vendors were on the Calle del Pestrin; bakers on the Pistor; fruit vendors on the Frutarol. The silk weavers in Cannaregio worked on the Fondamenta degli "Ormesini," a kind of silk originating in the Persian Gulf. The arrow smiths were on the Frezzerie near San Marco; the cloth sellers on the Mercerie; the sword smiths on the Spaderia. Murano attracted glassworkers from Padua, the Friuli, and the Balkans. Many other immigrants from the Balkans became domestic servants. Where priests (*preti*) and nuns (*muneghe*) trod, streets took their names. Great noble families also named the pathways leading to their principal locales, as did the immigrant groups from Dalmatia (Schiavoni) (see Fig. 18 in Chapter 4), the Ottoman empire (Turchette), the Armenians (Armeni), and the Germans (Tedeschi).

4. Urban Morphology

Despite Venice's commonalities with other Italian cities, it is important to underline at the outset that Venice's aquatic environment, and associations with foreign lands via the sea, inevitably endowed it with a uniqueness all its own. Venetian survival depended on taming the tides, in contrast with the land-borne cities that instead conquered their hinterlands, razing forests and irrigating arid soil. Unlike the inland settlements of Florence and Milan, for example, the city's wealth did not originate with agricultural productivity. Venetian women and men grew some produce, such as beets, cauliflower, and scallions, in small gardens and orchards, and they raised pigs and hunted small fowl in addition to fishing. However, they also boated in their victuals and raw materials from the Veneto, trading salt for other supplies. Moreover, they consumed entire forests to build their city, their watercraft, and their fleet. The inhabitants of this thriving port mainly subsisted on a diet of fish, still today an integral part of the city's cuisine, and profited from the swelling tides of trade. They supplied the hinterland valleys of the Adige, Brenta, Piave, and Tagliamento with fish and salt and depended on them for other alimentation and raw materials. The rivers were vital, both as a means of transport and as trading depots, for the tiny gardens on the lagoon could not adequately feed the city's inhabitants. The Sile north of Venice connected Venice and the greater lagoon to Treviso and from there overland to Germany. The Brenta linked Venice and Padua; from Verona, the Adige was a stepping-stone to Trent, Bolzano, and the Tyrol; while the Po and its many tributaries were major gateways to northern Italy.

Another distinguishing feature of the floating city was the absence of walls. Instead, the Adriatic Sea cushioned Venetians from potential marauders, making the development of a navy essential. Already by the year 1000 Venetians proudly hailed a small fleet that sailed around the Mediterranean, keeping competitors at bay. Elsewhere in Italy, towns fortified their perimeters heavily against bands of hungry potentates and raised or hired armies. Powerful feudal magnates, often bishops, were seizing the lands of feeble kings but were in turn being challenged by emerging cities. Most of northern Italy, save Venice, paid homage to a line of German dynasts after 962, while papal territory was a precarious Roman island stretching only part of the way across the width of the Peninsula. The clash between popes and emperors raised havoc in the Italian cities, as noble clans took sides and pitched battles. Venice, on the other hand, was removed from this medieval drama. With the sea as a natural barrier, the city only erected small fortifications at its outer limits: at Mestre, the gateway to Venetia, and at San Nicolò on the Lido, the principal route to the littoral islands and to the Adriatic Sea. Rather than being expended on feudal warfare, human energies were devoted mainly to creating a commercial empire, especially between 1190 and 1220. Moreover, as historian Elisabeth Crouzet-Pavan rightly emphasizes, the morphology of the islands, the climatic conditions of the lagoon, the isolated island parish settlements, and the constant effort to tame the seas and the tides required tremendous organization as well as a sustained concentration of human capital and energy.[3]

According to architectural historians, commercial expansion in the three centuries following the millennium became critical to the city's physical appearance. The Venetians achieved hegemony along the Adriatic coast and founded permanent colonies in the Aegean; they grew wealthy with the crusading expeditions of European Christians to the Levant (presently Cyprus, Syria, Lebanon, Palestine, Israel, and Jordan), supplying ships, food, and money; and with ad hoc shipping corporations that shared both the profits and risks of long-term travel and exchange. Their city became an important link between northern Europe, the Adriatic coast, Greece, Constantinople and the Black Sea, Egypt, and the Holy Land. As a result, the architecture of the newly enriched Venetian banking and merchant elites would differ from that of the inland cities' power holders. Their orientation was commercial rather than military. In central Italy, nobles who constructed urban residences in the twelfth century erected tall towers both to defend themselves and to represent their strength as clans. Venice, however, lacked both the local stone as well as the physical stability to engineer such structures. The merchants' waterfront palaces, in contrast to the fortified dwellings of Italy's landed elites, were arcaded, splendid constructions with which to mirror water and sky, but not protective barriers. They were distinguished by their *fondaci*, from the Arabic *fondouk*, signifying trading post, with docks to load and unload cargo from business ventures, as well as storerooms for merchandise, an appearance that did as much to exude peace and tranquillity as did the myth of Venice (Plate III).

Venice became a magnet for immigrant populations and an embarkation point for medieval pilgrimages, activities that are essential to understanding the medieval city's visual appearance. Both were in great measure products of the exchange with Byzantium, the Islamic world, and the Gothic in northern Europe. They also resulted from Venice's hosting and absorbing an array of peoples, including Germans, Slavs, Mamluks, Arabs, Greeks, Albanians, Jews, and a great variety of immigrants from mainland Italy. From the ninth century, the Giudecca had a refuge (*ospedale*) for travelers to the Holy Land. Another went up near the San Marco bell tower between 1253 and 1268. The city organized a regular galley service for tourists to the Holy Land, an enterprise that required furnishing lodging to pilgrims and creating employment for others.

Venice's town plan, according to architectural historian Deborah Howard, was a mirror of its medieval commercial experience.[4] The Venetians borrowed from Islamic typologies, recalling the great medieval cities of Damascus, Aleppo, Cairo, and Jerusalem. Merchants transported Islamic forms and modes of living, dividing Venetian space into industrial, public, and residential sectors. The major industries – shipbuilding, glassmaking, and supplying timber – rested on the fringes of the urban nucleus, as did the enclosed nunneries and mendicant orders. These enclaves cut off pedestrian circulation, similar to the *madrasas* and hospitals of the Islamic world. The central axis of the city, which ran from San Marco to Rialto, and vice versa, resembled an Islamic *suq*, or open-ended thoroughfare with artisans' and merchants' shops. Each end of this grand public artery opened into an expansive public space that recalled the major gathering places of cities in northern Africa and Southwest Asia. Behind Venice's public arteries lay a dense maze of footpaths, often dead-ended, that sheltered the private, residential space of its seventy-parish communities. Interestingly, in this regard Venice resembled the Mamluk capital of Damascus, which contained 70 separate residential districts and 120 canals. Moreover, the Grand Canal appeared somewhat like the great river arteries of Cairo and Baghdad. And the Venetian skyline, with its domes, crenellations, bell towers, and rooftop decks, were salient reminders of Islam's major cities (Plate IV).

The construction of Venice's principal focal points – the Piazza San Marco, the center of political, judicial, religious, and ritual affairs; the Rialto market, the commercial and financial center; and the Arsenal, the state shipyard and symbol of Venetian power – also rested on the medieval seafaring adventures of Venetians who had brought back religious stories, art forms, and merchandise from foreign lands. The port area, where the mouth of the Grand Canal flows into the lagoon basin, became the principal political and ecclesiastical center. The construction of a very large square, a basilica, and the palace of the doge followed the model of the Roman *palatium*, which also possessed a large, open square, a mausoleum, and the palace of the head of state.

Construction of the doge's chapel began three years after the relic of Saint Mark's body was laid to rest next to his palace in 829. The doge decided to model the structure after the sixth-century Church of the Holy Apostles in Constantinople. This first ducal chapel burned down in 976 and was replaced in 1063 by the impressive Greek basilica, foursquare, with low domes, modeled after the Church of the Holy Apostles and Hagia Sophia in Constantinople (see Plate I). The relics of St. Mark were lodged in the crypt of the basilica until the eighteenth century.

Contact with Constantinople and Alexandria underlay the iconography of the Basilica of San Marco.[5] From the outset it narrated Christian stories in the Byzantine pictorial language of gold mosaics, with settings that recalled the Islamic world, such as Joseph in Egypt amid the pyramids (Fig. 2). The vaults, domes, and upper walls of the interior depicted eastern saints; biblical narratives, such as the lives of Jesus and the Virgin; the apostolic message; and the life – and theft of the relics – of Saint Mark, set within the context of the Egyptian lands that Venetian merchants had visited and returned to describe. The atrium of the church also evoked Egyptian scenes of merchant travel and trade, complete with camels, tents, and buildings, in depictions of the Old Testament from the Book of Genesis. The floor, made of marble mosaic, resembled an Asian carpet. The visual program, infused with a Byzantine

Figure 2. Dome with scenes from the story of Joseph: *Joseph Gathering Up All the Food*. Byzantine mosaic, thirteenth century CE. Location: S. Marco, Venice, Italy. Photo credit: Scala/Ministero per i Beni e le Attività culturali/Art Resource, N.Y. Image Reference: ART408988.

stillness, was designed to teach worshippers the fundamentals of Christian history. After the Fourth Crusade in 1204, which permitted Venetians to study Greek writings in Constantinople, there were references to the classical tradition in San Marco as well. The visual language of the Basilica of San Marco was a dramatic departure from the Byzantine churches on Torcello and Murano, whose sober exteriors were made simply of brick. The façade was adorned with colorful mosaics and gold background, recalling the architectural style and mosaic art of the Great Umayyad Mosque in Damascus and the Dome of the Rock in Jerusalem. The mosaics adapted the visual vocabulary of Arab book illustrations as well as Byzantine artistry.

The twelfth and thirteenth centuries witnessed further transformations in the Basilica of San Marco that underlined Venice's ascendency as a commercial and naval power in the Mediterranean. The square outside the church was doubled in length, to accommodate the ceremonial meeting of Pope Alexander III and the Holy Roman Emperor Barbarossa, and work began on the offices of the Procurators of St. Mark, supreme magistrates and administrators of communal property. In addition, the Venetians designed a smaller square for the columns of Mark and Theodore. They also topped

Figure 3. Sixth-century columns from Acre transported in the thirteenth century. Location: South side of Basilica San Marco, Venice, Italy. Photo credit: J. M. Ferraro.

Figure 4. Replica of the Four Tetrarchs. (Originals, fourth century, Egyptian-Syrian carving in porphyry, are in the Basilica Treasury.) Photo credit: J. M. Ferraro.

Figure 5. The Horses of St. Mark's Basilica. Gilded copper. Hellenistic, fourth–third century BCE. The four horses were displayed in the hippodrome of Constantinople until the Venetians looted them in 1204, during the Fourth Crusade. Location: S. Marco, Venice, Italy. Photo credit: Vanni/Art Resource, N.Y. Image Reference: ART366558.

the basilica with the low, hemispherical domes that were characteristic of Byzantine churches. Throughout the thirteenth century, the Venetians elaborated on their most important religious edifice, with three Islamic domes topping the Byzantine cupolas; ivory and wood carvings providing intricate lacework, and Arabic portals and ornamentation recalling Islamic architectural forms (Plate V). Some of the decorations around the south façade next to the Doge's Palace were booty from wars and crusades, such as the two sixth-century Syrian pilasters from Acre and Byzantine reliefs on the wall (Fig. 3) as well as the fourth-century red porphyry Egyptian-Syrian Tetrarchs (Fig. 4). The body of St. Isidore, part of the Crusading booty of Doge Domenico Michiel in 1125, was housed in a chapel dedicated to the saint, and honored every year with a visit from the doge and other high-ranking magistrates. So too was the icon of Theotokos Nikopeia. Perhaps Venice's most famous war trophy, however, was from the notorious Fourth Crusade, the four horses pilfered from the Hippodrome at Constantinople in 1204 (Fig. 5). Venetians proudly commemorated their temporary conquest of the Byzantine capital with a celebratory ducal mass every sixth of December.

The northern European Gothic style mixed eclectically with this Venetian affinity for the East, but San Marco showed its strongest ties with Byzantium. In one sense the exotic iconography functioned as a collective merchant memoir, for those who had journeyed to foreign lands. In another sense it conveyed travelers' experiences to Venetians remaining at home in what was now a growing, multicultural entrêpot. The Islamic aspects of San Marco thus appealed to the developing cosmopolitan identity of urban residents.

Like the cathedral of San Marco, the Palazzo Ducale (Plate VI), which originated as a fortress-like stronghold for the head of state and was rebuilt in 1340 and 1424, also incorporated Byzantine, Islamic, and Gothic features collected from merchant adventures. It did not at all appear like the Italian municipal architecture prevalent elsewhere in northern Italy. While it borrowed from the Gothic north, it was distinctly oriented toward monumental Mongol and Mamluk architecture. What stands out first about the structure is the openness of the Palazzo Comunale facing the waterfront. Unlike other seats of communal government, it lacked fortification, light and air permeating its intricate lacework. It was more like the Mosque of St. Athanasius in Alexandria or the fourteenth-century hall of justice in Cairo than the municipal hall of Siena. Moreover, the pinnacled roofline, characteristic of Egyptian architecture with its mosque crenellations, looked more like the political space of sultans than Christians. Again, the visual experience of Venetian wayfarers – along the trade route to Alexandria and the Silk Road to Persia – was translated into Venetian public space. The lozenge pattern in the tiles on the upper half of the palace façade recalled the monuments of fourteenth-century Mongol rulers, save that the blue, white, and gold tile work became in the Venetian setting warm red and white, with Verona marble and Istrian stone. Howard has underlined that the adoption of these styles glorified Venetian commercial ventures on the Silk Route and with the Mamluk sultans during a delicate period when the commune was trying to obtain the papacy's permission to trade with the potentially lucrative Islamic world.[6]

The Palace of Justice on the Piazzetta, with its imagery of Solomon and seven philosophers representing the liberal arts and the wisdom of Venetian rulers, also referenced foreign prototypes. The Porta della Carta (Fig. 6) was crowned with a figure of Justice, an iconic reminder of Venice's wise rulers. Civic values adorn the capitals supporting the Bacino wing of the Palazzo Ducale. Some pay homage to skilled craftsmen; others depict the peoples with whom Venice came in contact – the Latins, Tartars, Turks, Hungarians, Greeks, Goths, Egyptians, and Persians; still others illustrate the Pythagorean-Ptolemaic cosmological model. The life cycle of the Venetian patrician merchant is also part of this assortment of themes carved on the Palazzo's stone shafts.

Figure 6. The Porta della Carta, by Giovanni and Bartolomeo Bon, begun 1438. Location: Venice, Italy. Photo credit: J. M. Ferraro.

San Marco and the Palazzo Ducale, representing the apogee of civic power and pride, were not entirely otherworldly; they also responded to the building programs of other Italian cities and competed with them to achieve superior beauty. Piazza San Marco, for example, began with a modest bell tower whose purpose was to mark time and to act as a beacon for ships, but as Italy's medieval towns competed to make their environments superlative, the Campanile grew to a height of sixty meters. The arches decorating the Palazzo Ducale both on the side of the Basin and that of the Piazzetta are also superior examples of the Flamboyant Gothic style, originating in

Figure 7. Jacopo de' Barbari (c. 1460/70–c. 1516). *The Arsenal.* Detail of *The Map of Venice.* Location: Museo Correr, Venice, Italy. Photo credit: Erich Lessing/Art Resource, N.Y. Image Reference: ART151954.

northern Europe. The Porta della Carta, a ceremonial gateway linking the Ducal Palace with San Marco, built by Giovanni and Bartolomeo Bon, is one of Venice's most important late Gothic monuments, together with Ca' d'Oro, a patrician palace on the Grand Canal.

Venetians chose the eastern edge of the city as the site for state building of boats, and merchant and war galleys, the vehicles that connected the floating city with the larger Mediterranean and the northern European world. The Arsenal, from the Arabic *darsiná* (signifying a locale of manufacture), symbolized Venice's growing commercial and naval strength, but it also represented the city's largest medieval industry (Fig. 7). Established in 1104, it was modeled on Byzantine precedents. Four parishes of shipbuilders, some with military training, supplied the Arsenal's labor force, with women making sails and men involved in all aspects of construction. The Arsenal workers built superior ships to accompany improved navigation, particularly after 1330, and the state-sponsored *muda*, a convoy of merchant galleys with armed crews of about two hundred men, guaranteed the Venetian spice trade as well as other precious cargos.

5. Social Geography

After the first millennium, every town in Italy from Rome to Milan grew dramatically. The Italian peninsula's position on the Adriatic and Mediterranean seas, between northern Europe and the Levant, coupled with fertile soil and a rising birth rate, fueled a significant economic and urban growth to the mid-fourteenth century, when the Black Death ravished Europe and reduced the population. Up until then, agricultural productivity, the Crusading expeditions (1096–1204) to the Levant and Byzantium, and long-distance trade, banking, double-book accounting, insurance, monetary exchange, and textile manufacture – all benchmarks of the medieval commercial revolution – generated great riches, propelling the newly wealthy to the acme of the Peninsula's social and political hierarchies. Everywhere the population soared, releasing an excess of agricultural laborers to the growing cities. Venetian figures were among the highest in Europe, reaching 120,000 by 1300, an important underpinning of its urbanization.

Social organization in Venice changed during the twelfth and thirteenth centuries. Parishes ceased to be exclusive, family estates, and the singular power of the doge waned in favor of shared, noble governance. This transformation corresponded with the city's greater role in international commerce, a development that endowed successful business denizens with preeminence. Noble investors made commercial contracts, called *commende*, with traveling partners in an effort to collectivize both risk and profit. They also accumulated great wealth through banking and investments in a variety of manufacturing enterprises, wealth that enabled them to influence the direction of urban affairs. In 1284 they minted the gold ducat, which they named *zecchino*, after the Arabic word *sikka*, meaning mint.

The municipal government, through its leading families, assumed a prominent role in urban development. The city was divided into units, and magistrates called the Giudici del Piovego were assigned responsibility for maintaining and improving streets, bridges, canals, and modes of transportation. While the parish remained an important urban division, in 1171 it was subsumed into one of six districts, called *sestieri*, whose administrators, called *capi*, were laymen representing the public good. Snaking through the city, the Grand Canal balanced the social weight of these six districts, with three *sestieri* on either side, each with an administrative head. Castello, San Marco, and Cannaregio were on the left side; Santa Croce, San Polo, and Dorsoduro on the right. Historian Robert Davis tells us that the bureaucratic division, primarily for policing and tax collection, may have fostered popular factionalism in addition to neighborhood self-consciousness.[7] The inhabitants in the districts closest to the mainland – Cannaregio, San Polo, and Santa Croce – identified with the "peoples from the land" and had named themselves Cannaruoli by the late thirteenth century, after the dockworkers and cattle butchers of Cannaregio. Those settled in the three seaward districts of San Marco, Castello, and Dorsoduro named themselves "Islanders," and eventually Castellani. There was then a factional boundary running at roughly right angles to the Grand Canal. The government established six Lords of the Nightwatch to patrol a city now rife with the rivalries of the Nicolotti fishermen on the right bank and the Castellani arsenal workers on the left.

Neighborhood divisions were also balanced with common space that brought residents back together as a whole. Foremost was the Piazza San Marco, the seat of civic and religious powers, with the inner harbor at the Bacino San Marco, linking Venice with the Mediterranean world. Arriving visitors would first sight the two monumental columns sustaining the symbols of Venice, the patron Saint Theodore and the Winged Lion of St. Mark. The magnificent Byzantine basilica that served as the chapel of the doge stood proudly at the eastern end of the grand Piazza, exhibiting the city's war trophies and eastern orientation. Adjacent to its southern edge was the Palazzo Ducale, the residence of the doge and the meeting place of the ruling class. The Rialto, a world marketplace and financial center, was a second important urban axis, together with the Grand Canal, the city's major artery of transport and communication. The third axis was situated in the eastern quarter of the city, home to the state's shipbuilding facilities and military arsenal as well as the storehouse for hemp and a rope factory. The fourth axis lay to the west, nearest the mainland. It housed manufacture, with the exception of the glass furnaces, relegated to the island of Murano (see Plate VII) because of the danger of fire. In fact, many of Venice's medieval industries were situated outside the home. Making glass, soap, dyes, tiles, bricks, saltpeter, or metal products required furnaces, leaching pits, boiling vats, and other equipment more appropriate to the medieval "factory" setting.

Venice underwent a great deal of construction between the twelfth and fifteenth centuries. Between 1250 and 1350, the commune reorganized the commercial center at Rialto. In fact, from early on the area was destined to become a commercial rather than a residential district. The process began when one large landowning family, the Orio, willed their property to the city at the end of the eleventh century, designating that it be used as a market. The area then commercialized, and in 1157 it housed the first private banks. Housing around the Rialto markets became denser and buildings

grew taller. Nobles in the vicinity thus steadily transferred to the opposite side of the Grand Canal, where the German warehouse (Fondaco dei
Tedeschi) was built in the 1220s. As this area filled, new families settled along
the Salizzada San Lio, adopting the Veneto-Byzantine style, with tall and
narrow buildings and relatively small windows. Other noble families chose
to live near the doge, around the Piazza San Marco, making the Rialto–San
Marco axis an area of prime real estate. Beyond their own residences, the
urban elite owned a variety of other real estate, including houses, shops,
canteens, grain mills, and waterways for fishing, hunting, and drying seawa-
ter to extract salt.

Patrician merchants used their homes both as showplaces for their success
and as headquarters for their commercial ventures. Their homes also defined
the public identity of the Venetian ruling class, an identity that changed
over time. The earliest architectural example of aristocratic housing was the
Veneto-Byzantine palace of the twelfth century. The Palazzi Loredan (Fig. 8)
and Farsetti (Plate III) (currently Venice's municipal hall), and the Fondaco
dei Turchi (currently the Museum of Natural History) date from this period.
Each had a two-story arcade facing the waterfront, where merchandise
was loaded and unloaded. The ground-floor portico led to the Great Hall
(androne), which housed storerooms, offices, cooking facilities, armor, and
whatever else the family wished to display. On the floor above were the family's living quarters. Each room led off a great T-shaped central room called
the salone or portego. The distribution of rooms on either side of the portego's
large space permitted better ventilation. Behind the palace was a courtyard,
an essential open space that permitted light to enter the dwelling; a well;
and an exterior staircase to access the upper floors. Servants occupied the
top floor of the residence. This type of building could also be found in the
Levant. Most likely, Venetian merchants adapted their model from the Arabic
fondouk, or trading post. They too named their warehouses fondaci. Away
from the canals, the architecture of Venetian elites took a different form,
as exemplified in the thirteenth-century palaces on the Salizzada San Lio
(Fig. 9). These houses, lining a commercial artery, had shops on the ground
floor opening onto the street. The first floor housed residents' living quarters,
and the upper floor was for servants.

Whether on the Grand Canal or not, Venetian exteriors were highly decorated, a luxury that elites on the mainland could not afford because their
palaces were designed, like fortifications, to protect them. Only Venetians
could enjoy the tranquillity of an arcaded water frontage – ephemeral
façades, narrow bays, slender columns, and tall stilted arches, just the opposite
of the heavily fortified palaces of central Italy. They adorned their exteriors

Figure 8. Ca' Loredan, early thirteenth century. Location: Venice, Italy. Photo credit: J. M. Ferraro.

with reused friezes and imported medallions, marble slabs, and Byzantine reliefs looted during the Crusades. Not all their decorations were stolen; they also engaged masterful Lombard stone masons to carve their capitals and cornices.

During the thirteenth century, the leading families consolidated their hold over Venetian trade, both in the colonies and at home. They held major interests in shipbuilding, forced loans to the government that earned interest, and, in the fourteenth century, the state galley convoys. Venice as a commercial power was represented with the new Gothic style that gradually

Figure 9. The Salizzada San Lio. Location: Venice, Italy. Photo credit: J. M. Ferraro.

eased out the preceding Veneto-Byzantine tradition. Along the Grand Canal, noble palaces decorating Venetian waters with their lacy reflections commemorated trading conquests as well as each dynasty's status within the ruling circle.[8] Both the height and the front of the palace were important, the uniformity of the former projecting social and political cohesion and the latter celebrating family memory. During this period, the state offered financial help to families building palaces on conspicuous urban sites, such as the Grand Canal.

The Rialto was left, thus, to become a commercial center. In fact, owing to the Crusades and the establishment of a seaborne empire stretching from the Adriatic to the Aegean and the Levant, it became an international emporium. Between 1250 and 1350, the streets of parishes in the vicinity were extended into the marketplace; canals were dredged to rid them of fetid water; watercraft circulation was improved; building projects for wharfs, stalls, shops, and custom houses were undertaken; and sale sites received specialized designations, such as large-scale trade; victuals; merchandise; and banking, insurance, and finance. Warehouses were also built along the canal, underneath the prime real estate 3's most prosperous families.

The arrival of mendicant orders from central Italy during the thirteenth century also integrated the different parts of the city. They brought with them a unifying Gothic building style for large churches, noble palaces, and confraternities (called *scuole*; the singular is *scuola*); they established major axes of pedestrian circulation; and they marked out the city's sacred space, providing a sense of both community and identity. Dominicans (or Preacher Friars), Franciscans, and Augustinians brought in boatloads of timber from the mainland to construct churches above the level of the sea, their façades later adorned with brick and stone. Among the most important were the Dominican Santa Maria Formosa (1234) and San Giovanni and Paolo (Plate VII), built on the northern edge of the city between 1246 and 1258 and remodeled between 1333 and 1368; the Franciscan Santa Maria Gloriosa dei Frari (1250–1330) (Fig. 10) and San Francesco della Vigna (1300); and the Augustinian Santo Stefano (13th–14th centuries). These structures were a departure from the older parish churches, built in the Veneto-Byzantine style, some of which had been constructed from wood and covered with thatched roofs. With generous donations from the great Venetian families and the commune itself, the mendicants built larger, more embellished structures. The Gothic ornamentation from northern Europe was in vogue, but the Venetian churches could not have vaulted ceilings because of the physical instability of the soil. Instead their ceilings were flat, albeit beautifully decorated with wooden beams.

The city's major families also undertook large building initiatives during the thirteenth century, favoring Gothic ornamentation for their façades. Domestic architecture mirrored the city's social hierarchy. At the pinnacle of society and politics were the Badoer, Contarini, Falier, Michiel, Morosini, Polani, and Ziani families. Directly underneath them were the *cittadini*, a hereditary citizen caste of merchants, notaries, lawyers, and bureaucrats. Everyone else comprised the commoner class of *popolani*, but there were obviously great variations in wealth and status, ranging from the butcher,

Figure 10. Exterior view. Location: Santa Maria Gloriosa del Frari, begun 1330 Venice, Italy. Photo credit: Scala/Art Resource, N.Y. Image Reference: ART183806.

the baker, and the candlestick maker to surgeons and apothecaries. The city's top families chose the landed sites that gave them access to the port, the commercial hub at Rialto, and the Grand Canal, the conduit for transport but also the most coveted aesthetic setting. Until the fourteenth century, the Grand Canal housed boatyards and stone yards, but thereafter it became the residential area for patrician palaces as well.

Space was always at a premium in Venice, forcing architects to look for creative ways to expand the dwellings of the rich. The obvious way was up, but the soft ground limited physical stability. Another way was to build the house out over a public street, with the street passing underneath through an arcade called a *sottoportego*. Yet a third solution was to project the upper stories a short distance over the street, supported on wooden or stone corbels, as exemplified on the Calle del Paradiso (see Fig. 17 in Chapter 4), which traverses the Salizzada San Lio. There the Foscari and Mocenigo families built blocks of rental units. Venetian palaces and modest flats were heated with fireplaces, situated on outside walls, one above the next and sharing a chimney. Decorated, terra-cotta chimney pots, shaped like inverted bells with a conical top, confined the sparks and cinder to the flues and sheltered the openings from rain.

BUILDING CONSTRUCTION

Foundations: Laborers hammered pilings deep into the mud, to the rhythm of song. The wood piles passed through alluvial clay and sand reaching 12–15 feet in depth. A raft of larch planks cemented with stone and brick was constructed atop the pilings. Where the layers of clay and sand were too deep to be reached, the building site was contained within a wooden barrier. Then it was drained and fortified with baulks of oak and larch. The tops of the piles lay approximately ten feet below the high tide level. Stone structures were built atop the raft, while the walls of building sat atop the piles, which carried the most weight. Floors began with an oak foundation. Then stone and marble shards were firmly packed into a layer of mortar. Architects designed foundations with materials and structure that lent themselves to lightness and flexibility.

Façades: Usually of brick and in one of two colors: pale grey or red.

Roofs: Began with a layer of flat, hollow bricks. Roman tiles were placed on the rafters. Stone gutters around the roof were linked by drainpipes to the wells down below.

Materials: Reddish-brown bricks and tiles manufactured on the mainland for walls and roof tops, respectively. Powdered brick, marble grains, and lime produced a stuccoed cover for the bricks. White limestone from Istria was carved and decorated for capitals, cornices, balustrades, and doorways. Portals and fireplaces were made of Verona's red marble. Some marble came from Constantinople's constructions. Piles were made of Dalmatian oak. The Friuli region and Treviso also supplied oak for ceiling timbers and roof beams. The Dolomites and Cadore supplied the more preferable larch and spruce, lighter woods that worked better on Venice's soft soil. Floors were either of wood, or in the richer households, of ground tiles and bricks set in cement and polished. The homes of the wealthy also had glass windows. Iron was necessary, but used sparingly in the damp, corrosive climate.[9]

Another space-saving innovation in Venetian palace building was the "L-shaped" plan, common in areas where land was at a shortage and very expensive. In contrast with the "T-shaped" central *salone*, the "L" plan situated the great hall to one side of the edifice, stretching from the façade to the back. (Ca' d'Oro is a prime example.) The smaller rooms were placed on the opposite side of the building. Such palaces were often built back to back between two canals so that each had access to both a street and a waterway. The canal frontage afforded the interior the much-needed light, but in addition these palaces had adjacent courtyards behind them for illumination. In the fifteenth century the courtyard was placed on the side of the building rather than in the back to furnish even more light (e.g., Ca' Foscari).

Commoners' houses, in contrast, were arranged around a shared courtyard and water well, or along a side street.

Rising prosperity, a climbing birth rate and immigration, and a growing building trade encouraged new reclamation and construction between 1280 and 1340, giving birth to the districts of Santa Croce and Cannaregio as well as the Giudecca Nova. With them came new alleyways, quays, and bridges, and the first paved streets. Cannaregio also housed the state foundry during the fourteenth and early fifteenth centuries, where copper bars and bronze were produced for artillery. When the foundry was no longer able to satisfy the growing need for artillery, it was transferred to the state Arsenal in the 1430s.

The state also rebuilt the Palazzo Ducale in the mid-fourteenth century, adding Gothic ornamentation to the Veneto-Byzantine and Moorish elements. Prospering citizenry continued to build a host of new palaces in the Gothic style as well as artisan cottages for rentals. Thriving merchants and craftsmen erected confraternities, essentially brotherhoods, as places to meet, to assist the needy, to stage rituals and pageants, and to represent all parts of the city. The major ones, or *scuole grandi*, included the Carità, San Marco (Plate VII) (currently the Hospital), and San Giovanni Evangelista (1260); the Misericordia (1308); and much later San Rocco (1478) and San Teodoro (1552). The minor ones, or *scuole piccole*, accommodated the growing communities of Albanians, Greeks, and Slavs as well as minor craftsmen and traders. This flurry of construction reached its acme in 1348, when the bubonic plague brought most activity in Venice, and Europe as a whole, to a temporary but dramatic halt.

The floating medieval city continued to face engineering problems germane to its configuration. One was securing sufficient drinking water, achieved by constructing artificial wells that collected rainwater. Wells were costly to build; thus the first ones were private, belonging to the most prosperous families. The structure consisted of a clay-lined cavity as deep as sixteen feet below the level of the highest tide, to secure it against the invasion of salt water. At midpoint was a central shaft, topped with sand that filled the cavity up to the street pavement. The well was capped with a stone lid containing several slits. Conduits attached the well to drainpipes, which in turn linked the rain gutters surrounding the city's roofs. Eventually there were also drains in the paving surrounding the well. The rain water spilled into the sand, which acted as a filter, before accumulating in the central well shaft. Vital to the survival of the population, wells became important social sites, joining rich and poor alike. Families attached to a noble household through service shared the aristocrats' amenities. However, each public square also had at least one well to furnish the less fortunate with water. When engineering improved after the fifteenth century, making wells more common, there was greater social segregation, with noble households enjoying private cisterns while poorer households shared responsibility for the construction and maintenance of these vital sources of potable water. By 1500 there were some 4,000 private wells and only 100 public ones. Crouzet-Pavan tells us that even rain gutters mirrored the city's social hierarchy, with stone and marble adorning aristocratic households and more transient, wooden conduits serving the needs of ordinary people.[10]

The supply of potable water depended upon precipitation. During dry spells, water bearers (*acquaroli*) brought in boatloads of water from the Brenta River and sold it by the pail. The government purchased water and distributed it to the poor. Venetians kept a variety of water pails, separating those carrying potable water from the ones serving hygiene and other household needs. Even the salt water that served sanitary needs, however, had to be protected from pollutants, and the city early developed an ecological consciousness. Ordinances prohibited dumping cloth dyes, spoiled meat, and other pollutants into the canals. Instead, the lagoon was designated as the principal receptacle for refuse. House drains did discharge effluent into the canals, or into covered drains that spilled into nearby waterways. Houses far from the water, however, needed cesspits.

Much of Venice's foundation and overall design was in place by the end of the fourteenth century. Architectural historians have concluded that commercial interaction between the tenth and mid-fourteenth centuries, perhaps more than anything else, had defined Venice's architectural fabric and material culture. Despite later claims of Greco-Roman ancestry, a Renaissance fashion made manifest in Venetian interiors after 1400, the city's most enduring features originated in northern Africa and Southwest Asia, the spheres of its medieval, maritime ventures.

FURTHER READING

Architecture: G. Bellavitis and G. Romanelli (1985); D. Howard (2000, 2005, 2007a–c); P. Maretto (1986); E. Trincanato (1948). *History*: E. Crouzet-Pavan (1992, 2002); R. Davis (1994); F. Lane (1973); L. Martines (1988); D. Romano (1987).

2

THE RICHES OF ASIA, EUROPE,
AND NORTH AFRICA

1. Crusading Ventures

Venice established the commercial and cultural connections that made it a world city during the three centuries following the first millennium. The remarkable course of maritime expansion began with the establishment of trade agreements with Constantinople, under the leadership of Doge Pietro Orseolo II (991–1008). Throughout the eleventh century Venice cultivated this lucrative alliance, lending critical assistance to the Byzantine emperor in 1082 in his struggle against Norman marauders. Venetian loyalties were in turn richly rewarded with permission to traffic the waters of the eastern Mediterranean.

The renowned Crusades soon followed, creating a series of opportunities for further gain between 1099 and 1204. When the pope galvanized Europe's restless warriors and pilgrims to reconquer the Holy Land in 1095, Venice became both a pilgrim stop and a point of departure on the way to adventure. The Crusading movement inaugurated the Venetian tourist industry, for the wayfarers required victuals and lodgings during their stopovers. At the same time, Venetian galleys offered crusaders passage at sea, another lucrative business opportunity. On these expeditions merchants opened up new trade routes in the southern and eastern basins of the Mediterranean. Applying their maritime technology, naval strength, and business acumen, the leading families made Venice a Mediterranean power on equal footing with its former Byzantine rulers.

The Venetians' avaricious ambitions emerged quickly after the pope's summons in 1095. They happily responded to the religious mission under the pretense of expressing Christian piety but began by affording themselves a leisurely sojourn in the Greek territories (named "Romania" because they were regarded as part of the Roman Empire). Only after they had pilfered the relics of Saint Nicholas for their church on the Lido and had secured

Figure 11. Jacopo Robusti Tintoretto (1518–94). *The Conquest of Constantinople in 1204. Episode of the Fourth Crusade*. Location: Palazzo Ducale, Venice, Italy. Photo Credit: Scala/ Art Resource, NY. Image Reference: ART104914.

strategic trading ports in the Aegean did they continue on to Palestine, where they proceeded to ransack Jaffa and Haifa. A few decades later, in 1123–4, they made inroads into the Muslim territories of Ascalon, Acre, and Tyre, heaping gold, silver, and spices into their cargo ships and securing for themselves and other European crusaders the principal trade routes between Asia and Europe. The Venetians proceeded to amass great wealth in goods, antiquities, relics, and slaves as much through pillaging, piracy, and colonial dominance as through trade (Maps 2 and 3).

Market conquests in the Adriatic, Aegean, and ports of the eastern Mediterranean Sea contributed significantly to Venetian prosperity at home. The maritime adventurers traded timber and slaves in Egypt for alum, linen, cotton, silk, and spice, which they carried back to Venice via the Adriatic.

THE MARRIAGE OF VENICE TO THE SEA

The "Marriage of the Sea," one of Venice's most important civic rituals, celebrated the city's dominion over the sea. The ceremony, scheduled on Ascension Day, was established during the eleventh century to commemorate the initiation of the campaign to conquer Dalmatia under the leadership of the Doge Pietro II Orseolo. Orseolo had begun his quest on Ascension Day, and thus it became a date of celebration. The ritual took the form of a solemn procession of vessels that followed the doge in the state's ceremonial ship, the Bucintoro. It set out to sea via the Lido (see Plate XIV) with the prayer, "for us and all who sail thereon the sea may be calm and quiet." The participants were then sprinkled with holy water and the rest was thrown into the sea. Priests chanted from the seventh verse in the fifty-first chapter in the book of Psalm, "Purge me with hyssop [a garden herb used in medicines] and I shall be clean." In 1177, Pope Alexander III gave the ceremony a quasi-sacramental character in gratitude for Venetian services against the Holy Roman Emperor Frederick I. The pontiff gave his ring to the doge to toss into the sea. The ritual of marrying Venice to the sea was then performed every year on Ascension Day. As the ring was tossed overboard the Venetians chanted, "We wed thee, sea, in the sign of the true and everlasting Lord."

The ritual of the Sensa also inaugurated a renowned fair in Venice that attracted both the peasantry from the countryside and visitors from other Italian and European states. For fifteen days, Piazza San Marco was the site of a grand market, with exotic food and dress as well as a vast array of other items for consumption. Venetian merchants were obliged to close their shops and set up stalls, distributed through guild lotteries, in the square instead. Venice put an assortment of gold, perfume, needles, swords, knives, rosary beads, woodwork, glass, mirrors, shoes, books, and icons on display.

Between 1125 and 1149 they netted coastal Dalmatia and the island of Corfu, giving them strategic dropoff and loading zones for their cargo as well as hegemony over the Adriatic. The Dalmatian coast was essential, for the early cargo ships could not carry great weight. A series of ports, used as stepping-stones, facilitated loading and unloading from short distances between Venice and the greater Mediterranean world. The Venetians also began to transport wheat from the shores of Apulia and Sicily to their warehouses and to those of their neighbors. Moreover, they dominated commercial exchange on the Adriatic by obliging all ships to bring their cargoes to the lagoon where Venetians could in turn re-export the merchandise.

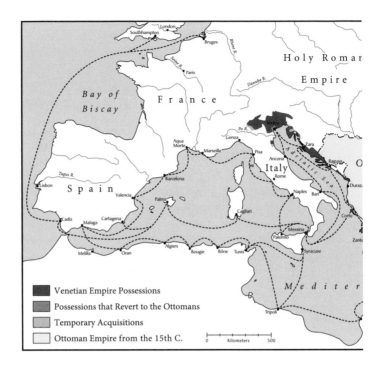

The road to profit, however, was not one of linear progression but rather of detours and even dead ends. As the twelfth century came to a close, Venetian commercial enterprise encountered a series of temporary adversities before reaching a new hiatus. But then the Fourth Crusade (1202–4) brought the maritime power another half century of commercial hegemony, albeit at heavy cost to its reputation for the rape and plunder of Constantinople. Thanks to Venetian mythmaking, the four bronze horses now housed within Saint Mark's Basilica scarcely commemorate the atrocities, instead standing as war trophies in the company of sacred relics. Further conquests during the Fourth Crusade made Venice the preeminent power on the seas linking Constantinople to the Adriatic. The city emerged with substantial influence over the Latin empire, including the temporary allotment, until 1261, of three-eighths of the Byzantine capital. It also established a series of naval bases that amounted to a Greek colonial empire. Negroponte, the "Black Bridge" between Crete and Constantinople, served as a commercial stepping-stone to Crete, which was purchased and parceled out to soldiers, landlords, and merchants. Venice also acquired Modone, on the Ionian Sea, and, for a few years, Corfu, as well as the city of Zara in Dalmatia. Importantly, Venice, like Genoa, played an

Map 2. Major Trade Routes. Europe, North Africa, Asia. Based on Janet Abu-lughod, *Before European Hegemony: The World System, A.D. 1250-1350* (Oxford: Oxford University Press, (1989), 123. Map by Harry D. Johnson, Department of Geography, San Diego State University.

instrumental role in linking Europe to the world economy of Asia, via the Levant, which received the goods from East and Southeast Asia via overland routes.[1] But 1261 was once again a turning point in the system of trade. When the Latin Kingdom fell and Venice lost its hold over Constantinople, it shifted its commercial gaze southward, toward the Mamluk Sultanate (Map 4).

Thanks to the development of the nautical compass, an Arab construction that replaced the needle-and-bowl, by the 1290s convoys of galleys and cargo ships, called *mude*, traversed the seas each autumn along two main routes: the muda to Romania commuted to Constantinople; the other one toured Cyprus, Little Armenia, and Syria. Both of these routes, which continued through the late fifteenth century, were linked commercially to China. Later the Venetians added a southern muda to Alexandria, which loaded cereals, dye-plants, spices, and pharmacopoeia that had originated in the Moluccas and the Indian Ocean (Indonesia, Ceylon, India). The southern route was vital through the sixteenth century but contained by Mamluk forces. The first major sea caravan departed Venice for the Greek mainland and the Aegean, picking up wine, oil, fruits, and nuts to take to Egypt and bringing back wheat, beans, and sugar. It also

exported silk from Sparta and Thebes. At the same time a large colony of
Venetians made Constantinople their home base, supplying the Byzantine
capital with grain, salt, fish, furs, and slaves from Soldaia and collecting
Asian wares from the Black Sea to market in Europe. East Asian goods
were transported through the vast Mongol empire, stretching from the
Sea of Japan to the borders of Hungary. From Constantinople, Venetians
also visited the rivers of Iran and Iraq, passing through the Khanate of
Persia, eventually reaching the Indian Ocean and thus the spices of India
and the Indian Ocean. The second major sea caravan departed Venice for
Cyprus, Syria, and Palestine, making exchange between western Europe

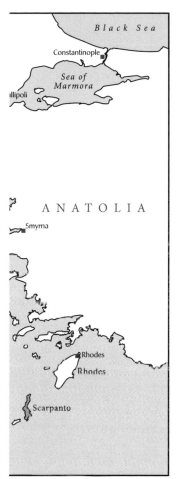

Map 3. Greek Locales at Times under Venice. Based on Frederick Lane, *Venice, A Maritime Republic* (Baltimore: Johns Hopkins University Press, 1973), 177. Map by Harry D. Johnson, Department of Geography, San Diego State University.

and the Levant instrumental. Venice transported woolens and metals from its western European suppliers to the Levant and returned to Europe with silk fabrics from Constantinople; red dye from the Peloponnese; wax, honey, cotton, and wheat from various ports; furs and slaves from the Black Sea; and sweet wines from the Greek islands.

The Venetians were not just supplying transportation for goods. They became major colonizers and controlled the processes of production. Crete, a stepping-stone to Haifa, was home to large Venetian estates that produced grain, wine, oil, and fruits that were marketed back in Venice as well as in Jaffa, Acre, and Damascus. The other great Venetian colony was in Acre, the

GALLEYS

Teams of carpenters, sawyers, caulkers, and cordage and sailmakers could put a merchant galley afloat in a couple of years. The vessels belonged to the state, which in turn chartered them out to merchant associations that shared both profits and risks. Oarsmen propelled these galleys built by the state arsenal workers. The galleys were incapable of carrying heavy tonnage, which was left to the privately built round ships (called cogs). Instead they transported cargo for short distances, unloading and loading from port to port. They traveled in convoys of eight to eleven, called *mude*, for mutual protection. The arsenal workers also constructed the state's war galleys. In the fourteenth century there was a reserve of twenty-five. This doubled by the end of the fifteenth century as the Republic engaged more frequently in naval conflict. With the sixteenth-century Ottoman menace, the fleet reached 100, engaging between two to three thousand workers. The early galley oarsmen of the thirteenth and four-teenth centuries considered theirs to be a respectable profession, but after that point the Republic had a difficult time recruiting oarsmen. Many Dalmatians and Greeks entered this service. From the sixteenth century the Republic decided to draft criminals to the galleys, who were kept at work in chains.

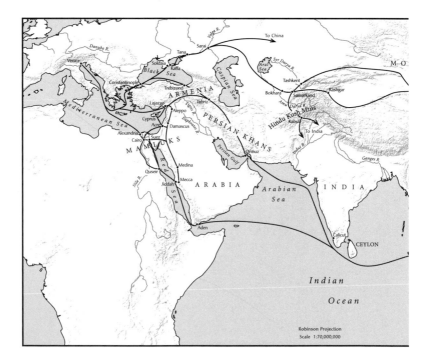

city that became the center of all business during the Crusades and the meeting place of the trade routes that tapped the wealth of Asia and the Spice Islands. Acre was the home of an international community of Muslim merchants, Christian Arabs, Armenians, Jews, and Greeks. Venice's Genoese rivals also settled in the city, vying for business opportunities. Bales of eastern drugs and spices arrived at the gates of Acre on the backs of camels traveling from Mecca to Damascus along the old caravan route. Other suppliers reached Acre from Egypt. This caravan also brought alum, sugar, wheat, wood, metals, and slaves. The Venetians constructed country estates around Acre and grew lemons, oranges, almonds, and figs for export.

Venice once again experienced commercial setbacks in the fourteenth century. Trade wars with the Genoese weakened the Republic's grip over its eastern sea routes. However, the period also witnessed the opening of additional markets between the Mediterranean and the North Sea, with new Venetian colonies in London and Bruges and an annual spring convoy to northwest Africa and Aigues-Mortes in Provence. The northern European cities supplied metals, wool, and textiles in exchange for the exotic products from the Mediterranean and Asia. Further, after 1368 Venetians, under the lead of the Cornaro family, made heavy investments in sugar mills, irrigation systems, and slaves on the island of Cyprus. They

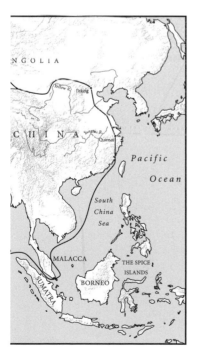

Map 4. Trade Routes of Greater Asia. Based on Frederick Lane, *Venice, A Maritime Republic* (Baltimore: Johns Hopkins University Press, 1973), 71, 78. Map by Harry D. Johnson, Department of Geography, San Diego State University.

THE POLO BROTHERS

Among the most famous Venetians who set up business activities in Constantinople were Nicolò and Matteo Polo. The two brothers sailed from Venice to the city on the Bosphorus in 1261 and at the Black Sea they traded Russian and Turkish products. They traveled from Soldaia to Sarai on the Volga River, remaining with the Mongols for a year. Then they continued east along the Silk Road until they reached the Great Khan in China. They returned to Venice in 1269 and picked up Nicolò's son Marco. The three journeyed to China between 1271 and 1275 via Syria and Tabriz, joining the Silk Road to the north of Hindu Kush. They reached the Great Khan in China once again in 1275, where Marco remained for seventeen years. Marco made the return journey to Venice between 1292 and 1295 via the China Sea, the west coast of India, and the Persian Gulf. Between 1298 and 1299 he chronicled his observations about merchandise, taxes, and administration in China. He also described how the Mongols had opened up the land route to the Spice Islands, and observed the marketability of sugar, spices, silk, and cotton for his native Venice. From his travel notes, Venetians, and Europeans in general, learned about new ways of life, culture, and technology.

also imported cotton, a plantation crop produced in Syria, Anatolia, and the southeastern Balkans.

2. The Rialto: Mirror of the World

If Venetian seafaring adventures shaped and colored the visual representation of the Basilica San Marco, the Palazzo Ducale, and the palaces of the merchant nobility, the island of Rialto captured the medieval merchant and colonial experience and infused Venice's inhabitants with worldly tastes (Fig. 12). Originally the residential area of powerful noble families, Rialto began in the ninth century with a few butcher stalls and a fish market. When in the eleventh century the commune inherited the properties of the noble Orio family, the island became the seat of the government agencies that regulated economic affairs. Soon it was a center of finance, with the first private banks appearing around 1157. It underwent reorganization between 1250 and 1350, with the older Rialto Vecchio, centering around the church of San Giacomo, designated for large-scale trade, credit operations, and marine insurance, and the newer Rialto Nuovo, at San Mateo, specializing in the sale of victuals.

Figure 12. Aerial view of Rialto Bridge. Photo: Pubbli Aer Foto. Location: Venice, Italy. Photo Credit: © DeA Picture Library/Art Resource, NY. Image Reference: ART349675.

The entire area also developed into a giant warehouse, not just for Venice but for Europe as a whole.

The strategic position of the Rialto island made it a natural magnet for shops and stands displaying the world's material goods to rich and poor, whether they could afford to purchase the showcase of exotic merchandise or not. It was linked by watercraft via the Grand Canal to Venice's port district, the area around San Marco where the lagoon channel met both the Grand Canal and that of the Giudecca. Winter convoys arriving from the Levant anchored at San Marco and unloaded their precious cargos, which were in turn transported via boat or on foot to Venice's shops and stalls. On foot from the port, the winding shopping street, called the Merceria, led to the Rialto Bridge, Venice's only crossing on the Grand Canal until the nineteenth century. The structure was first made of a platoon of boats (1172), then of wood (1200–60), and finally carved in stone (1591). A ferry service on the Grand Canal across from the fish market, at the Fondaco dei Tedeschi, transported Rialto vendors to their food suppliers in the Po Valley and brought to Venice merchants from other parts of Italy as well as from Vienna, Augsburg, Nuremberg, Regensburg, Ulm, and other transalpine commercial centers.

The Rialto market became the medieval jewel of international emporia thanks in part to the Venetian naval conquests of the twelfth and thirteenth centuries, which had propelled Venetians into the Levant and Byzantium. Exotic goods and home products intersected in the commercial district's shops and stalls. Vendors exchanged Venetian salt and metals mined in the Harz, Bohemian, Carpathian, and Bosnian mountains, for timber; they sold produce grown on the mainland and fish from their lagoon; they consumed and exported grain from the Levant and southern Italy; and they introduced wealthy consumers to the exotic spices, dyestuffs, silks, and gems from Byzantine and Islamic markets.

The market district was segmented into specialized areas that are still evident in the names of streets and squares today. Wine was sold on the Fondamenta del Vin, on the southern side of the bridge adjacent to San Silvestro. This pedestrian thoroughfare was also named Del Ferro, for iron was marketed here as well. The wine vendors formed their own guild and confraternity in 1505. The porters (*portatori*) and bottlers (*travasadori*) followed in 1569. Wine was unloaded on the Riva del Vin, a walkway intersecting the Grand Canal, and stored in warehouses or delivered to the taverns (*bacari*) that served refreshment. There were also designated warehouses for oil and flour in the vicinity, as well as the stalls and shops of the cloth merchants, apothecaries, and furriers. The goldsmiths occupied an alley named Ruga degli Oresi (goldsmiths in Venetian dialect) adjacent to the Rialto Arcade, where many shops still stand. Along the right bank of the Grand Canal, near the Riva del Olio (where *sagomatori* unloaded their casks) and the wharf that received timber shipments, was the renowned Campo della Pescaria, where fishermen brought their daily catch. A wooden structure was built in 1332 that sold birds as well as fish; this burned down in 1531 and was rebuilt in 1884. Facing Cannaregio on the Grand Canal, the Erberia and the Fruttaria housed the vegetable and fruit stalls, respectively, with home products from the islands and the mainland. The poultry vendors were their neighbors. New butchers' stalls, named the Beccarie, were built around 1339 in the campo near San Giovanni Elemosinario. A specialized government office in the vicinity regulated each of these products. Not everyone, however, shopped at Rialto. Each neighborhood had its own market on a specific day of the week in its parish square. There were also two larger markets, at San Polo on Wednesdays and San Marco on Saturdays. San Marco, like Rialto, had market stalls with fresh victuals and cooked meals as well.

3. An International Food Court

The Crusading expeditions played a critical role in fostering a cultural pluralism that was integral to Venetian daily life. They made the city not only
a leader in long-distance trade and an international emporium but also a
magnet for religious tourism and the home of peoples from Byzantium
and the Levant. Greeks, Turks, Egyptians, Persians, Arabs, Jews, and other
Levantine peoples introduced a variety of new culinary tastes that became
not just "Venetian" but through trade also the cosmopolitan cuisine of
Europe. Food in Venice began to carry both regional and national signifiers.
On the one hand, the lagoon and its islands supplied the primary materials
of fish, game, salt, and garden vegetables, each a source of regional and community pride. On the other the primary materials were embellished with
signifiers from other nations, including Dalmatia, the islands of the Aegean,
Byzantium, the Jewish nations, and the Islamic world.

Which foods reached Venetian consumers once they left the markets? The
answer depended on a number of shifting variables, but above all was financial means, governed by wages, prices, and taxes. Other factors included
class status and ethnicity. The majority of Venice's inhabitants, like most
Europeans, had marginal incomes and limited purchasing power. They subsisted largely on bread, gruels, and local fish. Grains were Venice's most basic
staple. They were not a home product for much of the Middle Ages, until
agriculture became a primary investment in the late sixteenth century. Even
then, famine consistently threatened the city, and in order to maintain public
order the government had to keep grain reserves that could be distributed at
reasonable prices. Thus state officials closely regulated the grain warehouses,
keeping stocks of millet, a long-lasting cereal; wheat, a more expensive product imported from the Black Sea; and barley, rye, spelt, and after 1540, maize
from the New World that was planted on the mainland.

Wheat had been prevalent in Italy during Antiquity but was lost during
the early Middle Ages. During the Crusades it became a Levantine import
that transformed the Venetian, and European, diet. In 1300 Venice became
the principal granary for northeast Italy, importing many of its stocks from
the Levant. An imposing grain warehouse at Terranova, the small island
next to Piazza San Marco, proudly advertised the Republic's position as a
major supplier. The dough makers (*pistori*) transported the cargos of cereal
to grinding mills with their own boats. In 1333 they established guild regulations with the bakers (*forneri*), adopting San Rocco (Saint Roch) and San
Lorenzo Giustiniani as their patron saints. Wealthy houses had their own gra-
naries and ovens. They usually made their own dough at home, as did people

of more modest means, but those who did not have their own ovens took their dough to the bakery ovens. Rialto housed twenty-five bakeries during the fourteenth century, on the Calle delle Beccarie, which was also named Panateria. The other major conglomeration of bakers, numbering nineteen, was situated in San Marco, near the bell tower. Every neighborhood also had an oven and a main street for retail commerce.

Venetian officials supervised the quality of bakery dough as well as the weight and price of bread, which was fixed daily. Bread mirrored the socio-economic hierarchy. Only the rich could afford *albo*, or white bread. Most people consumed brown bread, named *de tuta farina* or *massarìn*; or common brown bread, called *traverso*. *Pan biscotto*, often shaped in rings called *bussolai*, was made for the navy as well as for ships' passengers because it lasted longer. The dough makers were obliged to make it for the government within three months of having received a shipload of grain. *Pan biscotto* was so important that it had its own warehouse near San Biagio in order to supply the Venetian fleet. There was also a luxury bread for the old and sick called *buffetto* that only a few *pistori* were authorized to produce. Soft and spongy, it was very white and made with pure flour; at times butter and sugar were added to it. During periods of famine *buffetto* was prohibited.

Famine was a regular occurrence in Venice, as in the rest of Europe. The early fourteenth century made this structural vulnerability particularly apparent when the fertility of the land could no longer accommodate the dramatic demographic growth of the previous three centuries. In Venice in 1339 the Doge Bartolomeo Gradenigo built a grain warehouse near the fish market for times of famine. The Republic elected men to sift and tend the grain for the public. They had to sift a daily quota. Others measured and weighed it. Owing to Venice's damp climate, the grain had to be taken out of the warehouse several times a year and dried in the sun so it would not get moldy. Periodically it had to be cleansed as well.

Next in importance to grain were Venetian *menudi* (Italian: *menuti*), or minor foods, often used in soups and gruels. These supplementary cereals, including pulses, lentils, beans, peas, and chickpeas, were a cheap source of protein. As important as wheat were pulses, with which Venetian merchants loaded their boats in Alexandria. The corn exchange arrived much later, after 1540, and became a renowned antidote against famine throughout the Venetian empire. From the seventeenth century, maize was ground for polenta, a corn pudding made with water and oil, and became a standard part of the diet. Polenta itself, however, was not a novelty: in Roman times it was made from spelt and minced broad beans. Throughout the Middle Ages, the standard diet of the poor included a gruel made of barley grains, which were toasted and ground and then mixed with millet to make a coarse polenta. Corn polenta, both white and yellow, remains a main staple of the Venetian diet today. It accompanies fried fish, cheese, and a variety of dishes with sauces.

Venetians living abroad after the Crusades brought home many new tastes.[2] Ancient Romans had relied on wheat to make dried pasta, but the practice had disappeared. Jews in Venice, on the other hand, began using wheat to make *bigoli*, a thick and coarse spaghetti often mixed with a sauce of anchovies and onions. Another food that the Crusading experience reintroduced was rice, which was familiar in Greek and Roman times and was common to Muslim Spain after the eighth-century Arab invasions. Medieval Venetians imported it directly from the Arab world of the Levant, and it was sold as a luxury item in spice shops. The cultivation of rice on the Italian mainland in early modern times, however, brought the price down, and *risi e bisi*, rice and peas, became a standard Venetian dish, especially during the feast of St. Mark (April 25). For the wealthy, raisins from Zante, which Venetians call *sultane* (supposedly after the sultan who dropped a handful of white grapes in the sun as he fled an approaching tiger; they dried into raisins), were mixed with rice to make Turkish rice pudding, a luxury treat. Oil was another important Levantine import brought after the Crusades, one that transformed the medieval diet by introducing vegetable rather than the prevalent animal fat for wide consumption. Cheese from Apulia, Dalmatia, and Candia (Heraklion, Crete) became a source of cheap protein for Venetians as well as one of the five basic staples of sailors, together with ship biscuits, wine, salted pork or sardines, and beans.

Of course in Venice and on the islands of the estuary, fish was a main staple from the beginning. Sardines, anchovies, crab, shrimp, eel, oysters, and other seafood, either boiled or roasted, were basic. On Murano, fish was roasted after work in the glass furnaces. A typical meal was *bisato su l'ara*, or roasted eel. Salt, like fish, was a Venetian product, especially from the ninth century when Venice controlled the mouths of the Po and Adige rivers. It became essential to worldwide trade and was used to preserve sturgeon, tuna, cod, and sardines (as well as sausage and pork). *Schinale*, the spine of sturgeon, was salted and smoked; *morona*, a salami made of sturgeon, was either dried or preserved in oil; Baltic cod was salted and dried and sold as *baccalà*. *Bottarga*, or fish roe, was also popular. Typically, however, anything that was preserved, such as meat or fish, was relegated to a lower station in the hierarchical food chain. Fresh fish from the deep sea (rather than local waters) and meat usually adorned the plates of only the wealthy.

The consumption of fish also followed a social hierarchy, based on abundance or scarcity. Blue fish was more available than white; fishing in the deep sea was more labor intensive than catching fish from the lagoon and thus sea fish were more expensive. But all fish came under government regulation, with certain communities, such as the residents of San Niccolò dei Mendicoli, given the privilege of fishing and supplying the Rialto market, and the public health (Sanità) officials supervising quality while the Giustizia Vecchia adjusted daily market price.

Although fish was a home staple, medieval trade had an impact on its preparation. The fifteenth-century revolution in salting, together with the Byzantine practice of using vinegar to preserve food, brought new tastes to the table. Ordinary people adapted, combining salted fish; onions, which were brought by the Turks; and the combination of sweet plus salty (in Venetian, *saor*), a taste shared by the Turks but originally from Constantinople. Saor was made with the raisins from Zante. Venetians also prepared sweet and sour pork by combining vinegar and white wine with raisins and pine nuts. Although saor is a very popular Venetian dish today, it is not strictly Venetian: the method was used in Italy, Spain, southern France, Portugal, and North Africa, and it originated from a Persian stew called *sikbaj*. The saor recipe in Venice became from the seventeenth century one of the standard dishes served at the Feast of La Salute on November 21, an acknowledgment of the diet of workers who built the monumental church of Santa Maria della Salute.

Meat was not as common to the Venetian diet as fish, not only because it was expensive but also because Christian rituals limited its consumption for 166 days out of the year. The church required Catholics to abstain from meat, eggs, and other dairy products that came from animals during Lent. Fish was lighter and more preferable. Fasting was obligatory prior to receiving communion at a Catholic Mass, and there were many other feast days that required abstention. Still, there was some meat consumption, and it too can be placed into social categories. Venice imported herds from Dalmatia. They were slaughtered on the Lido, and offal, a kind of tripe, was an everyday food for the poor. Moreover, a variety of animal innards, or scraps from the butchers' shops, also found their way into Venetian recipes. Calf's liver, made with onions, was one of them. Others included heart and *nervetti* (chopped up tendons and meat from the foot of the calf). Since the seventeenth century, one of the two traditional dishes to celebrate the Feast of La Salute besides saor has been *castradina*, or mutton stew, also part of the workmen's diet at the construction site of the great baroque church. In principle, pork and mutton were at the bottom of the meat chain, while beef and veal were intended for the urban prosperous. Birds, with the exception of chicken, held more prestige than quadrupeds, and the lagoon supplied game meat, particularly quail and duck, shot in the sandbanks as well as hare, rabbit, heron, partridge, woodcock, larke plover, and teal. Jews made wider use of duck and goose, encouraging their integration into Venetian cuisine, but they were luxury products. The government attempted to limit the consumption of partridges, pheasants, and peacocks during times of hardship produced by war and the need for more tax income, or famine. Some meat, like pork, was local and often slaughtered at the start of winter. Much later, in 1549 Venetian inventories listed turkey as a luxury meat brought in from the New World. Peasants brought in chickens and eggs for consumers of all social stations. Most meat was finger food, but aristocratic tables adapted the Byzantine *piron*, or fork, after the eleventh-century Doge Domenico Selvo married the princess Teodora from Constantinople.

Jewish immigration to Venice in the twelfth century also made a lasting imprint on the city's cuisine. The Jews introduced Venice's inhabitants to eggplant, originally from the tropical gardens of Southeast Asia but central to the cuisine of Baghdad and the Middle East. Venetians and other Italians initially thought eggplant would make them crazy. The word *melanzana* derives from *malum insane*, an ailment believed to cause insanity. Other Jewish delicacies that made their way into the Venetian diet included almond puff pastries; *frisinal*, a *pasticcio* of macaroni with either cheese or meat or vegetables; *cugoli* (breadcrumb dumplings); and artichokes. Because Jews abstained from pork, they popularized roasted duck and goose salami using birds from the lagoon's marshes, and later they consumed the more expensive turkey meat from the New World.

Onions, lettuce, and cabbage were common, but new vegetables and fruits from the Levant entered the Venetian diet after the Crusades. Besides eggplant, they included spinach from Persia, dates from Maghreb, apricots from Damascus, bananas from Egypt, fava beans from Turkey, white garbanzos from Salonico, and asparagus from Armenia. After 1450 Venetians prepared artichokes (*kharshüf* in Arabic; *articiòco* in Venetian) from the Nile, which were considered an aphrodisiac.

Perhaps the most renowned culinary revolution derived from the importation of spices, used both for cooking and for attaining the good health attributed to them by medieval Arab medics. *Sacchetti veneti*, small pouches of mixed spices, were widely used in the city and beyond to flavor cooking. Black pepper was like currency, and cinnamon, cloves, cumin, nutmeg, ginger, and saffron – all spices for the rich – came from the Levant. The poor used thyme, marjoram, bay leaves, savory, aniseed, coriander, garlic, sage, mustard, and parsley, often grown in their own gardens. Caraway, mint, dill, and fennel were also common; inherited from Roman times, all were used to flavor foods. In the Middle Ages they were also used in honey-coated confections.

But the twelfth century produced a spice craze for the wealthy, with all kinds of pepper: black, white, and long, used in meat, fish, and soup. *Saracinesca* sauce (sauce of the Saracens), a mixture of almonds, raisins, ginger, cinnamon, cloves, cardamom seeds, galangal, and nutmeg, embellished aristocratic cooking. Cinnamon (and the cheaper cassia) was used in macaroni with sugar, also a luxury dish. Cinnamon was also an ingredient of *panada*, bread crumbs cooked in broth or milk; and in *pevarada*, a sauce for meat made with ground cloves, nutmeg, and ginger. Other spicy sauces used on meat included a green sauce made from crushed parsley, ginger, cloves, and cinnamon as well as tartar sauce made with garlic, almonds, cloves, sugar, egg yolk, and vinegar.

Spice shops also sold sugar, Arabic in origin, and a popular item of consumption that often substituted for honey among elites in Venice after the Fourth Crusade. Sugarcane was grown on the island of Cyprus, a Venetian possession from the thirteenth century; the sugar industry was then developed by *spezieri da grosso*. In the sixteenth century Venice published the first manuals

---

A VENETIAN SPICE RACK

Foods were not always fresh, so spices helped preserve them and conceal their less than fresh taste. Venetian cooks used the following spices:

Black pepper: From India but also from islands like Java, Sumatra, Borneo, the Philippines, and Malaysia. Venetians acquired it in the Levant.

Ginger: Widely used during the sixteenth century. Green ginger came from India and was used on fish and meat, in sauces and soups, in gelatin, and in foods with pepper. It was also put in aromatic wines and on fruit.

Cinnamon: Imported from Ceylon and India. It was used in soups, omelets, fish, and sugared confetti.

Cloves: A costly spice. Used on roasted meat and in stews.

Nutmeg: Introduced by the Arabs for therapeutic reasons. Used in drinks, soups, gelatin, and spice bags. It was brought to Venice from India. Fruit was marinated in salt and vinegar and then boiled with water and sugar to make a laxative.

Saffron: From Asia Minor or Persia, but it was also grown in Italy. Its main function was to color food yellow. Put in fritters, torets, salami, tripe, sauces, and soups.

Sugar: Originated in India, Indochina and southern China. The Arabs used it in the Persian Gulf. Italian merchants purchased it in Syria and Cyprus after the year 1000. It was used sparingly until the fifteenth and sixteenth centuries. Used in pastries and sauces as well as dishes made with almonds, pine nuts, pistachios, and eggs. It was used to make a syrup for fruit; to sweeten confetti, fritters, and marzipan; and to make decorations for noble tables.[3]

for a European readership on how to refine sugar and make sweets. The sugar refiners obtained the raw material, placed it in a large container filled with water, and boiled it. At aristocratic tables, meals sometimes began with an *apéritif* (from the Latin *aperire*, "to open"), such as sweetened wine or milk and ended with a digestive, such as lumps of spiced sugar or spiced wine.

Wine, the primary table drink, came from a variety of regions. Trade with Cyprus brought the heavier raisin wines and malmsey, while maraschino, a Venetian monopoly, came from Zara. Other grapes came from the Tyrol, Brescia, Vicenza, Friuli, Istria, and Dalmatia. Some were made into a heavy liquor called grappa. The barrel makers' guild, located near the church of San Silvestro west of Rialto, organized their regulations in 1283. Wine shops were named *malvasie*, after the grape that Armenians sold on the Riva degli Schiavoni. Taverns, called *furatole*, also sold wine, while *bacari* as well as open stalls served bite-sized snacks and drinks. Wine was also a trading commodity. The Venetians exported Cretan wine and malmsey, a sweet dark wine from Cyprus and the Morea, to England and Flanders in exchange for wool.

What was the daily menu for upper-class Venetians? Historian Evelyn Welch examined the account books of the patrician Bernardo Morosini for 1343 and learned that the noble family purchased salad vegetables such as cabbage and lettuce twice daily in the morning and evening. They consumed meat approximately twice a week, and bought wine every three days. They also bought in-season items, such as peas and beans in winter and figs and almonds in spring. Sweeteners, such as honey and sugar, were used more sparingly. Like most nobles, they made their bread at home but then sent it out to be baked. Cheese, oil, and drinking water were also part of their usual expenditures. Two centuries later, the Priuli family, also nobles, were purchasing similar items. Like other Europeans, at the start of winter they slaughtered a pig and purchased the spices needed for sausage-making. They also had eggs delivered to their door. Ordinary households, of course, ate more modestly.[5]

TAVERNS (*BACARI*) AND INNS (*OSTERIE*)

A variety of taverns in Venice catered to clienteles of differing social stations, offering clues about modes of socialization. Prior to 1355 some taverns received state privileges to serve the more costly white wines that came from Romania and Candia as well as Ribolla from the Friuli. The upper classes would consume something sweet, paired with the more robust Malvasia wine prior to a meal. (Their assumption was that sweet things prepared the stomach for the courses that followed.) Ordinary people, on the other hand, drank barrel wines.

The innkeepers received their own *scuola* at San Matteo in the vicinity of the Rialto in 1355. Each establishment cultivated a specific clientele, not only according to class but also at times according to ethnicity. The Germans, for example, largely stayed at the Aquila Nera, the Lion Bianco, or the San Zorzi establishments; these were exclusively for transalpine peoples. In addition, the Fondaco dei Tedeschi, supervised by three Venetian nobles, was a virtual community of German merchants. It had eighty rooms, including offices, store rooms, a kitchen, and refectory that separated the merchants from Ratisbon from those from Nuremberg. There were also Trentini, Bohemians, Poles, and Hungarians. The Ottoman Turks, Persians, Greeks, Armenians, Luccans, Albanians, and Florentines also had *alberghi* and private lodgings recognized by the state. The Jews, however, were a separate case. They were subdivided into nations but were treated like one foreign community because of their religion. They were supervised by an assortment of officials including the Five *Savii* of Trade. There were a few lodgings for businessmen who were Greek, Moldavian, Bulgarian, Serbian, Bosnian, Albanian, and Macedonian. Other places catered to the aristocracy, such as La Campana. Still others were for religious entities like the monasteries of San Lorenzo and San Servolo.

The state auctioned off public inns to renters. By the sixteenth century the Collegio dei Sette Savii supervised the inns and taverns, and taxed consumption. These state-owned establishments were at the top of the hospitality pyramid, while *locande*, *alberghi*, houses, and rooms catered to the lower classes. There were also places that just offered food. The *furatole* provided soups or fried fish to the poor, and there were stalls that served tripe, sausage, animal heads, pigs' feet, and small fish.

Rialto and San Marco were the two main sites for taverns and inns. Those in the Rialto were all grouped between Ruga Vecchia San Giovanni and Campo delle Beccarie, in narrow alleyways named after the establishment: Scimmia, Campana, Due Spade, Torre, Anzolo, Bo, Donzella, Sole. Campo San Giacomo was the pulsating heart of the market. The hostelries at San Marco were better furnished and better staffed. Rizza and Pellegrin faced the Piazzetta dei Leoni. Some inns were reputedly closed to prostitution, including the Bo at San Matteo di Rialto, the Melon, the Sarasin, and the Stella. The Gambero, the Due spade and the Anzolo watched for prostitutes outside their doors. Whether this was strictly regulated is highly doubtful.

Public Hostelries: Fourteenth–Eighteenth Centuries

Rialto: Due Spade; Torre; Sole; San Zorzi; Scimmia; Anzolo; Sturion; Campana; Donzella; Gambaro; Scoa.

San Marco: Luna; Cappello; Cavalleto; Corona; Pellegrin; Salvadego; Rizza; Lion Rosso; Cerva.[4]

4. Textiles from Asia

Textiles, like food and cuisine, were also important historical markers of Venice's intersection with the cultures of Asia, Europe, and North Africa. From the sixth century, Venetians were exposed to the fashion aesthetics of the Greek east, viewed through the iconography of church mosaics. But it was the Crusades of the eleventh to thirteenth centuries that ushered in a new textile lexicon, at the very moment when Venice was establishing its own cloth industries. The result was a multicultural fusion catering largely to people of means. Besides *calicò*, a kind of cotton from Calcutta, the Venetians quickly adapted a variety of costly silks: *damaschìn*, a precious fabric with gold and flower designs, from Syria; *levantina*, from the Levant; the Arabic-derived *tabino*, a heavy silk woven for luxury dress, from a district of Baghdad; and *ormesin* from Ormuz, an island in the Persian Gulf. Venetians established their own production of *ormesin* in the district of Cannaregio on the Fondamenta degli Ormesini. Other new textile inspirations included *taffeta* from Asia; *rassa*, a coarse woolen cloth used in gondolas, for bed covering, and for women's dresses, from Serbia. Venetians began to weave *rassa* on the Riva degli Schiavoni, an area filled with Dalmatian immigrants. There was also a coarse wool called *schiavina*, used for pilgrims' cloaks and the coats of fishermen and sailors. The word in Venetian dialect was *schiavo*, signifying a Slav from Dalmatia.

Like alimentation, fashion and dress were hierarchical and reflected financial means, class, ethnicity, but also gender. Second only to food, textiles were a very important commodity in Venice, involving a broad segment of the population. Among the raw materials, wool was the most essential, given the cold, damp winters on the lagoon. In summer, cotton or linen provided relief from the high temperatures and humidity. But there were variations in the quality of these fabrics that reflected the broader, societal hierarchies. Cotton and linen from Egypt and Syria clothed both rich and poor, but the wealthy wore finer weaves; the poor were clad in homespun, coarser blends. Cotton brocades also ornamented the wardrobes and furnishings of the rich. Wool, from England and Flanders, came in similar variations. The raw imports arrived at the Venetian homes of ordinary people, where women spun thread, wove cloth, sewed for their families, and furnished merchants with cloth for fairs and markets. They also remade clothing from used garments and worked with flax and hemp, making bed linens, undergarments, working clothes, ropes, and canvas sails.

Silk was the social marker of the aristocracy, signaling wealth and ostentation. It first came to Venice from the Byzantine Empire and was widely available to wealthy Venetians after the Fourth Crusade. Other silks came from China, through Iran and Anatolia (Turkey), together with gold- and silver-wrapped thread. We know from inventories and wills such as Marco Polo's that Asian textiles were plentiful in Venice by the fourteenth century, but between 1300 and 1500 artisans began to adopt the eastern techniques of textile making to produce home products. Notably, in the early fourteenth century several families from Lucca immigrated to Venice. They were already familiar with Islamic techniques, owing to their affiliation with Sicilian workshops, and they readily adopted both Persian and Turkish designs for both clothing and home furnishings. Velvets and gold- and silver-wrapped braid were also used as diplomatic and commercial currency. Production of silk, including velvet, satins, and brocades, peaked in Venice in the sixteenth century. Thereafter raw silk production moved to farms and households of the mainland Veneto, where mulberry plants were cultivated. Rural women unwound silk cocoons, combing and spinning them to sell to the dyers and weavers who supplied the markets. Venetian sumptuary laws aimed in vain to attenuate the consumption of luxury silks. They were an important part of the self-definition of Venice's constitutional elite. Patrician women lined their garments with silk and decorated them with gold and silver embroidery. Their dress styles required lots of fabric because of their puffed sleeves and the high-heeled *zoccoli* shoes they wore, as skirts had to be long enough to conceal them. Pregnant women especially liked wide skirts that required lots of fabric.

All of the products Venetian entrepreneurs both grew and transported eventually reached the ports on the lagoon, the warehouses of the merchant aristocracy, and the city's markets. The food and wares from the trade fairs of Champagne; the ports of the Low Countries and England; the rivers of southern Russia; the markets of Damascus, Acre, and Alexandria, and the Aegean colonies were all plied at the Rialto emporium, bringing new modes of living to the people on the lagoon. Merchants recounted their travels, describing other ways of life and infusing the city with new cultural aesthetics to include cuisine and dress as well as interior design and material artifacts. Venice had indeed become a world emporium and city by the twelfth century.

FURTHER READING

Documents: D. Chambers and B. Pullan (1992). *Economy*: B. Arbel (2001); F. Braudel (1972, 1986); J. Ferraro (2007); D. Jacoby (1999); F. Lane (1973). *Empire*: E. Dursteler (2006); M. O'Connell (2009). *Fabric and Dress*: G. Grevembroch (1754); M. Rosenthal and A. Jones (2008); A. Vitali (1992). *Food and Drink*: F. Braudel (1986); M. Costantini (1996); M. Dal Borgo (2005); A. Fabris (1990); G. Maffioli (1982); E. Welch (2005).

3

A PRIDE OF LIONS

1. From Dukedom to Commune

The history of the Venetian patriciate is central to the city's medieval metamorphosis from a scattering of island communities on the fringes of the Byzantine Empire to a major Mediterranean power and Italian regional state. By the tenth century a group of family dynasties held the reins of power. At this time, other parts of Italy were ruled by feudal magnates or bishops, many tracing back to a line of German kings. Venice, on the other hand, followed a different course of political development. Family dynasties kept their independence, remaining oriented toward Byzantine culture and focused on commercial enterprise. Although they embraced the Byzantine model of monarchy with the election of a doge in the eighth century, between the ninth and the thirteenth centuries the position became more ceremonial than real. Instead, competing families with great fortunes in banking and trade rose in status and shaped the course of events.

Dynamic economic expansion in the Adriatic, eastern Mediterranean Sea, and the Levant during the eleventh and twelfth centuries produced marked social differentiation at home, distinguishing the most successful families from the rest of the population. The commercial leaders who had strengthened Venice's power on the seas, subdued the Istrian and Dalmatian coasts, and profited from trading privileges with the Byzantine Empire also invested in real estate around the Rivoalto and in the fertile Po Valley. Accumulating great riches, they in turn constructed powerful clientele networks in Venice and dominated high offices like the dogeship.

Family dynasties such as the Candiano, the Partecipazio, and the Orseolo all attempted to make the dogeship hereditary during the tenth century, but their struggles came to naught, for in the 1050s still other lineages, greatly enriched by financial and commercial ventures, emerged and propelled Venice in the

Figure 13. Giovanni Bellini (1430–1516). *The Doge Leonardo Loredan*, 1501–4. Oil on poplar, 61.6 × 45.1 cm. Leonardo Loredan was the Doge of Venice from 1501 to 1521. He is shown here wearing his robes of state for this formal portrait. Bought, 1844 (NG189). Location: National Gallery, London, Great Britain. Photo Credit: © National Gallery, London/Art Resource, NY. Image Reference: ART373875.

direction of oligarchy. Among them were the Badoer, Giustiniani, Michiel, Morosini, and Contarini, who regularly served as tribunes. A council of wise men (*sapienti*) fostering the idea of communal governance made inroads in 1143 under the leadership of Pietro Polani, an event that signaled the advent of collective urban authority and presaged the restriction of ducal power.

The turning point came in 1172 when a hostile council assassinated Doge Vitale II Michiel. Six years later the Rialto oligarchy formed an electoral commission to select the doge, an announcement that power now lay with the commune rather than its figurehead leader. By 1192, the major offices were chosen by lot, among "old" families like the Dandalo and "new" families enriched in business ventures like the Ziani and the Orio, a rivalry that dominated medieval Venetian politics for centuries. Communal power took the form of councils and groups of family associations enriched by international commerce, some of which would go on to develop a complex state apparatus to serve their need for international trade and a market economy. Several new magistracies sprang up: a six-member minor council that functioned in tandem with the extant larger assembly; a public prosecutor; offices specializing in justice, police, and finance; and a treasury. At first the general assembly, called the *arengo*, represented the city's six districts and their respective parishes, grouped by twos to form thirty units (*trentaccie*). Three electors were selected from the *trentaccie*, who in turn chose the members of the various councils. Eventually the general assembly dissolved and was replaced with a legislative body of men over the age of twenty five named the Great Council, from which the majority of officials were elected. The main responsibilities of this Council included voting on legislation, verifying the legitimacy of its members (this later shifted to the State Attorneys, the main law officials of Venice), and electing governors and council members. The Great Council in turn delegated some of its jurisdiction to other councils, including a Council of Forty for criminal appeals, established between 1207 and 1220; and the Council of the Rogati or Pregadi, a sixty-member senate to oversee commerce and navigation, and later, international affairs, diplomacy, and defense. There were also other offices, like the Giustizia Vecchia, that supervised the handicraft guilds beginning in 1173; the Piovego (1224) that oversaw urban planning and development; and the Giustizia Nova that regulated foodstuffs, inns and taverns, and the wine trade (1261), as well as various assemblies. Officials were placed throughout the seaborne empire as well.

Crouzet-Pavan has correctly identified the role of environment in fostering communal unity in Venice. The city was in many respects the product of human effort, its precarious fabric subject to the flow of the tides. Taming the environment required magistracies to supervise navigation channels and protect the shores that sheltered the lagoons from the Adriatic. Such efforts required continual cooperation and may have built both social and political cohesion. Historian Luciano Pezzolo also cogently argues that shared commercial interests between the patriciate and the rest of Venice's inhabitants fostered cohesion, especially before the fifteenth century.[1]

At the same time, the lineages at the helm of power developed an elaborate ceremonial symbolism to reinforce the notion that the doge was merely a conduit between the people, the state, and Saint Mark, and not the head of a political dynasty. Until the sixteenth century, his investiture included his entering the Basilica of San Marco barefoot and prostrating himself before the altar, while the people "stole" his clothes and "ransacked" his house, a powerful reminder that his honorable office came with serious limitations. Nor did his wife, the dogaressa, play any role in these induction ceremonies, a practice that deliberately removed her from the political stage. Instead, the people, through the guilds, choreographed a separate entrance for the ducal spouse, meticulously situated, historian Holly Hurlburt tells us, within the gendered arena of marriage and motherhood.[2] With great pageantry the people accompanied the dogaressa through the city to San Marco, visiting the Basilica before entering the ducal palace to feast with the doge and the members of the guilds who visited them. The first woman of Venice upheld the universally prized virtues of wife and mother. Marriage was the glue that held the leading families together, and her introduction to the people took the form of a wedding ritual that celebrated the ducal couple's union to state service, not as dynasts but as the temporary custodians of a ceremonial office.

2. The Workings of Oligarchy

The late thirteenth century was a critical time in Venetian political history, at home and abroad. The period witnessed increasing hostility from Genoa, Venice's commercial nemesis, as well as shrinking markets in the Levant. Gradually between 1286 and 1323, the government formed an exclusive social caste, effected through a shift in power to governing councils, which in reality signified a group of family dynasties. The Great Council admitted nine Syrian families to its ranks when Venice lost Acre in 1291, but in 1297–8, under the dogeship of Pietro Gradenigo, it enacted a First Closing of membership, a measure that made the participating families into a constitutional, hereditary elite. Only those lineages that had been members of this deliberative body since 1293 would acquire permanent membership. The legislation served both to restrict the parameters of nobility and the benefits of office-holding, making both the privilege of a genealogical caste composed mostly of merchants and bankers. Further legislation based on birthright followed to restrict membership: by 1323 only men who had had male ancestors in the Great Council or who had held high offices in the commune could obtain this privileged political status. In essence, these restrictions created an exclusive nobility that in 1328 inscribed their names in a Book of Gold, establishing that only their direct descendants were eligible for government office.

The Closing of 1297 was not seamless, nor was there a firm commitment to political equality. First, the constitution was never formally defined and became the subject of debate from the late fourteenth century as patricians weighed the merits of monarchy and aristocracy. Second, a concept of hierarchy developed early within the ruling families, because their social weight varied in measure with their wealth and political acumen. At the head of the complex and evolving state apparatus was an executive council, or Signoria, which included the doge, the six members of the Minor Council representing the six city districts, and the three heads of the Tribunal of Forty. It eventually replaced the idea of a commune in the fifteenth century, when the *arengo* was abolished (1423) and the Senate became the main legislative organ and governing body. Some of the doges succeeded in wielding extensive authority; yet others enjoyed no more than ceremonial influence. Following the Signoria in political power were the sixty nobles in the Senate, elected to serve one year terms. The authority of this body grew exponentially in the fourteenth and fifteenth centuries. It added a Zonta (Venetian for "addition") of twenty patricians in 1361–5, which was enlarged to forty in 1413 and became a permanent body of sixty in 1450. There were additional bodies that sat with the senators, including the governors of taxation, the supervisors over salt, the Council of Ten, and the Tribunal of the Forty. The members of each of those bodies were entitled to vote with the Senate. On the other hand, the six councilors of the doge, who joined the Senate in 1396, did not have voting privileges. The Senate, the majority of whose members were patricians with maritime interests, had a broad array of powers, deciding on war and peace and matters of finance, and mediating relations between Venice and the territories under the lion's wing.

There were factional rifts in the patriciate that resulted in the formation of a new magistracy, the Council of Ten, in 1310. It was composed of ten patricians, but the doge and his six councilors also sat with this body and were entitled to vote. The State Attorneys, on the other hand, joined the Ten in deliberations but did not vote. The purpose of this group was to oversee grave dangers to the state, after Biamonte Tiepolo and Mario Querini conspired to overthrow the doge and to challenge some of the parameters of oligarchy established in 1297. The Ten became a permanent governing body in 1355 after sentencing to death Doge Marino Falier (1274–1355), who had conspired to restore a ducal monarchy. This important tribunal was chosen from the ranks of the most powerful senators, each representing a different family dynasty. Ostensibly to guard state security from subversion, the powers of this institution increasingly grew into the early modern period to include minting money; regulating forestry, mining, and water usage; making diplomacy; policing grave crimes such as sodomy and treason; conducting secret inquiries; and supervising finance, taxation, and defense. At the end of the fifteenth century the Ten co-opted fifteen additional patricians as a Zonta. All of this movement within the patriciate exposes its lack of internal cohesion, however it appeared to outsiders.

It is apparent that this composing and recomposing of various groups served as a valve to release pressure and attests to the way in which the patriciate maintained the Republic's constitution over the long term. The hereditary elite periodically maneuvered to restrict its ranks, but it also allowed for some flexibility, particularly in times of financial need. For example, there was a brief hiatus in 1381, when thirty new families were admitted to the patriciate as a reward for helping to finance the war with Genoa. Following this, the rigorous screening process for admission to the Great Council continued. Most young men went through an examination of family credentials at age twenty-five, but by the fifteenth century some were able to compete in a lottery (called the Balla d'Oro, or Barbarella because the ceremony took place on Saint Barbara's Day, December 4), for early admission at age twenty (for a brief period the age limit was eighteen, but this was revoked in 1418 because the Great Council was becoming too large). The ritual registration, signifying that the claimant had passed the test for nobility, marked his passage from adolescence to political adulthood.

A series of laws between 1414 and 1430 related to social pedigree, marriage, age, and gender advanced the overall process of exclusion, a process that historian Stanley Chojnacki has described as a Second Closing.[3] First, the patriciate enacted a law in 1414 making Barbarella registration obligatory, a change implying that admission to the patriciate was not as closely monitored during the fourteenth century. Second, the 1422 law of the Great Council focused on mothers of claimants to office, bringing them under close scrutiny by the State Attorneys to ensure they were not low born. Third, a law in 1430 required fathers to formally present proof of their sons' credentials to the State Attorneys. A century later, further laws separated the patriciate from other social aspirants, a development Chojnacki describes as a Third Closing.[4] From the sixteenth century, noble births (1506) and marriages (1526) by law had to be registered in the Golden Books of the patriciate in order to ensure the purity of the body politic. The iconography of Figure 14, depicting the State Attorneys in the company of the Virgin Mary, highlights the emphasis on pedigree and purity. The progeny of patrician

Figure 14. Leandro Bassano (1557–1622). *The Virgin in Glory and Portraits of Three Avogadori.* Sala dell'Avogaria. Location: Palazzo Ducale, Venice, Italy. Photo Credit: Cameraphoto Arte, Venice/Art Resource, NY. Image Reference: ART126541.

daughters who married outside the caste would not be admitted to the ruling circle; legitimate heirs of patrician sons would, but marriage exogamy was highly discouraged. In effect, these laws made the patriciate a social caste, keeping the illegitimate out and making the state the guardian of noble marriage whereby birth determined nobility.

The emphasis on social pedigree and purity of blood made marriage and female virginity central to Venetian political ideology and iconography as well as to the institution of a patrician class. Patricians expressed their civic identity in gendered language – in iconic Venetia, Justice, and Liberty, all feminine words. Venice itself claimed virginity, for according to legend the city was founded on the anniversary of the Annunciation to the Virgin Mary.

This ideal was consistently made manifest in civic rituals such as the entrance ceremonies of the dogaresse, which became more elaborate during the four-teenth and fifteenth centuries. The guilds continued to accompany her in her journey from the private to the public sphere, but by 1329 the ceremony was transferred from the land to the sea. The dogaressa boarded the ornately decorated Bucintoro, the state's ceremonial vessel that also commemorated the Annunciation of the Virgin and the Marriage of Venice to the Sea, and floated down the Grand Canal with a trail of boats and barges behind her to the ducal palace, where she offered a feast to guild members. By the fifteenth century, the staging had become even more elaborate, and the status of the dogaressa's natal family was given more weight. She represented all married patrician women, whose duty it was to produce heirs for the state in order for a purebred nobility to survive.

The heirs of the state experienced a childhood and adolescence filled with responsibility. A boy began his training at an early age. Historian Margaret King's study of the life of Valerio Marcello, an eight-year-old who died pre-maturely in 1461, details the care with which patricians trained their young.[5] The character of the infant Valerio's nurse as well as that of his tutor were of critical consideration to his parents. The precocious Valerio had a personal teacher by the age of five. He was expected to pursue the humanist edu-cational program of Italy's ruling elites, learning Greek and Latin; the skills of oratory, debate, and poetry; the moral lessons of history and ethics; and the geography of the Venetian empire. Like all other boys of the ruling class, athletics and military training would be included in this program, in some ways a mirror of education in the city states of ancient Greece. Learning the names of armaments and equipment, the art of navigation, and the kinds of seagoing vessels important to Venetians was as essential to Valerio's training as imbuing him with civic responsibility and obligation of service to the state. This kind of preparation was particularly important for the small group of wealthy patricians who would serve as ambassadors to foreign lands. The humanistic approach, which encouraged a knowledge of geography, envi-ronment, and people outside Venice, helped inform government policies at home.

While all males in Venice legally became men at age twenty, according to the law of 1299, patrician adulthood, Chojnacki has shown, was also defined by the processes of business and government.[6] Before reaching that stage, patrician sons underwent a long period of socialization, where their moth-ers supplemented the lineage affiliation of the paternal line with that of their own kinsmen. Teens also went through a period of social puberty until reaching the age of eighteen or twenty. During this time they joined the

Companies of the Hose (Compagnie della Calza), elite social clubs that exposed them to the public arena. The Hose sponsored public entertainment, a function that developed out of performances at private banquets and at secular and religious festivals, such as Carnival. They also staged vernacular dramas that ridiculed social behavior. At age twenty, patrician males entered the Barbarella and commenced their training in government, reaching full political adulthood at age thirty. Those tracked for marriage then completed the process to adulthood with astute nuptial unions, while bachelor brothers tacitly agreed not to start legitimate family lines themselves. Outside the constitutional hereditary elite, prosperous youth of lesser wealth and status, especially the *cittadini* that served as state secretaries in the chancery, underwent similar humanist training but instead of participating in the *calza* they entered crossbow contests, vying to be selected as galley bowmen, places of high honor. Prosperous males, whether patrician or not, married in their late twenties or early thirties if that served the estate planning of their parents.

While male patrician adulthood was defined by business and government, the adult status of patrician women hinged upon reproduction and marriage. Until 1299, girls of any social rank became women at age twelve; thereafter they were defined as adults at age fourteen, unless married, in which case they became adults earlier. Some patrician families were in a hurry to marry daughters early because of the political, social, and financial gain such unions would bring. Venetian prescriptive literature, however, cautioned against early marriage. Both the Franciscan writer Paolino di Venezia in the early fourteenth century and the patrician humanist Francesco Barbaro a century later advised families to allow their daughters to reach the age of eighteen before they were married. Nonetheless, some patrician girls married at thirteen, beginning their reproductive years early.

With political adulthood patrician men acquired certain responsibilities vital to the preservation of the aristocratic Republic: marrying and producing future leaders; ensuring the patronage of poorer nobles and nobles with less power, and, in turn, building loyal clienteles; and applying their education in philosophy and the liberal arts. Before this time, nobles had acquired their learning from their fathers or uncles, whom they followed on business trips and political or naval missions in order to learn about trade and war, as well as in schools that offered merchants business arithmetic. But in the early fifteenth century the nobles established endowed lectures at Rialto that focused on the study of Aristotle and the embodiment of aristocratic values. This group held a close affiliation with the university at Padua, one of the oldest universities in Europe, with strengths in law and medicine, and the only university that Venetian nobles were permitted to attend. (However, they were excluded by

law from professorships.) Like ancient Spartan citizens, their primary duty
was to family dynasty and to the state, to benefit the Republic. They were to
be models of virtue and pious Christians who upheld an austere morality for
the entire body politic, practicing self-control and self-sacrifice for the good
of the whole. The sons of the nobility growing up in the early years of the
fifteenth century also utilized the humanistic skills they acquired from their
grammar teachers in Venice to reinforce the idea of rule by the few through
aristocracy. By the mid-fifteenth century there was an important state grammar school at San Marco that taught advanced Latin to both nobles and the
future state secretaries who would work in the chancery. From the late fifteenth century, students there also availed themselves of the great humanistic
library that Cardinal Bessarion had bequeathed as well as the Aldine Press, the
most important press for Greek and Latin works in Europe. Writing in elitist
Latin rather than the more popular vernacular prevalent during the fourteenth century, these humanists defended aristocratic ideals.

A word here must also be said about the Venetian citizen class whose
members had important government responsibilities. From 1478, the oldest
families in this group, the *cittadini originari*, enjoyed a legal monopoly of the
eighty-odd posts in the Ducal Chancery that supported elected magistrates
and diplomats. The secretariat of the chancery, which included secretaries to
the Senate and the Council of Ten, provided the technical skills and continuity in government that patricians, who rotated in and out of office, could
not. In addition to the Grand Chancellor who served the Great Council and
led the elite corps, there was a Chancellor of Candia as well as numerous
ambassadorships. Other *cittadini* enjoyed important positions as notaries for
the criminal tribunal of the Forty, the Collegio, and the doge. These offices
were coveted, and passed down from generation to generation. The political
weight of these officeholders is still unknown. It may be that their activities
held equal or greater significance to those of patricians rotating in and out of
offices. Researchers are currently studying their importance in government,
in policy making, and in Venetian political success, and we shall have to wait
for further assessment.

3. State Development

Venice's political orientation shifted dramatically after 1400. While Genoese
competition waned, the Ottoman Turks loomed ominously on the
Mediterranean. On the Peninsula, the major powers engaged in intense
territorial aggrandizement to net resources. Ensuring a landed base along
the Po and Adige rivers of the northeast, and its sources of raw materials

and alimentation, had been vital almost from Venice's beginnings. But from the mid-fourteenth century, when competition among all the major Italian cities for trade routes and resources dramatically increased, Venetian patricians had no choice, however contingent the circumstances, but to build a regional state that both protected their access to mainland trade and reinforced their maritime interests. For almost two centuries they debated that decision, questioning whether the turn to the land had become a formula for political and moral disaster. Some clung to their seaborne orientation, for the commercial empire was substantial, while others set their sights on the West, making Venice a two-faceted empire. (Map 5).

The first phase of the largely ad hoc process on land involved harnessing the seigniorial powers encircling Treviso, Padua, and Verona. Venice preempted the Carrara lords' territorial consolidation by annexing Treviso in 1389; Vicenza in 1404; and Verona and Padua in 1405. The Republic followed in 1420 by taking the Friuli, again to block territorial consolidation by local lords as well as to protect its Istrian possessions. The final phase of expansion, designed to keep Venice's powerful Milanese rivals at bay, to control the trade routes into northern Europe, and to protect patrician landed investments, extended to the Lombard cities of Brescia in 1426 and Bergamo in 1428, a move that definitively made Venice one of the five major territorial powers driving the political and economic rivalries of the Italian Peninsula.

Venice was at once regarded with suspicion, its aristocracy sharply criticized by its neighboring Italian states for being greedy and impious. By this time, however, the same individuals who governed the city also dominated intellectual life. Humanism, the educational program of the ruling class, endowed patrician writers and orators with something beyond military might. They wielded literary power. When Venice's Italian rivals sought to debase the aristocracy by accusing them of being lowborn fishermen tainted by their commercial activities, patrician humanists, who were particularly fond of history, refashioned their origins. In his *Defense of Venice,* humanist patrician Paolo Morosini (c. 1406–82) fabricated a story about the first nobles of the city deriving from the defeated heroes of Troy and thus of excellent blood. Moreover, he justified mainland expansion by claiming that the subject territories had requested annexation, preferring the milder rule of the Republic over the seigniorial lords who had previously dominated them.

Venetian apologetics did not, however, assuage the city's Italian rivals, who thwarted all further attempts at expansion. Venice eyed the Po Valley but failed to secure it in the War with Ferrara in 1481–4. At the start of the next century the Republic set its sights on papal Romagna, an ambition that propelled its Italian rivals to ally with the monarchs of Europe and Pope Julius

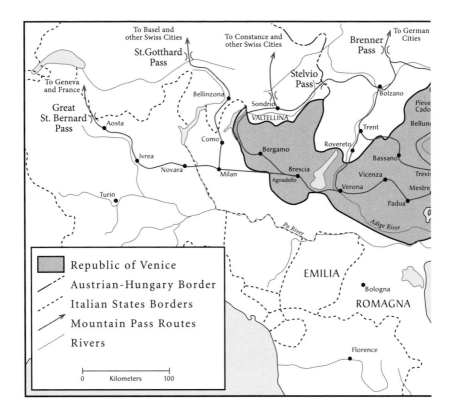

II to put down the Venetian army at Agnadello in 1509. French and imperial forces occupied much of the Venetian mainland, and many Venetian subjects turned their backs on the Republic. But then the pope, content to have reacquired the Romagna, abandoned his imperial and French alliances to side once again with Venice, and within ten years the Republic managed to regain almost all of its lost mainland territories. Venice thereafter was more than just a city-state. It was a major regional Italian state.

The expansion of the regional state throughout the Veneto, Lombardy, and the Friuli triggered further state development (Fig. 15). It also effected a second shift in the Republic's identity, the first being from "dukedom" to "commune." Now Venice was no longer a "commune." The "Signoria" possessed a "dominion." Thus it came to be referred to as Il Dominio, La Dominante, or La Serenissima Signoria. The government grew in measure with its territorial expansion, although again this was more in response to contingent circumstances than a planned process, and much of local governance was still left to local power holders. Specialized Venetian

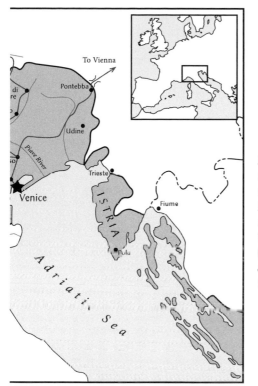

Map 5. The Mainland Empire after 1426. J. M. Ferraro, *Nefarious Crimes, Contested Justice: Illicit Sex and Infanticide in the Republic of Venice, 1557–1789* (Baltimore: Johns Hopkins University Press, 2008), 16. Map by Harry D. Johnson, Department of Geography, San Diego State University.

magistracies were established to deal with water, fiefs, sanitation, grain, forests, mines, common lands in rural districts, borders, fortresses, and artillery. Two commissions with an additional ten men joined the Senate in making law in addition to the prestigious Savii di Consiglio (established in 1321 and added to the Senate in 1396), which drew up the Senate's legislative proposals and oversaw ecclesiastical affairs: the Savii di Terra Ferma (established around 1420), keepers of the territorial state and military defense; and the Savii agli Ordini (1442), which oversaw maritime interests. Together, the Signoria and the sixteen Savii became the "Pien Collegio" and represented some twenty-six of the most prestigious members of the urban patriciate. Moreover, the number of offices in state administration more than doubled from 1350 to 1450, obliging some 831 of 2,600 male nobles to serve the state on a rotating basis. Among these offices, 550 pertained to Venice itself, while the remaining ones dealt with the administration of the landed and seaborne dominions. The fifteenth century also witnessed the establishment of ambassadors, chosen from the

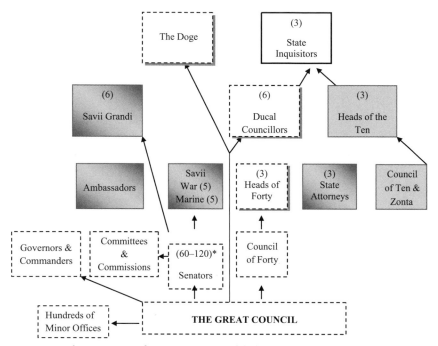

Figure 15. The structure of government. Modeled on F. C. Lane. *Venice: A Maritime Republic* (Johns Hopkins University Press, 1973), 429. Chronological development is illustrated by dashes (established prior to the fourteenth century), light gray (fourteenth century), dark gray (fifteenth century), black outline (sixteenth century). Shadows identify the *Signoria*; arrows indicate elective bodies. There were sixty senators prior to the fourteenth century; eighty by the fourteenth; 100 by 1412; 120 from 1450.

most prestigious patrician dynasties, who put forth their most educated scions. Venice sent ambassadors to all the major European states as well as a *bailo* to its former medieval possession, Constantinople, which still retained a Venetian community.

The Great Council elected patricians to serve as governors of the subject cities. Each city had a *podestà* for civil and criminal affairs and a *capitano* for defense, who rotated through the mainland as part of their *cursus honorum*. The larger cities of Brescia, Padua, and Verona held more prestige than the smaller ones, and a governorship in these cities required substantial private wealth to meet the social and political demands of the office. Patricians held greater administrative control over the provinces nearest the lagoon – the Padovano, Polesine, and Trevigiano – and delegated the government of smaller urban centers to local power holders. The Friuli, on the other hand, remained in the hands of an entrenched local nobility.

Venice's relations with its subjects were contractual. Patricians respected local statutes and worked through local administrative structures. Local officials collected indirect taxes and parceled out property and income taxes; they ran tribunals and supervised legal procedure. The Venetian governors, on the other hand, presided over criminal justice as well as important civil disputes. They also supervised grain provisioning and the institutions of charity, the granting of local citizenship, and the establishment of municipal law and ordinance, competencies that were mostly under the jurisdiction of the local urban councils – essentially hereditary oligarchies – on the mainland. Citizenship in Venice and the mainland cities was mutually exclusive, but Venetian subjects enjoyed negotiable trading rights.

The principal challenges for Venice's provincial governors included maintaining order and stability during periods of military and/or economic crisis; protecting charities; organizing the cereal market and regulating grain prices; netting fiscal resources; obliging local elites to meet their fiscal responsibilities; and presiding over tribunals of local justice. These were enormous tasks, requiring an expanding state apparatus. The government drew resources from indirect taxes on food products and articles of consumption. However, their protectionism also invited resistance, smuggling, and the flight of laborers to other states. Moreover, their transit and custom taxes suppressed local incentive to produce.

Besides supervising their acquisitions on the Italian mainland, Venetian patricians also had to oversee their Greek and Albanian territories.[7] (See Map 3). Among the Greek possessions under direct Venetian sovereignty, patricians served as dukes at the Cretan capital of Candia (1204–1669); and parts of the island were a virtual Venetian fiefdom. Patricians also served as *baili* for Negroponte (1204–1470) and Corfu (1396–1797), respectively. An assortment of Venetian governors were assigned two-year commissions in Argos and Nauplia (1394), the fortresses of Modone and Corone, the Aegean island of Tenedo and port of Pteleos; the Cretan ports of La Canea and Rettimo; the Saronic island of Egina (1451); and Skyros, Skiathos, Skopelos in the Sporades Archipelago (1453). Tessalonika had a *provveditore* for the seven years it was under Venetian rule (1423–30), and when Venice acquired Cyprus (1489–1571), patricians appointed a lieutenant. Other Greek territories were under foreign sovereignty, but Venice was entitled to govern its own merchant communities, called *fondaci*, applying civil justice with Venetian law (see Map 2). The most important were Constantinople and Trebisond, each with a *bailo*. The ports of Tana and Sinope also fell into this category until the second half of the fifteenth century. Egypt, Palestine, and Syria, lands subject to the sultanate of Egypt, also had Venetian *fondaci*. Whether under direct sovereignty or not, Venetian patricians governed together with local councils and were obliged to negotiate with an assortment of local centers of power. The security of their commercial empire was at stake. Moreover, after 1430 Venetian taxation in the areas under its control became vital. The Dalmatian and Albanian coasts, particularly the mouth of the Adriatic, also required protection. To this end many of the inhabitants in these areas joined the Republic's military forces on land and sea. Among the Republic's possessions were Durazzo (Durrës) (1392–1501); Shkodër and Drivast (1396–1479); Antivari (Albanian: Tibari) and Dulcigno (Albanian: Ulqini) (1406–1571); Zara (1409); Sebenico and Trau (1412); and Spalato (1420). Each was supervised by a Venetian patrician, who worked together with local officials.

Patricians thus ostensibly ruled a vast seaborne and landed empire whose operations and defense grew more demanding over time. Prior to the twelfth century, the indirect taxes levied on trade and consumption had covered expenditures, but by 1200, the wealthy were required to assume interest-bearing loans on behalf of the state to supplement these revenues. Patricians also used some of their commercial capital to finance military operations. The people of Venice, on the other hand, pitched in by joining the workforce. Through the fourteenth century, merchant ships served as Venice's fleet in times of war, while urban neighborhoods supplied free oarsmen in times of need.

Both the Ottoman menace and the Italian Wars of the fifteenth century, however, demanded greater military enforcements and with them broader popular support and state revenues. For the Venetian regional state this included the establishment of a standing army and permanent state structures to organize and compensate the regiments. For the seaborne empire the members of the guilds and confraternities were asked to either help man the ships of war or provide money.

The sixteenth century brought even greater challenges. The crisis of the League of Cambrai and the debacle at Agnadello in 1509 compelled the Republic to establish a fortifications program that extended from the western frontier of the mainland empire across the Mediterranean to Cyprus. It also conscripted a peasant militia in 1522 and formed its first convict galley in 1545. At the same time, Ottoman expansion demanded greater defense expenditures, ones the Catholic polity willingly provided in the face of Muslim aggression. Venice had already lost some of its bases in the Peloponnese as well as in Albania and Greece. To finance the series of wars the Republic devised an efficient system of taxation that doubled its revenues over the course of the sixteenth century. The preponderance of state income came from its territories, saddled with new levies on goods as well as direct taxes, and from Venice's own guilds and confraternities. These income sources also financed the late seventeenth-century campaigns to capture the Peloponnese, the failed effort to retain it during the eighteenth century, and Venice's armed neutrality during the War of the Spanish Succession. Mainland taxpayers did not willingly offer revenues. Smugglers artfully evaded indirect taxes on consumer goods, and urban oligarchies and other power holders foisted direct taxes onto their rural neighbors. The Republic was burdened with complex negotiations across the sociogeographic spectrum and suffered from a shortage of bureaucratic structures to cope with both the evasion and the cacophony of protests. Nonetheless it succeeded in multiplying state revenues between the fifteenth and eighteenth centuries. It was less successful, on the other hand, at integrating the various components of its regional state and seaborne possessions or in improving military organization on land and at sea after Lepanto in 1571.

In Venice itself, the expanding government did not develop through any smooth or linear process. On the contrary, as political historians such as Gaetano Cozzi and Robert Finlay have demonstrated, there were overlapping jurisdictions, rivalries, and serious conflicts of state as the actors in Venice's oligarchic circles vied for wealth, prestige, and authority.[8] The need to supply the new subject territories, rife with civil and criminal conflict, with an efficient system of justice, as the extensive work of historian Claudio Povolo has shown,[9] presented enormous challenges. It also shifted power within the patrician councils. The State Attorneys lost jurisdiction in the 1470s to other magistracies, including the Auditori Novi, who reviewed the verdicts of the provincial governors; the Council of Forty, who oversaw criminality in Venice; and the Council of Ten, whose power grew exponentially over the late fifteenth and sixteenth centuries.

There were also many moments when the patriciate compromised its principles, succumbing to corruption and scandal. Shrinking maritime and mercantile fortunes during the fifteenth century and the prohibition during the sixteenth century for nobles to engage in commerce and industry contributed to a growing body of poor patricians, who were left out of power and corruptly forced to sell their votes. At times the election process was corrupt. In theory, all members of the Great Council had an equal chance to serve by drawing lots, but in practice the same men habitually won the most important offices, through bribery, private negotiations, and secret voting. Some nobles, as historian Donald Queller has shown, avoided the more onerous and expensive positions; others did not perform their duties; still others, hungry for resources, were corrupt.[10] Between one and two hundred occupied the major offices in the Senate, the Collegio, and the Ten, and the most important embassies, governorships, and ecclesiastical offices. Even the episcopal head of the church in

Venice, the patriarch, was a layman chosen from among patrician ranks. There were marked differences in the quality of these offices, some holding more prestige, others requiring more experience or preparation, still others weighing more or less on the officeholder's financial resources. Together, all of these developments shattered the notion of an aristocracy of peers.

Over the course of the fourteenth to sixteenth centuries, officeholding became increasingly more important to those whose fortunes in long-distance trade dwindled. The shift in orientation began during the War with Genoa in 1379–81, a conflict that had produced financial setbacks. The next two centuries witnessed further challenges when the Ottoman Turks seized Venetian possessions and established an empire that stretched from Albania to the Levant and most of North Africa. By 1510, the proportion of aristocrats in trade had declined, as they placed greater investment in seeking public office and making personal loans. The withering spice trade after 1570 encouraged further withdrawal from commerce. Thereafter agriculture, industry, and governorships lured nobles away from the sea to the Venetian mainland. Gaetano Cozzi has emphasized that the number of nobles in government had become excessive by the 1540s, and that this trend caused the Republic to lose some of its political equilibrium.[11]

The shift to officeholding, owning real estate, and lending, however, was not unique to Venetian oligarchs. One by one the mainland cities that came under the Lion of Saint Mark in the fifteenth century evolved in the same direction, developing a noble consciousness among the civic elites who shut their doors to outsiders in order to more fully enjoy the benefits of offices and power. They increasingly distanced themselves from families that had engaged in commerce or manufacture, privileging the lifestyles of the landed aristocracy. For those who could use the proceeds from real estate and agriculture to their advantage, this worked well; for others, it exacerbated their indigence.

4. Elite Family Behavior

Elite family behavior, that is the strategies used to maintain status and power within the ruling circle, was critical to the longevity of Venice's patrician dynasty. Among its many choices, astute marital politics and estate management were essential and required careful treatment. Elites ruling other Italian cities, among them Milan, Siena, Brescia, Cremona, Genoa, Lucca, and Verona, followed a similar logic to separate themselves not only from the lower ranks of society but also from the rest of their own order. Particularly to achieve the latter, they had to retain superior wealth and high offices in church and state over the long term and in some instances also superior demographic strength. The biological extinction of some families and the cooptation of others helped this process along until in the last centuries of Venetian rule only a select few dominated the political arena. It is well worth examining these strategies, which Chojnacki has outlined in detail,[12] for to some degree they drove the history of the ruling class.

In Venice among the 190 families in the Great Council, about forty consanguineous patrician social networks dominated Venetian life. There were twenty-four old houses (longhi), families that had furnished doges prior to 1383 and based their prestigious status in antiquity. Among them were the Dandolo, Contarini, Dolphin, Gradenigo, Morosini, Corner, Giustinian, Falier, Querini, Sanuto; and sixteen new houses (curti), including the Donà, Mocenigo, Barbarigo, Loredan, Gabriel, and Venier, whose prominent status derived from wealth and astute connections. They occupied the dogeship from 1383 to 1612. The family names of these forty dynasties shaped identity and status, provided support networks, and conferred memberships to the most powerful political councils as well as to civic confraternities. The remaining 150 struggled to maintain their political positions, particularly because many of them did not enjoy the wealth of the great families.

The marriage legislation enacted between 1420 and 1535 reveals some of the fissures in this exclusive group, owing to the aforementioned disparities in wealth, antiquity, and officeholding. The poorer nobles, fearing financial ruin and greater political exclusion, coalesced to enact state laws that both defined noble marriage and set limits on dotal wealth to 1,600 ducats. On the other side were the wealthy new families that disposed of great capital, as well as the old families enjoying the benefits of selling their antiquity to the new houses able to offer exorbitant dowries and corredi (dotal goods in clothing and jewelry). Another law sought to limit the inheritances of married women by establishing that the excess of 1,600 ducats be invested in the woman's name in the state funds. While she could access the interest from such capital, the government sought to set the terms of the economic relationships between families that came together in marriage.[13] All this was to prevent the poorer nobles from being priced out of the noble marriage market. But it had far-reaching consequences. First, it strengthened women's social and economic position. Second, it created a pool of male nobles who remained unmarried, and more and more female nobles who went into the convent. The distinction between the married and the unmarried conferred upon the latter a second-class status.

The attempt to limit dowries, however, met with little success: between 1425 and 1524 they rose 83 percent. New efforts followed at the start of the sixteenth century. A law in 1505 limited dowries to 2,000 ducats, after the deduction of the husband's 1,000 ducat *corredo*. It also revised women's inheritance rights. Families had to register the marriage contract before the nuptials took place and then wait for official approval. Further, no widow could reclaim her dowry unless it had been recorded by the State Attorneys. That held her family to state norms. Limits were not set on women's non-dowry inheritance but on dowries themselves so that sons-in-law could be restrained. But married women were made vulnerable this way, for they could lose their inheritance if their fathers had violated these laws. The state was dictating estate practices so that fathers did not invest everything in costly marriage alliances. Again the underlying goals were to protect the poorer nobility from a rich minority and to establish equality in marriage possibilities. Fathers, however, ignored the measures of 1505, making it necessary for the Senate to enact further legislation in 1535. Magistrates raised the ceiling to 4,000 ducats. Furthermore, the bride's family was not to lose more than 1,000 ducats in the form of the husband's third, and the *corredo* third was reduced to a quarter. The husband would be fined one-half of any excess over 4,000 ducats. The rules were aimed mostly at bridegrooms living off their wives' dowries, but fathers who disobeyed would also be fined heavily.

Noble marriage thus evolved from being a private transaction to constituting state business. Moreover, such marriage became part of the patrician standard of maintaining purity and glory for the state. This was the product of common interests – between a majority that found it increasingly more difficult to meet the standards of noble social conduct that had been set by a wealthy minority and men at the apex of power (largely in the Council of Ten) who were concerned with the growing gap between rich and poor. The Senate represented the middling ground and sought to maintain a balance among the families at the two extremes.

The family network, however, was more than a means of social placement; it was also the site of capital accumulation, through business investments, dowry, and inheritance. On a financial level, patrician families organized their real estate and business operations into *fraterne*, or joint family firms among brothers. Prior to 1580, more emphasis was given to commercial investment; after 1620, it was oriented toward real estate, government bonds, loans, and shares of tax farming. Whatever the basis of wealth, there was a tacit agreement that only one brother would marry, in order to concentrate financial resources within the patriline. But human needs often led nobles to stray from this ideal template; historian Alexander Cowan's work reveals that they married secretly, with the recognition of the church.[14] Nobles at the apogee of power were cognizant of being the custodians of a family estate and that the political influence of the dynasty depended to a large degree upon wealth accumulation over the long term.

Politically astute patricians maximized their horizontal connections with the wider ruling group, forming kinship ties through marriage. Endogamy during the fifteenth and sixteenth centuries became a constitutional principle. Connections through the female line were as important as those through the patriline, such that Venetian council members excluded in-laws from participation when voting on issues involving individual patricians because they expected affinal collusion.

There was great variance among the constitutional elite, in terms of family size, structure, and wealth, important factors that underlay their status and effective political weight. The forty-some-odd old and new houses represented only a fraction of the 181 families that held political office in the mid-fourteenth century. Twenty-six families held political prominence between 1293 and 1379, guaranteeing a certain continuity; among them fourteen families held the highest honors. Political consolidation was often achieved through the biological attrition or expansion of the family; cooptation into the more powerful, smaller councils; the continuity of the lineage; and the conservation of wealth over the long term. The strength of the family hinged on its size and its wealth, but also on astute marriage and kinship alliances. Thus patricians made arranged marriages that emphasized dowry and bilateral descent, priorities that superseded religious ritual, in order to guarantee political preeminence. This was typical of most oligarchic regimes in Italy. Each family dynasty was intent on enlarging and protecting its sphere of influence by monopolizing wealth and taking advantage of high office.

How did some patrician dynasties reach the pinnacle of power? First, reproduction was essential to the continuity of the lineage, for it furnished the possibility of constructing both vertical and horizontal networks within and outside the family and ensured continuity. Second, career strategies helped consolidate the power of oligarchs. Prior to 1509, their wealth had been primarily based in banking and commerce; thereafter they turned increasingly to landed investment and loans. Officeholding in the church also advanced family interests. Natives to Venice held almost all of the regional state's forty-four bishoprics, and nearly all nobles had at least one kinsman who enjoyed a benefice. Third, financial strength over the long term was critical. It bound the destinies of families joined through marriage, giving patrician groups cohesion and logic. Ensuring rich heirs required practicing wealth conservation, through restricted marriage. In principle, both sons and daughters were ensured a fair share of the family inheritance, but in practice, political exigencies determined whether a daughter might receive a frighteningly large dowry to keep the family's political integrity intact, at the expense of her brothers. The *fraterna* limited marriage to one brother while other male siblings shared the family wealth and acted as an association. Although there are no firm statistics, there is also evidence that for economic motives some parents, by verbal and physical threat, compelled their sons to enter religious life rather than marry.[15] For similar economic and social motives, very few patrician daughters were dowered for wedlock, for parents avoided marrying them to outsiders or foreigners, nor would they permit them to marry down within the patriciate. But those women who did marry were richly dowered and wielded influence.

Chojnacki has shown that the conjugal fund was favored in Venice; wives and widows had an important impact on the elite marriage market by contributing to the dowries of daughters, nieces, and granddaughters.[16] In order to make an important match, the bride's natal female relations contributed significantly to her dowry. Elite women thus received large dowries, which in turn enriched their daughters' marriage prospects. At the same time, they inherited substantial resources. Such wealth gave women the opportunity to effect a change in expectations about appropriate social and emotional behavior for men and women. Their bequests and donations were oriented more toward affective ties with relatives rather than the traditional passing of wealth down the male line. In contrast to patrician men, patrician women demonstrated great personal regard and affection for their female kin rather than strict loyalty or obligation to the patriline.

Mothers and fathers, however, could not dower all daughters equally, especially because dowries rose to frightful levels during the sixteenth-century inflationary cycle. The Venetian ruling class worried that inflated dowries would ruin families. Yet Chojnacki has demonstrated that the very parents who feared dowry costs were inflating them, a result of family competition but also of changing female attitudes. Widows in possession of ever larger dowries increasingly dowered their female kin, fueling self-perpetuating upward pressure on dowries. Fathers as well, keen on arranging marriages and enlarging the dowries they received, also contributed to the inflation.

Patrician daughters who did not marry entered convents as gifts to God and the state. Nunneries had been in existence in Venice ever since the seventh century, with the founding of the Benedictine San Giovanni Evangelista at Torcello in 640. During the ninth century the two main aristocratic convents, San Zaccaria and San Lorenzo, were established in the center of the city. Gradually, many more sprang up on the margins of Venice, where space permitted buildings and gardens. Once the nobility had undergone aristocratic closure, these female sanctuaries came under the close supervision of the patriciate, in order to guard their endogamous purity. In fact, virginity became a central metaphor of political perfection: the Venetian ruling class was likened to a woman's untouched body, just as the Virgin Mary represented the city of Venice itself. Moreover, female spirituality held charismatic qualities that served Venice's civic ideology. In the convent of the Vergini, for example, the doge, who was its patron, married each newly consecrated abbess in a symbolic ritual, orchestrated by the Patriarch of Venice and in the presence of the executive council and the patriciate.

Because Venice's patrician nuns served as a kind of moral validation of the city's constitutional elite, from the fourteenth century onward the government attempted to control their behavior and their sacred spaces, legislating fines and imprisonment for male perpetrators who violated convent walls and female virginity. State sanctions, however, were continually repeated, an indication that they were often ignored. Indeed, some convents were havens of moral disorder, despite the state's warnings against criminal behavior and the preachers' claims that the sins of the flesh would bring on plague and other catastrophes.

But there was more to the narrative of religious enclosure than the preservation of the patriciate's immaculate state. Historian Jutta Sperling has convincingly shown that women were pawns in a system of gift exchange whereby if a daughter could not be given in exchange for a daughter-in-law of equal or greater value, then the daughter was removed from circulation.[17] Put differently, the exchange of dowries among patrician families was a means of circulating, and accumulating, wealth. Both the dowry and the wedding itself were a sizable investment for a patrician household. Aristocratic honor demanded conspicuous consumption in bridal exchange; weddings were exercises in displaying magnificence, and dowries remained on a drastic course of inflation. For this there had to be not only a return, but a return with interest. This requirement was even more critical after 1580, when patrician income derived mostly from real estate and loans rather than liquid capital. Fathers not only restricted the marriage of daughters, but of sons as well. Moreover, they entailed their possessions, so that their successors became merely the custodians of dynastic wealth but could not capitalize on the inheritance. Thus in the context of a shrinking economy, patricians accumulated wealth by restricting marriage for daughters and sons, by making widows fight for dowry restitution, and by disinheriting sons.

Venice was not unique in sending its aristocratic daughters to the convent. Monachization rates rose all over Italy during the sixteenth century, peaking between 1580 and 1650. Sperling estimates that in 1581, 54 percent of Venetian patrician women were enclosed. In 1619, there were around 2,000 "Virgins for Jesus" locked up in convents, ostensibly in patriotic service to the state. Historian Mary Laven estimates some fifty nunneries scattered around the city in 1650; thirty-three in the city and seventeen in the lagoon, housing some 3,000 nuns.[18] Ironically, the practice of enclosure reduced the number of patrician women available to patrician men and enhanced demographic decline, making the election procedures for political offices unworkable. In the fifteenth century, the rate of endogamy within the ruling class was around 90 percent. By the mid-seventeenth century it had declined to 75 or 80 percent, to the detriment of the body politic. The aristocracy then had to compromise its purity in 1646 by selling entrances into the Great Council for 100,000 ducats a seat in order to replenish its numbers and to raise money for the war with the Ottoman Turks.

To what might we attribute the longevity of Venetian oligarchy? Was it because seafaring built moral character as well as material gain, the contention of the diarist and merchant Girolamo Priuli (1476–1547)? A wise gerontocracy? To begin, strong political leadership and common commercial and environmental interests between patricians and *popolo* fostered popular cooperation in the city. Statecraft was not excessively intrusive, as evidenced by the practice of respecting civic traditions and reacting only contingently in both the landed and seaborne dominions. Second, astute estate management and wise investment guaranteed the wealth of a core group of leading dynasties, who could provide continuity over time. Third, and perhaps of the greatest importance was the patriciate's approach to the constitution, which was not static. Patricians permitted patterns of change when circumstances demanded them, either through new admissions to replace extinct lines or raise capital, shifting alliances, or a redistribution of political weight among the various councils and competing generations. This flexibility was also exhibited through their evolving public choreography and discursive constructions: from dukedom to commune and from commune to Dominion, the "Serene Signoria" shrewdly masked its internal divisions with Solomonic myths about continuity and peaceful endurance.

FURTHER READING

Marriage: P. La Balme and L. White (1999). *Mainland Cities*: J. Ferraro (1993); J. Grubb (1988). *Military Organization*: M. Mallett and J. R. Hale (1984). *Politics and the Patriciate*: S. Chojnacki (1998, 2000); G. Cozzi (1973); G. Cozzi and M. Knapton (1986); E. Crouzet-Pavan (1992, 2002); J. C. Davis (1962, 1975); R. Finlay (1981); H. Hurlburt (2006); M. King (1986, 1994); F. Lane (1973); D. Queller (1986); D. Romano (2007). *Religious Life*: M. Laven (2002); A. Schutte (2011); J. Sperling (1999); G. Zarri (1998). *Sexual Behavior*: G. Ruggiero (1985). *State Development*: G. Cozzi (1980); L. Pezzolo (2006); C. Povolo (1980).

4

IDENTITIES AND MODES OF SOCIALIZATION

1. A World City

Much has been said about the constitutional elite, whose dynastic lines to some degree provided great social continuity in Venice, but who in general were the Venetians? The progeny of the original island settlers, whether noble or common, would persistently vaunt their antiquity in the city's collective memory through the ages. However, Venice had shed its insularity by the year 1000 and, like all cities, its native population was regularly replenished with newcomers. Pilgrims, tourists, seamen, merchants, laborers, and exiles repeatedly infused the urban fabric with new energies.

There were several catalysts for immigration. Among them were the waves of catastrophic mortality, brought on by famines and epidemics. After the devastating Black Death of 1348–9, there were repeated visitations of the plague, with fourteen outbreaks between 1456 and 1528. The epidemics of 1575 and 1630 were particularly savage, taking between 25 percent and 30 percent of the population each time (Fig. 17). Each cycle of demographic depletion prompted concerned authorities to provide economic incentives to newcomers, not only to rebuild the labor market but also to repair the truncated families and to fill vacant houses. The Venetian turn to mainland Italy at the start of the fifteenth century, coupled with the disruption caused by the Italian wars, also attracted residents to the new capital city from the periphery. Villagers steadily migrated to the lagoon city from places in the hinterland as well as the Adriatic Coast to seek a better life. Many found work in the burgeoning woolen industry. Yet another development that triggered relocation to Venice was the collapse of Byzantium to the Ottoman Turks in 1453. The city attracted Greek and Jewish merchants and scholars. Similarly, the expulsion of the Jews from Spain in 1492 and the sack of Rome in 1527 triggered additional diasporas of talented groups and individuals to

Figure 16. Gentile Bellini (1429–1507). *Procession in Piazza San Marco*. Location: Accademia, Venice, Italy. Photo Credit: Scala/Ministero per i Beni e le Attività culturali/ Art Resource, NY. Image Reference: ART149371.

the Venetian lagoon. Finally, the Venetian economy was a powerful magnet for immigration. Trade incentives consistently brought droves of northern Europeans, particularly from Germany and Flanders, to the medieval commercial center through the fifteenth century, while in the sixteenth century, in addition to becoming a haven for intellectuals and workers in the printing industry, Venice developed into one of the most industrialized cities of Europe.

The steady supply of new people came as professionals, master craftsmen, skilled and unskilled workers, merchants, musicians and composers, artists, peddlers, sailors, soldiers, porters, rowers, exiled aristocrats, and miscreants banished from other Italian states. Women joined men in the textile industry and as domestic servants and servers in taverns and inns; they grew food in Venice's small gardens and orchards; they also provided services as chambermaids, wet nurses, and prostitutes. The migrants arrived from the hinterlands and cities of Padua, Vicenza, Verona, Bergamo, Brescia, and Crema as well as the territories of Istria, Dalmatia, Albania, Greece, Germany, Flanders, Spain, Portugal, Armenia, the Ottoman Empire, and the Levant, speaking Italian dialects and foreign tongues. Some acquired permanent domiciles in Venice and applied for citizenship; others were temporary. Among the itinerant labor force were German bakers and cobblers, butchers from the Grisons, shipyard workers from the Trentino, and journeymen printers from France and Savoy. Apart from the original core of early medieval island settlers, then,

Figure 17. The Plague Doctor's Dress; Calle del Paradiso, thirteenth–sixteenth centuries. Location: Venice, Italy. Photo Credit: J. M. Ferraro.

the population of Venice was fluid, and to be Venetian was often liminal. Far from insular, the population of this major port was part of a global economic system where peoples of varying origins circulated. It was home to foreign subjects, refugees, and tourists but also to Venetian subjects who had lived for lengthy periods in foreign lands and absorbed hybrid cultures.

Venetians categorized themselves in law as nobles, citizens, or common *popolani*. Historians attempting to reconstruct the associations of these legally defined groups within specialized studies of politics, religion, family networks and friendships, ethnic identity, and work, however, have discovered that their horizontal and vertical ties of socialization defy strict categorization. A wide range of social affiliations linked people of different stations together in more than one way, starting within the household and extending to the workplace, the tavern, the market, the parish church, the neighborhood faction, guilds, confraternities, ethnic communities, and sexual relations. Baptisms, godparenting, guardianships, marriages, marital dissolution, business relations, legal disputes, funerals, feasts, charity, religious events, ceremonies, games, and brawls brought families, parishioners, and neighbors – inseparable components of the island communities – together with foreign subjects, refugees, and tourists, again producing hybrid mixes of cultures that came to be known as "Venetian." A few examples will help to convey this broad interaction among different classes.

Households with servants and slaves are an ideal place to identify vertical social ties. Masters availed themselves of valets and gondoliers; mistresses supervised chamber and kitchen maids. Some women and men held ties of deep affection with both the same and opposite sex, as evidenced in their wills: a servant leaving a small token to an employer or naming him or her as an executor; an employer bequeathing goods, capital, or a dowry to a servant. Some noblewomen who took their abusive husbands to the patriarchal court, petitioning for marital separation, could rely on their chambermaids to testify to the abuse on their behalf. Masters provided annuities for their aging servants, and put them in hospitals. Both masters and mistresses served as godparents for the children of their servants. Nobles, citizens, and other prosperous people provided dowries, small sums of money, and/or goods to the less fortunate, tokens of loyalty and solidarity as well as religious faith. Still other masters and servants, however, had less than ideal relationships, ones spoiled by under compensation and sexual exploitation.

Prosperous Venetians were also served by slaves, the majority of whom were Russian, Tartar, Mongolian, and Circassian women. Venetians preferred non-Christian slaves, such as the Bulgarians, but there were some Roman Catholic slaves – Greeks from Crete and Candia captured in war or through piracy; and the Albanians escaping the Ottoman Turks in the fourteenth century. Because selling Christians was controversial, the slave trade shifted to the market centers of the Black Sea. Venetian ships leaving from Tana, Trezibond, and Constantinople transported male slaves to Egypt and female slaves to the Rialto market. By the late fifteenth century, these markets dried up and Venetians gathered more black males from Africa. Male slaves, however, remained a rarity in Venice. They appear in painting as the gondoliers and servants of the Venetian nobility. It was much more common in Venice to see female slaves working within the household. Emancipation did occur, and servile status was not transmissible.

The parish church and the surrounding neighborhood are also ideal places to view interclass social interaction. Churches were magnets for worshippers, life-cycle religious rites, and celebrations of the religious calendar, while neighborhoods provided yet another venue for life-cycle rituals along with banquets, ball games, bull or oxen runs, and collective group rivalries. Confraternity halls and hospitals brought together laypeople of similar trades who were devoted to charitable works and pious acts for banquets, feasts, festivals, and burials. Guilds provided vocational training as well as economic, social, and cultural affiliations. Citizenship conferred defining features on certain members of the Venetian community. Still further, ethnic groups formed communities with common customs and religious beliefs, while their business associations and economic activities linked them to the greater whole.

Gendered associations further complicate these tangled networks of social affiliation. There is some consensus among historians that until the sixteenth century, elite artisans, professionals, and merchants co-existed; thereafter the upper echelons of male society separated themselves from individuals who did any sort of manual labor. Less research, however, has been done on female sociability. Ordinary women were drawn together by a shared set of economic activities, such as cooking, cleaning, laundering, sewing, spinning, sailmaking, room letting, wet-nursing, obstetrics, and prostitution. These activities generally took place in the household, which was the site of domestic production and reproduction, as well as a place of social exchange. However, ordinary women also participated to a large degree in neighborhood life. Elite women, on the other hand, tended to be more isolated, devoting themselves to their kin and their servants. A large portion of the female nobility took the veil. For those who did marry, community involvement came more in the way of charitable work for poor girls and young women. Overall, female economies and networks of affiliation tended to be less visible than those of men.

Physically, nobles, citizens, and commoners settled in the same residential neighborhoods. Elite families coalesced around prime real estate but lived side by side with commoners in the same neighborhoods and parishes where religious rites legitimized marriage and children and brought friends and kin together in sickness and in health. Immigrants settled near the sites of commerce and handicrafts, bringing with them their own traditions but also integrating into Venetian life and taking up the customs and rhythms of the lagoon. Venetian residents in turn incorporated aspects of their cultures. Members of the religious orders peopled every neighborhood, interacting with both nobles and commoners. It was, in fact, not just the dominant families that named *calli* and *campi*, but also priests and nuns, together with oarsmen, furriers, pastry cooks, and weavers. Alleys and squares bore the names of those who labored and those who prayed as well as those who governed. Germans, Slavs, Greeks, Albanians, Ottoman Turks, and Jews also shaped urban geography, particularly after 1400, a material sign of their integration: rich merchants from Nuremberg, Ratisbon, and Augsburg at the Fondaco dei Tedeschi (Plate VIII), Rialto, and San Bartolomeo; Greek Orthodox scholars from the Venetian colonies in the eastern Mediterranean Sea and the Levant, at Castello; the nations of Jews – Ashkenazi moneylenders and secondhand clothes dealers; Sephardic and Levantine traders – at the Ghetto (Plates IX–X), the dumping site of a disused foundry, in Cannaregio; and the Ottoman merchants, subjects of the Sultan from the Balkans and Asia Minor, at San Giacomo dell' Orio.

Alongside this physical integration, manifested in residence patterns and topographical landmarks, there was nonetheless an implicit hierarchy in the city's social fabric, inscribed in law and the Christian religion and embedded in the rich visual representation of housing, works of art, codes of dress, ceremonies, and material culture. Class and gender were particularly apparent in dress, which was color coded to designate men's social station and women's sexual status. In public, nobles wore black, courtesans dressed in red, married women and widows were veiled in black, while maidens covered their heads in white, and servants wore the sober tones of taupe. Legislation cautioned naïve foreign visitors not to mistake prostitutes for honest women, as they sometimes cunningly garbed themselves in the dress of respectable females.

Hierarchy was also ingrained in relationships of power, at both the elite and the popular levels. It was most evident among the nobles who ruled the state and occupied the leading ecclesiastical positions, and its development as an organizing principle, with all the benefits of social worth, privilege, and authority, is best understood by the legal formation of the ruling class. Other social groups did not lend themselves to such strict categorization. On the contrary, social definition, at least among those outside the hereditary constitutional elite that ruled the city, was dynamic and inchoate, and the city's physical topography and modes of socialization encouraged broad interaction.

2. *Cittadini*, or Citizens

Demographic pressure in the years approaching the fourteenth century led to the establishment of restrictive laws of citizenship. Venice developed a second-tier elite, called "the *cittadini*," or citizens, whose legal status as a bureaucratic elite, scholars believe, was better defined than their social standing. Though it was rarely used, they had a formal appellation, *circumspectus et providus vir*, just as nobles referred to themselves as *nobiles vir dominus*. At the top of their hierarchy were the *originari*, native-born citizens with long-term residence in the city, who enjoyed membership by birth or by privilege. Other citizenship categories included *de intus et de extra*, men who had lived in the city and paid its taxes for at least twenty-five years; *de intus*, those with a minimum of fifteen years' residence (or eight years if they took Venetian wives) and a record of paying city taxes, and *per privilegio*, long-term residents with economic privileges. Clearly, citizenship was an important legal status that hinged on long-term residency, a criterion that defined this minor aristocracy against foreigners and more recent residents. *De intus et de extra* citizens, mostly men of commerce, were permitted to ship goods and engage in trade between Venice and the Levant. They paid lower customs duties than did foreigners. *De intus* citizens were eligible to join any of the guilds, to exercise trade in Venice, and to serve in minor public offices.

In addition to holding important bureaucratic offices that ensured the continuity of government, from 1410 citizens by birth also formed the *banche*, or members of the Great Confraternities, along with citizens by privilege who had been in the relevant confraternity for at least twenty years. There were six large religious lay confraternities that owned extensive property throughout the city. Like the patricians' Book of Gold, the secretariat had their own Book of Silver. This class accounted for between 5 percent and 8 percent of the population.

During the last third of the sixteenth century, the character of this social class shifted from its earlier foundations based on birth, residency, and the payment of taxes to one that emphasized social status, family lineage, and honor. In 1569, the condition (typical in other Venetian subject cities, such as Brescia) was added that neither the citizen nor his father nor grandfather could engage in the mechanical arts. Anna Bellavitis finds that the behavior of families in this class during the sixteenth century was critical to the formation of their bourgeois identity, owing to the laws that excluded the *ars mecanica* but also because of the role of women.[1] Citizen women, especially widows, astutely managed their assets, accumulating significant wealth over time. Those with substantial dowries and inheritance were able to influence the choice of marriage partners for their offspring, and those with smaller dowries brought wealthy foreign males to the citizen ranks through marriage because, unlike the patriciate, this class could transfer citizen status through the female line.

At this point scholars know more about the cittadini's political and economic roles, and about the laws defining their legal status than they do about their social status and ties, which are still being researched and debated. It appears that, similar to other second-tier elites in late sixteenth-century Italy, the intellectual prowess of physicians, lawyers, and notaries became ennobling.

Laws were enacted between 1517 and 1736 for them to serve in the criminal tribunal of the Forty. Those engaged in such professions were considered honorable, particularly from the late sixteenth century. There were some 400 posts in the Forty during the seventeenth century. The originari also served the Council of Ten, Venice's supreme judicial organ. In addition to education, cittadini also formed their social identities through marriage alliances. Like those of the patriciate, they tended to practice endogamy, particularly from the sixteenth century onward. Moreover, the natural sons of the patriciate also received cittadino status.

Art historians and ethnographers are also demonstrating the ways in which members of this group developed their own cultural aesthetic. Cittadini adorned the entrances of their residences with family crests, symbols of their status. The Amadi family choreographed expressions of popular devotion around the statue of the virgin they owned at Santa Maria dei Miracoli, transforming themselves into prestigious parishioners. It is more than likely that future research will uncover a variety of ways cittadini expressed themselves in social and cultural terms and also show the diversity of their interactions with members of other social groups.

3. Ordinary People

Ordinary people, who made up 90 percent of the population, ranged from the well-to-do to those struggling with subsistence. Those in the lower and middle ranges were obviously more preoccupied with modest wealth accumulation than with political hegemony. For them, marriage and family depended in large part on whether the new household unit would have the means to subsist. Sons who inherited vocations from their fathers had greater possibilities of marriage, for example, than seasonal laborers who migrated to the city from the neighboring farmlands or across the seas. Despite disenfranchisement from the government, commoners had their own forms of local representation and social identification in the seventy parishes or *contrade*. Each had a priest, chosen by the house owners of the parish before being installed by the bishop; and each had a parish leader, or *capo di contrada*. The *capi* were named and supervised by the doge and his council. They made tax assessments for forced loans and registered all adult males, supervising their selection for military-naval service. They kept watch over behavior in taverns as well as over foreigners. They served as police until the Lords of the Nightwatch were established during the thirteenth century.

Up until the late fourteenth century, the parish played an important role in the life of the people, organizing festivities and processions, and providing charity. The Festival of the Twelve Wooden Marys (January 31) is a case in point. It was celebrated from at least the mid-twelfth century to 1379, when it was temporarily abolished. Each year, two parishes, in addition to the parish of Santa Maria Formosa, sponsored formal banquets in patrician palaces, social gatherings of women, boat races, popular sports, and games. The origins of this distinctly Venetian festivity that was known throughout Italy are once again attached to one of Venice's many legends, harkening back to the tenth century and preserved through oral tradition. The story of the Twelve Wooden Marys begins with one of the annual Venetian celebrations of the Transfer of Saint Mark to the cathedral at San Pietro di Castello, commemorated each January 31. The doge and the members of the commune had just sponsored the weddings of twelve poor young girls, bestowing on them lavish dowries. Triestine pirates interrupted the church celebration, snatching the girls and their dotal wealth. Venetian menfolk became the heroes of the day by chasing the renegade pirates to the port of Caorle, named to this day the Port of the Maidens, and rescuing the girls on February 2, the day of the Purification of the Virgin, or Candelmas. To commemorate this good deed, which preserved the girls' sexual honor, marriage, and motherhood, the doge pledged that he and his successors would visit the parish of Santa Maria Formosa every year on February 1 and 2. Needless to say, the festivities were a favorite of medieval Venetian women.

The Festival of the Twelve Wooden Marys was temporarily suspended during the War of Chioggia with Genoa between 1379 and 1381. When it was reinstated, its physiognomy had changed to emphasize the centralizing aspirations of the city-state and to pare down the preeminence of the parish. Candelmas remained a parish feast, but its parameters were reduced to a local event. Instead the politically minded ruling class reconfigured the entire spatial pattern of the procession, cutting out the parishes and featuring instead the route from San Marco to the Marian center at Santa Maria Formosa.

Despite the growth of the city-state tradition, ordinary people still enjoyed other modes of leadership and sociability outside parish circles, ones which revolved around the professions and skilled work. The first arena included physicians, lawyers, and notaries, wealthy, educated commoners who often used the appellation *dominus* and who circulated within their own professional organizations. The second encompassed labor guilds, formed in the late twelfth century either to speak for employers of laborers (e.g., shop owners) or to protect employees (e.g., caulkers, masons, and carpenters). They fell into two categories of production, located at the Arsenal and the Rialto, respectively: shipbuilding and the handicrafts. The officials who supervised these activities formed yet another category of guilds. Further, the doge also had his own set of officials (*gastaldi*) to ensure that he received the labor services owed him, particularly from the shipwrights and ironsmiths. The number of guilds is too long to list, but among the principal groups were the range of textile workers, retailers, boatmen, victuallers, porters, and shipyard workers. Women enjoyed membership in the guilds of textiles and clothing; fustian weavers, comb-makers; cappers, tailors, doublet-makers; secondhand dealers; ironmongers; and haberdashers. It is important to note that none of these guilds regulated trade, which was the monopoly of the patrician elite. Guilds were not closed monopolies; qualified immigrants could set up shops in Venice, provided they paid dues and observed rules. Historian Frederick Lane has shown that some guilds were subordinate to merchants, who drew their main profits from foreign trade, such as the shipwrights and the cordage makers. Lane emphasizes that the suppliers of capital were in control of many branches of industry, and they were in the governing merchant aristocracy.[2]

The guilds remained subject to state regulation, with the tribunals of the Giustizia Vecchia overseeing the handicrafts and the Giustizia Nova supervising foodstuffs, taverns, and the wine trade. During the 1260s, a period when Venice experienced serious commercial losses resulting from the war with Genoa, the government attempted to contain guild power. The Great Council passed a law forbidding guilds to form sworn associations against the doge and his council or against the commune.

Even though in medieval Venice guild members were legally excluded from direct political participation, there were other ways their voices were heard and they were able to participate in the life of the polity. Historian Richard Mackenny's book on the guilds demonstrates that their public expression of the principle of brotherhood, a medieval civic tradition that all Venetians acknowledged, aided ordinary people in feeling that they were part of a Christian state.[3] The trade guilds of workers practicing the same occupation, or *arti*, achieved this through their confraternities (*scuole*), associations for religious devotion and mutual aid. The confraternities were federations of related trades. Beginning in the thirteenth century, each worker, whether Venetian or foreign, was obligated to matriculate in a confraternity, which held legal status, access to courts of law, and rights of appeal. There were Six Great Confraternities – San Giovanni Evangelista, Santa Maria della Misericordia, San Marco, Santa Maria della Carità, San Rocco, San Teodoro; and several Small Confraternities. Among the latter was the scuola of the Dalmatians (Fig. 18) and that of the Greeks, who were only permitted to have their own church in 1514. Until the fifteenth century,

Figure 18. Scuola di San Giorgio degli Schiavoni, begun 1480; rebuilt in 1551 by Giovanni de Zan. Location: Venice, Italy. Photo Credit: J. M. Ferraro.

Greek peoples, who were dispersed all over Venice, were referred to as the "Greek Nation," or the "University of Greeks." They were in a variety of occupations, as merchants, shipowners, captains at the port, custom officials, clerics, soldiers, physicians, pharmacists, teachers, book publishers, painters, and artisans. The studies of archivist Maria Francesca Tiepolo reveal them to be bicultural[4] – that is, both Greek and Venetian. The establishment of their scuola in 1498 gave them legal recognition and suggests that they were separate, and some of their customs and language did stand out. However, there is also evidence that over time they assimilated into Venetian life. Moreover, Greek vocabulary entered the Venetian dialect, Greeks lived in the same neighborhoods as other Venetians and had common interests with them, and they also intermarried. Albanians, Dalmatians, Milanese, Florentines, Bergamascs, Lucchesi, and Jews in the professions, trade, or crafts also had scuole that provided them the opportunity to mix with other residents of Venice. The Milanese were concentrated in the building industry; Dalmatians in seafaring; Albanians in military combat. Wealth varied in the membership of the scuole, linking rich and poor; nobles, citizens, and the skilled professions.

The confraternity took care of the brotherhood in several ways, such as providing a social club for banqueting; creating a means of distributing alms to the unfortunate; assisting at funerals or burials; commemorating the deceased at mass or the saints as intercessors; or doing good works in honor of a patron saint. While guild activities unfolded around the workshop or the marketplace, the confraternity operated in a much larger space, beyond workplace, parish church, or neighborhood affiliations, assuming a much broader social role in Venetian life, supported by spectacular visual representation and innovative music. As patrons, they commissioned great artists to produce paintings for church altars, and as crafts workers, they endowed their churches with beautiful handicrafts, such as candle holders, silver and gold work, and glass chandeliers. The confraternities, both great and small, were at the forefront of European musical developments, along with Venice's nunneries, monasteries, parish churches, and guilds. Musicologist Jonathan Glixon has found that they not only emulated the mainstream styles of sacred music advanced by Adrian Willaert and Andrea and Giovanni Gabrieli at their annual feasts, but they also sponsored religious celebrations accompanied with innovative chant, songs for family rites like burials, polyphonic poems, and instrumental ensembles for monthly ceremonies.[5] Music, like artistic representation, served a fundamental purpose of projecting the confraternities' corporate honor as well as encouraging music appreciation in the overall public.

The confraternity was a devotional group of pious Christians, joined under a patron saint for the purpose of honoring God through the dispensation of charity to one another (and not to the poor, who instead received alms from the Misericordia) (Fig. 19). Some, particularly among the *cittadini originari*, practiced flagellation, regular confession, and sexual abstinence. The Christian ones practiced regular liturgical exercises to promote the cult of a saint. Some scuole performed services of compassion, like accompanying the condemned to execution or aiding cripples. Others, like the bakers, the tailors, the silk throwsters, and the painters, founded hospitals, which, unlike our modern ones today, did not care for the sick but rather provided shelter

Figure 19. Jacopo Robusti Tintoretto (1518–94). *Fellows of a Confraternity*. Photo: Mauro Magliani, 1998. Location: Accademia, Venice, Italy. Photo Credit: Alinari/Art Resource, NY. Image Reference: ART332213.

to needy guild people. It is important to note that the medieval Venetian confraternities were not the product of the organized church but rather a community expression of the laity's desire to be involved in Christian life. A government magistracy, the Provveditori di Comun, regulated the smaller confraternities until 1360 when they came under the purview of the Council of Ten. It was only in the late sixteenth century that the church intruded into these brotherhoods. Nor were the medieval confraternities the expression of a singular parish, with the exception of Sant'Apostoli and Sant'Anna; the membership of each contained almost seventy parishes. Again this changed in the middle of the sixteenth century with the Catholic Reformation, when the parish church, with the encouragement of the state, assumed a greater role in lay devotion.

Venetian confraternities were also critical sites of human bonding. Historian Dennis Romano finds female servants bequeathing small sums of money to the *scuole piccole*, particularly ones that sponsored female saints. They often willed money to more than one brotherhood and showed a special fondness for the confraternity of the Blessed Sacrament, Saint Ursula and the eleven thousand virgin martyrs, the Virgin Mary, and other female saints. In churches scattered all around Venice they particularly enjoyed garnering indulgences for the souls of both the living and the dead.[6]

Confraternities had a political identity and as such belonged within the history of Venice rather than that of the church. They played a great part in feasts, festivals, and parades, all of which were instruments of government in Venice and critical modes of communication. They made public statements, such as greeting a newly elected doge or protesting his election, welcoming foreign dignitaries, and celebrating victories of war. They commemorated past victories. On the Fat Thursday of Carnival season, for example, blacksmiths butchered pigs to celebrate Venice's legendary victory over the Patriarch of Aquileia and the capture of his twelve feudal canons and lords in 1162. The captives were liberated with the proviso that the patriarch would send the Venetian doge an annual tribute of one bull, twelve pigs, and 300 loaves of bread. The loser agreed, and until the Patriarchate of Aquileia was dissolved in 1420, his successors continued to send payment, to the delight of the populace. In 1525 the aristocratic polity, increasingly concerned with decorum, shunned the coarse pigs and reformed the ritual to include the decapitation of one bull for the pleasure of the masses (Fig. 20).

The centrality of the confraternities was an affirmation that Venice clearly privileged Catholics over members of other denominations and that Catholicism served as a tool to foster the feeling that these religious brotherhoods belonged to a civic life. Protestants in Venice, on the other hand, were not permitted the kinds of organizations other Christians enjoyed. Nonetheless, as Germans, they enjoyed a privileged status because they were vital to the Venetian economy, first as merchants who augmented the riches of nobles and citizens and, second, as bakers, cobblers, weavers, physicians, printers, soldiers, porters, and servants.

Figure 20. Joseph Heintz the Younger (1600–78). *Bull Hunt in Campo San Polo.* Location: Museo Correr, Venice, Italy. Photo Credit: Cameraphoto Arte, Venice/Art Resource, NY. Image Reference: ART178833.

4. The Jews of Venice

The Jews of Venice, also vital to the economy, were subject to even greater restrictions than Protestants: they were permitted to reside in Venice proper only after 1516. Actively engaged in the city's commerce from the fourteenth century onward, Jews were nevertheless not permitted to settle in the city; instead, they were forced to live in nearby Mestre and commute to Venice. They did reside, however, throughout the Mediterranean, particularly on Salonico and Crete, as well as on the Italian mainland. During the late fourteenth century, the Venetian government decided to modify its restrictive residency policy. Adversities such as the Black Death of 1348–9, commercial rivalry with Genoa (1300–55), and the War of Chioggia (1378–81) had resulted in financial setbacks and created an urgent need for both the government and the less fortunate to borrow capital. Thus in 1381, the government issued a charter, called a *condotta*, officially authorizing the Jews to live in Venice and to lend money at rates of 10–12 percent. The charter, the first of many, was only a temporary contractual agreement. In fact, patricians vacillated repeatedly over whether to cancel or renew such agreements, at times voting to expel the Jews but then shifting policy in economic downturns that forced them to take stock of their assets. Despite an expulsion decree in 1395, some Jews were permitted to remain in the city, but for no more than fifteen consecutive days. They were required to wear a yellow circle on their clothing, a Venetian nod to the Fourth Lateran Council of 1215, which required that both Jews and Muslims be visibly labeled so as to prevent legally prohibited sexual relations with Christians. The Venetian government's aim, however, was not only to prevent intimacy or intermarriage but also to limit the financial operations of the Jews and to prohibit the open practice of their religion. Further, in 1443 the Senate ruled that Jews were not to teach games, dance, or music. Nonetheless, compared to the negative, restrictive treatment of Jews in other parts of Europe, Venetian policies appear relatively tolerant. The Jews came to play a vital role in all aspects of Venetian society as financial resource managers, skilled physicians, and learned scholars.

The War with Imperial and Papal forces at the start of the sixteenth century was a turning point in many ways for Venice, including its Jewish population. As the forces of the League of Cambrai advanced and captured Venetian territories, where Jews were free to live and practice moneylending, the government found it advantageous to house them in Venice where they could help alleviate the Republic's financial burden. They were thus permitted to reside in the city as long as they paid annual taxes and lent money, ostensibly to the urban poor whose numbers had grown during the war. In 1515, the Ten made an agreement with a Jewish banker residing in Mestre, Asher Meshullam, whom they called Anselmo del Banco, to begin moneylending in Venice for a five-year term. Meshullam and his associates paid 6,500 ducats for this privilege. The following year they obtained the right to sell used clothing (*strazzarie*, signifying "rags") and other used items for a three-year period in exchange for lending the treasury 5,000 ducats. The group opened nine stores that year and later, for an additional sum of money, a tenth. They thrived, catering to a broad segment of the resident population as well as to foreign visitors by renting furniture, carpets, and decorations for special occasions and state festivities. The latter included ornamentation for the celebrations at Fat Thursday during Carnival and for the Bucintoro, the vessel the doge used during the annual ceremony of the Marriage of Venice to the Sea.

The need for moneylending, an activity prohibited by canon law, and the usefulness of the secondhand business strongly contributed to the founding of the Jewish Ghetto, an urban space that segregated Jews from the rest of the population. Two islands associated with an obsolete foundry in the district of Cannaregio were the site of the new settlement. The island that had housed the foundry in the fourteenth century was named Ghetto Vecchio, while the other, where the foundry waste had been dumped, was named Ghetto Nuovo. The word that Jews later pronounced "Ghetto" is derived from *getto*, the Venetian word for caster, the form that shaped smelted metal (from the verb *gettare*, "to cast"; the verb also means "to throw"). The Ghetto Nuovo had housed the master cannon caster during the fourteenth century, when the foundry satisfied the state's need for artillery. That was no longer the case during the fifteenth century, when warfare escalated and metal production required more space. In 1434, the foundry was transferred to the state Arsenal, and the Ghetto Vecchio and Ghetto Nuovo (the onsite spellings in Venetian are Gheto Vecchio and Gheto Novo) were auctioned off. The open fields of the latter became an ideal place for adolescent nobles to practice with their crossbows and to set traps for birds. The area passed through various owners, who built housing, largely rented by textile workers. When the Jews moved into the area in 1515, they transformed the word *getto* into ghetto, a word that gained lasting and universal meaning around the globe.

The Jews continued to be vital to the Venetian economy, as moneylenders, textile merchants, and vendors of used articles. Moneylenders were actually pawnbrokers, who sat at counters (*banchi*) to receive pledges or pawns (*pegni*). The lenders were referred to by contemporaries as *banchieri*, but this is not the same as "banker." It referred instead to the lender who accepted pawns in exchange for loans. The Venetian government favored Jewish moneylending because it provided a source of cheap credit for the poor.

Not everyone, however, was disposed to housing the Jews, particularly the Franciscan friars. Other segments of Venetian society were also ambivalent, especially those who saw the Jews as economic competition. In 1524, one group of patricians proposed that Venice establish its own pawnshop, virtually removing the kinds of small lending activities that Jews had performed. The Ten, however, mindful of the Jews' usefulness as both lenders and a source of taxation, refused. In 1541, the Jewish district was enlarged to include the Ghetto Vecchio, and in 1573 once again the government debated whether to expel the Jews' charter, but despite strong voices advocating this they ultimately decided to renew. At this time patricians also expressed ambivalence toward the Ottoman Turks, with whom, in defense of Christian Europe, they were struggling in the Mediterranean. Still, the Jews were permitted to remain in Venice and to lend money, but now at a maximum rate of 5 percent.

The mid-sixteenth century witnessed a new wave of Jewish immigration to Venice, merchant communities referred to as Levantini (Eastern Mediterranean Jews) and Ponentini (Western Mediterranean Jews) whom the Venetians came to distinguish from their resident moneylenders, called Tedeschi (German) or Italiani. In 1496, the Inquisition reached Portugal, causing many Jews to flee to Venice. Shortly thereafter, many Jewish merchants also left the Ottoman Empire, returning to Venice as Ottoman subjects. Some of the Levantini may have originated in Spain or Portugal, where they had been forced to suppress their religion and practice Christianity, in 1492 and 1496, respectively, or flee. The Spanish had given them the derogatory name Marrano, signifying pig. Scholars refer to them as Crypto-Jews. Venice served as both a center of transit and a place of settlement for these people, whether they were hiding their Judaism and living outside the Ghetto or had converted back to Judaism and were living within its confines. But Venice banned converts to Christianity suspected of secretly practicing Judaism in 1497 and again in 1550, forcing those who wished to remain to live in the Ghetto and practice Judaism. In 1589, Daniel Rodriga, the consul of the Sephardic Jewish merchants, persuaded Venetian rulers to make the Ottoman merchants Venetian subjects. The Republic needed them to generate trade with the Dalmatian port of Spalato. The Senate responded, issuing a charter to Levantine, Spanish, and other Jewish merchants, some no doubt of New Christian origin, that permitted them to stay in the city for ten years and allowed them to import and export merchandise without restriction. The Crypto-Jews were required to revert to Judaism.

Thus the patricians in power persisted in protecting Jewish residency because it was in their economic interest to do so. However, the proscribed space of the Ghetto, linked to "Christian" Venice by two bridges, speaks to the limits of Venetian hospitality. Gates were constructed at the two access points to the area; they were closed at sunset and opened at sunrise, preventing Jews from having access to Venice at night. Physicians with special permission, however, could leave the Ghetto to attend their patients after hours. The Jews were obliged to pay the salaries of four Christian guards who resided at the access points. The two sides of the Ghetto overlooking small canals were sealed off by high walls, and quays were bricked up to prevent access. The Jews also had to pay for the two boats circling the area around the clock to keep them contained. When they left the Ghetto they were obliged to wear dress that identified them: initially a yellow skullcap, then a yellow or red turban.

Within their own community, the Jews were permitted to self-regulate. There were between two and three thousand of them in the sixteenth and seventeenth centuries, with 199 dwelling units in 1582 and 618 in 1661. They had their own butchers observing dietary laws and bakers for unleavened bread. They had several tailor shops and moneylending offices. They had a home for poor Tedeschi, a hostel for visiting Levantines, and a hospice for unmarried girls. They also prepared feasts, ceremonies, and spectacles, attracting Venetian Christians and tourists during Carnival as well as at other times of the year. There were many attractions in the Ghetto, including dice games and shows, as well as bookstalls.

The Jews availed themselves of Christian notaries living in Cannaregio in the vicinity of the Ghetto. Historian Carla Boccato's studies of the activities of two notaries in the neighborhood of San Marcuola show that Jewish women interacted with the people who lived in the residential zones around the ghetto, that is, at San Marcuola, dell' Anconetta, della Maddalena, and Ponte degli Ormesini.[7] The witnesses who signed their wills included Christian shopkeepers, artisans, boatmen, and porters. While the wills are usually written in Italian, some contain Iberian words from Sephardic Jews; others are strictly in Venetian; and others have Hebrew words. There was also a kind of Judeo-Venetian that was a local dialect in the Ghetto. It consisted of Venetian infused with Hebrew, German, Spanish, and Portuguese. Boccato's work suggests that Jewish women were strongly integrated into the city of Venice as evidenced in their relationships with neighbors, their donations to Christian hospitals, and their assets in the Venetian Mint. However, this did not necessarily extend to marriage. Some women's wills specify that their daughters would be disinherited should they marry Germans or Italians.

The Jews were allowed to practice their religion only within the Ghetto. They built their own synagogues, which they referred to as *schole*, similar to those of the Christian confraternities. The synagogues included the Grande Tedesca (1528) and Canton (1532), which were Ashkenazi; Italiana (1575) (Plate X); Levantina, or Eastern Mediterranean (1575); Spagnola or Ponentina (c. 1580–1635), Western Mediterranean, both of which were Sephardic. Like the Christian confraternities, the *schole* had a set of regulations, administered by representatives who were elected from among the membership. They held fiscal and moral authority, provided clothing for the poor, treated the sick, buried the dead, secured the release of prisoners, paid ransoms to pirates to release captured Jews, and arranged marriages for poor girls.

There was some confluence between the artistic culture of Venice and that of the Jews. At the level of high culture, Venice became a major center for the printing of texts in Hebrew, Ladino, and Yiddish, and thus an ideal place for Jewish education, which included publishing sermons, prayers, ethical writings, dedicatory poetry, and commentaries on Hebrew texts. Some Venetian nobles studied Hebrew and read these works as well, particularly those by notable Jewish scholars such as Leon Modena (1571–1648), Menasseh ben Israel (1604–57), and Simone Luzzatto (1583–1663). With respect to daily life, a great deal of interaction between Christian and Jewish workers took place. Despite official proscription, both groups sublet rooms or attics in the Ghetto. Moreover, the area gave employment to many casual laborers from both faiths, including porters, street cleaners, water carriers, attendants of stalls, and peddlers, thus allowing for cultural exchange.

5. Other Modes of Sociability

Over the fifteenth to sixteenth centuries, the Great Confraternities, along with all other Catholic expression in Venice, gradually lost their medieval spirit of corporation. Historian John Martin argues that the sacred was split off from the corporate and placed increasingly under the control of both secular and clerical elites.[8] Within the Great Confraternities, citizens and professionals no longer mingled with skilled artisans but instead embraced a more aristocratic conception of politics and society. Late humanist philosophy reinforced this fundamental elitism, which affirmed hierarchal differences. Moreover, religious life no longer provided ordinary people with a connection to civic institutions. The patrician class placed the religious under greater control, while the Counter-Reformation church sought to tighten morality and enjoined parish priests to vigilantly supervise marriage, midwifery, and sexuality. The patrician state also began to exercise greater control over religious cults, such as the one surrounding the Marian church of Santa Maria de Miracoli. Martin concludes that by the end of the sixteenth century there was a great disjunction between the way Venice described itself, as a free Republic, and the new emphasis on hierarchy and social control.

The onslaught of the religious schisms brought on by the Protestant Reformation cannot be ignored in retracing social affiliations in sixteenth-century Venice. Martin's "hidden heretics," evangelicals, Anabaptists, and millenarians who flooded the city as itinerant priests and friars, publishers, book vendors, merchants, artisans, and missionaries brought in the new brands of Christianity and effected splits in Venice's social landscape.[9] Evangelism had infiltrated segments of the aristocracy by 1540. Thereafter it attracted elite artisans, professionals, merchants, mercers, publishers, printers, jewelers, tailors, and silk weavers, most of whom were literate and receptive to the ideas of Luther and Calvin. Evangelists tended to be antihierarchical, but they were not unified, for the professionals emulated the nobility, mingling in secret with nobles and citizens at the Fondaco dei Tedeschi, the Giudecca, or San Giorgio, while elite artisans congregated within their own social milieu to discuss religion in the streets, shops, taverns, and public squares. Workers constituted the overwhelming majority of Anabaptists, although there were some professionals. Most were poor and illiterate cobblers, textile workers, and swordsmiths who argued for communal property. Millenarians, on the other hand, were literate members of elite crafts, who, unlike the evangelicals, accepted the extant social and political order. All three of these groups advocated reading (or listening to) scriptures and interpreting them themselves, in distinct opposition to the Catholic ruling class which sought to control all aspects of the sacred.

Factionalism, which included armed conflict, was yet another mode of socialization among ordinary people. With its own cultural space and timing, factionalism offers a much different perspective on the way groups in Venice organized than do the guilds and confraternities. The latter participated in official culture, which included ducal processions and banquets, state cere-monies, religious holidays like All Saints' Day and Christmas, or pagan festi-vals like the Lenten Candelmas. But at the close of these civic celebrations that reinforced the "Myth of the Most Serene Republic" thousands of work-ers, together with their wives, relatives, and neighbors, departed from the ceremonial sites of San Marco, Merceria, Rialto, and the Grand Canal to enact their own violent neighborhood dramas.

Factionalism had long-standing roots in Venice. According to one foun-dation myth that was well established by the sixteenth century, the ninth-century settlers had already begun to sort themselves into two groups, "peoples from the land" and "islanders." The first came from the mainland, especially the Byzantine city of Heraclea; the second from the islands around the lagoon. The refugees from Heraclea settled the landward areas of Venice, at Cannaregio, San Polo, and Santa Croce, while the islanders established enclaves facing the sea, at San Marco, Castello, and Dorsoduro. Urban lore described them playing out their social and cultural differences with stick battles and ritual brawls on marshy banks and grassy fields in the center of most islands as early as 810. Another foundation story from the last quarter of the thirteenth century told of one Bishop Polo who tried to force five neighborhoods in Dorsoduro to pay a tithe from which they felt they were exempt. An angry mob tore him to shreds, but the question of tax exemp-tion also split the district into factions. Five parishes lined up with the dock workers and cattle butchers in Cannaregio. This new alliance was at the cen-ter of a third story. Some 250 years later, the five Dorsoduro parishes with the dock workers and cattle butchers of Cannaregio lined up with the fish-ermen of San Niccolò and challenged the Castellani faction to a showdown. The challengers lost. They took the name Nicolotti and fashioned red caps in memory of the assassinated Bishop Polo to wear to their battles.

It is plausible, according to historian Robert Davis, that the formation of urban districts in 1171 further fanned the fires of these two factions, kept alive by generational hostility. The first surviving documentary evidence of their existence, however, dates from only 1369, when the government issued

Figure 21. Gabriele Bella (fl.1700–50). *Combat Scene on the Ponte dei Pugni* (Bridge of Fists). Location: Galleria Querini Stampalia, Venice, Italy. Photo Credit: Cameraphoto Arte, Venice/Art Resource, NY. Image Reference: ART171810.

an edict encouraging competitive battles so that its peoples would develop the martial skills to defend the city.[10] Whatever their origins, and there was more than one urban legend about Venice's two great factions, this factionalism became an important organizing principle, like parish structure, the division into social classes, and gendered meaning.

These public displays of disorder evolved from stick battles in the neighborhood campi to wars of the fists by the late fourteenth century, occurring primarily on the bridges – a phenomenon that endured until the beginning of the eighteenth century (Fig. 21). The neighborhood brawls drew a large crowd of partisan spectators that crossed class, generational, and gender lines. Nobles, cittadini, priests, monks, nuns, Jews, and children all rallied in favor of the gladiators outfitted in helmets and shields who pummeled each other. The battles amused foreign visitors as well.

What interests us here is how factional lines were formed, according to Davis. The factional boundary ran at right angles to the Grand Canal, cutting across worker districts and effecting a seaward/landward fissure in Venetian society. Those closest to the mainland called themselves the Cannaruoli by the late thirteenth century and later the Castellani, led by the shipbuilders.

Those living in the three seaward districts, led by the fishermen, called themselves the Nicolotti. By 1500, the two had divided the city between them, taking in new immigrants and foreigners as they arrived. Their most popular sites of violence were the two fish markets at San Marco and the Rialto; the bridges of San Marziale and Santa Fosca in Cannaregio; and the Ponte dei Pugni, the Carmine, and Gesuati bridges in Dorsoduro. The greatest hostility was expressed by the workmen who lived at or near the boundary lines. In those cases faction trumped occupation. Davis has shown, moreover, that factionalism influenced marital endogamy and godparenting, thus critically impacting both family and community. The compelling evidence of this violent factionalism over the generations may be yet another antimyth against the patrician and humanist ideal of Serenity, unless in fact the government's repeated encouragement of this behavior – by ignoring its own mandates and by noble attendance at the brawls – was in fact a clever way to afford the populace a means of letting off steam. Moreover, it was a means of readying the populace in the martial arts lest the city without walls succumb to invading marauders from the menacing Ottoman Empire to the southeast.

Carnival was another occasion when the government ignored its own mandates to curb rowdiness and permitted commoners to parody ducal processions and republican sovereignty as well as to publicly invert the social and hierarchical structure. The eighteenth-century playwright Carlo Goldoni described Carnival as "The World Turned Upside Down" (*Il mondo allo roverso*). The festivities began on December 26 and ended the day before Ash Wednesday, when the forty-day Lenten season of fasting and bodily restraint began. The mysterious figures dressed with black silk hoods and lace capes (*bauti*) over bulky cloaks (*tabarri*) razed social rank to the ground. Other disguises derived from the figures of the *Commedia dell'Arte*. People thronged the campi, dancing, singing, carousing, playing games, and staging parodies of civil and religious life (Fig. 22). Carnival was a time of sensual licentiousness when people gorged, got drunk, and indulged sexually prior to the Lenten demands for abstinence. Aristocratic youth in Companies of the Hose, distinguished by the patterns and colors of their silk stockings, organized imitations of ancient Roman entertainments, bull-baiting, and wheelbarrow races. There was also rough play. The ritualized violence was both symbolic and real, as benign as tossing stinky eggs or as lethal as murder.

Theorists of city ritual have explained the nobility's willingness to tolerate comical disorder and the mocking of authority as ways to protect communal values and justify political, religious, and gendered hierarchy. Laws were held in abeyance, while costumes and masks – already a craft industry by the fifteenth century – disguised social class and gender. Role inversion served as a

Figure 22. Pietro Longhi (1702–85). *Carnival Scene in Venice*. Location: Accademia, Venice, Italy. Photo Credit: Erich Lessing/Art Resource, NY. Image Reference: ART60973.

means of organizing social relationships that were not contractually defined. Commoners who could afford the costumes dressed as the doge or as patricians; courtesans wore the jewels of married ladies; and women dressed as priests. One could even imagine mice chasing cats down alleyways, as they do during Carnival masquerades today. Nonetheless, it would be mistaken to characterize the Venetian nobility, or commoners for that matter, as homogeneous groups, for there were also conspicuous fissures, owing to generational and gendered differences.

There are many ways to reconstruct Venetian social networks. Venue lends itself well to sorting people out, with descriptive texts and illustrations of daily routines and life-cycle rites in the household; the neighborhood with its campi, bridges, taverns, and water wells; the synagogue or parish church, convent, or monastery with its burial sites; the workplace, guild hall, or confraternity; the smaller marketplaces and the large one at Rialto; fairs; the shipbuilding industry at the Arsenal; the port at San Marco; Piazza San Marco, the site of dramatic public spectacle as well as political life; and on water through the labyrinth of canals, the lagoon, and the open sea.

Urban space spanned a mere seven square kilometers. People recognized one another as they routinely trod the footpaths and rowed through the waterways and as they glanced down from their houses and balconies to observe human activity. There was little privacy in that densely populated space. Women working at doorsteps or on their balconies could observe daily routines as well as irregularities. Families heard and witnessed one another's squabbles, and gossip quickly brought information to the peopled calli and campi. Moreover, the calli and campi afforded opportunities to stop and chat, or flirt; play games and sports; fetch water; cool off on a warm night; purchase vegetables, fruits, and fish at a local stand; or stop for a drink in a tavern.

6. Forming Families

While Venetian topography helps us identify the sites of sociability, it nonetheless does not entirely explain the organizing principles of social interaction. As we have seen, religion and religious rites such as baptism, marriage, and funerals; ethnicity; law; gender; and informal operational codes such as male and female honor both fostered cohesion and underlay rifts. It is also important to consider the family as a unit of social organization, with its life-cycle stages of childhood, adolescence, and adulthood. In some senses this is an ideal because legally family required marriage and legitimacy, something not all Venetians could attain. Financial means and gender played important roles in setting the parameters of whether people would marry. Children in families of very modest means, for example, were burdened with labor responsibilities. They began as early as seven to conduct menial tasks, such as sweeping or fetching water. Puberty defined womanhood for girls, and boys were considered capable of doing the full work of men by the age of fourteen. Boys entered the apprentice system some time after age eleven; girls spun and sewed as well as learned all the tasks associated with reproduction and nurture. Both sexes helped their parents with whatever production activities unfolded in the household. Did they enjoy no adolescence? Probably not, by modern standards. Still, they engaged in games and social activities that we would define as the ritual observance of adolescence, such as charivari, bull runs, the wars of the fists for boys and the factionalism the fist competitions generated for girls. There were also lots of children who either lost their parents to one of life's many misfortunes or had parents who could ill afford them. If they were lucky, they might enter domestic service, becoming part of the extended family of a prosperous household; acquire guardians; or enter orphanages. If not, they ended up on the streets. It is important to emphasize, thus, that despite the tenet upheld by church and state that marriage was critical to the social fabric, many Venetians could not marry to form legitimate families.

For those who were able to take vows, forms of courtship were determined in part by social standing. At the upper levels of society, marriage was a business arrangement. Parents, not spouses, made the match, generally employing such criteria as the purity of the bloodline, status, wealth, and family reputation. Upper-class patriarchs carefully assessed a prospective marriage alliance in terms of the family dynasty's standing in political and social life, as well as its wealth. Betrothals were arranged with the help of allies and kin. In contrast, young people's initiation of marital agreements had more success further down the social ladder, where wealth and standing were lesser concerns. Still, parental consent was desirable, and property was an important consideration. Parity in the match remained the most common criterion for suitability.

Bellavitis's study of Venice's citizen class of merchants and lower government officials is exemplary: most of the families in these circles married within their own ranks. However, the wealthiest and most successful sought to elevate their status by allying with the upper ranks of society and by situating their offspring within a diversified but beneficial range of social contexts. My own monograph, *Marriage Wars*, identifies couples from the same artisan ranks marrying, but also documents mésalliances between the upper and lower ranks of society. The marital litigation between Foscarina Memo and Giovanni Battista Misserini in 1612 is emblematic.[11]

Foscarina's social standing was much more ambivalent than that of her husband Giovanni. She was the illegitimate daughter of a prominent Venetian patrician, Giovanni Francesco Memo. Her father had died and her mother was left with a meager income. Thus Foscarina had little hope of living in noble standing. Giovanni, on the other hand, was the rich son of a prosperous book publisher. His father would never have approved the marital union, so Giovanni married Foscarina in secret and maintained a double life, one as his father's son and the other as a clandestine husband. It is not clear why he chose Foscarina, but the evidence suggests that she was attractive and was compensating for her mother's paltry income by letting herself out as a courtesan. Giovanni was smitten, and the union was consummated. After three years, however, the marriage went sour and the disillusioned husband petitioned the Patriarchal Court for a formal separation, alleging that his wife had loose sexual mores. What followed was a long legal battle over their possessions. Foscarina aimed to keep the jewels, furniture, and other gifts she had received from Giovanni, while the disaffected husband, with his father's help, tried to recover as much property as he could. Mésalliances like that of Foscarina and Giovanni Battista were not uncommon. Other instances reached the Patriarchal court, especially when noble bachelors tried to dispose of their common-born concubines.

Giovanni Battista and Foscarina had not, obviously, followed social protocol. When couples expressed mutual consent to marry, their courtship was transformed into a serious relationship that then involved an insider circle of family and friends in the alliance. Consent had to be expressed in front of public witnesses before it was taken seriously and considered a binding promise. This had not always been the case, and many couples prior to Giovanni Battista and Foscarina had gotten into trouble by not observing this ritual. Until the Council of Trent in 1563, marriage rites varied. Marriage among humbler folk may not have entailed formal negotiations at all; some couples just started living together. The man publicly kissed the woman and presented her with a ring or some other gift, whereupon they proceeded to have a sexual relationship. Of course, this caused great confusion if at some point either of the spouses, usually the husband, reneged on his commitment. The ecclesiastical courts were flooded with such breach of promise suits. Thus in 1563, theologians at Trent, who characterized such behavior as sinful, established firmer requirements: that couples announce their banns in advance, publicizing them at least three times in their community; that they marry before their parish priest and at least two witnesses; that they affirm and publicize their mutual consent; and that they register the marriage.

The formalized rituals allowed the community to recognize publicly the new commitment, giving it greater cohesion. While it was traditional for fathers to arrange marriages, at times mothers or guardians, theoretically in the presence of witnesses, made the matches and concluded the symbolic exchange of property. The marriage contract provided for the costs of banquets, transportation, and clothing. The betrothed exchanged gifts and sometimes love notes. The community of witnesses served as social cement, at times coming to a troubled couple's aid to remind them of their nuptial commitments. Thus the union of two families, at whatever social level, was a recognized community affair, with rites and festivities evidencing its public nature. Betrothals, marriage contracts, and weddings involved kin, friends, and community, all of which helped to sustain the bonds of both the conjugal couple and their wider network of family and friends over time. Moreover, courtships, betrothals, and weddings were occasions of social drama where families forged new links. Both the social activity leading up to the wedding and the actual ceremony furnished occasions to publicize these new relationships of solidarity

Marriage also served the secular state as a means of regulating inheritance and reproduction. At the upper ranks, it forged alliances, advanced inheritance strategies, and supported patronage systems that permitted generations of families to endure over time. For the lower classes, marriage united the work skills of a man and a woman, together with their offspring, into one economic unit at the household level. For women this was especially visible in the cloth industry, where female labor was highly valued. At all levels marriage defined people's identities and was a mechanism of capital accumulation based on dowry and inheritance.

Marriage also held religious significance. One of the seven sacraments of the church, its essential function, according to Catholic dogma, was reproduction. Sex for pleasure alone was a sin; the couple's purpose was to procreate and suitably educate children. Catholic tribunals regarded mutual consent as the essential requirement for a valid marriage. Church services celebrated the union, making it public and secure under law, but it was the couple's mutual agreement that made it binding in the eyes of God.

There were no firm rules determining age at marriage. Some couples married young and lived under the authority of one set of parents. Most women were engaged at puberty and usually married between the ages of fourteen and eighteen, while grooms were between twenty-five and twenty-eight. There were gaps in the ages of brides and grooms among the working classes, as males delayed marriage in order to advance their earning potential. Household structure also varied, ranging from multigenerational to nuclear. Wealthier families had the capacity to house several generations, and their children could marry earlier. In contrast, the urban worker could not afford to support an extended family nor supply employment to all offspring. Thus his or her household did not extend beyond its nuclear origin. Sons and daughters married if they could establish separate households, the groom with a vocation and the bride with a dowry. If not, they remained unmarried.

Economic trends in Venice over the long term affected marriage patterns. Marriage rates normally rose following high mortality resulting from famines and epidemics, such as the plagues of 1348, 1575, and 1630. The reduced labor force necessitated earlier marriage. Age at marriage dropped in these downward cycles, multiplying the number of childbearing years. In contrast, in periods when the population was swollen, the marriage rate dropped and age at marriage rose. More people remained unmarried during these demographic cycles. This was generally the case during the sixteenth century, a period of dramatic demographic growth accompanied by inflation. The last three decades of the century brought religious war, plague, and famine, relieving population pressure and encouraging earlier marriages.

Many Venetians, however, did not take wedding vows for a variety of reasons. The poor faced severe obstacles in setting up a household, while the rich kept their wealth concentrated within the dynastic lineage. Most elite males in Venice were legally bachelors, and most patrician females took the veil. Patricians practiced restricted marriage in order to limit the number of collateral branches formed in each generation. They were also trying to avoid the dispersion of patrimony. The ideal was to maintain family size both in numbers and branches by having only one male in each branch reproduce. It meant that many bachelors spent their lives, according to historian Guido Ruggiero, outside the "boundaries of eros," or the "official borders of sexuality."[12] For women, similar economic concerns meant that many would not marry; these considerations were formalized by the institution of the dowry. Thus the ideal of marriage as the required place for normal sexuality was undermined by the realities of that institution itself.

Many of Venice's inhabitants found other sexual outlets, beyond the confines of accepted behavior. Ruggiero found a fourteenth- and fifteenth-century culture of illicit sexual behavior, mixed with the dominant culture of marriage and childbirth.[13] The patriarchal vision of sexuality permitted males considerable flexibility while restricting females' activity exclusively to the marriage bed. In almost every case, save violent rape, male family members were identified as victims rather than perpetrators of crime. Both seduction and adultery were defined from a patriarchal perspective. The daughter or wife were pieces of family property, subject to collective shame and dishonor. Adultery, for example, created property problems if the wife stole goods that belonged in law to the husband. The goods the husband gave to his wife, such as clothing and jewelry, remained legally his. So this was a problem when adulterous couples ran off together. In the fourteenth and fifteenth centuries the Venetian government, under the auspices of the tribunal of the Forty, stepped in to discipline adultery to protect property, maintain social distinctions, and keep women in place. Later, other tribunals, including the State Attorneys, the Forty, and the Ten would continue to keep sharp surveillance over the boundaries of marriage and property.

7. Contracts and Estates: The Secular Dimension of Marriage

Among the classes of substance, marriage contracts made according to secular law preceded and took priority over any clerical ceremony. Artisans, merchants, professionals, and patricians alike engaged notaries to record dowries, the exchange of consent, and dotal and wedding gifts. Patricians and cittadini paid the closest attention to the contractual nature of marriage and to the financial terms of the union, for marriage was of deep importance to their dynastic identities. The constitutional hereditary patrician class upheld endogamy; within the citizen class, the most successful merchant and bureaucratic families also tended to practice endogamy, while many physicians, lawyers, and notaries integrated into social circles in the landed dominions outside of Venice.

The secular dimension of marriage emphasized the importance of patrilinear descent and the disposition of dotal property within a lineage. Marriage created a new network that affected the cohesion of Venetian society in complex ways. Negotiations between the allying families, who were normally entering into a political as well as a social consortium, were mediated by common friends. The fathers, or alternatively the male kin of the future spouses, met, accompanied by close family and friends. At this meeting the terms of the marriage were set down in writing, and they were formally finalized at a later date in a notarial document. This betrothal ritual was as binding as the wedding ceremony.

The size of the dowry, the terms of dowry payment, the living facilities and clothes the husband promised to provide, and an itemized account of what the bride would bring to the marriage were all stipulated in the contract, and registered with the Giudici del Procurator. Women were expected to provide *corredi* that might consist of some clothing and household items, usually including the marriage bed and bedding for poor women, or vast amounts of cash, goods, or property for wealthy ones. The dowry was a statement of the bride's social status, publicizing her place in society as a whole. The dowry often substituted for a daughter's share of the family inheritance and increasingly did not include the land earmarked for the patrilinear lineage. Often that land was entailed, a legal restriction that made its recipient, through primogeniture, its custodian over his lifetime with the obligation to pass it on to the first male in the line.

The dowry was the central concern of contract negotiations. While in Roman times its purpose was to aid the groom with the expense of matrimony, in medieval and early modern times it was the bride's right to a share of her natal family's patrimony. Her husband could not alienate or consume it, and his own property was in jeopardy if he transgressed these rules. Legal restrictions over the governance of dotal resources were specified in Venice. Fathers, brothers, mothers, aunts, and other kin contributed to dowry resources, and these were registered in a special tribunal under the name *Vadimoni*. The well-dowered bride was a social asset. Wealthy women of the citizen class, especially widows, determined important nuptial choices for the family through astute management and disposition of their dotal property. In Venice, the sixteenth century was characterized by dowry inflation, making women and women's property increasingly important to marriage negotiations.

In practice, husbands had use of wives' dowries but did not own them. A widower was entitled to one-third of the dowry, and the rest went to surviving children. Women who thought their husbands were wastrels could sue them. The Republic established a special tribunal in 1553 to protect women's dotal property. Women might bequeath their dowries if they did not have an heir. Otherwise they were obliged to leave them to their children.

All of these laws were designed to cement social categories and ensure social order, but life often got in the way of official regulations and the prescriptions of the Catholic Church. Catastrophic mortality truncated households, leaving widows and widowers as well as orphans. Poverty prevented marriage but did not ensure celibacy. Also people, including vow-breaking patricians and clerics, simply made other life choices, bonding out of love, physical attraction, or economic necessity. The Venetian aristocracy subscribed to a strict marital regime, making arranged marriage one of the tenets of the Republic's stability. Whether patricians acknowledged it or not, however, this was also one of the city's many myths. Marriage and legitimacy remained an ideal that many could not attain, forcing magistrates to deal with the Republic's vices while they extolled its virtues.

FURTHER READING

Cittadini: A. Bellavitis (2001); J. Grubb (2000). *Charities*: B. Pullan (1971). *Confraternities*: J. Glixon (2003); R. MacKenny (1987). *Factionalism*: R. Davis (1994). *Greeks*: M. Tiepolo (2002). *Heretics*: J. Martin (1993). *Jews*: D. Calabi (2001); R. Calimani (1987); G. Cozzi (1987); R. Davis and B. Ravid (2001); B. Pullan (2001); B. Ravid (2001). *Marriage and Sexuality*: J. Ferraro (2001a, 2001b); M. King (1976); G. Ruggiero (1985). *Ritual*: E. Muir (1981). *Servants*: D. Romano (1996). *Social Classes*: D. Romano (1987). *Women*: M. Chojnacka (2001); S. Chojnacki (2000); P. La Balme (1984).

5

MATERIAL LIFE

1. Turning Tides

The Republic's commercial expansion reached the height of its development in the mid-fifteenth century. By then the Ottoman gaze rested firmly on Venice's seaborne empire. With a storm brewing on the horizon, the Venetians added two new sea routes. The first transported slaves, gold, hides, and cereals from sub-Saharan to North Africa, stopping in southern Spain and Barcelona and then heading south to Sicily and Tunis before returning to Venice. (See Map 2). The second docked at Alexandria, Tunis, and the Barbary coast. However, the submission of Constantinople to the Turkish Sultan Mehmed II in 1453 made Venice's position on the Aegean and the Adriatic tenuous. At first, diplomacy prevailed, but by the end of the century the Republic was engaged in a costly war (1499–1503). Modone and Corone fell to the Ottomans, who then went on to conquer Syria and Egypt in 1517. Another war broke out between 1536 and 1540, with Venice losing the Morea and the duchy of Naxos to its political nemesis. Thirty years later, Cyprus also came under Ottoman rule, despite the Christian victory of the Holy League of Venice, Spain, and the pope at the Battle of Lepanto (1571).

Despite the series of reversals, Venice enjoyed commercial vitality through the sixteenth century, thanks to the efforts of diplomats, merchants, laborers, and pilgrims. Moreover, the economy thrived at home, with one of the strongest industrial bases in Europe. Venice continued to be a powerful magnet for immigration, capable of strengthening its labor force even in the face of dramatic demographic fluctuation. In preparation for the Battle of Lepanto in 1571, for example, the Venetians built a hundred galleys with the aid of more than 2,000 arsenal workers. The plague of 1576–7, however, produced a dramatic setback, reducing the population of 168,000 to around 120,000, but by 1586 the number had climbed to 148,000. The thriving industrial base

Figure 23. Andrea Palladio (1508–80). Aerial view. Photo: U. Colnago. Location: Villa Barbaro, Maser, Italy. Photo Credit: © DeA Picture Library/Art Resource, NY. Image Reference: ART347727.

attracted droves of foreign peoples searching for employment in the merchant fleet and the navy, where new ships carrying cannon were being built; in port services; and in the crafts. Luxury industries, including lead crystal and plate glass, soap, silks, and jewelry, attracted a global market. Nearly 10,000 people labored in the wool and silk industries; others were stonemasons, glassmakers, sugar refiners, leather workers, coppersmiths, blacksmiths, goldsmiths, and printers. The wool industry flourished, specializing in medium-quality Spanish and Neapolitan wool. When tastes for heavy, high-grade broadcloth waned in favor of the English and Dutch worsted fabrics, the Venetians astutely shifted to silk production, with brocades and damasks, catering to both the middle and the upper classes. Urban finance complemented trade and manufacture: in 1587 the Banco della Piazza di Rialto was established as an important source for the payment of commercial bills of exchange.

2. Worldly Goods and Home Furnishings

The gradual decline in sea power had little impact on aesthetic tastes. Venetians had already absorbed the cultures of their seaborne empire by the time the balance of power had shifted to the Ottomans on one hand and the north Atlantic economies on the other. For more than five centuries, merchants, artisans, oarsmen, tailors, bakers, cooks, goldsmiths, pharmacists, and physicians had sojourned in the Venetian colonies at Constantinople, Aleppo, Tripoli, Cairo, and Alexandria in the midst of spices, cotton, silks, carpets, and precious gems. They had brought home their experiences as well as exotic goods, globalizing the city's material culture. This culture was also facilitated by the city's foreign merchant colonies of Spanish and Portuguese Jews, Greeks, and Armenians. These groups founded wide-reaching business networks throughout the Mediterranean world that ultimately contributed to the mix of worldly tastes and the continuity of material exchange.

The aesthetic repertoire of Venetian patricians embraced both the classical past as well as the medieval and early modern connections to North Africa and Asia. In turning to the lands of the Venetian mainland and the construction of enormous villas and agricultural estates (Fig. 23), Venetian nobles adopted a more western Roman identity in the sixteenth century, emulating the latifundia and the lifestyles of *otium* of ancient Roman patricians. Still, the domestic interiors of their stately villas and palaces displayed their admiration for Islamic artifacts, such as saddles, stirrups, bridles with red velvet; weaponry; armor, carpets, metalwork; Isnik wares, and leather goods. In their private cabinets (*studioli*) by the late sixteenth century, Venetians exhibited both Turkish and Indian wares, reflecting a worldly aesthetic. They decorated their walls with world maps and navigation charts. Asian carpets warmed their floors and decorated their balconies on festive occasions. By 1500, knotted-pile wool and Iranian silk carpets from Ottoman Turkey and Egypt filled the homes of the wealthy and powerful as well as the great churches and religious foundations. The irony, then, was that despite the Ottoman Turkish enmity on the sea from the mid-fifteenth century there was a growing market for Ottoman exports at home.

At the same time Venetian manufacturers were exporting their own Islamic imitations. The glassworkers on Murano had borrowed heavily from Islamic artists in the thirteenth and fourteenth centuries, and by the sixteenth century some 20 percent of their production, catering to Islamic aesthetics, was exported to Syria and Egypt. There was a home market for these items as well: Venetians were purchasing Turkish-style, lacquered leather-covered shields and armor; Islamic metalwork, with gold, silver, or tin and *niello* ornaments, incised in brass; and numerous inlaid articles, like inkwells and candlesticks, bookbindings, and knife handles. These damascened objects, called Veneto-Saracenic, were late Mamluk metalwork made for export to Venice rather than objects produced in Venice by Islamic craftsmen. Some Venetian metalworkers, however, began to produce imitations of Islamic inlaid brass.

Collecting was very popular by the sixteenth century. Private cabinets mirrored the owner's social, economic, and intellectual identity. They were filled with exotic products, including inlaid Islamic metalwork; inkwells; candlesticks; knife handles; and lacquered wood. Noble Venetians also imported eastern ceramics from Damascus from the mid-fifteenth century; porcelain from China; *maiolica* from Syria; spice jars called *albarelli*, black with some red and white glaze; and Isnik pottery. It is possible that nobles were bequeathing such imports to loyal servants, for in 1638 we find a servant named Vettor della Rova living at Santa Maria Formosa in Corte Nova who listed two maiolica plates from Constantinople in his possession.[1] The demand for ceramics stimulated a domestic industry of *maiolica*. Made *alla porcellana*, they were decorated with blue and white arabesque ornament and related to Turkish Isnik ware called golden horn style.

While Venetian ceramics emulated inlaid or damascened Islamic metalwork, in textiles there was a cross-fertilization of decorative designs and techniques between Venice and Turkey with wool, silk, and cotton. There were also Moorish-style bookbindings, for religious or classical texts as well as mosque lamps. Not just noble homes exhibited Turkish wares and local imitations, but those of merchants and artisans contained them as well. Ordinary Venetians were filling their homes with Ottoman artifacts and images of Ottoman Turks.

Ordinary people, however, could afford little for their homes as most of their income went for subsistence. They made do with the bare essentials: a bed with modest linens, an iron pot or two for soups and stews with a hanging chain, cooking pans, water pails, lamp and candlestick holders for lighting, benches, and stools. For example, Zorzi de Dimitri Caristo, a Greek from Negroponte living in the district of Castello, listed a very modest inventory of used garments and sheets, copper pails for water, two flasks, a bed warmer, twelve forks, and a bit of furniture.[2] Clearly, consumption was a phenomenon of the well-to-do, who had surplus income for purchases beyond basic necessities. Brides of modest means brought an assortment of goods to the domestic hearth, including various kitchen items; a few copper pails to hold drinking water, for washing one's hands, or for discarding refuse; a jar or two; a flask; iron or copper pots and pans; stirring spoons; chains to hang the pots over the fire; and even iron forks, called *pironi* (the rich possessed silver forks). For the bedroom, their dowries included linens and pillows, and often a bed warmer. If they brought any furniture at all, it was a storage chest made of walnut, the most common of the furniture woods. Some furniture was made of pine, while the upper classes could afford more expensive woods like ebony. Men from the working class brought knives and forks and candleholders as well as chests, benches, and tables. Men's inventories also often list pictures. Even the humble possessed a religious picture or two, of the madonna or the crucifix. Pictures were always first on the list of these inventories. The rich also possessed these basic items, but more of them and of much higher quality. The inventories of ordinary people often list items as used or old, particularly clothing items but also bed and table linens and furniture.

Venetian inventories also give us a picture of the kinds of cloth used in domestic interiors. Again there was a material hierarchy of fabrics, from fine to coarser weaves listed in wills, inventories, and dowries. Women's dowries are a good source from which to gather this information because it was usually the bride who brought the bedding and kitchen linens to the marriage. Their inventories were carefully registered at the time of marriage in the tribunal of the Giudici del Proprio so that later on, upon their husbands' deaths, they could rightfully claim them. Included in the inventories are cotton and linen sheets; wool blankets and bedcovers; silk bedcovers for the warmer months; and wool-stuffed mattresses. Cloth napkins came in cotton and linen. Cotton was also used for handkerchiefs and underwear. A few examples from various social classes will illustrate the variations in usage. In 1598, the spinner Zuanne di Cortenovi received a dowry from his mother-in-law, Madonna Fiore, for his wife to be, Marietta. What was most important for the future bride to bring was her own clothing, plus bedding, linens, and cooking utensils. The clothing and linens were generally made of old, recycled cloth of lower-quality cotton or linen. The humble classes rarely possessed silk. The bride came with three beds, four pillows, and four cushions; two old bedcovers made of coarse wool; three used blankets, and large bed sheets. She also brought eleven cloth napkins, made of the remnants of low-quality linen; seven old cotton handkerchiefs; and eleven white linen pillow cases, which were old and used. In terms of clothing she brought a dress made of used cloth; and for the cold winters an old, used, wool, herringbone tweed dress and two old furs; an assortment of twenty-nine women's blouses, all used; two pairs of socks; and two pairs of old sleeves. She also contributed seven pails, which would be used to fetch water, wash clothes, and dispense with refuse; an old candleholder; four bed warmers; a cooking pan; a stirring spoon; various household utensils; five stirring spoons made of wood; a couple of old iron pots; eight cloth napkins of old coarse cotton. All this was valued at 106 ducats.[3]

Nine years later, in 1607, Dona Natalina, the widow of a silk weaver from Oderzo, brought similar items to her second marriage. In addition, she had a walnut bed, two mattresses filled with wool, six blankets, and a fur bedcover.

She also owned a small picture of the crucifix. She had various dresses, made of coarse green cotton or Scottish wool, and of lighter wool; a hat; and a new fur. She had several bedcovers: there were two yellow ones of heavy, coarse wool; four red ones; and five old ones. She had nineteen old blouses and six handkerchiefs; seven shoulder veils; two pairs of socks, one of silk. She brought a cloth for the table. Natalina also brought a walnut chest, a mirror, and a comb. For the kitchen she had an iron pot and a chain to append it over the fire; a pan; a grater; two pails; a couple of copper vases; and a pine chest. Her dowry amounted to 114 ducats.[4] The goldsmith Domenico di Brazzi's bride, Antonia, brought sheets made of hemp; blouses of local cloth and of hemp; aprons of Cambria (a fine cloth) with lace; a cushion made of Dutch cloth; and a pair of sleeves. She also brought some jewelry, including a rose stone with seven turquoises; a pair of pearl earrings and another of agate; and some silver buttons.[5] Antonio Marca Zarotti, whose title of doctor indicated a university degree, received from his wife Margherita Cordeli a long list of items of higher quality than those of the craftsmen's brides. She had red silk, brocades, and damask; two ebony desks and two black tables; a big mirror, another ebony desk trimmed with ivory; and walnut furniture.[6] Higher up the social scale, among the ranks of the nobility, the dowries were much richer, to accommodate the social station of the bride. In 1614, Dona Angelica married Francesco Da Mosto. The year before, her widowed mother, Faustina Loredan had promised Francesco 1,600 ducats. Of these, 700 ducats were in cash and 900 were in dotal goods, including 200 ducats' worth of linens. In addition, the bride brought silk clothing, gold jewelry, and pearls.[7] Likewise, when Giovanni Battista Ballarin, a secretary of the Council of Ten married Clarissima Prudentia Perea, his noble bride came with a diamond mounted in gold; a gold necklace and earrings; black velvet dresses; velvet and Venetian silk cloth; a bedcover; silk embroidered blouses; all the furniture in her villa; her carriage; plus other real estate.[8]

3. New Food, Drink, and Pharmacopeia

Although most of the cultural pluralism inherent in the Venetian diet derived from new encounters in medieval trade and immigration, sixteenth-century contact with the Americas also had an important impact. Maize, also called Turkish or West Indian grain, was the New World's most vital contribution, saving most of northern Italy from famine in the period after 1540, when several cloudbursts, heavy rains, and broken river banks produced acute food shortages. Grain supplies were at the mercy of the weather, and the popu-lation was rapidly expanding. Thus, polenta, consumed in great quantities,

ON THE USE AND ABUSE OF CHOCOLATE

In 1775, Giovanni Battista Anfossi published a medical-historical dissertation entitled *On the Use and Abuse of Chocolate* dedicated to the Venetian patrician Pier-Vettore Pisani, the Procurator of San Marco.[9] The Inquisitor General of the Holy Office of Venice approved the manuscript for printing in June 1775. Anfossi's recipes offer glimpses of how Europeans adapted the flora of the Americas, including cacao and vanilla beans, aromatic flowers, and a variety of spicy chile peppers. The most prominent ingredient they added to the Mesoamerican drink was sugar, whose consumption increased exponentially from the sixteenth century.

Anfossi marveled that the Spaniards had discovered many good things to make the body healthy. One was chocolate, which the author likened to ambrosia or nectar. In one popular recipe, created by Bartolomé Marradón, a doctor in Seville, cinnamon, sugar, pepper, cloves, vanilla, and anise were added to cacao. The measurements were 700 grams of cacao, a pound and a half of sugar, two ounces of cinnamon, fourteen grains of pepper from Mexico called chile or pimento, half an ounce of cloves, three beans of vanilla, or instead of vanilla two ounces of anise, and a seed called *achiote* (from the Yucatan, a spice with slightly bitter and peppery textures). Anfossi emphasized that the drink was very well received. There was another chocolate mixture, however, attributed to Antonio Colmenero, a professor in Andalusia, that competed with the first one. In this mixture, for each 100 grains of cacao one added two grains of chile pepper, or, peppers of Mexico (which are larger and are called chipotle), or if not that then two granules of pepper from India (the latter, he counseled, were less spicy, and different from the Spanish ones); a fistful of anise and two vanilla seeds. Flowers, such as Alexander roses, could be used for flavoring. The mixture also called for two drams of cinnamon, a dozen almonds, a dozen walnuts, a half pound of sugar, and lots of achiote, enough to color the paste. A third and most simple recipe included twenty pounds of roasted cacao beans, eight pounds of sugar, six ounces of fine cinnamon, and three ounces of vanilla.

Anfossi commented that chocolate was a controversial item of consumption. Some people argued that it was too spicy; others that it was too viscous. Anfossi, however, reminded readers that chocolate was nutritious and was a daily staple before the Spanish arrived in America. He believed that the inhabitants who ground cocoa beans lived to be 100 years old. Anfossi also addressed the alleged side effects of chocolate consumption, denying that it caused constipation, weak stomach, loss of breath, or adverse effects on women's uteruses. Green cacao beans might cause such difficulties, just as it was not healthy to eat raw beets, squash, or onions. Cacao, Anfossi concluded, could help digestion and stimulate the appetite. Moreover, it strengthened and nurtured.

became a lifesaver. At the opposite end of the spectrum, turkey as a luxury meat reached aristocratic tables. Chocolate and vanilla beans arrived in the seventeenth century and acquired great appeal at eighteenth-century aristocratic cafés and gambling houses. Chili peppers by themselves never caught on, but tomatoes gained popularity in Venice and Italy in the nineteenth century, once the Venetians were convinced that they were not harmful. The Venetian diet continued to welcome new food and drink into its recipe books through the nineteenth century, when Austrians brought wurst, breaded veal cutlets, cream-filled doughnuts, goulash, dumplings, and strudel to Venetian tables, and spritzers to the bars and cafès, all very popular to the present day.

Spices continued to flow into Venice, reaching the tables of the wealthy who had grown accustomed to using them in cuisine despite the ups and downs in trade of this commodity. Nearly every district in the city had a street, courtyard, or portico marking the apothecaries, who were called *spezieri*. The first half of the sixteenth century witnessed a slight depression in spice trading, owing to the new sea route of the Portuguese, which reached the Indonesian spice islands quicker than the traditional, medieval landed caravans. However, Venice compensated for this setback at mid-century by reviving the Egyptian and Syrian spice routes, losing hegemony to the Dutch only after 1620. The spices that came from Egypt, the Levant, and Asia Minor continued to be in steady demand in Venice, particularly as medicines. The pharmacy industry grew exponentially during the late sixteenth century, from seventy-one shops in 1565 to 100 in 1617 (Fig. 24). These shops offered a variety of herbs, liquors, and minerals to treat impotence and infertility, issues of great importance to married Venetians. Other remedies included cloves for a toothache; mace as an astringent and diuretic; and sugar as a tonic. Spice shops also sold the popular *triaca*, of Greek and Arabic origins, approved for sale by the Venetian Health Magistracy (Sanità) in 1603, and also sold in the Levant. From the Greek *theriake* meaning antidote, it was used for animal bites and poison.

The nobility enjoyed an array of luxury supplies from the city's spice shops in the seventeenth century. A good example is from one Pietro di Nobili, who in 1674 left his widow and children an inventory of the spices and victuals in his two centrally located shops at the fish market and San Marco, respectively. The first shop held an assortment of beans, lentils from Puglia and Alexandria, rice, German barley, spelt, coriander, canary grass, Veronese fennel, starch flour, minor fennel, old cumin, Spanish almonds and almonds from Candia, boxed figs, linen seeds, and soap. The second shop marketed

Figure 24. Pietro Longhi (1702–85). *The Pharmacist*. Location: Accademia, Venice, Italy. Photo Credit: Cameraphoto Arte, Venice/Art Resource, NY. Image Reference: ART 123753.

various handcrafted waxes; tiles; refined spices and sweet spices; crushed and whole cloves; ground, whole, and slivered pepper; nutmeg; mace; raw and refined sugar, sugar candy; chopped pine nuts; ground and whole saffron; cloved cinnamon; ginger; Levantine berries; molasses; and aged pistachios.[10] A century later, in 1772, the apothecary of *confetti*, Giovanni Battista Ferrari, sold similar items, including rice, almonds, coriander, fennel, chocolate, candied citrus, honey, burnt sugar, raw and refined white sugar, cinnamon canes and ground cinnamon, red cloves, ground saffron, coffee from Alexandria, *mascabà* sugar (a red sugar, described in Boerio as very ordinary), melon seeds, mace, raisins, pine nuts, and ginger from Cyprus.[11]

Among the new consumer items in the early modern period was coffee, a Turkish import, first brought to Venice in 1638 via Yemen, Mecca, and Cairo as a precious medicinal. The Venetians had already learned about coffee from one of their ambassadors to Constantinople, who in 1585 described the blackened drink before the Venetian Senate. The Ottoman Turks, he wrote, blackened their water with a grain called *kahave* that is roasted and ground. First sold in spice shops in Venice after 1640, it became popular by 1660. Venetian magistrates realized by 1676 that the sales of this product were an important source of revenue. The first coffee shop opened in Piazza San Marco near the Procuratie Nuove in 1683. The "black drink" began as a panacea for a stomachache before it became commonplace in social interaction among the wealthy. Coffee shops, numbering as many as 206 by 1759, were important geographical markers, giving names to many streets in Venice. Some of the cafés were no more than taverns, but others, such as the Florian (1720) and Quadri's (1775) at San Marco, were important sites of upper-class socialization.

The inventory of one café owner, Osvaldo Valentin, in the centrally located *frezzaria* near San Marco in 1762, indicates how luxurious some of these places of refreshment and conversation were. The shop had a copper sign with the owner's name engraved on it. In the anteroom was a painting of his shop, mirrors in gold, a gold lamp, Bulgar arm chairs, a water container, and containers of black coffee beans. Also listed in the inventory were white vanilla beans, chocolate beans, a medium-sized sugar container and some ordinary-sized ones, rosolin liqueur, small glasses for liqueur, boxes of sugar, cups for sorbet, glass spoons, and tin sugar spoons. The furnishings and equipment included a walnut counter with pine drawers, funnels and measuring utensils, sieves, sorbet containers, a glass window at the bar, a large coffee pot, medium coffee pots, pots to make large and small coffees, scales and weights, a coffee canister, a pot to make chocolate with its own frother and cover, a grinder, and a stone stove. The main room was large, with prints, bar tables, and a pine ceiling. Other rooms were decorated in gold and iron, with small walnut tables and pine benches. Smaller, interior rooms had their own private tables, an ice chest made of pine, candleholders, and iron fireplace utensils.[12]

4. The Meaning of Food

Clearly, the consumption patterns of Venetians mirrored the hierarchy of class and financial means, and there were stark differences. Perhaps none was more important than food, humans' most basic necessity. It thus became an important social and political tool for Venetian magistrates in order to cement civic loyalty. Food was used to display prosperity and largesse on feast days as well as during visits from foreign dignitaries. While banquets were clearly for the rich, on these occasions there was room for the poor to indulge as well, particularly during the sixteenth century, a period of population growth and price inflation that required greater generosity on the part of the government. Thus in 1509 the doge began to offer the pork butchered on Carnival's Fat Thursday to the monasteries and the prisons rather than to the patriciate. Guildsmen shared the meat as well. And the aristocratic Companies of the Hose, renowned for their own sumptuous banquets, provided bulls and pigs for the consumption of all. Carnival was the last chance before Lent for Catholics to eat meat, and an occasion to sponsor banquets for the less fortunate.

Also in the sixteenth century it became a practice for doges to be openly generous to commoners rather than to patricians. For example, on Palm Sunday flocks of pigeons were released from the roof of San Marco to be caught by the poor for their Easter dinner. Moreover, in 1521 the doge canceled guildsmen's traditional obligation to supply him as lord of the woods and marshes with 3,000 mallards and capons, which had in turn been dispensed to patricians and leading citizens. Thereafter he was to make offerings to commoners of the city instead.

Venetian sumptuary laws repeatedly called for moderation in the staging of banquets. Wedding expenses were also targeted from the fourteenth century on, as the sumptuary law of 1525 exemplifies. According to this legislation, the groom could offer only two meals, and certain foods were prohibited, including partridge, pheasant, peacock, mountain birds, baby doves, confections of large pine-nut cakes, pistachios, round filled pastries, sweetmeats, confections, marzipan fruitcakes, and sugared fruit on penalty to both the host and the chefs.[13] Yet according to the diarist Marin Sanudo, these very prohibited treats adorned the public banquet table elevated in St. Mark's square for the visit in 1530 of the duke of Milan. Spectators below observed members of the Companies of the Hose present elaborately molded sweets with political symbols to both state leaders. For the duke, a large St. Mark's lion and a Visconti snake with a Guelf in its mouth, and for the doge, a large St. Mark's lion with the Gritti coat of arms and the ducal *corno* and then a sweeping array of sugared meringues in animal shapes. There was, thus, still a time for extravagance despite repeated calls for temperance, during state functions but also, abusively, during private feasts as the artist Veronese documents in his 1563 painting, the *Wedding at Cana*.

Food played a prominent role during the many feast days throughout the year, not just at the state and religious levels but also in the celebrated factional rifts played out in Venetian wars of the fists. Following the public brawls on the city's bridges, local patrons provided free food and drink in the neighborhood campi, where all social classes enjoyed lasagna, eels in milk, and barrel wine. Significantly, when the city's two major factions, the deep sea fishermen from San Niccolò and the cattle butchers of Cannaregio, quarreled, the fish markets at San Marco and Rialto were among the principal sites of violence. There were even more refined internal divisions involving the hierarchy of food and food provisioning. The Nicolotti fishmongers snubbed the squads of eel fishers and fishermen in small boats on the lagoon, who lived in the parishes of Sant'Agnese and San Trovaso, forcing them to join the opposition. Food porters and workers who unloaded sacks of flour each formed their own cells, acting out their occupational and social rifts on the Feasts of Santa Giustina, All Saints Day, Christmas, San Stefano, and Candelmas. The city thus could be divided up in as many ways as one sorts food and drink and every other aspect of material culture, while the sites of food production and consumption – bakeries and taverns, for example – became after hours the sites of ritual violence as well as of food for comfort.

Neither these sites of socialization nor the descriptions of banquets and displays of governmental largesse, however, should disguise the serious instability resulting from periodic famine. Between 1520 and 1540, for example, real wages shrank and land subdivision increased, causing panic migrations to Venice from the countryside. Some of the migrants were accommodated in Venetian industries, but the government now also had to increasingly care for the poor. Magistrates drew up poor laws and encouraged philanthropy from private associations. However, between 1540 and 1575 the situation grew even worse, making almsgiving from the Great Confraternities and pious testators insufficient to feed the growing numbers of beggars. The government began to resort to taxation to support social welfare when the great plague of 1575–7 swept away a significant portion of the hungry. By 1590, however, famine reach severe levels not only in Venice but in the entire Mediterranean. In the local hinterland, the rye and bean crops that peasants relied on for subsistence had failed. Ordinary people resorted to eating millet and other cheap crops such as maize, in stark contrast to the bounty found on the banquet tables of the nobility.

5. Clothing and Representation

Venice had a dress code that made cultural constructs abundantly evident: it used color and fabric to reflect social and material definition by vocation, marital status, gender, and class. Dark colors, particularly black, expressed in public the high status of patrician men and women, who also displayed their wealth with precious stones and gems, pearls, alabaster chains and belts, gold, silver, and furs. Colors of importance were *pavonazzo*, a shade of violet-blue inspired by peacock feathers; *berettino*, a shade of blue or ash gray used in ceramics; *viride*, a shade of green; *albo*, white; *nigrum*, black; *grana* (cochineal, the name of a red dye); *turchino* and *biavo,* shades of blue; *morelo*, purple; *cremesino*, a blood red; *rubeo*, ruby.

Dress reflected collective modes of socialization and representation. A few examples will illustrate such categorization. The published sources are both Cesare Vecellio's sixteenth-century costume book and Giovanni Grevembroch's eighteenth-century encyclopedia of fashion. In addition, archival sources provide inventories of dotal goods. There was a difference between how people were expected to dress in public and how they dressed in private. The public attire of women, whether aristocratic, working class, or poor, signaled whether they were married, single, or widowed. Their sexual behavior was marked in code as well, in terms of whether they were concubines, high-class courtesans, bordello prostitutes, or street whores. Sober colors connoted honesty, or fidelity among the married. Black was first and foremost the color of the aristocracy, and the preferable color for married women going about in public. Their dress was layered with undersilks and aprons, often in black but adorned with gold braid, gold chains, necklaces, lace, and pearls. Underneath might be an embroidered dress, with a gold braided belt at the hem and an expensive gold chain at the waist, and silver pendants. If the Senate, urging restraint if not parsimony, forbade silver accessories on their dresses and purses, these women braided their hair and held it in place with little gold crowns, or with jewels or pearls. They adorned themselves with coral necklaces, silver buttons, and gold sashes, and they cooled themselves with gold-handled fans. In the sixteenth century, aristocratic women wore gathered white collars with fabric from Cambrai, but by the seventeenth century they were covering themselves with transparent veils, black for the married and widows; white for maidens. Colorful garb was more appropriate for the home, away from the public eye or visiting guests; if worn in public, it suggested waywardness.

Women's dress often reflected either their own occupations or those of their husbands. Among the more prestigious categories was black. The wife of the Procuratore di San Marco, whose duties included bestowing gifts to charity and protecting orphans, dressed with sobriety, in black, as did the wives of the major notaries and secretaries from the citizen class. Down the social scale, a castellan's wife wore a simple silk headdress, a toga of *porpora* (a dye whose color varied from bright red to purple, extracted from mollusks

Figure 25. Titian (Tiziano Vecellio) (c.1488–1576). *Portrait of a Woman Known as La Bella*, detail. Post-restoration. Inv. 1912. n.18. Location: Galleria Palatina, Palazzo Pitti, Florence, Italy. Photo Credit: Scala/Ministero per i Beni e le Attività culturali/Art Resource, NY Image Reference: ART424645.

in the Levant) or *giacinto* (purplish blue), and half sleeves, and a silk skirt. Household maids, usually from Dalmatia or Friuli, wore aprons in a variety of colors. Even some of the poor followed dress protocol in public, unless they were reduced to rags. *Poveri vergognosi*, citizens who had lost their fortunes and went about asking for charity, wore long black sacks with hoods covering their faces until 1438, when such disguises were prohibited.

The dress of aristocratic and other wealthy women at home could be less sober (Fig. 25). They liked to adorn their hair with copper, silver, and gold silk ribbon, as well as roses, pearls, and jewels. They loved silk dresses that opened both at the sides and at the shoulders to expose even more luxurious fabric underneath. Another variation was a colorful skirt with a low-cut silk blouse and a gold bodice. A white, silk shawl rendered the revealing upper garment more modest. Some aristocratic women wore purple, but blood red (*cremesin*) and green were also favorites. Among the common fabrics were *ormesin*, or silk made in Venice; *damaschino*, or silk with gold from Damascus but then made in Venice; *levantina*, or silk from the orient; *tabino*, a heavy silk or taffeta with gold and silver; and *cendà*, a very lightweight silk that women wore on their heads.

Whether in public or at home, noblewomen were expected to carry themselves with decorum. Aristocratic maidens wore sober colors like teal blue in public. Their skirts and puffed sleeves were often embroidered, hardly disguising the silk lining underneath. Similar to married women, they wore silk shawls around their shoulders, jeweled pendants, and pearl earrings. By the seventeenth century, unmarried women of the noble or citizen class covered their faces with white veils of linen or silk, at times masking themselves so that only their relatives recognized them. Once a noble maiden was betrothed, however, she could visit her future husband dressed and veiled in black. Widows also dressed in black and were expected to go about the city with great modesty. Within this group, but at the other end of the social scale, were the *pizzocheri,* usually widows who lived on charity and under the care of a religious order.

Modesty, in fact, was the measure of all things when it came to women. Venetians even had a hierarchy of immodesty, which included, in hierarchical order, concubines, courtesans, *meretrici*, whores, and bordello prostitutes. Concubines were forbidden to wear pearls, so as not to confuse them with "honest" women. Instead, they wore imitation pearls, or gold and silver chains and embroidered gloves. They dressed according to their means, in silk or ordinary cloth. The more prosperous had crystal beads or ornate buttons, silk skirts and hats, embroidered stockings, and Roman shoes. Unlike the nobility, they could go about the city in bold colors, especially red. Prostitutes and courtesans could wear *braghesse*, or pants. Some cross-dressed, wearing men's shirts. They wore aprons and belts over shirts. Others had *braghesse* underneath. Up until the sixteenth century *braghesse* were men's long underwear. As time went on they became women's long underwear. Prostitutes would pull a cord to expose the underwear under their dresses.

The costly dress of Venetian women was of continual concern to certain segments of the patriciate. A special Venetian magistracy, the Pompe, established dress standards that prohibited certain lengths and widths of costly fabrics and set limits on jewelry and adornments. Wealthy women circumvented or ignored these prohibitions, braiding dresses with pearls and jewels and decorating them with gold or silver thread, wearing pearl necklaces and gold brooches, and donning full sleeves that went from shoulder to elbow and were lined in silk. They wore silks under costly gold and silver brocades and braided their hair with gold and silk, jewels and pearls. Their expensive accessories included gold chains, fans with gold handles, coral necklaces, silver buttons, and gold sashes.

A sumptuary law of 1511, reported by the diarist Marin Sanudo, identifies the limits placed on costly apparel: ornaments to the head in gold- and silverwork could not exceed the value of 15 ducats, and headdresses with pearls and jewels were prohibited. Only a strand of pearls could be worn at the neckline. Gold and silver fabric and expensive silks and wools used for sleeves were limited to a specific measurement, and cheating by slitting open the sleeve to expose further lavishness was strictly forbidden. In principle, the use of precious fabrics was constrained. Nor could over-gowns be lined with lynx, sable, marten, ermine, squirrel-back, or covered with silk. Waistbands, kerchiefs, or aprons could not be made of gold, silver, silk, or linen.

Time and again, the rules for simplicity were ignored and the sumptuary regulations had to be repeated. Upper-class Venetians were very creative when it came to circumventing rules. In 1529, the diarist again reported legal transgressions. The wealthy had substituted chains of gold and pearls with those decorated with alabaster, crystal, lapis lazuli, carnelian, green quartz, mother-of-pearl, quartz, jasper, agates, porcelain, rock crystal, embroidery, and filigree. Those who could afford to simply paid the sumptuary fines and continued to abuse the law, showing off their luxurious treasures.

What did both the legislation and the disobedience mean? There was a disjunction between the patrician men who drafted the legislation and those who dressed their wives in violation of the law. At one level the dialectic of legislation and disobedience reflected conflicts among men. Within the Venetian ruling class there were rich nobles and poor nobles. The poorer nobles attempted to set limits in order to protect themselves from the rich minority. It was a desperate attempt to set the terms of their economic relationships. If they were ruined, they would lose what little status they had, even to men outside the patriciate with greater wealth. The patricians at the summit, on the other hand, wished to preserve their superior status and keep their honor by proclaiming their magnificence. Here the Venetian patriciate was split philosophically, and it manifested itself in all material ways, including housing, banquets, and other forms of material consumption. Patrician wives used their imagination to display the power of their husbands, but that was not all. Their elaborate dress was also a means of presenting themselves, distinguishing themselves, and like their husbands, competing with other families of the ruling class. The literary feminist from a wealthy citizen family, Moderata Fonte (Neé Modesta Pozzo 1555–92), penned a lively defense against male writers who criticized women as frivolous and vain or of using clothing to advertise sexual availability. In *Il merito delle donne* (1600) Fonte argued that choice of clothing is a form of self-expression, and that sumptuary legislation was men's way of limiting women's freedom of expression. The theme is also reiterated in the work of another famous feminist writer of the age, Lucrezia Marinella (1571–1653). In her *Nobiltà et eccelenze delle donne* (1600), this prosperous daughter of a physician and writer argues that women's choice of fine dress is a reflection of their human dignity and worth.

The language of competition, distinction, and emulation reached beyond the circle of Venice's powerful and prosperous. Men and women of superior financial means outside the patriciate also arrayed themselves in high fashion in order to emulate the nobility and distinguish themselves from commoners. There was also the importance of projecting a world image: as a world power in the medieval period; a princely power in the fifteenth century period of territorial state building; a shattered power in the wake of defeat at Cambrai in 1509; and a declining economic power with the rise of the Atlantic economies after 1620. The ruling class needed to proclaim self-magnificence, whether on the rise or falling into the shadows of greater territorial powers. Thus the wives of patricians governing the Republic's subject cities dressed with grandeur, using damasks, *tabino*, and black silk lavishly decorated with lots of gold, silver, jewels, and necklaces, and with veils decorated in gold.

If women dressed according to their marital status, and inherently according to their sexual behavior, men's dress was oriented more toward social station and vocation. Aristocrats wore black, as did the robed physicians, lawyers, and judges who in winter wore damasks and velvets and in summer Venetian silks, velvet belts, silver buckles, black silk socks, and velvet hats. The plague doctors wore juniper-scented linen and wax masks greased with oils to ward off unhealthy vapors (Fig. 17).

Venetian citizens serving in the chancelleries, a kind of second-tier nobility, were garbed in sober teals with velvet stoles. Young Venetian men of means wore taffeta in summer or wool jackets in winter, lined with colored taffeta; gold buttons; velvet, linen, or silk berets with matching trousers; silk socks; Moroccan shoes from Spain; and coats. Men's professions or vocations were also collectively marked, whether they were apothecaries, doctors of law or medicine, plague doctors, merchants of various wares, goldsmiths, fruit vendors, grain sifters, street sweepers, lantern keepers, or grave diggers.

Each wore a kind of uniform, making it easy to differentiate one vocation from another. Even the poor had a dress code. In 1619, the government prescribed how beggars must dress: with a black overcoat, blue vest, brown pants, white shirt, long white socks, and shoes. Orphans were assigned colors according to the hospital that sheltered them: the Incurabili had turquoise; those at San Giovanni e Paolo wore white; those at the Pietà dressed in red; while the Mendicanti wore black. On feast days they all wore either black or the uniform of their institution when in public.

Venice was a multiethnic city by the twelfth century, and each immigrant group preserved much of the traditional dress of its country of origin. In fact, many names for Italian clothing items originated in the Levant: *giubba* for jacket; *caffettano* for caftan; *tabarro* for cloak. The city housed Armenian monks, Greek prelates and nuns, ambassadors from everywhere, Turkish and Armenian merchants, Arabs, and Greeks, all wearing the native dress of their homelands. Jews in the ghetto, on the other hand, wore black. From 1425 by law they had to wear a yellow cord; after 1515 yellow berets; and after 1680 red berets. The costume books of Vecellio and Grevembroch specify the kinds of wool used for dress in winter; and cotton and silk in summer.

There is also an ethnic dimension to the Venetian inventories, evident in the names of the fabrics and the styles of clothing. For example, in 1580 one merchant described the women's dresses he possessed as "of coarse wool and in Turkish style."[14] A doctor listed his Turkish carpet in 1583.[15] Marina De Allegri also listed a Turkish-style dress.[16] There were "damasks" and "Flemish cloth," as well as *scotto*, a herringbone tweed, the finest of which came from Scotland. A servant named Vettor della Rova living at Santa Maria Formosa possessed a Dalmatian hat. There were also Moroccan shoes.[17]

★ ★ ★

TO CONCLUDE, THE SHIFT IN VENETIAN ECONOMIC ORIENTATION from sea to land is easier to measure than the city's consumption patterns. Ordinary laborers were vulnerable to the ups and downs of food supplies, taxation, wages, and debased coinage, factors that limited their purchasing power and in large part excluded them from exotic worldly aesthetics. The situation was quite different for people who retained purchasing power. The setbacks at sea did not hinder their consumption, nor did they produce a shift in aesthetic tastes. Upper-class Venetians retained their fascination with both the Western classical tradition and the aesthetics of greater Asia and North Africa, as evidenced in their home décor, collecting, and textile and glass production. They also exhibited an avid interest in recovering the material culture of the ancient Roman world, whose artifacts they encountered not just in Italy as a result of intensified peninsular interaction but also across the Mediterranean world in their trading expeditions over centuries. The city thus availed itself of a multicultural aesthetic, the fruit of commercial enterprise and its attraction of diverse immigrant groups.

FURTHER READING

Fabric and Dress: P. Allerston (1998, 2000); G. Bistort (1969); F. Braudel (1986); Grevembroch (1754); M. Rosenthal and A. Rosalind Jones (2008). *Food*: M. Dal Borgo (2005); G. Maffioli (1982). *Home Interiors*: R. Sarti (2001). *Islamic World*: S. Carboni (2007); G. Curatola (2007); W. Denny (2007); D. Howard (2000, 2005, 2007a-c). *Pharmacopeia*: R. Palmer (1985). *Production and Consumerism*: J. Ferraro (2007); B. Pullan (1971); E. Welch (2005).

6

CITY OF MYTH

1. The Politics of Mythmaking

The Venetian turn to the mainland during the fifteenth century signified a great deal more than territorial expansion: annexation of the towns to the west opened up new cultural horizons in letters, science, and the visual arts. Previously the Mediterranean basin, Asia, and the Gothic north greatly influenced Venice's cultural and intellectual developments. From the fifteenth century, however, the history, literature, and artistic traditions of the Italian peninsula took on new meaning. Greco-Latin and Arabic foundations were thus added to traditions the Venetians had encountered on their trading ventures. The internationally renowned university at Padua offered significant advancements in anatomy, medicine, the mechanical sciences, botany, and agronomy. It also endowed Venice with an auspicious circle of humanists who immortalized Aristotelian philosophy and physical contact with Roman archaeological remains that were scattered throughout the territories. The famous poet Petrarch had given Venice humanism in the mid-fourteenth century, but the fifteenth-century contact with the Italian mainland was heavily responsible for the development of Renaissance culture in the two centuries that followed.

The generation of Venetian patricians growing up after 1430, when mainland expansion was complete, both broadened their spectrum of knowledge and used it to their political advantage. Political writers embellished Venetian culture with Aristotelian ideas and Catholic orthodoxy. Moreover, they sharpened images of the so-called myth of Venice that surfaced in writing around 1380 with claims that the city was encapsulated in timeless stability. They developed an elaborate panegyric and iconography to justify this belief. To begin, it was alleged that the entire community offered unquestioned loyalty to the city, an assertion that recalled the ideals of the

Figure 26. Bonifacio de' Pitati (1487–1553). *Apparition of God the Father.* Below Piazza
S. Marco and S. Marco, Venice. Location: Accademia, Venice, Italy. Photo Credit: Scala/
Ministero per i Beni e le Attività culturali/Art Resource, NY. Image Reference:
ART146271.

Greek polis, where even family dynasty but certainly individual interests
were sacrificed for the good of the whole. In addition to the devotion of
the people, humanists wrote, Venice also enjoyed special favors: from God
and from Saint Mark, whose relics protected the city and whose images

adorned churches and civic monuments. Still further, they reiterated that
Venice was blessed with excellent rulers and superior institutions, including a citizen navy. Venetian nobles were, according to the humanist Lauro
Quirini, the direct descendants of the Romans who established political
institutions modeled on the revered Roman Republic. This ideal nobility
was immune to factionalism and pure of blood. Venice's great family dynasts
were especially born to govern, and they brought only harmony and liberty
to their peoples. By providence, this ideal city and its immaculate ruling class
were destined to endure forever.

The dissemination of patrician political ideology was greatly assisted by
the development of the printing industry in the last decades of the fifteenth
century. Moreover, the patrician writers who saw their words in print were
also the beneficiaries of the Greek Diaspora that followed the Ottoman
capture of Constantinople in 1453. They were trained in Greek as well as
the Latin language and history, subjects that shaped their speech, their writing, their governing skills, and their lifestyles. Many devoted their energies
to staffing the printing press as well as to writing and classical learning.
They were avid collectors of books, and when the former Greek patriarch
of Constantinople, Cardinal John Bessarion, donated his library to the city
in 1468, they made plans to build the Library of Saint Mark's (now the
Biblioteca Nazionale Marciana), begun in 1537. Thus by the early sixteenth
century the certainty of the myth was reiterated via a plethora of humanist
writings. After most of the Italian peninsula succumbed to the invasions of
France and Spain at the close of the fifteenth century, non-Venetians also
gave currency to these political myths alongside patrician humanists, marvel-
ing that Venice retained its independence and its constitution.

2. The Iconography of Mythmaking

There were many themes running through Venice's civic myth.[1] Among the
most prominent were the city's miraculous birth, its association with the
Virgin Mary, its favor with God and the saints, its providential mission, and
its omniscience and largesse. These messages were conveyed through pictorial language and pageantry as well as humanist writing. There were few limits to the penchant for self-glorification, and the construction of a Venetian
version of history lent itself well to this self-promoting view.

The city's story began with its miraculous birth on water on the day of the
Annunciation of the Virgin. It was favored by God, who founded the free and
Christian Republic on the same date that the Archangel Gabriel announced
the coming of a savior. Venice thus was a new Jerusalem, associated with

political salvation as the first free Republic after the collapse of Rome. By
the thirteenth century, the Annunciation appeared in the sculptural deco-
ration of the Basilica's façade, and it became ubiquitous in the political and
religious centers of the city, along with the Archangel Gabriel. By the end
of the sixteenth century, it was featured in the commercial center of Rialto
as well, across the arch of the stone bridge. Moreover, in the Ducal Palace,
the painter Bonifacio de'Pitati produced a canvas for the state bond office in
the 1540s with God the Father and the Holy Spirit soaring above Piazza San
Marco (Fig. 26), explicitly proclaiming that God had created Venice to bring
political salvation to a free peoples. Originally hung in the state loan office,
the two side panels announce the Incarnation of Christ; in the center God
and the Holy Spirit soar above the Piazza San Marco and the Basilica.

The messianic Republic was also blessed with saintly favor. First came
Saint Theodore, harkening back to the city's Byzantine associations, but there
was also the Dalmatians' Saint George and the Greeks' Saint Demetrius.
Foremost, of course, was Saint Mark the Evangelist, whose body, hidden in
a basket of pork to pass through Muslim inspection, was pirated in the ninth
century, fortifying the city with the powers of his relics. The winged Lion
of Saint Mark, one of the four winged beasts of the apocalypse prominent
in Ezekiel's visions, became the quintessential symbol of Venice and proclaimed its dominion over landed and seaborne empires (Fig. 27).

With the strong humanist interest in the classics by the late fifteenth
century, the Christian themes were given a pagan gloss. Jacopo de' Barbari's
monumental view of Venice, carved in wood in 1500, announced that in
addition to God, the Virgin, and Saints Mark and Theodore, the classical
gods Mercury and Neptune were watching over the chosen city as well.
At the Scala dei Giganti in the courtyard of the Palazzo Ducale, the venue
for the doges' inaugurations, the architect Jacobo Sansovino (1486–1570)
thus designed a staircase in the second half of the sixteenth century with
statues of Mars and Neptune, each representing Venice's domination of
land and sea.

The Palace of the Doge is among the best venues for tracing Venetians'
self-fashioning of their history. Both sculpture and painting documented the
city's mythical foundations and its greatest military victories, including the
sack of Constantinople in 1204, the victory over its commercial rival Genoa
in 1380, and its survival of the War with the pope, France, and Spain in the
League of Cambrai in 1509. In the fourteenth century, significant events
were documented in pictorial programs and manuscript illuminations. They
were replicated once again in the fifteenth and sixteenth centuries. A great
fire, however, destroyed much of this work in 1577, requiring the Procurators

Figure 27. Vittore Carpaccio (1455 1525). *The Lion of Saint Mark.* 1516. Location: Palazzo Ducale, Venice, Italy. Photo Credit: Erich Lessing/Art Resource, NY. Image Reference: ART126686.

of Saint Mark responsible for the rebuilding program to commission new decorative works during the final two decades of the sixteenth century.

By the time of the 1577 fire, Venetian painting had reached the height of its influence in Europe. The genre got a late start relative to Tuscan artistic development, for Byzantine models from greater Greece and Constantinople had prevailed to the fifteenth century, along with the florid Gothic that reached Venice during the thirteenth century. It was Venetian territorial expansion in the first two decades of the fifteenth century that facilitated bringing both Tuscan and classical influences to the lagoon. The sojourn of the Florentine master Gentile da Fabbriano in 1421 launched a new pictorial emphasis that prioritized color and light, in harmony with Venice's aquatic environment, rather than the form and mass of central Italian painting. The Bellini family workshop in Venice – Jacobo and his son Gentile, along with Jacobo's son-in-law, the Paduan Andrea Mantegna – was the harbinger of a new classical style. Jacopo had worked in Florence and Rome in the 1420s, learning the Renaissance principles of painting and acquiring a taste for classical antiquities. Little of his work has survived, save two albums of drawings. His son Gentile (1429–1507), on the other hand, is greatly appreciated for his recordings of the contemporary Venetian scene, as evidenced in *The Miracle of the Holy Cross* (Fig. 28), produced for the Scuola of San Giovanni Evangelista, with its detailed description of Venetian life, people, and topography; and his *Corpus Christi Procession* (Fig. 16 in Chapter 4), which renders a fairly accurate depiction of the Piazza San Marco, minus the unsightly latrines and criminals in cages. Gentile also represented Venetian fascination with Islamic subjects and style. He had spent some time as the guest of the Sultan Mohammed II in Constantinople between 1479 and 1480,

Figure 28. Gentile Bellini (1429–1507). *The Miracle of the Holy Cross*, 1496–7. Location: Academia, Venice, Italy. Photo Credit: Erich Lessing/Art Resource, NY. Image Reference: ART130538.

an experience that prompted him to record the life of Southwest Asia for Venice. Two of his portraits capture this, one of Mohammed II (1480) and the other of a Turkish woman (c. 1479–80). Moreover, his painting of Saint Mark preaching in Alexandria (1507) is also a reminder of the long-standing cultural links between Venice and the birthplace of the city's patron saint in North Africa (Fig. 29).

Gentile's brother Giovanni (c. 1430–1515) absorbed the family's interest in Antiquity but was especially adept at capturing the visible world. For this he is credited with being the first Renaissance Venetian painter. A beneficiary of the oil techniques introduced by the Sicilian artist Antonello da Messina, Giovanni drew attention to the mountainous landscapes of the Venetian mainland, the stage for saintly madonnas painted for the Hospital of San Giobbe and the Church of San Zaccaria. The San Zaccaria Altarpiece is an important example of Bellini's translation of the Renaissance classical style into a Venetian idiom. The designs in the apse and the glass lamp are distinctly Turkish or Islamic, but they are framed within the classical Roman

Figure 29. Gentile Bellini (1429–1507). *Saint Mark Preaching in Alexandria*. Painting finished after Gentile's death by his brother Giovanni Bellini in 1508. Oil on canvas, 347 × 770 cm. Location: Pinacoteca di Brera, Milan, Italy. Photo Credit: Erich Lessing/ Art Resource, NY. Image Reference: ART137538.

half dome and Corinthian pilasters. The apse is filled with color and light and exhibits a mastery of the perspective that Florentine artists had skillfully developed.

As Giovanni Bellini's career entered its final years, Giorgione, also a master of landscapes, and Titian, with his portraits, mythologies, and religious subjects, inaugurated a golden era in Venetian painting. Tintoretto and Veronese shone brilliantly during the mid-sixteenth century; and these renowned painters were joined during the final years of the century by Lorenzo Lotto. The Procurators of Saint Mark, themselves connoisseurs, gave many of these artists state commissions. They also maintained the Basilica and the Piazza, appointing head architects, called *proti* and *protomaestri*. While the scuole seemed to have preferred Venetian-born artists like Vittore Carpaccio (c.1460–1526), the state's connoisseurs looked outward for masters with peninsular reputations.

The first-floor rooms of the Ducal Palace were reserved for exalting Venice's triumphs, with paintings by Paolo Veronese, Palma the Younger, and Bassano, while the third floor exhibited some of the most important iconographical manifestos. Tintoretto's ceiling of the Sala delle Quattro Porte presents the foundation of the city with Jupiter leading Venice into the Adriatic (1577). This artist also replaced another important painting destroyed in the fire, Guariento di Arpo's fresco of the Coronation of the Virgin (1365–68) in the chamber of the Maggior Consiglio. The canvas personifies Venice as the Queen of Heaven. The crowned figure presiding atop a leonine throne also represents Venice as Justice, another important component in the city's self-fashioning.

Justice, which functioned as another name for Venice and was depicted in the figure of a woman, was everywhere around the political center, holding swords and scales and sitting on thrones flanked by lions that conjured up the memory of King Solomon, who also sat on a throne with two lions. The Piazzetta at San Marco is named the Piazzetta della Giustizia and nearby Sansovino's library commemorates the wisdom of the ruling class. Justice is also above the Porta della Carta, which Pietro Lombardo decorated with statues of Strength and Temperance and Antonio Bregno those of Prudence and Charity (see Figure 6 in Chapter 1). A woman, Justice is often accompanied by Temperance, Prudence, Fortitude, and Charity, all virtues of the Republic. With this feminine figure, the palace of the doge was likened to that of Solomon, so that at the corner of the structure that was adjacent to the Porta della Carta, Bartolomeo and Giovanni Bon carved the Judgment of Solomon above the capital of a column in 1438. Beneath are illustrations of law-giving in history that include Aristotle and Moses, raising Venetian rulers to the status of the ancient sages.

The painter Paolo Veronese, assigned the ceilings in the chambers of the Council of Ten and the Collegio, also illustrated Venice's association with Justice. In the first he rendered a vivid allegorical painting of Jupiter's wife Juno showering Venice, the Queen of the Adriatic, with fabulous riches. The message was that Venice, like Venus, born of the sea, was blessed not only with commercial wealth but also with wise rulers (Fig. 30). For the ceiling of the College, often the venue for the reception of foreign dignitaries, two decades later the artist rendered the Republic enthroned and ruling in the company of Justice and Peace (Fig. 31). Venice thus was an ideal state, politically wise, and favored both by Christendom and the ancient Greek world.

This iconic mythmaking did not just take place at the seat of government. The confraternities advanced it as well. The city's lay confraternities sponsored some of the most important art projects, some with the backing of the Council of Ten. The Scuola of San Marco, for many years the city's richest guild, housed Tintoretto's *Miracles of St. Mark* as well as canvases by Palma the Elder and Paris Bordone. The Carità exhibited Titian's *Presentation of the Virgin* (1534–8), a mural whose pink and white lozenge patterns in the marble wall were a specific reference to the Doge's Palace. On the left the artist's rendition of the Pyramid of Gaius Cestius connected Venice to Rome; and on the right a reference associated Solomon's wisdom and justice with Venetian rule.

Figure 30. Paolo Veronese (1528–88). *Venice Receiving the Ducal Horn*. Location: Palazzo Ducale, Venice, Italy. Photo Credit: Cameraphoto Arte, Venice/Art Resource, NY. Image Reference: ART378.

Figure 31. Paolo Veronese (1528–88). *Allegory of Justice before Venice Enthroned*, Sala Collegio. Location: Palazzo Ducale, Venice, Italy. Photo Credit: Cameraphoto Arte, Venice/Art Resource, NY. Image Reference: ART372.

The confraternities also vaunted their importance in civic life and their place in the civic hierarchy. That of San Giovanni Evangelista held Gentile Bellini's celebrated *Corpus Christi Procession* (1496) (see Figure 16 in Chapter 4), which suggested the wide participation of the city's lay associations and fostered a sense of inclusion and commitment to the common weal that deceptively suggested broad participation in government. The Corpus Christi parade attracted thousands of spectators, who watched the long procession beginning with the members of the Great Confraternities, guildsmen, the small confraternities, and other congregations. These groups of non nobles *preceded* the ducal procession, which included the patriarch carrying a tabernacle containing the Host, and the senators. The order of the procession was very important for it gave a place to nearly every corporate body in Venice. Bellini's other celebrated painting, *The Miracle of the Holy Cross* (also called *The Recovery of the Relic of the True Cross at the Bridge of San Lorenzo*; see Figure 28), depicts a perfectly organized spectacle, with a disciplined public standing in assigned places within a precise hierarchy. These are just a few of the many examples throughout the city of the way sculpture and painting reinforced the notion of a peaceful society governed by wise rulers.

3. The Roman Renaissance: Building Projects

The patrician turn from the sea to the land ushered in a new era of conspicuous spending that transformed aristocratic dwellings as well as public buildings. In private space, noble palaces became more elaborate. Great halls, tapestried in green damasks and taffetas, crimson silks, and linens trimmed in gold, accommodated lavish banquets, balls, and parties. Moreover, there was a massive building program on the mainland, where patrician dynasties erected magnificent country villas and amassed important art collections (Fig. 23). The home continued to be a metaphor for the values of the nobility. Well heads, tympanum reliefs above entry doors, stuccos, and paintings justified a hereditary nobility that was visually personified by symbolic images of justice, temperance, prudence, charity, constancy, and hope, while religious paintings, bas-reliefs, and sculpture projected spiritual devotion and a Christian morality.

The more lavish consumption patterns represented a major shift in the patriciate's social and political agenda. To the mid-fifteenth century, nobles within Venice's ruling circle had projected an ethos of equality and discretion, evidenced symbolically in their public attire in black robes. However fictitious the idea, they wanted to appear equal before the public. In some ways the palace of Ca'd'Oro (1450) (Plate XI) was an exception, presaging what was to come. A century later, the patrician psychology of restraint, art historian Patricia Fortini Brown tells us, gave way to unabashed material consumption.[2] The medieval Gothic style had emphasized austerity, even parsimony, and the fictitious equality of the leading families was portrayed by all houses being built of similar height. That trend gave way first to a stylistic pastiche and then to classical magnificence, signaling both a change in sensibility and a change in cultural orientation. The references to noble seafaring ventures on palace façades was replaced with an iconography hailing ancient Rome as several Venetian families became obsessed with tracing their roots back beyond the foundation of Venice to the ancient capital.

Figure 32. The two Giustiniani palaces and Ca' Foscari, all begun c. 1450. Location: Venice, Italy. Photo Credit: J. M. Ferraro.

Treatises on living noble and emulating Rome permeated noble consciousness, effecting a change from the austere to classical grandeur.

A stroll through the city today still documents this archaeology of architectural styles. At one end is Ca' Foscari (Fig. 32) built by the Doge Francesco Foscari in 1452 in the traditional Gothic idiom that conformed with the palaces of Foscari's peers. But at the same time it was much bigger and occupied a more prominent place at the junction of the major Rio Nuovo and the bend in the Canal Grande. It also contained visual references to the Palazzo Ducale. In the middle of the cultural transition is the Ca' Corner-Spinelli, a palace that the Lando family had engaged the Bergamasc Mauro Codussi to fashion in 1490. It belonged first to Giovanni Corner, nephew of Caterina, Queen of Cyprus, and then to the Spinelli, a family that owed its prosperity to the silk industry. The structure foreshadowed what was to come, blending traditional Venetian Gothic with new Lombard and Tuscan motifs and reflecting Venice's newly established commitment to its mainland empire, to humanist scholarship, and to Renaissance classicism. Then came the shock of the international Battle of Agnadello in 1509, when the Republic lost its subject cities to the Holy Roman emperor. The shattered ruling class needed a new basis for its self-proclaimed magnificence, a renovation, which rested on its own Byzantine-Islamic-Gothic glory and perfection but also suited the new gentlemen who had left the sea for the land.

It was during this period of renovation, between 1510 and 1560, that the patriciate split philosophically into traditionalists who sought to preserve the façade of equality and the new proponents of conspicuous material consumption. The former turned to Cassiodorus's ancient description of rich and poor fishing peoples living in harmony together with relatively equal housing. In line with this philosophy Doge Andrea Gritti built a restrained house on the outskirts of the city at Francesco della Vigna in 1525. Likewise, Francesco Zen built a house between 1533 and 1553 in the interior of the city at Cannaregio rather than on the prestigious Grand Canal and decorated it with his family's history in trade, arms, and diplomacy in the Mediterranean and the Levant. Some classical motifs were used but mainly the decorations celebrated the family's medieval history. The new and bolder ostentation came, in contrast, with Ca' Loredan, now Vendramin-Calergi, which Mauro Codussi constructed for Andrea Loredan around 1510 (Plate XII). Fortini Brown has characterized this building, which is now the municipal casino of Venice, as the first Renaissance residence, its Corinthian capitals mirrored majestically on water.[3] The structure blended elements of the Tuscan Renaissance with Gothic Venice. The twin bay windows, three classical orders, accentuated cornice, and all-stone façade were new. It was followed by the palace of Zuanne Dolfin in 1536, which was still not Roman but employed classical geometry and language such as the Doric, Ionic, and Corinthian orders and the row of lions' heads in the top frieze of the façade. The epitome of the new Roman style in private residences, however, came with Ca' Corner della Ca' Grande, fashioned by the architect Jacobo Sansovino between 1545 and 1560 for Zorzi Corner, who hailed from one of the patriciate's old dynasties. The bas-reliefs of cuirasses, shields, war trumpets, and Roman armor were all planned to publicize the Corner family's Roman genealogy as heirs to the Scipios. The palace, in formal, classical language, soared over other patrician residences, ignoring the symbolism of equality. Ca' Corner della Ca' Grande, famous for its monumental size and rich interior, including a bedroom with wall coverings in gold, triggered a widespread exhibition of classical grandeur on the part of Venetian families mingling with the papal court in Rome. Ca' Dolfin (1536), Ca' Corner della Ca' Grande (1545–60), and Ca' Grimani (Michele Sanmicheli, 1556) – the last built for the procurator of San Marco Girolamo Grimani – no longer ascribed to the politics of parsimony. The Grimani palace (Fig. 33) was boldly assertive, with a protruding façade, enlarged classical features, and height. The tie to Rome is featured in the triumphal arch of its central bays. The deceptive size of the palace, seeming bigger than it is, matches the Venetian penchant for mythmaking. Much as patricians aspired to be the successors

Figure 33. Palazzo Grimani, San Luca, by Michele Sanmichele, begun 1556. Photo Credit: J. M. Ferraro.

of Rome's ancient civilization, in fact, they were not. But in Roman fashion, patricians abandoned the altruistic dimension of the Venetian myth in favor of more selfish interests like the ostentatious display of material wealth. In the sixteenth century, patricians gradually retreated from their social responsibilities to enjoy the *otium* of their country villas, where they truly emulated the patrician lifestyles of the ancient Roman nobility.

The most significant transformation in architectural style took place between 1530 and 1570, yet another critical period in the Republic's history. First, the temporary but dramatic loss of Venice's subject territories in the first decade of the century was a catastrophe that presaged the ominous triumphs of the Holy Roman Emperor Charles V. Then Imperial troops sacked Rome in 1527, and by 1530 the Spanish Hapsburg presence in Italy was substantial. Venice was constrained to guard its independence more vigorously. Second came the resurgence of the Counter-Reformation church, sustained by the Hapsburg throne, a development that divided the patriciate into pro- and antipapal factions and fostered controversy over governing policies. Finally, Venice incurred weighty losses to the Ottoman Turks: Modone and Corone in 1537–40, followed by Cyprus in 1571.

In the face of these new challenges one segment of the Venetian ruling class sought to redefine both itself and the public image of the state by creating its own imperial aura. The first phase, between 1530 and 1570, was in the hands of the pro-papal old guard, who, under the leadership of a Cambrai war hero, Doge Andrea Gritti, undertook the Romanization of public space. The sack of Rome by the Holy Roman emperor's army in 1527 encouraged Venetians to fill the vacuum created by Rome's humiliation and temporary political decline. Artists and architects fled the ancient capital, bringing to Venice the renowned Jacopo Sansovino. The Veronese technician of military construction, Michele Sanmicheli (c. 1487–1559), joined him, while the Bolognese Sebastiano Serlio offered the Venetian intelligentsia a new classical idiom in the Mannerist style in his publications of the building of the ancients.

It was primarily Sansovino, influenced in Rome by Bramante, Raphael, and Michelangelo, who implemented Doge Andrea Gritti's program for a second Rome between 1537 and 1554 through the new design of the Piazzetta of San Marco, the construction of the Loggetta in front of the bell tower, the Library of Saint Mark's with its Doric arcades, and the New Mint (Plate XIII). Sansovino rejected the medieval past, lauding instead the precepts of Vitruvious and the classical grandeur of Rome. The Library (completed by Vincenzo Scamozzi between 1588 and 1591) replaced a seedy row of twelfth-century hostelries and taverns, a meat market, and bakers' stalls. In their stead were reminders of ancient Rome in the way of obelisks and garlands as well as Doric and Ionic orders. It was a Roman illusion filled with grandeur. The real centerpiece of illusion, however, was the Loggetta, a meeting place of the patriciate, decorated in red, white, and green marble with an elaborate sculptural program extolling Republican Venice. The classical gods Apollo, Peace, Mercury, and Minerva represented Venice's good government. Finally, in realigning the south side of Piazza San Marco, Sansovino had created a new Venetian forum with the regularly shaped trapezium of the New Procurators' Offices.

Gritti and his patrician supporters thus visually projected Venetian supremacy, defining the city as the new Rome. Moreover, in tandem with the new architectural monuments, the doge strengthened the smaller executive councils in government, allowing a small group to retain the emergency war powers they had acquired during the War of Cambrai. An addition to the Senate, in Venetian named Zonta, behaved more elusively, while an exclusive number of nobles held the most important offices and ambassadorships. All the while the young guard, who opposed both the papacy and the Spanish presence in Italy, rejected the values of the ruling gerontocracy. In 1582, however, their time would come. In alliance with some of the patriciate's newer as well as poorer families, they would repeal the Zonta in 1582, face down the papacy with the Interdict of 1606–7, and change the way the Venetian Republic would represent itself.

Sansovino and Sanmicheli had brought the Roman Renaissance style to the palaces of some of the richest pro-papal families in Venice: the Dolfin, the Corner, and the Grimani. The last two families together held five of Venice's eight cardinalships between 1500 and 1550. Sansovino designed Palazzo Dolfin on the Grand Canal in 1538 according to the classical canon and took his inspiration for Palazzo Corner della Ca' Grande at San Maurizio (1545) from Bramante's "House of Raphael," while Michele Sanmicheli designed the Corner palace at San Polo (1545) and the monumental Palazzo Grimani with its Roman triumphal arch and three-storied Corinthian order on the Grand Canal (1556) (see Figure 33).

Sansovino's death in 1550 cleared the way for Andrea Palladio to continue the classical idiom. Palladio's more radical designs, however, did not readily win over the patriciate. Instead, his most influential work in the city was in the sacred space of the church. His remake of the façade of San Francesco della Vigna (1565), financed by the Grimani family, with classical columns in white Istrian stone, was unprecedented in size. With the Refectory (1560–62), the church of San Giorgio Maggiore (begun in 1566) (Plate XIV), and the church of the Redentore (begun in 1576) (Fig. 34), Palladio embellished "classical" Venice with interlocking Corinthian temple fronts. The monumental order of columns and geometric forms of these gigantic church façades evoked imperial grandeur and played a central role in the processional routes of the Republic. Here was Venice's love for the votive, with all its drama. Unlike the more restrained San Giorgio Maggiore, which was financed by the Benedictine monks, the Redentore was the work of the Venetian Senate, now intent on making specific references to both ancient and contemporary Rome.

Palladio's success in advancing the classical idiom to church architecture, however, did not extend to the "temple" of the state, the Ducal Palace. The Palazzo Ducale remained in the hands of the anti-Roman faction of the Senate. When Palladio proposed in 1577 to remake the palace, badly damaged by fire, in the classical mode, he was turned down in favor of rebuilding the Gothic structure that represented the stability and longevity of the Republic.

Figure 34. Church of the Redentore, by Andrea Palladio, begun 1577. Note the pontoon bridge on the left that is laid out for the annual procession. Location: Venice, Italy.
Photo Credit: J. M. Ferraro.

One more votive temple, in addition to that of the Rendentore, served
as a stage for the state's ideological program at the city center, the church
of Santa Maria della Salute, executed by Baldassare Longhena beginning in 1631. The Marian church, dedicated to the Virgin at the end of

a catastrophic plague epidemic, extolled the virtues of the mythical city, whose foundation date was also the feast of the Annunciation of the Virgin. More than one million piles, a virtual forest, were driven into the sea to support the gigantic structure that would be the site of an annual procession and celebration.

4. Theaters of Political and Religious Drama

Architecture and painting were but two of the media that conveyed Venetian identity. Another, which complemented the first two and engaged the entire spectrum of the city's inhabitants and its foreign visitors, was pageantry, something the Venetians developed with great skill and refinement. Pageantry served to remind everyone of how special the Serenissima was. At the same time it was meant to be an organizing principle across social classes. Loyalty to state and the Christian calendar and creed were the common denominators holding these public spectacles together. Each celebration had a special purpose that historian Edward Muir has aptly categorized: to immortalize history; to emphasize the limits of the doge's authority; to punish malefactors; to receive a foreign emissary; to celebrate a secular or sacred event; and to pay homage to God.[4]

The Venetian ruling class had a long tradition of constructing and immortalizing the city's history to its liking. Among its favorite events were the annual celebration of bringing back St. Isidore's body with the Crusading booty of Doge Domenico Michiel in 1125. The Conquest of Constantinople in 1204 was another celebratory event. Every December 6 the reigning doge would attend mass to commemorate this Venetian victory. Likewise victories over Venice's commercial rival, Genoa, were celebrated on Saint Martial's day, July 1; Mary Magdalene's day on July 22; and the beheading of John the Baptist on August 29. The recovery of Padua in 1509 was the focus of a July 17 celebration with an elaborate procession of secular and ecclesiastical officials and members of the high government to the parish church of Santa Marina. The 1510 post-Cambrai lifting of the Papal Interdict was the occasion for processions in Venice and the subject territories. The members of the Scuole Grande of San Rocco built a tableau with statues depicting Justice, Saint Roch, St. Mark, and a woman dressed as Venice holding a dove representing the Holy Spirit. The Venetians tipped their hats to the French Catholics in 1563 in their victory over the Huguenots. Another female saint, Justina, was given the honor on October 7 for the celebration of the Venetian triumph over the Ottoman Turks at Lepanto in 1571. On that day, the doge attended mass at the parish church of Santa Giustina and then returned to San Marco to view a procession of the great confraternities and the regular and secular clergy. During the Papal Interdict of 1606–7 ritual served to mount a strong anticlerical stance. The pope's failures were contrasted with the righteous attributes of the Venetian state. Most of the clergy marched in procession with secular magistrates to invoke a separation of Venice from Rome. There was even an inflammatory float representing a collapsing church supported by the doge and the great mendicant Saints Dominic and Francis. Both saints were portrayed exalting the doge. It is notable how many of these occasions honored parish churches and incorporated both the secular and regular clergy and the confraternities before making the political space of San Marco once again the focal point of the celebration.

It was also important to patricians, ridden with rifts between rich and poor, to remind themselves and others that the doge was a figurative head of state and not a true monarch. St. Vitus Day commemorated the Querini-Tiepolo conspiracy of 1310, when factionalism reached a dangerous level. Every June 15 the Venetians staged a ducal procession from the church of San Vito to San Marco with all the magistrates, congregations, friars, and monks to give thanks to God for the preservation of domestic peace. St. Isidore, on the other hand, served the function of condemning the overly ambitious Doge Marin Falier, who was decapitated in 1355 for his grandiose political aims.

The political consistency of Venice's aristocratic regime earned the admiration of many European aristocracies. The marching order of the processions at times reinforced the aristocratic hierarchy. However, the wide participation of the city's lay associations, such as that of San Giovanni Evangelista, documented in Gentile Bellini's painting of *The Corpus Christi Procession*, also fostered a sense of popular inclusion. The Corpus Christi parade began in Rome in 1264 with Pope Urban IV and was first celebrated in Venice in 1295. Initially, it associated the Venetian government with the support of pilgrimages. By the sixteenth century, however, the organizers had developed high-tech pageantry with portable tableaux displaying allegorical and dramatic images. The floats were adorned with silver liturgical objects and three Old Testament tableaux and were designed to display Venetian riches and divine blessing. The religious drama of the Corpus Christi procession carried important political meaning. It attracted thousands of spectators, who watched the long procession beginning with the members of the great and small confraternities and other congregations. In Bellini's painting (see Figure 16 in Chapter 4) the Piazza also looks deceptively calm. Moreover, he has groups of non nobles *preceding* the doge, the noble senators, and the leader of the Venetian church carrying the tabernacle containing the Host.

The rituals of the Catholic Church, such as the cult of saints and the veneration of relics with supernatural powers, and the church calendar also assisted in this process of representing Venice as "The Most Serene Republic," with wise rulers and broad participation. Another of Gentile Bellini's paintings, *The Miracle of the Holy Cross* (see Figure 28), depicts a perfectly organized spectacle, with a disciplined public standing in assigned places within a precise hierarchy, while this dramatic spiritual scene of retrieving a piece of the true cross that accidentally fell into the water took place. This could hardly have been the case on the many feast days when Piazza San Marco and the city's other great monuments were transformed into public theaters filled with emotional drama. The underlying purpose of such spectacles was to capture spectators' loyalties and infuse onlookers with a sense of religious piety and civic pride. That accomplished, however, the crowds then scurried off for the real fun: to watch the famous fistfights on Venice's bridges, where men pummeled one another and knocked each other off bridges as excited fans cheered them on (see Figure 21 in Chapter 4).

Public punishment was also a way to remind the people that the repressive forces of Venice's secular tribunals were there to regulate and even annihilate the perpetrators of crime. Convicted criminals were publicly condemned in judicial processions and then transported through the city to places where they were mutilated or executed. Venice's judicial magistrates used these processions as a way to remind the public of their authority as well to redress various injuries publicly. Such rituals were another way patricians reinforced the "Myth of Venice," as the dispenser of social stability. A malefactor might be made to wear a crown decorated with devils and to stand all day on a stage situated between the two columns of Justice in the Piazzetta next to the Ducal Palace. Edward Muir explains that the offenders, at times liars or immodest women, were transformed into ritual objects, and they served to purify the community from guilt and wrongdoing.

Another way to purify the community was to pay homage to God, the saints, and sacred relics. Not all public display masked the dark social realities troubling the city. Beneath the ideal templates inscribed in laws and projected in colorful iconography and grand public processions, Venice was filled with adversity, poverty, and vice. At times it experienced price inflation and wage reduction, and it was ridden with food shortages and disease. Floods and earthquakes, and repeated visitations of the bubonic plague struck terror in the hearts and minds of the people, weighed on the consciences of guilt-ridden sinners, and called for pious supplications for God's mercy and promises of moral reform.

Saint Roch, the patron saint of the Scuola of San Rocco, was called upon to give protection from outbreaks of pestilence. Confraternity members had transported the saint's body to Venice from Germany in 1485, his finger among the most precious relics they displayed in their processions to ward off disease. And the repeated visitations of devastating plague, transmitted by infected fleas, gave them ample opportunity to react, along with all the other confraternities. In despair, lay men and women built shelters for the sick, sometimes engaging unemployed prostitutes to wash and bind victims' sores, while St. Roch looked after them.

There were fourteen outbreaks of plague in the seventy years between 1456 and 1528, but the epidemics of 1575 and 1630 were among the most ferocious, decimating between 25 percent and 30 percent of the population each time. The Venetian confraternities staged penitential rituals, beating themselves to placate Divine wrath. Their dedication to making votive offerings to God and the Virgin Mary is responsible for the building of some of the city's greatest landmarks. Among the best examples are those of the Redentore (1576) and La Salute (1630). In the first case, the Senate implored the religious houses to pray continuously and to organize frequent processions asking God to end the savage plague that had begun in 1575. Senators commissioned Andrea Palladio to design the famous Church of the Redentore, a votive temple of pilgrimage and state ceremony that sits like a great piece of scenery on a stage. To this day, in July a pontoon bridge is laid from the Zattere bank across the Canale della Giudecca to Palladio's church. There is an immense procession from San Marco to the Zattere and then across the temporary bridge (Fig. 35). The procession is spectacularly theatrical, with the great church, raised up high like a sanctuary, appearing to be floating on water. But the plague paid another savage visit in 1630. Lasting sixteen months, it killed nearly 50,000 people. Thus the Venetian government called upon the architect Baldassare Longhena to build yet another votive temple, this one dedicated to the Virgin, who was also the protector of health. Here again on a prominent site, where the Giudecca and Grand canals join, a spectacular procession takes place every November 21. A temporary bridge is built across the Grand Canal to link San Marco with the Church of Santa Maria della Salute, so that Venetians can walk to the church and express their devotion and eternal gratitude for redemption from the plague of 1630.

Figure 35. Joseph Heintz the Younger (1600–78), *The Procession on Redemption Day*, detail. Even today, a pontoon bridge is laid from the Zattere bank across the Canale della Giudecca to Palladio's church Il Redentore. Oil on canvas. Location: Museo Correr, Venice, Italy. Photo Credit: Erich Lessing/Art Resource, NY. Image Reference: ART95904.

5. Setting the Sacred and the Secular to Music

Music, like processions and religious feast days, played a very important part in Venetian daily life. The city was filled with private concerts, serenades, and musical boating parties on the lagoon. With the advent of printing, the Republic also encouraged music by granting copyright patents to notable instrument makers and to printers. But more important, music played a vital role in the Venetian sacred ritual and secular pageantry described above. It was yet another way, along with poetry, to reinforce the messages the aristocracy wished to convey. The development of musical styles in Venice came relatively late: in the fourteenth century there was an established tradition of motets celebrating ducal authority at ceremonial events, but it was not until the sixteenth century that both vocal and instrumental music flourished. The initial stage in musical development culminated with the appointment of the renowned Flemish composer and musician, Adrian Willaert (c. 1490–1562) as concertmaster of St. Mark's Basilica in 1527. Doge Andrea Gritti's engagement of this preeminent composer was part of a deliberate cultural agenda that placed Venice on the European musical scene as a trendsetter. Willaert was instrumental in the development of both sacred music and the poetical, secular madrigal. With respect to the former, he developed music for double chorus at the Basilica San Marco, whose structure lent itself to two conversing, or "antiphonal" choirs. This polyphonic mode, of Franco-Flemish origin, came to be known as the Venetian School. There were two choir lofts in the Basilica, one on each side of the main altar of St. Mark's, each with an organ. Willaert divided the singers into two groups, using them either antiphonally or together. All of Willaert's successors used this style through the seventeenth century.

Venetian polychoral music reached its peak with the early Baroque composer Giovanni Gabrieli. It extended from the sacred compositions of San Marco to the secular vocal pieces, called madrigals, written for several voices. The genre had originated in the affluent northern courts of Italy, where patrons encouraged singers to set Petrarchan sonnets to music. The result was a kind of text painting. It was, however, the Venetian poet and scholar Pietro Bembo (1470–1547) who had the most decisive influence on the development of the madrigal. Bembo, born into an aristocratic family, traveled extensively with his father, a Venetian ambassador. In Florence he developed a love of the Tuscan form of Italian and Petrarch's poetry. He also studied Greek and was influenced in Florence by Lorenzo de Medici's Neoplatonic court, along with the philosophers Ficino and Poliziano. Bembo subsequently enrolled at the University of Padua. In his *Prose della volgar lingua* he asserted that Petrarch's verse was a perfect model for expressing emotions ranging from bliss to tragedy. This work was applied to music and to the development of the madrigal form. Madrigal singers used Petrarch's tropes for noble self-fashioning, singing his poetry in salons to melodies of sensual beauty. Noble decorum and luxury was expressed through the sonnet. There were also witty poetical texts for sophisticated audiences. Salons grew in number through the sixteenth century, providing important venues for the exchange of ideas and art forms such as the madrigal.

Cipriano Rore (c. 1515–65) and Orlando di Lasso followed Willaert, using more elaborate chromaticism, while the theorist Giuseffo Zarlino elaborated on the technical issues of this genre in 1558 in the *Istitutioni harmoniche*. Rore, Willaert's successor in Venice in 1562, was one of the most influential composers of the sixteenth century, principally through his madrigals, where in 1542 he established five voices rather than four as the norm. His ideas influenced madrigal development into the next century. His music, along with Willaert's, was sponsored by the Florentine exiles Neri Capponi and Ruberto Strozzi. The former headed Willaert's music academy while the

VERONICA FRANCO

Veronica Franco[5] (1580–1625) was a poet famous in her own time who made her living as a courtesan. She received her training from her mother, who was also a courtesan until she married. The Franco family was of relatively high birth for Venice, coming from the *cittadini* class. However, the early death of her father left Veronica without the financial possibility to wed. Instead, she studied the humanities, as well as music, art, and dance, becoming an intellectual courtesan, or *cortigiana onesta*. The members of this group of "free women" earned their living by entertaining men of wealth and stature, especially the (married) Venetian patriciate.

Franco began her education at an early age. She studied the biographies of elite Venetian men whom she later lauded in commissioned sonnets. At elite social gatherings for men, she played the lute and the spinet, recited her poetry, and discussed Greek and Roman literature. She also kept abreast of works by contemporary artists, writers, and politicians.

Franco was a prolific poet, publishing her own collection of verse (*Terza rime*) in 1575. In this volume, Franco included seventeen autobiographical poems regarding her life as a courtesan, a work that attempted to distinguish the courtesan from illiterate women who sold sex. Other poetry, filled with dedications and accolades, described Veronica's relationships with male patrons. Much of the poetry was erotic and designed to tantalize clients. Franco's explicit eroticism was a departure from Petrarchan love poetry, an established genre at this time. Aware of her feminine sexual powers, this honest courtesan used her poetry to undermine ideal templates of women as silent and unapproachable. Her bold sensuality earned the scorn of male writers like Maffio Venier. Venier lambasted Franco with obscene verse, a challenge she accepted with relish, deftly neutralizing Maffio's attempts to publicly humiliate her. Besides herself, Franco defended all women who had been victimized physically and/or verbally by men.

In her fifty *Lettere familiari a diversi* (*Family Letters to Different People*), published in Venice in 1580, Franco exhibited a variety of skills. These writings contain biographical sketches of contemporary notables as well as snapshots of her daily life. She also commented on the events and situations represented in her *capitoli*. As a moralist, Franco used her *Letters* as a vehicle to place her private life on the public stage and to testify to the fairness, virtue, reason, and wisdom of the courtesan.

Franco was brought before the Inquisition in 1580 on charges of placing men with whom she had relationships under her spell. Prior to her death at the age of forty-five she helped found an asylum for wayward women.

latter sponsored Rore's motets. Capponi and Strozzi were rich aristocrats with musical abilities. They sang domestic music and played the viol as well as serving as important musical patrons.

Even the madrigal heritage, like architecture and the visual arts, displayed some of Venice's societal fissures. The patriciate sought ennobling text to inflate their status. Gottardo Occagna and Antonio Lantani printed vernacular music to exalt noble fame. At the other end of the spectrum was Girolamo Parabosco, a bourgeois writer from Piacenza, who emphasized virtue over birthright. Along with the famous poet and courtesan Veronica Franco, Parabosco straddled the fence, on the one hand praising the Serenissima but on the other also challenging aristocratic norms. Franco was careful to respect the noble patronage that enabled her to excel as a poet. Her patron, Domenico Venier, educated at San Marco in the humanities, was devoted to Bembo's ideas of noble decorum. On the other hand the famous courtesan, along with another female poet, Gaspare Stampa, wrote in defense of the female sex and advocated improvised female singing.

Besides gaining fame in poetry set to music with the madrigal form, Venice took the lead in Europe in the manufacture of musical instruments. The city became a center for building organs, a Byzantine invention, along with making harpsichords and plucked and wind instruments. The Venetian-born Andrea Gabrieli (1532–85), a composer heavily indebted to Rore, was appointed official organist at St. Mark's in 1566, one of the most prestigious musical positions in all of Europe. Within the unique acoustical space of the Basilica, which lent itself to dual choirs, Andrea Gabrieli developed a grand ceremonial style for the Venetian state. Andrea's nephew, Giovanni, became even more famous. He became the principal organist of San Marco in 1584 and was the first composer to assign specific instruments to accompany the choirs. Large groups of brass instruments sounded prominently, while chorus and instruments dialogued with echo effects. Giovanni Gabrieli's fame rose across Europe, and musicians traveled from afar to learn about Venetian musical styles.

Musical instruments in general began to receive more prominence, alongside voice. In 1568, the government was able to engage permanent instrumental musicians for feast days as well as to accompany the polychoral singing in San Marco. There were lavish performances in the Basilica as well as the Great Confraternities, such as the ones designed to sustain the "Myth of Venice" after the victory at Lepanto in 1571 or to welcome the French king Henry III in 1574.

This brief excursus into high musical culture traces the well-known evolution from a cappella Renaissance style to multiple choir concerts to sacred and secular Baroque concerti. Willaert, the Gabrieli, and Monteverdi are the most visible composers shaping the history of musical forms and styles, and Venice was most certainly in the vanguard of this art form. The Great Confraternities were also at the heart of Venice's innovative musical scene, sponsoring music for celebrations and pageantry, along with the aristocratic Companies of the Hose. Like the Ducal Chapel and aristocratic patrons, they also commissioned the best composers, singers, and instrumentalists of the day. But as musicologist Jonathan Glixon's important work on the confraternities has demonstrated, Venice's lesser venues – small confraternities, nunneries, monasteries, and local parishes – also deserve attention in the master narrative, for they gave employment to hundreds of singers and instrumentalists throughout the city and brought music to the entire population. Ordinary people heard singing in processions and at funerals; from priests, chanting to organ accompaniment; from humble friars singing harmonized music at funerals as well as the more sophisticated polyphonic laude, instrumental ensembles, motets, and masses. The series of annual feasts provided great employment opportunities for lesser singers and musicians. In their desire to honor God, non noble citizens, merchants, and ordinary people within the great and small confraternities paid for and sponsored hundreds of musical events. Glixon estimates that the scuole commissioned music for approximately 300 days each year in more than 100 of Venice's churches throughout the city.[6]

★ ★ ★

THE VERSATILITY OF VENETIAN ACHIEVEMENT IN THE TRANSITION FROM the medieval to the Renaissance age was remarkable. Venice began the fifteenth century as a maritime power and international emporium, but it rapidly became a cultural leader as well, drawing visitors from near and far to marvel at its classical grandeur, mesmerizing stagecraft, and innovative music. The city's festive proclivities did more than charm observers: they invited viewers to participate in the rituals that promoted judicious government and loyalty to the common weal. Credit must be given to the confraternities that patronized the visual and musical arts as well as to the *popolani* who staged and witnessed the civic fanfare. Only with their support could the aristocratic myth of serenity and divine favor continue to serve as a panacea for the hardships of daily life.

FURTHER READING

Architecture: T. Cooper (2005); D. Howard (2005); M. Tafuri (1984, 1989). *Carnival*: P. Burke (1987). *Cultural History*: O. Logan (1972). *Documents*: P. La Balme and L. Sanguinetti-White (2008). *Humanism*: M. King (1986). *Iconography*: D. Rosand (2001). *Music*: J. Glixon (2003). *Painting*: R. Goffen (1986, 1997); P. Humphrey (1997). *Palace Building and Private Life*: P. Brown (1997, 2004). *Ritual*: E. Muir (1981).

THE SERENISSIMA'S WAYWARD SUBJECTS

1. The Age of Religious Dissent

The myth of an ideal Republic of enduring stability, clearly articulated in the pageantry, music, and visual arts, was a calculated antidote to the city's underlying disorders, which magistrates defined in social and gendered terms. Moreover, the imagination offered flight from the religious and political subversion sweeping across much of Europe during the sixteenth and seventeenth centuries. To the north, in Wittenberg, an ardent Augustinian monk named Martin Luther, calling for church reform in 1517, had by 1521 unwittingly started the new Lutheran religion, rupturing nearly a thousand years of Roman Catholic unity. Further religions schisms soon followed throughout the Holy Roman Empire. Then, during the 1530s, Jean Calvin initiated a second wave of protest, this one more militant, in the Swiss cantons, and by mid-century Calvinism was spreading rapidly to disaffected elites in France and the Spanish Netherlands. Catholic prelates began to take up reform in 1545, convening for nearly two decades in the city of Trent to study how to improve the priesthood, care for the sick and poor, and preserve the sanctity of marriage. They also strictly affirmed traditional Catholic doctrine. But by this time the followers of Protestant beliefs were entrenched and encroaching on Catholic lands. As a result, religious wars racked most of Europe well into the seventeenth century. Protesters' differences with the Catholic Church did not stop with theology, but rather with the entire way society was organized. Seeking freedom of religious worship but also to throw off the yoke of class difference, diverse groups with different aspirations temporarily joined together. The Venetian state and local church, of course, sided with the Catholics, staging celebratory feasts when they obtained victories over the Huguenots in 1563 and the Ottoman Turks at Lepanto in 1571.

Figure 36. Paolo Veronese (1528–88). *Feast in the House of Levi*. Location: Accademia, Venice, Italy. Photo Credit: Cameraphoto Arte, Venice/Art Resource, NY: Image Reference: ART393.

Remarkably, throughout the age of religious wars Venice succeeded in holding religious and political subversion in check. This is not to say that their Catholic world was free from conflict. At the intellectual level considerable religious skepticism was generated by the philosopher Cesare Cremonini and the mathematician Galileo Galilei, both professors at the University of Padua, and by the Servite monk Fra Paolo Sarpi (1552–1623) in Venice, who excised God and Fortune from historiography. The younger patricians in the Great Council were receptive to this secular approach that challenged the authority of an increasingly militant Post-Tridentine Church. Nonetheless, the patriciate as a whole continued to adhere strictly to Roman Catholic theology and to the ideal standards of Christian morality, despite their infamous temporal independence from Rome. Moreover, they not only upheld but also tightened their rigid notions of hierarchy, particularly with respect to arranged marriage, and the purity of the nobility. Statues of the Virgin Mary adorning bridges at the intersection of canals and above alleyways served as visual reminders that the Republic of Venice and its hereditary rulers were the keepers of women's chastity and virtue as well as overall justice and stability. Ritual life structured society and articulated historical interpretations that would foster belief in the aristocracy's ideological myths. At the same time Venetian magistrates shrewdly manifested a new sensitivity to the material and spiritual needs of beggars, orphans, and wayward women who had fallen victim to poverty and disease, encouraging philanthropy but also enacting legislation to confine or remove those who violated their ideal norms.

There were no dramatic upheavals in Venice to write about during the "Age of Religious Wars," but the government did experience some constitutional difficulties in 1582–3 and 1627–8. The rifts were strictly within the sphere of the nobility. The first instance exposed generational differences. A group of young patricians, called the party of the Giovani, challenged the gerontocracy-centered Council of Ten, effectively curtailing its broad powers as well as its control of the Mint. Over the sixteenth century the powers of the Ten had ominously expanded to include defense and expenditure. There were also Provveditori who at times intervened with extraordinary powers. Alarmed by the old guard's consolidation of power, the Young Party reduced the jurisdiction of the Ten to justice and matters that affected state security, while the Senate took charge of finance and

---

PAOLO SARPI (1552–1623)

Paolo Sarpi, the son of a Venetian tradesman whose given name was Pietro, became a prominent cleric and voice of the Venetian Republic. Orphaned early in his youth, Sarpi was tutored by a maternal uncle who was a Servite monk. Sarpi also entered this religious order and took the name "Paolo." He began his professional career as the court theologian in the Duchy of Mantua. There he pursued mathematics and Asian languages. In 1575, he became an advisor to Cardinal Borromeo in Milan but soon moved to Venice to teach in a Servite monastery. Sarpi's criticisms of Aristotle as well as his advocacy for a Venetian church separate from Rome soon earned him the censorship of the Roman hierarchy. When the Venetian Senate recommended him for the bishopric of Caorle, the request was denied. After the death of Pope Clement VIII in 1605, the Venetian Republic made Sarpi a canonist and theological counselor. He trumpeted the Republic's cause to limit the church's acquisition of property in the Venetian territories.

In April 1606, Pope Paul V excommunicated the Venetians and placed their dominions under interdict. Sarpi entered the controversy and republished the antipapal opinions of Jean Gerson. Shortly thereafter, in an anonymous tract called *Risposta di un Dottore in Teologia*, he attacked the papacy's authority in secular matters. The Republic awarded Sarpi the distinction of state counselor in jurisprudence with free access to the state archives. An attempt was made on his life, but he recovered from the attack and spent the remainder of his life in cloister. He is remembered as a Venetian patriot who tolerated Protestantism over the decrees laid down at the Council of Trent and who advocated a separate, Venetian church.

defense. The rejuvenating reformists then championed an anti-Ottoman and anti-Hapsburg stance, advocating an aggressive foreign policy over neutrality. Moreover, under their spokesman Fra Paolo Sarpi, they rejected Roman authority over the Catholic faith in favor of a more evangelical, Venetian church. They also protected from Roman censorship professors at the University of Padua who were engaging in scientific experimentation and open-ended empirical research. The second instance underlined inequities and further divisions within the aristocracy. The patrician Renier Zeno, sympathetic to the large concentration of poor patricians, mustered support to protest the Ten's jurisdiction over crimes committed by nobles. In neither instance did ordinary people participate in the crisis of authority, and Venice's international reputation for political wisdom weathered the storms.

At the constitutional level the myth of enduring political stability did have some basis, for Venice remained ruled by aristocracy for 500 years, but as we have seen, in private that aristocracy continually evolved and allowed for internal patterns of change. Moreover, social reality diverged from the ideal templates that secular magistrates and religious authorities demanded in their laws and projected in their iconography and grand public processions. Daily life was filled with adversity. Plague epidemics were frequently accompanied by typhus, called spotted sickness, and as the armies of France and Spain descended onto the Peninsula, syphilis emerged in virulent form and women were targeted as the source of infection. Poverty and its partners, disease and crime, were present and became increasingly the responsibility of anxious state authorities. Against this backdrop of hardship, social and political subversion emerged playfully during Carnival season, the last hurrah before the stringent Lenten demands for fasting and bodily constraint. Ordinary people dressed up as rulers; commoners appeared as nobles; and wives commanded husbands in the campi and along the narrow alleys of Venice. Figures dressed as Bernadon reminded people of the horrors of syphilis, whose endemic presence made comic release a necessary cultural construction, while others masked themselves as plague doctors to release tension. Carnival was an opportune moment for frivolity. Pent-up steam escaped, with hostile fantasies turning into public spectacle. Masked figures defied the challenges of daily life, mostly in playful ways, but at times frustration was solved through violence.

Apart from pageantry and Carnival play, however, was a darker side; the activities of Venice's criminal tribunals exposed authorities' growing anxiety over the poor, the diseased, and the immoral. The Venetian patriciate, together with the Catholic Church, had developed an elaborate judicial network by

the sixteenth century, and court depositions are filled with stories of trans-
gression, where priests reneged on vows of celibacy; nobles wed outside
acceptable circles; Christians read heretical writings; peoples of differing religions formed households; women feigned sanctity and used magic to remedy
the ailments of the lovesick; soldiers and prostitutes spread syphilis; and female
virginity was defiled. Venetian records reveal that not everyone participated in
Christian culture in the same way. In the interests of living their lives, people
fled the travails of life and the intrusions of church and state authorities. Their
names largely forgotten, they are the fascinating subjects of alternate historical
narratives, ones that escaped the pen of Venetian panegyrists writing about La
Serenissima but that contemporary adjudicators denounced as blasphemers
or heretics, prostitutes, concubines, sorcerers, and practitioners of love magic,
feigned sanctity, abortion, and infanticide. There were perpetrators of rape
and incest as well, albeit documentation for the latter is very scarce. The city
of myth, it turns out, was a city of vice as well as virtue, something the satirist
and poet of whoredom, Pietro Aretino (1492–1556), noted with enthusiasm
in 1527 when he settled in Venice. But it is also important to emphasize that
the initiatives to repair societal ruptures during the Reformation Age came
not only from the church and state but also from neighborhood communities
and voluntary associations that demonstrated the wisdom both to regulate
disorder and to express their piety through community service.

2. Church, State, and the People

Unlike many of the areas that suffered both religious dissent and political
violence during the Reformation period, the Venetian church rested on a
strong popular tradition. The property owners in the seventy parishes each
elected their own parish priest, a unique custom that many groups of religious protesters elsewhere in Europe were fighting for during the years lead
ing up to the Reformation. In Venice, the entire parish was responsible for
the appointment of the priest, who was educated within the community
rather than in a religious seminary. Priests, thus, were embedded in their
communities and vice versa. They served as marriage and family counselors,
especially to married women, as well as dispensers of spiritual succor. When
the Venetian Patriarch Gerolamo Querini tried to have this local tradition
abolished in 1530, he failed, signaling the degree of strength the communities
still held over the direction of parish affairs.

Venice also enjoyed the right to ordain its clergy on the basis of the service
they rendered the church. Most of the forty-four bishoprics in Venice and

the Venetian mainland thus were held by the Venetian nobility; the appointments were made by the Venetian Senate. Moreover, the patriarch of Venice came from a very different tradition than that of other bishops in western Europe. He was not a cleric but rather a Venetian patrician who had already served in a number of secular commissions. Even the title patriarch deviated from the Western tradition: Venice had remained attached to the medieval Byzantine model of patriarchates, linked to Constantinople, Antioch, and Alexandria rather than to Rome. Also in the Byzantine tradition, the Basilica San Marco was the doge's chapel and not a cathedral, and the Friulian rite of Aquilea prevailed rather than the Roman liturgy.

Politically, a large percentage of the patriciate supported containment of the temporal power of the Roman church and ecclesiastical patronage. One of the thorniest issues was the expansion of ecclesiastical holdings within the Republic, owing to both the sale of property and to gifts and bequests. Added to that were the kinds of privileges and immunities the clergy held that reduced the fiscal resources and judicial powers of the Venetian state. The Republic retained the right to punish clerics who had committed crimes and to tax resident clergy. Venetian pamphleteers like the Servite monk Paolo Sarpi, the Republic's official theologian, trumpeted strong opposition to priestly authority. In contrast, a few Venetian dynasties, such as the Grimani, the Pisani, and the Cornaro, were loyal to the papacy, largely because they benefited from the great bishoprics bestowed upon them.

The families of the Young Party, however, pursued policies that ignited public conflict with the Holy See. When the pope announced that there would be an apostolic visitation of Venetian parishes in 1580–1, the Republic refused. Moreover, at times Venetian magistrates proceeded against the clergy for transgressions other than treason or wicked vice, matters that were technically not under their jurisdiction. Relations reached a boiling point in 1606 when Venice forbade laypeople to return land leased from the clergy to their ecclesiastical owners. Pope Paul V placed the city under interdict in 1606, virtually excommunicating Venetians. Significantly, in times of crisis like that of the interdict, the state could call upon the people to support and express its position separating church and state. A good example of this popular allegiance comes from the *scuole grandi*, whose governors were strictly lay citizens and not members of the clergy. The Grandi disseminated political propaganda to ordinary people, supporting the stance of the Republic, with showy tableaux invoking separation of church and state and depicting the infamy of the pope. In turn, the domesticated clergy, parish priests, several religious orders (save the Observant Franciscans, the Jesuits, the Capuchins, and the Theatines), and the lay religious institutions stood behind the state, holding services despite the interdict. One group of friars constructed a float showing a collapsing church supported by the doge, who was aided by saints Dominic and Francis, with the motto "long live the doge." European rulers as well as Venetian patricians themselves took sides in the showdown between the Republic and the papacy. Venice represented good and just government for anti-Spanish and antipapal forces, while the opposition exposed the tensions within the Republic, including the flaws of oligarchy. This anti-Roman puffery, however, was not deep-seated. When the French proposed a compromise enabling both sides to save face, the pope lifted the interdict and the Republic retained its reputation for political wisdom.

The political drama with the papacy did not impede the Venetian state's growing relationship with its local church. Together both oversaw the moral as well as material life of the civic community. Magistrates professed that the riches of Venice depended on the piety of its people. Time and again church authorities had reminded both rulers and people that the travesties that befell the city were linked to its sins. Recalling tales of prostitution, sodomy, venereal disease, and incest, confessors urged repentance when an earthquake struck Venice in 1511 and a devastating pestilence severely reduced the population between 1575 and 1577. In 1576, the Senate asked all religious houses to pray and organize processions to ward off the plague. They engaged Palladio to design the church of the Redentore and promised to hold an immense procession very year on the third Sunday in July when confraternities, monks, friars, congregations of priests, and ordinary people would walk from San Marco across a temporary bridge on the Giudecca Canal to the votive temple of the Redentore.

For Venice, the control and alleviation of dire poverty, through the discipline and education of the indigent, became of utmost importance. The impetus for reform came from several sources. At the state level, several secular institutions arose in the sixteenth century to cleanse the city of vice and purify civic identity. Among them, a magistracy to supervise convents and monasteries (1521); and the Executors of Blasphemy (1537) to prosecute those who insulted nobles, the state, and God and the Virgin Mary, and in 1539, to control gambling and prostitution. At the ecclesiastical level, with the Council of Trent (1545–63), local priests and preachers were encouraged to supervise the social and moral welfare of the people; from Rome came the repressive force of the Holy Inquisition (1547); and the Venetian Patriarchal Court took up the regulation of failed marriage (1563). At the community level, the confraternities as well as individual testators, strove both to save souls and to address the urgent social needs of prostitution, poverty, and crime. A home for repentant prostitutes, called the Convertite, began in the 1530s on the

Giudecca; in 1551, the women cut off their hair, pledged a life of austerity, and took up the rule of St. Augustine; in 1562 they became cloistered. Another institution, the Zitelle Periclitanti, sponsored by the Paulines in Venice, took in virgins in peril between the ages of nine and twelve; the mothers of some of these girls were prostitutes. The girls learned to cook and sew and were given small dowries to either marry or enter a convent. For married women who no longer lived with their husbands and were in danger of losing their modesty, the Venetian community established the Soccorso in 1577. Women in failed marriages, wives with abusive husbands, and wives evicted by husbands because of committing adultery found safety there. The fear was that if they were not enclosed in the Soccorso, they would be in danger of losing their modesty and of contracting syphilis, which had become endemic. These organizations, the result of caring priests as well as members of the laity, offered shelter for the young as well as a chance for salvation for adult females who had gone astray. Some of those who were afflicted with venereal disease had the chance to enter a specialized hospital, such as the Incurabili, established by the Company of Divine Love. In this case incurable meant long-term care. Those who refused aid, on the other hand, were expelled by the ministers of public health. Historian Laura McGough sees this as a gendered response to venereal disease. Control signified confinement or removal of women, while greater care was given to curing men, whose affliction was considered more a badge of honor than a source of shame.[1]

The government and society of Venice, thus, adhered strictly to the Roman Catholic belief that the charity of donors and the repentance of sinners saved souls. Perhaps this tradition of local influence over ecclesiastical institutions as well as the loyalty of the people to the common weal avoided the kinds of subversive tensions troubling northern European territories in the age of Reformation. But at the same time, the presence of the Bestemmia and the Inquisition signified that the Republic's peoples, especially women, were not entirely free to do as they pleased. The outcasts whom the voluntary charities failed to reclaim, as well as those groups and individuals who openly followed unorthodox ways, encountered the repressive forces of the state's tribunals as well as that of the Holy Inquisition, with whom the patriciate collaborated.

3. The Inquisition

Venice and Rome established the Holy Inquisition in the city in 1547 for the purpose of defending the Catholic faith against the protestant heresies that were disrupting religious unity. Rome staffed the tribunal with an auditor, an inquisitor, a fiscal lawyer, and a notary. In addition, however, three Venetian noblemen chosen by the doge sat with the tribunal, ostensibly furnishing opinions but in actuality serving in a supervisorial capacity. The sentencing was the competency of the auditor and the inquisitor, while a constable ordered by the Council of Ten carried out punishments. Clearly the presence of three noblemen was to give Venetian oversight to the process.

In its early years the Inquisitors concentrated on the confessional issues of Lutherans and Anabaptists, who, as challengers of Catholic doctrine, were considered threats to Venice and its territories. A flood of Lutheran, evangelical, Anabaptist, and millenarian ideas were reaching the city through a variety of foreign sources, including itinerant priests and friars, boarders lodged in the city's rooming houses, and the large colony of German merchants and laborers concentrated in the parishes near Rialto and around the German Exchange on the Grand Canal. Many artists and thinkers had established themselves in Venice as well, after Imperial forces sacked Rome in 1527. They were joined by journeymen printers from France and Savoy who came to work in Venice, the European center of the printing industry. Moreover, in nearby Padua, university students from the Holy Roman Empire and France also circulated a variety of Protestant ideas ranging from Lutheranism to Calvinism. Book vendors in parish stalls carried many of these new heresies to a popular readership. Catholic authorities were leery of all of these groups, and censorship reached beyond the bookstalls to any sort of iconography that referred to the so-called German heretics, such as Paolo Veronese's *Feast in the House of Levi* (Fig. 36). Originally entitled *The Lord's Last Supper*, the painter was forced to change its title after Catholic authorities objected to Germans and dwarfs depicted as sharing supper with Christ.

Historian John Martin tells us that evangelism in Venice first made inroads with the Venetian aristocracy, but by 1540 a popular following had emerged of both women and men, native and foreign.[2] They included lawyers, physicians, notaries, merchants, mercers, publishers, printers, jewelers, tailors, silk weavers, instrument makers, and a variety of workers in the service guilds. They were literate, and they were reading Luther and Calvin. Apart from their religious interpretations, these elite artisans, merchants, and professionals reacted to the rigid class structure of Venetian nobles, including the upper clergy. Increasingly in the sixteenth century, nobles were detaching from commerce and industry, devaluing manual labor and excluding those with any associations to it from their ranks. By 1560, lawyers and physicians were also attracted to these aristocratic values and hoped to join ranks with patricians as well as the citizen class. In reaction, the evangelists argued for greater social equality. Venice was a great industrialized city at this point, and skilled workers, master artisans above all, had attained a degree of wealth and autonomy. They sharply criticized the wealth and privileges of the Catholic hierarchy. The literate evangelists spoke about their religious and social ideas in Venetian alleyways and shops, in the public squares, and outside Catholic churches. They met secretly and discussed biblical Scripture, rejecting the Catholic calendar and the worship of saints and icons.

Evangelicals also reacted to patrician control of sacred time and place. For centuries, modes of socialization had revolved around Catholic culture – in churches, monasteries, guilds, and confraternities. Moreover, urban life was steeped in Catholic ritual, welding together secular political ideals with religious iconography and instilling popular loyalty in Venetian institutions. However, urban magistrates and Catholic authorities began over the course of the sixteenth century to intrude more in every walk of life, placing religious institutions under state scrutiny, staffing the Inquisition, advocating greater enforcement of clerical celibacy, and using parish priests to censor marriage and sexuality. Patricians also took greater charge over religious cults, such as the Marian following at Santa Maria de Miracoli. Martin notes that evangelical resistance formed around increasing state regulation of religious and moral life. He identifies the tavern as a comforting setting apart from sacred space. German clientele frequented the Aquila Nero and the Leon Bianco near the Rialto; there they came under the watchful eyes of Venetian magistrates fearing subversion. The apothecary at Due Columbini was another meeting place where heretical ideas were discussed over a chess game. These are clearly male spaces of socialization and tell us less about the thoughts and actions of Protestant women. It may also be that as long as Protestant women did not preach they did not present as much of a threat to male authorities.

Class differences were also at the heart of Anabaptist discussions but on another level. Their ranks were filled mainly with the poor and illiterate who were seeking better material circumstances, such as holding property in common. These Protestants also questioned the sacraments of the Catholic Church and the divinity of Christ. In contrast, another heretical group, the millenarians, were members of elite crafts and were literate. Less interested in overturning the social and political order, they desired religious autonomy, including the right to read and interpret Scriptures for themselves. Thus issues of egalitarianism mixed with those of alternative forms of worship.

Venetian magistrates and Inquisitors expressed greater toleration for Jews and other non-Catholics whose presence was important to commerce and lending as long as they did not proselytize, but those who had accepted baptism were expected to follow the precepts of the Catholic Church. Thus the authorities kept a watchful eye over baptized Christians who flirted with Judaism, primarily through the Inquisition. Most of those who came before this tribunal were Portuguese immigrants of Jewish descent and of modest social standing. Many were transient and not well established in the city.

By the last two decades of the sixteenth century, most of the heretics who were in danger of coming before the Venetian Inquisition for challenging Catholic doctrine had fled Venice. The men presiding over this tribunal then changed direction, focusing on other disturbing phenomena among largely ordinary people. The Inquisitors took on cases of alleged witchcraft, magic, and superstition; dishonoring God, the saints, and the church; and misusing the sacred and spiritual powers of the church. The papal nuncio in Venice Alberto Bolognetti (1578–81) reported back to Rome a litany of incantations and practices designed to ensnare love or material gain.[3] His descriptions reveal certain upper-class male anxieties for which women were to blame: impotence owing to female incantations; noblemen imprisoned by lower-class prostitutes; others who married the low born because they were under spells. Clearly, interclass marriage was as deep an anxiety as failed sexual performance, and this crossing of boundaries could only be explained comfortably by the supernatural forces that had overtaken the weaker sex.

Historian Guido Ruggiero's examination of Inquisition narratives exposes the hidden, topsy-turvy world: abbesses ruling houses of prostitution rather than convents; the host of the eucharistic ceremony binding the love not of God but of men and women; courtesans marrying nobles; and women vying with priests. His findings reveal much about popular beliefs and their diversion from the ideal templates advanced by magistrates and clerics. Much of this was linked to the limited earning potential of women.[4] Historian Sally Scully, tracking the lives of women accused of witchcraft, argues persuasively that it was a career option. So too was managing rooming houses, something my own work on unwed mothers reveals.[5] Indeed, among the few options open to women trying to eke out a living was the management of herbs and other healing potions; unofficial midwifery; and a kind of therapy service for women and men suffering the travails of love. All of these activities got them into trouble with church authorities who were trying to keep marriage and the family strictly under their realm.

Another group that became the target of the Inquisition by the seventeenth century were charismatic women. Historian Anne Schutte concludes that anxious inquisitors suppressed women's spirituality to ensure that reform impulses remained under male institutional supervision.[6] Ordinary Venetian women, continuing in the tradition of living saints, were claiming sanctity by controlling their bodies. Some claimed not to eat or to subsist only on the communion host; others abstained from bodily pleasures like sex. While not heretical, these claims attracted the attention of groups of followers, diminishing the stature of the male clergy in an age when the church was becoming more formally institutionalized. Holy women of all sorts, including nuns and unmarried women who did not join religious orders but took vows of chastity and poverty, were deemed suspect because of their unorthodox practices as well as because of the deep misogynist strain of the male clergy. Women, it was believed, were most susceptible to the wishes of the devil, and in this sense holy women with special claims to sanctity were no different than witches.

SARA COPPIA SULLAM (1542–1641)

Sara Coppia Sullam, the Italian poet, was born in 1592 to Simon and Ricca Coppia in Venice. Coppia Sullam's education was broad, encompassing both Jewish and Italian cultures and ancient Greek, Latin, and Hebrew. She married Jacob Sullam, a prominent Jewish community leader and businessman around 1612. In their home, they held salons for both Jewish and Christian poets, artists, clerics, and intellectuals.

Her fame lies in the discursive literary tradition of the seventeenth century. It revolved around the writings of the Genoese monk Ansaldo Cebà, especially his drama *L'Ester*. In 1619, Coppia Sullam herself performed a passage from it in a musical rendition. Her poetry praises Cebà and expresses a spiritual love for him. Cebà carried on a correspondence with her for four years, in hopes that she would convert to Christianity. The exchange, which included gifts and poems, was both literary and erotic, and the two playfully worked around Sara's maiden name, Coppia. As Cebà, who was twenty-seven years older than Coppia Sullam, characterized them as a Christian couple because her surname meant "couple" in Italian, Sara removed one "p" to alter the meaning. It appears that Cebà hoped to couple with Sara, if not in this life then in the next, but only if she were a Christian. In their exchanges they prayed for one another's conversion to the opposite religion. In 1623, Cebà's fifty-three letters to Coppia Sullam were published. Her letters to the monk are lost.

Coppia Sullam's poetry demonstrated a familiarity with both Old and New Testament scripture. She also displayed her knowledge of Aristotle and Josephus. Her most renowned work was *The Manifesto of Sara Copia Sulam, a Jewish woman, in which she refutes and disavows the opinion denying immortality of the soul, falsely attributed to her by Signor Baldassare Bonifacio* (1621). It was a response to Bonifacio's treatise *On the Immortality of the Soul*, in which he makes the serious accusation that she does not believe in the soul's immortality. But for her defense, she was almost tried by the Inquisition for heresy, and many of her friends abandoned her. Coppia Sullam sent a copy of her *Manifesto* to Cebà, who responded by urging her once again to convert to Christianity. She died in February of 1641.

Figure 37. Giovanni Antonio Guardi (1698–1760). *The Parlor of the Nuns at San Zaccaria.* Oil on canvas, 108 × 208 cm, eighteenth century. Location: Museo Correr, Venice, Italy. Photo Credit: Universal Images Group/Art Resource, NY. Image Reference: ART423398.

In much of Europe during the age of Reformation, whether Protestant or Catholic, the anxieties over heresy gave way to fears about the powers and sexuality of women. For this reason, Catholic authorities at the Council of Trent in 1563 ordered that all nuns be segregated and cloistered. It was a means of controlling both religious practice and the dangers of feminine subversion. Authorities erected high stone walls, similar to the harems of the Sultans, to conceal the women in convents. Nuns were veiled and placed beyond iron grates to ensure against contact with visitors as well as with unwanted intruders. Even the communion window where the women received the host from a cleric was grated to prevent the temptations of lust (Fig. 37).

Convent builders, historian Mary Laven tells us, intended them to be virgin colonies. Her research, however, shows that some of these brides of Christ were prone to vice and indiscipline.[7] This was indeed one of the Protestants' major criticisms of feminine religious communities. For centuries, writers such as Boccaccio and Chaucer had poked fun at the sexual dalliances of the male clergy, a danger to the women of the cloisters. The attack did not stop with Protestants. Within Venice itself, polemicists exposed the lustful deviance of Catholic clerics. Nuns who did not choose enclosure, on the other hand, did not blame male clerics but rather denounced the tyranny of their fathers, who had subjected them to convent life. Arcangela Tarabotti's tirade about the deprivations of nuns provides compelling evidence of some women's resistance to the system of arranged marriage. The nun denounced the paternal greed that fathers freely satisfied with the complicity of church and state through such practices as entailing the estate, limiting succession to one son, and cloistering daughters. Postmodern researchers corroborate this: Sperling's convent dwellers tell the compelling stories of coerced nuns while my own work on annulment petitions describes a similar discursive rhetoric for unwilling brides.[8] We must be cautious, however, in attributing this point

---

ARCANGELA TARABOTTI (1604–52)

Arcangela Tarabotti, née Elena Cassandra Tarabotti,[10] entered the Benedictine convent of Sant'Angela at age eleven. The eldest of nine children, she had been enclosed against her wishes by her father, in all likelihood so that her family could avoid the expenses of a dowry and marriage. Tarabotti took the veil as Sister Arcangela in 1620, later completing final vows. The nun became a prolific writer and the voice of feminine protest against involuntary female enclosure, complaining that she held no religious calling. Through her writings, she denounced the wholesale confinement of patrician women, the cruelty of paternal power, and the politics of a state that protected noble wealth by denying women access to education and condemning them to a life of confinement. Tarabotti lambasted men who spent lavishly on wives and prostitutes to promote their own vanity. She advocated recognition of the intelligence and judiciousness of women. While her writings came widely under fire, she also enjoyed the support of many noble women and several open-minded men.

Tarabotti's first work, *La tirannia paterna* (*Paternal Tyranny*), is perhaps her most famous. In it the unhappy nun decried the unjustness of her coerced enclosure and criticized patrician fathers and the state for their self-serving interests. A version of this work was published in 1654 under the title *La simplicità ingannata* (*Simplicity Deceived*). Her second work, *L'Inferno monocale* (*Convent Hell*), described the misery of daily life in the convent. It never went to print, but its sequel, *Il paradiso monocale* (*Convent Paradise*), was published because, uncharacteristically, she expressed remorse for her earlier protests and appeared to accept her fate. She reverted once again, however, to lauding the talents of women in the *Antisatira* (*Antisatire*) in response to Francesco Buoninsegni's *Contro il lusso donnesco* (*Against the Luxuries of Women*). She maintained that women were ignorant only because they had been deprived of formal schooling. She refuted the notion that co-ed schools would lead women to sin and placed the blame for women's educational deprivation on the lust of irresponsible men.

of view to all women in religious orders. There is also evidence that some nuns were content with their lifestyles.[9]

Laven's research, on the other hand, raises another problem in the cloister: nuns who were brought up in prosperous families desired the same finery as their lay sisters. They liked to dress up in luxury with fine cloth and jewels and to defy sumptuary legislation by using expensive flour, eggs, and almonds to make cakes and pastries. Convents in Venice were upper-class havens where the daughters of patricians, secretaries, physicians, merchants, and notaries mingled – not the poor. These women no more had religious callings than their mothers. Now and then a scandal emerged, exposing a concealed pregnancy, reminders that the high walls and iron grates were not impenetrable.

Alongside religious women, sexually free women were increasingly confined to defined areas where prostitution, something magistrates considered a necessary vice to cleanse the Republic and protect its virtue, was permitted. Authorities characterized prostitutes as sinners but not criminals. With the escalation of the Italian wars, prostitution in the sixteenth century had spread from the Rialto area to thirty-one locations, near the homes of major noble families. Magistrates passed a number of sumptuary laws aimed at identifying and limiting the material display of prostitutes. They were not only dangerous because they spread syphilis but also because they might be mistaken for being noble. A number of Venetian institutions kept a watchful eye on these wayward women, including the Provveditori alle Pompe, Public Health (the Sanità), and the Esecutori alla Bestemmia, while the asylums became part of the system of disease prevention and care. But the known locations for prostitution were the obvious places for authorities to find them. There was also a hidden world of married women, whose numbers cannot be quantified, whose abusive husbands forced them to sell sex in order to supplement meager incomes. Perhaps the most compelling evidence of widespread sexual commerce, however, comes from McGough's study of syphilis: it was not just rampant among soldiers and prostitutes; it was endemic in every Venetian neighborhood and was evenly distributed, a telling comment once again on women's limited access to employment outside the sex industry.

4. Protecting the Blood of Venice: Seduction and Rape

Both ecclesiastical and secular authorities were intent on regulating women's sexual commerce in order to uphold the interests of patriarchy as well as family honor and Catholic morality.[11] They had long considered the female to be the weaker of the two sexes. However, Ottoman ascendancy in the

Mediterranean, religious conflict, recurrent outbreaks of plague, and the spread of syphilis further exacerbated their anxieties. There was also concern that undisciplined, diseased men would debilitate the Republic's military vigor. Ideally therefore, women were either to marry or to submit to some form of enclosure in convents or charitable asylums to protect their chastity. Those who fell into harm's way and found themselves pregnant and unmarried were pressed to relinquish their infants to Catholic foundling homes like the Venetian Pietà.

Long-standing social customs frequently interfered with institutional regulation of sexual relations. Some couples, generally those outside elite circles, agreed to intercourse on promise of marriage, even though such practices had repeatedly flooded the church courts with breach-of-promise suits. In response, theologians at Trent in 1563 insisted that, in addition to mutual consent, a valid marriage required registration and publication of the banns. But some still ignored the rules. The Venetian state also weighed in on this problem by punishing male suitors who falsely promised marriage for sex. The Esecutori alla Bestemmia ordered the violator to provide the deflowered woman with a dowry or marry her. Seducers who did not comply faced exile, for defloration outside of marriage injured family status and disrupted estate management. Still, the onus was on the woman to furnish full proof of injury. Venetian law in 1520 specified that her claim alone did not suffice, and corroboration from eyewitnesses was required. Legal theorists assumed women were fabricating stories to improve their social and financial positions and that men of superior social station needed to protect themselves.

The seventeenth and eighteenth centuries witnessed further diminution of women's rights to claim damages for lost virginity, in both Venice and throughout the Italian peninsula. Authorities were particularly intolerant of interclass unions, even in cases where the woman was pregnant, in order to protect the nobility from interlopers. A misalliance between a nobleman and a common woman brought dishonor to his family and interfered with inheritance plans. Thus, rather than restore women's honor, as was the custom in the sixteenth century, lawmakers and judges thereafter cast blame on them for engaging in premarital sex. The scandal that illegitimacy would bring to fathers was considered worse than the fate of unwed mothers and children born out of wedlock. Hence, there were no paternity regulations to protect pregnant unmarried mothers.

Women who claimed they were victims of rape also faced greater difficulty in proving these charges in secular courts during the eighteenth century. Judges explored the alleged victim's participation in her first experience with sexual intercourse to determine whether her loss of virginity

was involuntary or voluntary. A verdict of involuntary *stupro* signified that
the woman had been raped, and the punishment for the violator was death.
However, if it was found that the woman had consented or relented, she
no longer had any legal recourse. The difficulty with this legal premise was
that, as in modern rape cases today, without eyewitnesses or visible signs of
violent injury, it was difficult to prove whether the sex was forced or con-
sensual. Authorities tended to be suspect of women's claims, assuming they
mostly agreed to sex. If their protests during alleged rape were not audible to
others, nor injuries immediately revealed to potential witnesses, victims had
no defense. Most of the court cases regarding rape were in settings outside
the home. However, my research has uncovered a very few cases of incest,
a largely unreported crime, as well as sex with one's religious confessor.
These cases were generally only discovered when the woman was visibly
pregnant.

5. Fault Lines in the Marital Regime: The Patriarchal Court

Some children, following their hearts, refused to respect parental wishes for
marital unions based on wealth and status. There is evidence across class lines
of resistance to arranged marriage. Ironically, my own research, presented in
Marriage Wars, shows that the Tridentine reforms that defined how a marriage contract became binding offered some unhappy couples hopes of dissolving their vows.[12] Thus they petitioned the Patriarchal Court to achieve
this end. Married women, more often than married men, called upon this
ecclesiastical tribunal to dissolve unwanted unions. Females were more cred-
ible than males in asserting that they were physically forced into marriage.
Men, on the other hand, had more to lose by disobeying their parents if
they faced disinheritance. Moreover, as husbands, they could simply aban-
don their wives or form new relationships without legal assistance. Generally
they turned to the secular courts if they feared losing dowry resources or
hoped to net control of them. The recognition of free will on the part of the
Church in Venice also encouraged women to seek the assistance of priests and
the Patriarchal Court in hopes of refashioning their lives. Ordinary women
were more inclined to be successful than patricians, who were locked into
systems that protected their lineages. Patrician daughters facing marriage or
convents perhaps had the least freedom.

There were several routes to dissolving marriage in the Patriarchal
Court. The first was via an annulment, signifying that the union never took
place. Legitimate reasons to obtain an annulment included forced unions,
no hope of consummating the marriage, and consanguinity and affinity in

relationships of third cousins or closer. A marriage between a Christian and non-Christian was also inappropriate unless the non-Christian converted. Taking vows of chastity or holy orders impeded marriage, as did secret vows to wed someone else. Godparents and godchildren were forbidden to marry because they shared a spiritual affinity, and a godchild could not marry the child, or sibling of a godparent. Legal guardianship created the same impediments. It was, moreover, inappropriate to marry someone convicted of fornication or adultery. Coercion under grave danger to life and limb also invalidated consent to marry.

With the assistance of parish priests and ecclesiastical lawyers as well as kinsmen, servants, and neighbors across generational, class, and gender lines, ordinary people marshaled evidence to demonstrate the invalidity of their unions, drawing from a repertoire of popular tropes that were attentive to canon law. Community gossip assisted their cause and also served to organize codes of conduct and regulate behavior. It was quite common for women forced to marry at a young age to petition the Patriarchal Court in their thirties for an annulment. They appeared to be disaffected by the dramatic age gap between them and much older husbands. This was not a legitimate objection in the Patriarchal Court, but it was a popular theme in erudite comedy and the improvised comedy of the commedia dell'arte during the mid-sixteenth century. The playwright Andrea Calmo (1510–71), reputedly of working-class origins, made the senile old merchant who was passionately in love with a much younger (and horrified) woman the object of ridicule. This was also a common theme in the theatrical farces of his contemporary, Gigio Artemio Giancarli (c. 1500–61), while Orazio Vecchi (1550–1605) and Adriano Banchieri (1568–1634) composed the musicals *Happy but Penniless* (1597) and *The Madness of Old Age* (1598), respectively, on this subject. The actress Isabella Andreini also criticized the age gap in marriage in her stage roles. The comedies and musicals served up an array of avaricious old fathers, unhappy daughters, lovers plotting elopements, and loyal servants assisting the young in their rebellions against the traditions of the old.

Playwrights who crafted plots that broke social or age barriers or defied parental authority met with aristocratic disapproval and themes of this nature were a thorny issue for writers such as Girolamo Parabosco (1524–57). Moreover, the reality was that older men had the financial means to wed young women, who were generally without resources. The inferior financial status of women in general – even those with resources often could not dispose of them independently – was a vulnerability that feminist writers like Moderata Fonte and Lucrezia Marinella readily identified in their defense of women, but this was a conflict left unresolved.

Separation was the other route to marital dissolution. Canon law defined marriage as a permanent union before God and the church, based on Matthew 19:6, but certain circumstances permitted a separation of bed and board. Among them were life-threatening abuse, leprosy, and adultery. Adultery was also a legitimate reason to be granted a separation. Husbands were rarely found guilty of this, but there was incentive for them to take their wives to court in order to keep their dotal resources. Women in failed marriages where their husbands were at fault retreated to one of Venice's asylums. Husbands were obliged to continue supporting them and to take responsibility for the children.

In tandem with the church, which reviewed the petitions describing couple's problems, the Republic established an assortment of tribunals to address the property issues associated with marital dissolution. Adjudicators were careful to provide for the financial welfare of married women as well as to safeguard their dotal wealth. Venetian patricians attempted to exercise greater regulatory powers over marriage in order to guarantee social stability. In the eighteenth century, the Council of Ten, lamenting past practices of the Patriarchal Court and ecclesiastical lawyers, asserted that it was entitled to review petitions for separation. The flood of petitions for marital dissolution were yet another threat to the Republican myth of peace and stability.

The broader community of friends and neighbors also played an important role in regulating marriage. This included encouraging the cohesion and continuity of the family and its wider networks of alliances and mediating property disputes. Priests acted as family therapists, while midwives counseled and assisted women in their childbearing years. Female servants assisted new brides as well as distraught wives. Neighbors censured misbehavior and upheld firm gender expectations. Husbands were expected to maintain their spouses and treat them well in exchange for fidelity. Thus the role played by Venetian communities in regulating marriage and family was critical. We must exercise caution in placing too much emphasis on marital breakup. Neither it nor marital satisfaction or bliss can be quantified. There is evidence for loving marriages, as Chojnacki demonstrates in his study of fifteenth-century patrician couples.[13] The wills of husbands and wives reveal mutual trust and generosity as well as mutual respect. It is difficult to reconstruct a history of marital relations and emotions, and we must be very careful not to overemphasize stories of marital breakup. At the end of the day, we cannot know the degree to which the desire for marital dissolution was common or the exception within society at large. However, the marital litigation recorded in the Patriarchal Courts does give us important insights into the challenges people faced in their intimate lives.

Orthodox Christians

Orthodox Christians deserve a separate note, for the Venetian state permitted those who were its subjects to keep their family laws.[14] Orthodox Christians sought redress from their bishops without interference from civil authorities. In Venice the Bishop of Philadelphia led the Greek Orthodox church, following canon law and the decrees of the orthodox emperors, under Byzantine law. While for the most part dissolution of marriage was discouraged, in special cases it was allowed.

The Greek Orthodox bishop did not address civil disputes, which were taken up in the Venetian tribunals of the Procurator and the Proprio. Both Byzantine and Venetian law penalized an adulterous wife by awarding her dowry to her husband. If the husband remarried, she could wed once again as well. Until then, the Giudici del Procurator assigned the wife a maintenance stipend, calculated at 6 percent of the dowry. In the case of an adulterous or abusive husband, the wife retained the entire dowry, and if the husband had dissipated her resources she could bring suit for restoration. The Giudici del Proprio, on the other hand, both registered dowries and returned them to widows, whether Greek Orthodox or Roman Catholic.

The Venetian civil tribunals also decided which of the spouses received custody of the children, just as in Roman Christian marriages. Byzantine and Venetian legal practice were the same. During the period of litigation, the father retained custody, while the spouse who was not held at fault ultimately was awarded care of the children.

---

8. Unwed Mothers, Invisible Fathers, and Infant Casualties

While theologians at the Council of Trent had reminded Catholics that marriage was the only legitimate path to reproduction, the exhortation was impossible to enforce.[15] There were times when both monogamy and clerical vows were breached, and lovers, family members, masters and servants, priests and concubines, Jews and Christians, nobles and commoners followed their own impulses. The widespread practice of restricted marriage and arranged marriage at the upper ranks of society encouraged men to make living arrangements with women of lower classes, and thus contributed to the problem of illegitimate births. Priests who found celibacy difficult added to the problem as well. They too were tracked, even coerced, early on to a vocation for which they did not necessarily have a calling, and they strayed.

Ordinary women who cohabited with men were particularly vulnerable under Tridentine rules, for their offspring were denied legitimacy and they were deprived of motherhood. The state upheld these standards, especially during the eighteenth century, by freeing men from claims of paternity. In Catholic areas, infant abandonment to foundling homes and infant death spiraled in consequence. In contrast, Protestant territories took a different approach, obliging partners to support their offspring. Moreover, women were entitled to file paternity claims.

Within the Venetian state, both Venice and its subject cities became secret refuges for unmarried pregnant women from rural areas who, sometimes with their partners, took temporary lodgings, gave birth, and then deposited their infants in foundling homes such as the one at the Church of Santa Maria della Pietà in Venice. This practice, motivated to avoid dishonor, has been documented throughout Italy since the thirteenth century, but it was more frequent in times of demographic growth and high levels of poverty.

Infant death was a graver disturbance than infant abandonment to foundling homes. In cases of suspected homicide, Venetian authorities depended on urban and rural neighbors to alert them and shed light on the circumstances surrounding the crime. Ordinary people complied when summoned to supply information, but they did not necessarily share the viewpoints of authorities. Instead priests, physicians, midwives, neighbors, parents, and siblings exercised their own judgment in what to offer their interrogators. Clerics and statesmen had defined the crime, but the community in certain circumstances was more forgiving. They had the power to be so because Venetian judges depended upon their version of events to construct their cases.

The procedures for Venetian justice, which shared common elements with judicial systems in other parts of Italy, merit comment. Investigators, who depended on the testimony of eyewitnesses, weighed credibility in terms of social class, biological sex, and manifest emotions during interrogation as well as overall reputation. This was the competency of the state attorney in Venice and the podestà in various parts of the empire. Inevitably this involved the prosecutor's own gender and class biases, but the quiet intercession of the community, through testimony from gossip networks, influenced the outcome of the investigation in important ways. In essence, gossip informed law and judicial praxis.

The prime culturally constructed perpetrator of infanticide and abortion was the unmarried woman. Her partner, perhaps a nobleman, a cleric, or a close male relative, remained invisible. Save for the latter, they were all protected by law. Hidden crimes are very difficult for the historian to document. My own research has uncovered just a few priests and laymen visiting apothecaries and mixing abortion potions or abandoning infants. Moreover, there is even scarcer evidence for incestuous relationships, which were rarely reported not only because of the shame and dishonor they brought to families but because the punishment for such nefarious crimes, to use contemporary terminology, was decapitation and incineration.

Venetian governors upheld legitimate marriage and reproduction in order to maintain social stability. Sexual practices outside the marital bond created both social and financial liabilities for the state. Thus, authorities were regularly called upon to regulate sexuality and domestic abuse. Sexual commerce between Christians and people of other religions was discouraged, together with intraclass unions. Incest and sodomy, on the other hand, were punished by death.

Asylums for women were one way to avoid such tragic consequences both for women and for male perpetrators of sex crimes. Asylums and other forms of female enclosure proliferated from the late sixteenth century, an emphatic comment on male anxiety over women's sexuality and fear about the spread of disease. There was also the need to protect the inheritance system of entail and primogeniture that the nun Arcangela Tarabotti had denounced and that her literary predecessor, Moderata Fonte, had fought by suing for a share of her own father's estate. In this regard, Schutte has pointed out in her study of the years between 1668 and 1793 that victimization was not necessarily gender-specific, for parents forced sons to take monastic vows as well as daughters.[16]

It is important to emphasize, however, that not all women shared the view about convent experience expressed by Tarabotti and Fonte. Historians have supplied rich evidence that nuns enjoyed happy intellectual and cultural lives, and that remaining single spared them the dangers of multiple pregnancies. The family of the noted fifteenth-century humanist Francesco Barbaro is a prime example: three of his five daughters appear to have voluntarily entered convents. The eldest was devoted to studying the classics as well as Christian antiquity. Barbaro was certainly wealthy enough to arrange marriages for his children, but they expressed other choices, and he valued the spiritual succor they brought to him.[17]

The age of enclosure corresponded with the persecution for witchcraft, though Italy had far fewer witches than northern Europe. Both were part of the male culture of honor that exculpated men and stigmatized women who freely expressed their power and sexuality. Witness the gendered rhetoric: asylums "rehabilitated whores." There was no equivalent for unmarried, sexually active men. The eighteenth-century courts in Venice quickly excused men who had impregnated unmarried women when the accused brought in a variety of male witnesses to testify that the woman had had sex with all of them. Class bias prevailed as well. A peasant or worker had little hope of defending his male honor before a nobleman who had cohabited and impregnated his sister. The aristocratic state honored rank and privileged the male sex. Married women, on the other hand, had better recourse.

Unmarried women risked everything, but many had no choice but to cohabit in order to subsist. If, however, both church and state failed them, the community must be given credit for assisting them. Among these unmarried women were so-called free women, who were probably considered prostitutes. They offered lodgings to unmarried pregnant women, often from the countryside, assisted in childbirth and postpartum care, called for additional assistance from priests, and counseled women on how to remove themselves from harm's way. Free women were an important presence in both urban and rural environments, together with midwives and village healers. Thus unwed mothers were not alone.

In conclusion, Venetian notions of order, stability, and social hierarchy often overlooked how people lived. Orthodox Christianity had not permeated all segments of society; nor was religion only in the hands of priests. Moreover, something was amiss in the systems of arranged marriage, female virginity, and clerical celibacy: sex and the body got in the way of the secular model of family estate management as well as Catholic morality. Neighborhoods and groups stood behind their friends. Diverging from the legal frameworks of church and state, they quietly turned upside down the hierarchies of class and gender professed by Venetian clerics and lawmakers.

FURTHER READING

Asylums and Charities: S. Cohen (1992); B. Pullan (1971). *Convents and Monasteries*: A. Schutte (2011); J. Sperling (1999); E. Weaver (2002). *Documents*: D. Chambers and B. Pullan (1992). *Judicial Institutions and Case Examples*: G. Cozzi (1958, 1976, 1980, 1981, 1982); R. Derosas (1980); E. Horodowich (2008); C. Povolo (1980, 1996, 1997). *Intellectual History*: W. Bouwsma (1968). *Inquisition*: P. Grendler (1977); P. Ioli-Orattini (2001); B. Pullan (1997). *Marriage and Alternative Lifestyles*: A. Cowan (2007). *Religious History*: J. Martin (1993). *Sexuality and Disease*: J. Ferraro (2001b, 2008); L. McGough (2011); G. Ruggiero (1985, 1993, 2001, 2007). *Witchcraft*: R. Martin (1989). *Women's History and Writings*: V. Cox (1995); J. Ferraro (2001b, 2008); M. Fonte (1997); R. Goffen (1997); D. Hacke (2004); M. King (1991); P. La Balme (1981); M. Laven (2002); M. Rosenthal (1993); A. Schutte (2001). *Violence*: G. Ruggiero (1980).

8

THE BAROQUE STAGE

Venice's position as a European state and a global commercial force after 1630 lies in the shadow of its medieval and Renaissance glory. No longer a dominant Mediterranean power, the Republic also began to lose its status as a first-rank European state. By 1625 French, English, Dutch, and Hanseatic ships had assumed prominence in the Mediterranean. The rising cost of lumber and the difficulties in acquiring sufficient supplies of hemp made it too costly for Venice's shipbuilders to keep up with the foreigners' superior vessels. Moreover, the Venetians had continued to rely on antiquated navigational methods. Even Venetian merchants preferred to rent foreign-made ships rather than use the ones produced in their own shipyard. Venetian sea power also suffered because Mediterranean piracy escalated notably after 1570. Ottoman Turks, Albanians, Corsairs, Spanish, Maltese, Tuscans, Neapolitans, and Sicilians all raided Venetian ships, causing heavy losses. Uskok and Barbary pirates wore down the transport business, compelling merchants either to take less efficient overland routes or to send their cargo via foreign ships in order to avoid further losses from raiding marauders. Venetian patrician families, rich from centuries of trade, were unmotivated to take further risks. They substituted agents for themselves on the long sea expeditions that once occupied their energies.

The relative loss of commercial vigor in the decades following 1630 prompted several historians during the 1960s to conclude that the Venetian economy was caught in the throes of an irreversible decline, a conclusion that has triggered a long and lively historiographical debate. Revisionist studies of the 1970s, notably that of Richard Rapp, argued that the decline in foreign trade was relative rather than absolute, a position that has since gained considerable consensus. Rapp further maintained that workers in traditional crafts managed to maintain a uniform standard of living throughout the seventeenth century, a conclusion that generated further

Figure 38. Francesco Guardi (1712–93). *The Feast of Maundy Thursday in Venice,* Italy. Oil on canvas. Photo: Béatrice Hatala. Location: Louvre, Paris, France. Photo Credit: Réunion des Musées Nationaux/Art Resource, NY. Image Reference: ART166588.

controversy.[1] Most recently, some historians of the economy have diminished the importance of maritime trade altogether, casting deep doubt upon the concept of decline both in absolute and relative terms. Researchers in this group conceptualize Venice and its territories as one economic system, composed of autonomous but interrelated networks that produced a thriving regional economy.[2] These debates permit at best tenuous conclusions about the health of the Republic's economy during its last two centuries. First, not all sectors fell into absolute decline. The agricultural sector focused on the cultivation of maize, rice, and mulberries, crops that had a profitable outcome.[3] Second, the commercial sector underwent a temporary decline and transformation during the seventeenth century, but the Republic was financially vigorous enough to engage in war to conquer the Peloponnese (1689–99) and thus acquire another maritime colony. Further, after 1735 Venetian commerce tripled, especially with the Ottoman Empire. Finally, in the manufacturing sector, entrepreneurs readjusted to contingent circumstances, with certain industries making a full recovery in Venice and others developing within a regional industrial economy. At the same time, the city continued to exhibit considerable social and cultural vitality, a boon to its tourist industry.

Venice's economic history during the last two centuries of the Republic thus demands analysis from multiple perspectives. The view from the land is quite different from that of the sea. If Venice was no longer the Queen of the Adriatic, its maritime activities were still intact and vital. At the same time the Dominante became a flourishing city of spectacle, drawing an international clientele and capitalizing on the profits that derived from its eternal allure, while the Venetian mainland, the site of large-scale agriculture and rural manufacture, helped sustain family fortunes and the state coffers. Material life continued to thrive among the prosperous, and spectators effusively hailed the efflorescence of the Venetian Baroque and flamboyant Rococo.

1. The Political Theater

The seventeenth century opened with a political duel of international interest between the state and the Holy See as Venice asserted its right to restrict ecclesiastical wealth within its territories. The transfer to the church of real property, a vital state resource both for raw materials and tax revenue, was a concern that required decisive intervention. Increasingly over the sixteenth century the lands of the mainland had assumed primary importance in the Republic's economy and strategic importance within the fiercely competitive Italian-state system. They could not be sacrificed to pious donations. The state was determined to set limits to Counter-Reformation devotion. A confluence of mutual interests with the French Crown led the latter to mediate between Venetian rulers and the pope, who had reached a performative standoff before their European spectators. Rome ultimately relented and lifted the interdict, a victory that boosted the confidence of the party of young patricians at the helm of Venetian government.

A more perilous storm nonetheless was brewing: Hapsburg expansion on the Peninsula literally encircled Venice. The Spanish branch of this potent dynasty occupied Lombardy and all of southern Italy, while the Austrian one dominated the lands to the north and northeast of Venice. Under the leadership of Niccolò Contarini, the Young Party abandoned the Republic's century-long policy of neutrality and between 1615 and 1618 embroiled Venice in two wars. The first erupted on the northeastern frontier, on the lands of the Austrian archduke, which the Uskok pirates of Senj were using as a base to harry Venetian shipping. During the hostilities, the Venetians displayed their penchant for macabre civic ritual by showcasing the decapitated heads of their enemies in Piazza San Marco. The pirates retaliated, capturing a Venetian commander and consuming his heart. The skirmish ended with the arch-duke consenting to vacate the Uskoks, but Venice's eastern frontier was secure no more. Moreover, the Adriatic Sea, which ensured Venetian independence, was vulnerable to the designs of the Spanish viceroy in Naples, the duke of Ossuna. He soon deployed a squadron of Uskoks and Ragusans to occupy Venetian shipping routes along the waterways and encouraged Corsair pirates based on the southern shores of the Adriatic to capture Venetian vessels. Once again the Republic, under the Young, dodged the Hapsburg offensive, and at the same time mounted a counterdefense on the western front by generously subsidizing the Savoyards in their battle with the Spanish governor of Milan. Ossuna then plotted with the Spanish ambassador to Venice, the marquis of Bedmar, to overthrow the government, but the Council of Ten ferreted out the traitors and expelled Bedmar in 1622. One Venetian nobleman, Antonio Foscarini, was unjustly convicted of selling state secrets to the Spanish. He was acquitted postmortem, having been strangled and publicly hanged by a leg at the columns in the Piazzetta at Saint Mark.

The Republic managed to escape the Hapsburgs for the time being but was no match for their military or financial strength. When the Thirty Years' War broke out in 1618, the patriciate judiciously adopted a neutral stance and retreated to the lagoon. Unwisely, they ventured out once more in 1630, to aid the duke of Nevers in his bid for the duchy of Mantua, but failed mis-erably in the face of Hapsburg forces. The Holy Roman Emperor's armies sacked the duchy before retreating and gifted Venice with a plague that sav-aged 50,000 souls and crippled the Republic's military force.

On the eve of the 1630 plague, there were also festering sores in the Venetian leadership. In 1628, Ranieri Zeno challenged the authority of the doge, Giovanni Corner, a scion of one of Venice's oldest dynasties. Belonging to the "*Longhi*," the group of families that had held the dogeship regularly until 1381 but were then kept from high office until Corner's ascendancy in 1612, the doge's expanding influence raised alarm: his sons held both church offices and positions in the Senate, in violation of the laws of the Republic. Zeno, currying the favor of a disgruntled group of impoverished nobles, attempted to break Corner's hold over the Signoria. The reforming impulse, however, fell apart, and the dichotomy between rich and poor continued to create rifts.

Besides the travails of factionalism, the patriciate was also experiencing attrition: between 1550 and 1594 the number of male nobles shrank from 2,500 to 2,000; by 1631 there were only 1,666, or around 1 percent to 1.5 percent of the population. The drop generated animated discussion over whether to sell admissions to the patriciate to new families, a move that would ward off bankruptcy but also tarnish the purity of the aristocracy. Ultimately, bloodline was sacrificed to financial expediency and 127 new families entered the Great Council between 1647 and 1797. Among them were the Widmann from northern Europe and the Manin from the Friuli. Still, however, the new admissions did not stave off the decline in numbers. Throughout the eighteenth century a mere 200 dynasties prevailed, with forty-two actually running the government and filling approximately 700 government positions. Of these only a few – the Pisani, Corner, Manin, Labia, and Rezzonico – retained great affluence. When the Republic fell in 1797, 1,000 nobles remained. Neither restricted marriage nor biology had favored the endogamous constitutional elite in their efforts to reproduce dynastic lines.

On balance, throughout the seventeenth century Venice continued to earn the admiration of all of Europe for avoiding the kind of constitutional crisis that afflicted England and culminated with the decapitation of King Charles I. It had also escaped Hapsburg domination, unlike Campania, Sicily, and Lombardy. But the Republic had lost stature to the rising Atlantic states, and its seaborne markets struggled with marauding pirates and Ottoman dominance in the Greek archipelago and Dalmatia. As the plague subsided in 1631, an Ottoman fleet of 400 set sail from Constantinople to Crete, Venice's last colony on the eastern Mediterranean Sea and a key stepping-stone to Levantine commerce. The patricians mustered all their naval might, using the 100,000-ducat entrance fees of each of the new families as well as the tax revenues from the mainland to fortify the Republic's military complex. Between 1645 and 1716, they engaged in three wars with the Ottomans, in Dalmatia, the Aegean, and the Ionian Seas. The Republic proved to be more than able to hold Dalmatia, even tripling the size of the territories that came under St. Mark's Lion. The arduous effort to retain control of Crete, however, a struggle that endured for more than two decades, largely ended in failure, despite both moral encouragement and financial support from other Christian powers intent on keeping the Ottomans at bay. The noted admiral Francesco Morosini finally yielded Candia in 1669, retaining only a few minor naval bases on Crete as well as the Aegean islands of Tine and Cerigo. Nonetheless, the Republic suffered heavy losses in human resources and capital: 250 patricians perished in war or from disease. But the navy still proved to be strong and there were sufficient public revenues from the tax base to confront the Ottomans once again. In 1683, at the invitation of Austria, Poland, and Russia, Venice joined an anti-Ottoman alliance, along with Tuscan, Roman, and Maltese forces. Admiral Morosini recovered Athens (unfortunately setting off an ammunition explosion in the Parthenon that blew a hole through the roof) and the Morea (the Peloponnese) between

1685 and 1688. When he returned to Venice he was declared a hero and made doge. Both the Morea and the Ionian islands became Venetian colonies. Venice's allies then concluded the Treaty of Karlowitz in 1699, permitting the Republic a fifteen-year hiatus from military engagement. Significantly, the Republic's revenues were rich enough to finance armed neutrality while the Bourbons and the Hapsburgs plunged into a prolonged war over the Spanish Succession (1699–1714).

In 1714, the Ottomans took advantage of the exhaustion that the Spanish Succession War had brought to Venice's European allies and wrested the Morea from the Republic. Despite the loss, Venice continued to avoid involvement in the War of the Austrian Succession (1740–48) and to maintain naval strength, focusing largely on the protection of its commercial interests against marauding pirates. French, Dutch, and English commercial power had surpassed that of the Republic on Mediterranean waters, and rival ports such as Trieste (1719), under the aegis of the Austrian emperor, and Ancona, which the pope declared a free port in 1732, challenged Venetian hegemony on the Adriatic. Nonetheless, port traffic in Venice remained strong as did the shipping industry and ship construction throughout the eighteenth century.

FRANCESCO MOROSINI (1619–94)

Francesco Morosini came from a prominent patrician family that bestowed Venice with several military heroes and doges. He distinguished himself as a naval admiral in several of the Republic's conflicts with pirates and political rivals. He first rose in stature in 1650 at the Battle of Naxos as captain general of the Venetian Navy. From there he led a series of successful campaigns against the Ottoman Turks. During the siege of Candia he commanded more than 3,600 men with few provisions to defend the fortress. Although he and his troops fought valiantly, Morosini was forced to surrender after eighteen months of battle to the Grand Vizier, Ahmed Koprulu, on September 27, 1669.

Morosini also commanded a naval fleet with Venice's new seventy-gun ships against the Ottoman Turks in the Morea in 1685, allying with the indigenous Greeks to resist an Ottoman takeover. He succeeded in conquering most of the Morea with the assistance of the Swedish officer Otto Wilhelm Königsmarck. As a result, Morosini was honored as a *Peloponnesiacus*, or resident of the Peloponnesus. In 1687, Morosini laid siege to Athens, razing several historical monuments to the ground. He returned to Venice in 1688 to become doge. He led his final campaign in 1693 and lost Negroponte. He died the following year. Morosini's great naval expeditions were recorded in a collection of paintings currently kept in the Correr Museum.

Against the backdrop of Ottoman and European wars, the Venetian patriciate stayed its course, but not without internal schisms, calls for reform, and anxiety about attrition. One problem involved the unequal distribution of wealth and power. In the course of the seventeenth and eighteenth centuries, the number of patrician families that remained within the inner circle of influence diminished. A small oligarchy dominated the Ten, the Court of Forty, and the State Inquisitors. Between 1760 and 1780, nobles such as Angelo Querino and Giorgio Pisani challenged this narrowing basis of power. Pisani, an impoverished noble, wished to preserve the entire constitutional elite, including the poorer ranks whose indigence debased the aristocracy as a whole. He called for financial reforms to aid the less fortunate, such as placing ceilings on dowries and raising government stipends. He further advocated a redistribution of aristocratic power. Pisani, however, fell into disfavor with the more conservative elements of the patriciate and was imprisoned in 1780. In the wake of liberal revolutionary movements in France and the American colonies and a growing body of French Enlightened philosophers such as Voltaire, Rousseau, and Kant, who criticized political abuse, some rich oligarchs remained intractable. The exegeses of Hobbes and Locke on rights to liberty and property and Rousseau's call for social contracts fell on deaf ears. Reactionary oligarchs adhered to the hereditary privileges of aristocracy. Others, however, more in sympathy with Pisani managed to effect important, nuanced change by resuscitating the ancient Venetian practice of correction, that is, to adjust the extreme imbalance in power. Thus in 1780, some of the rich families relinquished control of the Council of Ten to the middling families and restored power to the Senate. This was the kind of flexibility that permitted the patriciate to endure as a constitutional elite for five centuries. Nonetheless, political power continued to consolidate in some magistracies, despite the corrections. The six Savii Grandi in the College controlled business and foreign affairs, while the three State Inquisitors gradually assumed the competencies of the Council of Ten. The Senate held moderate power with the ascent of some middling families, but nine men sat at the apex of oligarchy while a clique of nobles educated in law served on the Court of Forty. A portion of the patriciate remained poor and uneducated, a few receiving minor instruction at the Accademia della Giudecca. Referred to as the Barnabotti because they received government housing in the neighborhood of San Barnaba, they sold their votes to the powerful and acted as clients for great patrons in exchange for benefits.

A portion of the nobility also expressed anxiety about the superior wealth of men in commerce who desired a political voice. The patrician Andrea Tron, whose own family owned a woolen industry in the Vicentine, urged the nobility in 1784 to return to mercantile activities to reinforce their economic energies. At the same time he adhered to the more traditional principles of noble birthright and privilege that separated patricians from merchants outside the constitutional elite. The three State Inquisitors, who availed themselves of secret informers and police, supported Tron's stance.

The strength of the patriciate's inner oligarchy stemmed in great part from the fact that few nobles could afford to hold high office. In compensation, the secretaries from the citizen class who flanked the inner circle and over generations acted as an important second-tier oligarchy, ran the government, providing the continuity that the nobility, by rotating offices, lacked. Destitute patricians were willing to pay a fine rather than serve the state. The ambassadorships to other European capitals were especially expensive. In a sign of its resilience, the patriciate periodically took measures to address this problem. The Great Council accepted new admissions for the sum of 100,000 ducats per family during the Ottoman wars between 1645 and 1718. At this time 127 persons joined the patrician ranks. Approximately 20 percent were mainland nobles; another 20 percent had been trained as lawyers or chancery officials from the citizen class; and the other 60 percent were merchants who quickly abandoned commerce to undertake the obligatory lifestyles of rentiers. Again in 1775, the patriciate made a place in the Great Council for forty new families from the Venetian mainland who could prove their local nobility for four generations, but a mere ten families submitted applications, a reflection of the fundamental lack of cohesion between the Venetian ruling class and its provincial elites. In a further attempt to arrest their demographic decline, the patriciate adjusted the constitution to permit sons born of marriages between their order and the citizen class to enter the Great Council as well. There was, then, periodically an infusion of new blood into the Venetian patriciate in the twilight years of the Republic.

2. Economic Spheres

The economic dynamics of the Republic underwent restructuring after 1630, but the catalysts for change had begun in the sixteenth century. The long struggle with the Ottomans had weighed heavily on patrician resources, making investment near home more attractive to this particular segment of society. First, the loss of Cyprus in 1571 had been a heavy blow for estate owners who had relied on income from salt, sugar, cotton, and grain produced there. Cyprus had also been an important port for navigation to Syria. Second, the mounting costs of warfare helped to produce a credit run that toppled two of the three private banks in Venice in 1570, and the Pisano-Tiepolo bank followed in 1584. The banking crisis, however, created willingness to allow foreign merchant communities in Venice to have a greater share of the commercial markets. The Spanish and Portuguese Jews took over more of the import business with the Levant and marketed Venetian products there into the eighteenth century. Moreover, they gave employment to large numbers of sailors, under the command of Dalmatian shipmasters.

Venetian patricians turned to other forms of income. One outlet for investment was to buy a share of the fiscal profits of tax farmers. The state auctioned off the various consumption taxes to buyers, who took a certain degree of risk if they failed to make their bids. Thus nobles made collective investments, similar to the shared risk typical of the merchant insurance business. Another source of income was personal lending. Because usury was prohibited by the church, these loans were disguised as fictitious leases on real property. In the eighteenth century yet another avenue for accruing income was savings banks, established by the confraternities that had accumulated great endowments. Nobles came to favor these banks over investing in government bonds. Others turned in the late eighteenth century to the newly burgeoning shipping industry in Trieste. Two Venetians, Carlo and Balthazar Rossetti, began shipping coffee. The poorer nobles, on the other hand, sought military commands or minor governorships on the mainland that sometimes afforded opportunities for illicit profit.

The shift of the patricians away from the sea made the resources of the Venetian territorial state central to their wealth. For most, real estate offered a safer window of opportunity, for by the sixteenth century the growing population demanded greater cereal production. The seventeenth-century aristocracy gradually assumed much of the property that had once been owned by the peasantry, and in the eighteenth century they divested the church of some its holdings. As large landowners in the Veneto plains, patricians astutely undertook reclamation work and improved irrigation to increase the production of food, especially maize, to cushion against famine. This turn to agriculture was vital both to Venice and to the rest of the mainland population. Between 1540 and 1570, population pressure had become acute, and regions on whom the Venetians had relied for food were experiencing shortages. Moreover, the 1590s witnessed a great agricultural crisis in the Mediterranean. Thus the price of victuals remained high. After 1577, the population rose steadily on the mainland, from 1.5 million to over 2 million people. Eighteenth-century population levels exceeded those of the sixteenth century, making agriculture a profitable investment.

Increasing the food supply during the eighteenth century required improved technology. A small group of middle-class, physiocrat reformers recognized the importance of agriculture and carried on discussions about how to raise the status of peasants and interest them in developing the land. There were also discussions about freeing the grain trade from Venetian protectionism. In 1766, the Venetian patrician Andrea Memmo tried to arrest spiraling grain prices by establishing agrarian academies in every major city of the Venetian mainland. He had several models to choose from: within the Venetian state, that of Udine; in Tuscany, the Accademia dei Giorgiofili, whose gentlemen were trying to revive the poor Maremma region; in Vienna, Maria Theresa's Royal Agricultural Society. The most important model, however, was in Venice's backyard, in neighboring Padua, where Memmo created the Accademia di Scienze, Lettere, ed Arti in 1779. The academicians took on grave social and economic problems: pernicious labor contracts, obsolete taxes, unregulated hunting and grazing, peasant ignorance, and the growing body of advanced knowledge emanating from circles of agronomists. Information on the best and most advanced practices was gathered into an encyclopedia under the supervision of Giovanni Scola for the purpose of improving the agrarian economy. Academicians encouraged the Venetian Senate to study land reclamation, experiment with new crops, invest in irrigation projects, and adapt advanced hydraulics and engineering, efforts that paved the way in the nineteenth century for applying agrarian theory to landholding and government policy.

Late patrician reformers like Memmo, and to some extent Querini and Tron, thus turned to Padua, not France; to a tradition of science and technology linked to Galileo and later Newton that fostered improved agriculture, better terms of land tenure, improved practices at the Arsenal, and patronage of the sciences, arts, and letters. They were committed to preserving the intellectual vitality of the Venice-Padua nexus. It was at the university, which accommodated an international student body, that the practical, technical, and mechanical dimensions of culture had advanced since the mid-sixteenth century. Notably, the Venetian Senate had hired the mathematician Galileo Galilei in 1587 to teach fortifications and mechanics, and the famed scientist invented a hydraulic device for irrigation and drainage. The University of Padua also constructed the first institutionalized observatory and, with Vesalius, initiated a revolution in anatomy. The medical school led the European world with the rediscovery of Galen and Averroes in Arab science, while Girolamo Fabrizio d'Aquapendente founded the first anatomical theater in 1594 and Santorio Santorio designed medical measuring instruments. It was to Padua that the learned turned to study mathematics, botany, anatomy, and surgery. In addition to the university, a number of prominent agrarian academies had sprung up in the Venetian territories, notably in Padua and in Brescia, where gentlemen scientists were experimenting with new crops in order to go beyond subsistence and reach a level of commercial agriculture, an endeavor that would continue into the modern age.

The manufacture of goods also underwent restructuring after 1630, successfully adapting to changing markets. Venice and the towns of the mainland became smaller, more specialized centers of manufacture than their respective rural hinterlands. Moreover, regional structures acquired preeminence, intertwining urban and rural venues in important ways. Venice relied on country dwellers to supply it with a variety of products made in rural homes, but the central government of this important regional state was also careful to impose protectionist policies, such as obliging rural entrepreneurs to purchase their raw materials in Venice, in order to maximize profit. Moreover, Venice continued to import raw materials such as wool, cotton, dyes, leather, soda ash, and lead for its own urban manufactures through the seventeenth century.[4]

The labor force in Venice itself changed. In the sixteenth century, continual immigration to the lagoon had created a plentiful supply of arsenal, wool, and silk workers as well as printers, stonemasons, fullers, millworkers, glassmakers, leather workers, smiths, lead crystal workers, canal dredgers, and employees of sugar refineries and wax- and soap-works. However, in the seventeenth century, shrinking demand as well as state taxes and a government reluctant to support technological innovation made working in the city less attractive for certain crafts. The wool industry in Venice collapsed the earliest, by 1550, but it thrived in Bergamo through the seventeenth century. The silk industry, on the other hand grew in Venice and on the mainland until the fall of the Republic in 1797, exporting to European markets. Although no figures are available, one can suppose that the construction industry was healthy as well, given the number of patrician palaces and country villas that went up during the seventeenth and eighteenth centuries. Glass production in Venice dipped and then refocused, prioritizing popular items like beads and necklaces rather than luxury goods. Lace, printing, organ building, the manufacture of plucked and wind instruments, and gold castings for church ornamentation all survived in Venice. Moreover, the city's guilds as well as the government were apparently more flexible than previous historians have claimed, supporting the notion of a relative decline in seventeenth-century Venetian manufacture. In the following century, the patriciate evaluated the guilds and revived supervisorial magistracies to oversee them in order to improve economic activity and ameliorate unemployment.

Shipbuilding remained solid in Venice. The Arsenal was still Europe's biggest industrial center at the start of the seventeenth century. Between 1620 and 1660, it produced 350 fully armed light warships and sixty-five large ones plus numerous small auxiliary craft.[5] The government was successful in coopting workers' support by permitting them considerable self-governance. Moreover, the port, though stronger in imports than exports, retained its significance in the Mediterranean through the eighteenth century, and Venice continued to be populated with large numbers of sailors, fishermen, and boatmen.

Venice's richest Lombard possession, Brescia and its province, also enjoyed thriving industries during the seventeenth century.[6] The Bresciano was an important center for arms manufacture, catering to Lombard and northern European markets, and in the mountains north of this important subject city mining and metallurgy yielded vital metal goods, including buttons, farm implements, and cutlery. Warfare, which continued to escalate in Europe throughout the early modern period, heightened the demand for cuirasses, swords, pikes, harquebuses, cannons, and iron bullets, while cast iron was used to make utensils, cauldrons, saucepans, grates, andirons, fire-backs, and plowshares. Foundries in the mountain areas also produced metal sheets, bars, rods, and nails. Other examples of thriving industries on the mainland include the copper mines in Val Iperina north of Venice, which experienced growth, as did paperworks and sawmills. These industries, from which the Venetian government reaped taxes, created work for a peasant labor force at the ovens, forges, and waterwheels, as well as a demand for diggers, miners, and carters. Their productivity encouraged some patricians to invest in iron mines and gun factories.

While Venetians continued through the seventeenth and eighteenth centuries to specialize in a limited market of luxury silks, the production of most textiles shifted to the villages of the regional state. Small villages around Padua and Bergamo, endowed with water-power energy and abundant wood, became promising centers. In the Veneto a number of towns prospered from fulling wool cloth, but Italy's woolens overall, which were of high grade and finely carded, catered more to a small luxury market, while the new worsted textiles from England and Holland were less costly and thus in greater demand. Venice focused on brocades and damasks that were the rage of the aristocracy, while several other subject cities produced less costly grades of this fabric. Throughout northern Italy, small towns from Carnia to Brianza achieved regional recognition for their output of silk and silk thread, as well as linen, hemp, and wool. Verona and Padua were noted for their stockings and berets. In the foothills around Vicenza, a member of the Venetian patriciate, Niccolò Tron, established a textile factory on the English model in the late eighteenth century. Tron's entrepreneurship is not an isolated case among the

Venetian patriciate. Others invested in paper factories as well as small printing operations that would further fuel the demand for paper. Local nobilities
also effected improvements in manufacture in products ranging from silk to
bricks, ceramics and terra-cotta, cement, and medicines.

The proto-industries of the countryside are particularly important to the
history of women and children, for much of the activity took place in the
household, the basic unit of production as well as consumption.[7] Women
were spinners, weavers, embroiderers, and mercers as well as petty retailers, hawkers, and peddlers. Venice itself engaged women laborers as fustian
weavers, comb-makers, cappers, tailors, doublet-makers, secondhand dealers,
ironmongers, and haberdashers. Women in Venice also made cloth sails at the
Arsenal. Others were involved in the preliminary processes of silk making,
such as reeling, winding, throwing, and boiling silk filament. Furthermore,
they made soap; washed, bleached, and dyed fabric; and gathered feathers to
make pillows. With the gradual diffusion of the mulberry tree from medieval Sicily and Andalusia to sixteenth-century northern Italy, rural women
unwound cocoons of silk, combed them, spun them, and sold thread to
urban merchants. In mining areas they carried wood and salt, sorted and
washed ore, and prepared charcoal briquettes for use in smelting. In the
Bresciano, women made silk thread, silk buttons, and stockings and linen.
Finally, women were intrinsically involved in costume and dress, activities
that touch on raw materials, production, culture, and social hierarchy. We are
only just beginning to learn about them from historians of fashion and used
clothing. Most women, however, worked at home for little or no compensation in real wages; as a result, they elude the archival record.

To conclude, changes in agriculture and manufacture cannot simply be
seen as the product of patrician withdrawal from seafaring. Rather, they have
histories of their own, in the first case linked to climate, environment, and
demographics, and in the second to the labor policies of urban corporations
and governments, changing consumer markets, and international ascendancy
in specific manufacturing sectors. The plague of 1630 disrupted production,
accelerating some manufactures and slowing others, but the population had
recovered by 1660 (see Appendix I), and between 1660 and 1700 agriculture, proto-industry, and rural manufacture were growing. In light of these
cycles, historian Andrea Zannini suggests that we view the seventeenth century as a period of fluctuation with two phases, one of temporary adversity
between 1630 and 1660 and one of growth thereafter.[8] At the same time, it
is important to note that Venice was part of a changing world, one that was
becoming larger and more globalized. The Mediterranean and its caravels
shrank in size to one of many world ponds when better-rigged ships made

with northern timber and strong enough to carry cannon sailed the oceans to the Americas and Asia. Venice did not join the Atlantic powers colonizing world markets but instead its entrepreneurs readjusted, exercising dominion over northeast Italy, developing commercial agriculture and rural manufacture, sending out merchants to manage their commercial investments in the Mediterranean, and exploiting the tourist market at home, to which it offered a treasure trove of pleasures.

3. City of Spectacle

Trends in trade and manufacture are only part of the economic picture for the inhabitants of an alluring city that floats on water. The tourist industry offers yet another perspective. From the eleventh century, Venice had attracted pilgrims on Crusade to the Holy Land; businessmen from Southwest Asia, North Africa, and Europe; merchants attending the book, lace, and glass fairs; northern artists experimenting with Italian techniques and styles; and, increasingly from the sixteenth century, visitors eager to see the city's holy relics and treasures, majestic churches and palaces, paintings, and visual beauty. They were treated to a variety of music, from street songs to religious chant; spectacular processions, based on the religious and state calendars; the Ascension-day fairs (Fig. 39); Carnival season, which became increasingly commercialized; and professional theater and drama. By the eighteenth century, this center for international culture was an obligatory stop on the grand tour for young gentlemen like Edward Gibbon and Francis Drake, who were finishing their education and sharpening their political expertise. Moreover, approximately 30,000 of the city's 140,000 inhabitants were foreigners. Temporary visitors furnished steady income to innkeepers as well as those with simply a room to let, food vendors, taverns and inns, gondoliers and other boatmen, domestic servants, gambling hall and theater owners, courtesans, prostitutes, musicians, and the array of workers that staged spectacles. Codèga, or lantern-bearing guides who acted as bodyguards, accompanied the tourists through the dark labyrinth, where armed bands of robbers and assassins still lurked. Professional entertainers during Carnival season, partially funded by the Ten, included rope-dancers, acrobats, fortune-tellers, and exotic animal keepers who placed their beasts on display for a fee. Thus, from the sixteenth century Venice became increasingly Europe's entertainment capital (Fig. 38), and rulers wisely subsidized the city's attractions to encourage business.

The territorial wars that racked Venice's commercial empire did not hinder the splendor and innovation of culture at home, which developed in tandem with the tourist industry. Of particular importance, the city witnessed a

Figure 39. Gabriele Bella (fl.1700–50). *Old Fair of the "Sensa."* Location: Biblioteca Querini Stampalia, Venice, Italy. Photo Credit: Cameraphoto Arte, Venice/Art Resource, NY. Image Reference: ART163466.

revolution in music during the seventeenth century that resonated throughout Europe. To begin, San Marco's orchestra, soloists, and choirs developed a bass and harpsichord accompaniment, called *basso continuo*, that constituted a conceptual leap toward the Baroque cantata made so famous in the eighteenth century by Johann Sebastian Bach. Further, in 1613 the Procurators hired a pathbreaking singer and gambist from Mantua, Claudio Monteverdi (1567–1643), to be the conductor of San Marco. Monteverdi, a key founder of Baroque music, quickly absorbed Venetian musical culture and the city's penchant for staging elaborate public festivities. Unlike the Roman church, which subscribed to simple liturgical music, the Venetians favored ornate liturgy and pageantry. Works for solo voice, called monody, gained currency, leading the way to the first operas. The choir of San Marco soon was famous for its performances of oratorio and for singers and instrumentalists' musical virtuosity.

While the first opera was staged in sixteenth-century Florence, Venice came to fully develop the genre. The city had been filled during the sixteenth century with itinerant entertainers who enacted comedies in the streets and squares of the city, but the Jesuits, complaining repeatedly about their ribald performances, subdued the bacchanalia as the Counter-Reformation gained momentum. The entertainment world experienced a turning point in 1605–7, when the state, under interdict, expelled Loyola's religious order. The itinerant comics and musicians soon returned to the city, setting the stage for the development of opera. Benedetto Ferrari and Francesco Manelli directed the first traveling company to perform Monteverdi's work at the Tron family's theater at San Cassiano in 1637.

The success of the Tron encouraged other entrepreneurial families such as the Vendramin, Grimani, Giustiniani, and Contarini to capitalize on the popularity of Carnival season in Venice by also constructing opera theaters. Their business interests coincided with intellectual currents, incubated at the University of Padua, that had gained popularity among the more libertine patricians. The most influential intellectuals for opera were members of the Accademia degli Incogniti, founded in 1630. The Incogniti, signifying unknown or anonymous, was heavily attended by Venetian senators, officeholders, and foreigners, many of whom wrote libretti, novels, and moral and political essays. Followers of Cesare Cremonini, a philosophy professor at the University of Padua who was brought before the Inquisition for his unconventional interpretations of Aristotle, the academicians were well grounded in Greek mythology and Roman history, and they valued sensuality over Christian restraint.

Under the pen of Incogniti librettists, the research of musicologist Ellen Rosand shows, the myths of Venice, familiar to painters, sculptors, and pageantry makers, took on new artistic life with opera.[9] Theater productions during the early 1640s centered on the city's mythical origins and Roman legacy. Among them were Giulio Strozzi's La Finta Pazza, an opera stressing Venice's Trojan origins, and Francesco Busenello's La prosperità infelice di Giulio Cesare dittatore, where the city on water is represented on stage. In this production, the glory of Ancient Rome fades while Venice, escaping Attila's invasions, springs eternal. Themes around the birth of Venice gave way in the mid-1640s to exaltations of the Venetian Republic, which was purportedly modeled on Ancient Rome. In line with this kind of emulation, theater patrons like the Grimani compared their own opera houses with those of antiquity, vaunting their superiority. Operas framed in classical histories also made reference to contemporary events. By the 1650s, commercial rivalries with the Ottoman Turks occupied the stage, and the trading cities of the East provided backdrop for dramas lauding great naval heroes. The virtues of Venice repeatedly personified in the visual arts were now projected on stage and placed in the service of the state.

Opera also served as social commentary and criticism, as exemplified in Monteverdi's notorious Incoronazione di Poppea (1643), staged at the Grimani family's Teatro San Giovanni e Paolo. The librettist Francesco Busenello drew from Tacitus's *Annals of the Emperor Nero* for the main plot, which included a shocking climax by conventional moral standards. The emperor makes his adulterous lover Poppea an empress, a message championing infidelity over marriage. Edward Muir interprets the opera's appeal among contemporary audiences within the context of Venice's restrictive marital regime, where few patrician males were permitted to marry while the majority of patrician females were locked behind convent doors.[10] Despite the limits placed on marriage, celibacy was not the norm. Patrician males availed themselves of a wide assortment of concubines, courtesans, and whores, for which Venice was noted in all of Europe. These were largely women in poverty whose families could not afford to dower them or enclose them in convents and whose looseness, on the one hand, made authorities anxious but on the other fulfilled the sexual needs of certain segments of the male population. Seventeenth-century operas like *Poppea* featured women in the sex industry and underlined the disjunction between a society under the repressive governance of restricted marriage and the very human demands of the body. There is considerable irony in the fact that three years after *Poppea*'s debut the patriciate sold entrances to their membership, in a sense prostituting themselves by mixing their blood with the blood of outsiders. They thus abandoned their official responsibilities to protect the virgins of Venice and the purity of the aristocracy, duties indelibly etched in the city's iconography. Muir also reasons that musical theater was popular because it furnished masked patrons with a place to enjoy clandestine affairs in the privacy of their opera boxes.[11] Such licentious behavior was not a novelty for restless patrician youth. It was rooted in Carnival, and the absence of the Jesuits facilitated the libertine intellectual strain of the learned academies that rejected Counter-Reformation morality.

Opera became a major part of Venetian life and a world attraction. Several public opera houses, including the Teatro San Salvador, the Teatro Novissimo, the Teatro San Moisè, and the Teatro San Giovanni e Paolo, were open throughout the Carnival, from Ascension Day to June 15 and during September and November. The musical theater functioned as something much more than entertainment. Like ritual and pageantry, it conveyed messages and manipulated the emotions of spectators. It might celebrate a Venetian victory, such as that over the Ottoman Turks exemplified in Vivaldi's *Juditha Triumphans* (1716); or refer to political struggles, wars, and assassinations. Alternatively, through the more comic opera buffa, the audience was treated to the dilemmas of family conflicts like resistance to arranged marriage, abduction, and adultery. Venice had long availed itself of masterful technical entrepreneurs staging processions and Carnival spectacles. The innovative scenery of the seventeenth and eighteenth centuries served as a magnet for fans far and wide. The public was entertained and persuaded with such theatrical effects as collapsing buildings, gods and ghosts masked in fog and clouds, and simulations of lightning and thunder. By the eighteenth century, Venice housed some nineteen theaters, the last being La Fenice, or "The Phoenix," built in 1792. Patricians owned their boxes at La Fenice and passed them down to heirs over generations until the end of World War I.

The eighteenth century also witnessed a new spotlight for Venetian entertainment: the center of choral and instrumental music moved away from San Marco to the city's orphanages. Perhaps the most famous was that of the Pietà, the foundling home and church where the renowned composer Antonio Vivaldi (1678–1741) performed and trained orphan girls to sing. Between 1703 and 1740, Vivaldi wrote several compositions for female music ensemble. There were also performances of violin concertos, motets, large-scale choral works, and compositions for double chorus and orchestra. Vivaldi taught the orphans music theory and how to play musical instruments. The conservatory became so acclaimed that girls of legitimate parentage desired admission and musical training. As a result of conservatories like the Pietà and those attached to the Ospedali of the Incurabili, the Mendicanti, and the Ospedaletto, Venice attained further European renown for its music, another boost for the tourist industry. Drama and comedy were also popular cultural attractions.

Carlo Goldoni (1707–93) and Carlo Gozzi (1720–1806) turned away from the conventional French neoclassicism of the era and placed the peculiarities of Venetian culture in the limelight, using dialect that required the spectator to have some command of local vocabulary and an understanding of local traditions and idiosyncrasies. Both writers drew upon the commedia dell'arte, a genre based on improvised, unscripted characters with traditional plots, but their approaches to theater differed. With Goldoni, improvisation largely came to an end. His comedies, which appealed to both nobles and merchants, centered on the conflicts surrounding the human dilemmas of the middle class in love, marriage, social relations, and money. Gozzi, circulating in the Accademia dei Granelleschi, drew on folklore and employed more complex metaphors in his dramas. The works of both playwrights also found their way into opera libretti. Goldoni's closest contemporaries, Baldassare Galuppi (1706–85) and Antonio Salieri (1750–1825), adopted his plots, while Gozzi's narratives were also woven into the operas of Puccini and Prokofiev, during the nineteenth and twentieth centuries, respectively. Rooted in Venetian culture, the output of both writers ultimately reached a broad, European audience.

CARLO GOLDONI (1707–93)

The playwright and librettist Carlo Goldoni was born outside Venice in the province of Padua. The son of a physician, Goldoni obtained a classical education, studied law, and spent his early career practicing the legal profession in a variety of capacities. From an early age, however, he shared his grandfather's love for theater, reading Greek and Latin comedies. Like many men trained in letters, he decided to devote himself to theater rather than law.

Under the pen name "Pastor Arcade," Goldoni transformed Venetian theater, which had been largely based on the commedia dell'arte (improvised comedy). Instead of employing the stock of masked characters from the *commedie*, he introduced realistic depictions of daily life, documenting provincial life and manners. Goldoni combined honesty and wit to dramatize the daily life, values, and conflicts of the middle class. He is known for using the Venetian language and local colloquialisms.

Critics derided Goldoni for abandoning the poetic charms of Italian comedy, but his plays became very popular. Fans found his depictions of humanity witty and charming. There was also a universal familiarity in his writings that spoke to both human interaction and to intellectual currents. Ignoring religious themes, Goldoni instead promoted the secular values of rationality, civility, and humanism. He also drew attention to the importance of the middle class. Goldoni spurned aristocratic arrogance, intolerance, and the abuse of power, calling instead for temperance and dignity.

Venice played a significant role in the development of modern journalism at the beginning of the eighteenth century. Apostolo Zeno and Scipione Maffei founded the *Giornale dei Literati d'Italia*, while Gasparo Gozzi published *L'Osservatore Veneto* and *La Gazzetta Veneta*, papers that reviewed the plays of Goldoni and the ideas of Voltaire. Francesco Griselini's *Giornale d'Italia*, on the other hand, covered the natural sciences and agriculture, while the *Giornale Encyclopedia* carried reports and debates on Venetian history and contemporary events. Literary scholar Rebecca Messbarger also categorizes the eighteenth century as "The Century of Women," for women increasingly engaged in intellectual exchange not only through their salons but also by entering Italy's scientific academies.[12] This activity was qualitatively different from the Renaissance discursive tradition, a literary genre that had little effect on the political arena. The 1720s witnessed a serious discussion at the Accademia of the Ricoverati in Padua (founded by Galileo in 1599) over whether women should be admitted to the sciences as well as government. Aretafila Savini De'Rossi wrote a stinging rebuttal to Antonio Conti's argument that women were incapable of governing or engaging in science and the military. Along these lines, Francesco Algarotti (1712–64) was teaching a kind of Newtonianism for Ladies as enlightened citizens.

Discussions about literature, theater, science, and philosophy during the eighteenth century extended from the newspapers, fashion magazines, salons, academies, masquerades and balls, and gaming houses to the new, public coffeehouse. Coffee had become the craze in Venice since the 1660s; also wildly popular was chocolate from the new world, which was sweetened with sugar, making it just as addictive to the pleasure-seeking as coffee. Venice established one of the first cafés in Europe in 1720, with the name Triumphant Venice, ironic as the Republic had just relinquished the remnants of its Greek possessions to the Ottoman Turks. It was soon renamed Caffè Florian after its new owner Florian Francesconi. Florian's was an elegant establishment that served exotic drinks in porcelain cups with sugared pastries and chocolates. There philosophers like Rousseau held debates, lovers held trysts, rogues like Casanova seduced women, and masked figures celebrated Carnival in disguise, acting out fictitious roles. Caffè Florian hosted the famous cultural figures of the eighteenth century, including Goldoni, the Gozzi brothers, and the sculptor Canova. In the nineteenth century, Balzac frequented this renowned establishment for men of letters as well as Goethe, Byron, Proust, and Dickens. Besides Florian, there were two other popular meeting places in the eighteenth century, one on the Riva del Vin at Rialto and another in Campo San Stefano. Each disseminated the news of the day. Foreigners called upon the proprietors to ask for directions or other information about the city. At some point after the middle of the eighteenth century, according to Goldoni's plays, these coffee shops fell into ill repute, particularly because they became gambling houses, and in 1767 the government forbade women to enter them. After much contestation, the ban was softened, and women were permitted entrance at certain times of the year, if they wore masked disguises.

Venetian culture thus was entrepreneurial and designed to encourage international tourism. Visitors came for Carnival or other civic occasions like the Marriage of Venice to the Sea or the Ascension Day fairs, to see a play or an opera, but also to gamble. Gaming houses became very popular. They took their name from the Venetian word for a small house, *casinò*. The principal one was the Ridotto, established in 1638, in Palazzo Dandolo on the Grand Canal near San Moisè (Fig. 40). It had several rooms for gaming and refreshment. Many of the games like roulette, baccarat, and poker, came from France but their variations assumed Venetian names. There were also private gambling parlors, like those of Elena Venier, Caterina Sagredo Barbarigo, and Marina Sagredo Pisani. Nobles also gambled in cafés, theaters, and barbershops,

Figure 40. Pietro Longhi (1702–85) (after). *Il Ridotto* (Theater Lounge). Location: Ca'
Rezzonico, Venice, Italy. Photo Credit: Scala/Art Resource, NY. Image Reference:
ART 58378.

while the state held its own lottery. There was some fear over licentiousness in
these gaming venues, but the primary anxiety, in the context of a state always
looking for revenues and trying to balance the public debt, was that many
nobles were gambling away their patrimony. The State Inquisitors closed
Barbarigo's establishment on the Giudecca in 1747, and the Great Council
shut down the Ridotto in 1768. Caterina Dolfin Tron was holding salon at
the San Giuliano casinò, a perceived hotbed of radical ideas from France, until
the Inquisitors closed it down. Other parlors, however, sprang up, and there
were some 150 gambling houses until the end of the Republic. The memoirs
of Giacomo Casanova (1725–98), the immortalized seducer, tell endless tales
of debauchery in these establishments.

Entrepreneurs readily accommodated tourists wishing to take home
mementos. There were glass objects, lace, and cityscapes. Venice held such
natural charm as an aquatic city whose monuments seemed to magically
float on water that view painting became an important genre. Canaletto and
Bernardo Bellotto spearheaded the movement. Francesco Guardi followed,
but unlike the first two painters his renderings of the city were more imagi-
nary than real. What stands out about Venetian culture during this period

besides its entrepreneurial purpose is its intense localism, whether in music, theater, or landscape painting. Venice remained the central subject holding the spectator's gaze.

4. The City as Stage

Spectacle remained a primary means of making political statements in Venice, and the grand processions and elaborate music required monuments that measured up to the pageantry. Venetian ideology during the Counter-Reformation lent itself to the construction of landmarks symbolizing the Republic's political values. While Rome was adorned with dramatic visions of spiritual ecstasy, exemplified in such statuary as Bernini's *Saint Teresa*, Venetians retained their secular sensibilities. They had triumphed over the papacy and the interdict at the start of the seventeenth century, boosting the confidence of a Young Party that was both antipapal and hostile to the Spanish Hapsburgs. Church architecture would reiterate not Rome's but Venice's brand of Catholicism, which was both pious and theatrical. This tradition was already evident in the building of Palladio's Redentore in 1576, the site where Venetians annually made votive offerings to God and the Virgin in thanks for final deliverance from the plague of 1575–77. The structure, resembling a piece of stage scenery, was more a classical temple of pilgrimage (bearing a remarkable resemblance to the Pantheon) and state ceremony than a church. The same technique was rendered in the construction of Santa Maria della Salute following the 1630 plague (Plate XV). The government called upon the architect Baldassare Longhena to build another votive temple, this one dedicated to the Virgin, the protector of health. The ruling oligarchy chose a symbolic site, on a narrow strip of land where the Giudecca Canal meets the Bacino di San Marco, so that the Salute, as the church was called, carried on a conversation with both the Basilica San Marco and the Redentore, the two other state-financed religious monuments. Its position, next to the Customs House, made it the protector of both trade and health.

The design of La Salute, a church deliberately assigned to the Somascan order to make obvious Venice's independence from Rome, found a place in the repository of Venetian myths. According to a priest of that order, Lorenzo Longo, Longhena had dreamt of the Virgin showing the doge a model of the church, thus miraculously planting the design in the architect's mind. But the design of La Salute eventually evolved in tandem with the patrician factions that rose to power. At mid-century, a more pro-papal group replaced the Young Party in government, reversing previous policies.

In need of capital to finance their wars with the Ottoman Turks, they permitted the Jesuits to return to Venice in 1657, and with this some of the more conservative Counter-Reformation themes found a place in the church's iconography. La Salute proclaimed the purity and perfection of the Immaculate Virgin and stood as an expression of Venetian self-confidence. In Giuto Le Court's group of statues over the high altar, the Virgin is flanked on one side by a personification of Venice and on the other by the flight of an old hag, representing the plague and the enemies of Catholicism. It appealed to the pro-papal, conservative branch of the patriciate.

Private investors, however, did not share the sobriety of the pro-papal party in power. Instead, like the libertine theater owners, they were commissioning lavish palaces, to adorn the city and exhibit their family crests, and enormous villas in the countryside, made with costly materials and decorated in flamboyant style. In this context, Longhena became a great visual artist, building the Palazzo Belloni-Battagia (1645–49) in Santa Croce, with Corinthian pilasters on the *piano nobile* and a façade decorated with the family coat of arms and admirals' obelisks. The architect also began building Ca' Pesaro in 1652, with its frightful monsters and theatrical masks. The putti and genies are a dramatic counterweight to the more sober architectural design. Other architects who subscribed to this more flamboyant style were Giuseppe Sardi, who designed the façade of Santa Maria del Giglio, and Alessandro Trimignon, who crafted that of San Moisè. Giovanni Scalfarotto's Church of San Simeone Piccolo and Giorgio Massari's Palazzo Grassi may be included in this list.

In the late seventeenth and eighteenth centuries, the richer patricians were staging elaborate parties and balls as well as frequenting gambling halls for their entertainment. Between 1670 and 1796 the wealthy constructed some forty new palaces in Venice itself and 600 villas on the mainland, primarily along the Brenta River and in the vicinities of Vicenza, Verona, and Treviso. Ca' Rezzonico on the Grand Canal is emblematic of this lavish building trend, with all its gloss and glitter. The commission was originally given to Longhena by the Bon family, but neither the patrons nor their client saw its completion. Longhena died before the first floor was finished, and the Bon family went into financial ruin. Thus the construction project fell to the nouveau riche Rezzonico family, bankers of Genoese origin who purchased Venetian nobility in 1687 for 100,000 ducats. The family was intent on making a social splash. It engaged Giorgio Massari to complete a monumental palace. Parisian fashions had gained currency by this time, both in dress and interior décor. The Venetians designed rococo divans and lavish bedrooms draped in silk, velvet, and damask (Fig. 41). Interior rooms were adorned with putti, flowers, and angels as well as Venetian girandole mirrors. Murano

Figure 41. Stuccowork probably by Abbondio Stazio of Massagno (1675–1745) and Carpoforo Mazzetti (c. 1684–1748), probably after a model by Gasparo Diziani of Belluno (1689–1767). Bedroom from the Sagredo Palace, Venice, eighteenth century (c. 1718). Wood, stucco, marble, glass, H. 25 ft. 2 in. (767.1 cm), W. 18 ft. 2 in. (553.7 cm), D. 13 ft. 2 in. (401.3 cm). Rogers Fund, 1906 (06.1335.1a–d). Location: Metropolitan Museum of Art, New York, NY, USA. Photo Credit: Image copyright © Metropolitan Museum of Art/Art Resource, NY. Image Reference: ART376913.

chandeliers decorated walls and ceilings. Lacquered furniture depicted scenes of everyday life as well as allegories. On Ca' Rezzonico's *piano nobile*, where guests were received, was a grand ballroom that typified noble interiors of the period. It was furnished with gold-gilt, lacquered furniture and decorated with silk wallpaper. There were desks with ivory inlays and marble tables. Chinoiseries were in vogue, recalling the Empire of Cathay. Other furniture pieces were actually designed by sculptors. Walls were fitted with marble paneling and expensive draperies or Flemish tapestries. Paintings in trompe-l'oeil (on a flat plane but rendering a three-dimensional illusion) of the Greek gods put the Rezzonico palace on a level with Olympus. The family engaged the most notable artists of the period to decorate some of the palace ceilings. The most famous, Giovanni Battista Tiepolo, chronicled the Rezzonico history in 1758, placing the family annals in the company of Greek gods and illustrating the virtues of nobility through allegory. Gian Battista and his son Domenico were not only painters but also superior interior decorators during this period.

Nobles such as the Rezzonico and the Labia, families that enjoyed notoriety for their feasts and balls, dressed extravagantly for these occasions, sparing no expense with costly textiles and jewelry. Eighteenth-century women adopted French fashion, using expensive silks to make ballooned skirts that were so wide special chairs had to be constructed to accommodate them. Their high-heeled clogs (*zoccoli*) also required longer skirts, made of precious fabrics, with flounces, pleats, puffs, hoops, and bustles. These women piled their bleached and powdered hair high in pyramids, baskets, and towers, and carried fans made of parchment, silk, and fine paper with handles of ivory, silver, gold, and tortoiseshell. Some were assisted in their makeup and dress by a *cicisbeo*, or gentleman companion, who served as an escort, valet, and, reputedly, a lover. Men wore waistcoats with flared skirts, tight breeches, tunics with laced wrists, white silk stockings, shoes with gold and silver buckles, tricornered hats in black felt, and the obligatory powdered wigs. Both women and men made heavy use of gold, gems, and pearls to decorate shoes, masks, and other clothing items. To some extent this was a masquerade, a performance of identity, the last gasp in the nobility's failed bid for power, and families like the Pisani at Strà, who ruined themselves hosting King Gustav III of Sweden, are a prime example. The lavish dress, parties, and balls were part of a cultural fiction that the aristocracy performed in the twilight years of a dying Republic.

Some of Venice's eighteenth-century artists meticulously documented noble fashion and lifestyles, giving us snapshots of life in a palace like Ca' Rezzonico. Gabriel Bella (1730–99) (see Fig. 21 in Chapter 4 and Fig. 39) depicted customs and daily life as well as political institutions, state receptions, ceremonies, feasts, and sports. Rosalba Carriera (1675–1757), an internationally renowned portrait artist working in soft pastels, realistically reproduced the textures of noble dress, including fabric, gold braid, lace, and other accessories. In her youth, the artist had made lace patterns for her mother, a skill that she later translated into painting. Carriera's pastel portraits show patricians in repose, free from problems but also free from meaning. Another

Figure 42. Salon with frescoes by Tiepolo (1753). Location: Palazzo Labia, Venice, Italy. Photo Credit: Cameraphoto Arte, Venice/Art Resource, NY. Image Reference: ART359601.

painter who gives us insight into material life during this period was Pietro Longhi. As a genre painter, he illustrated domestic activities among masters and servants, shop scenes, music, and dance, often in humorous fashion, and gave us snapshots of Venetian dress, residential interiors, the tailor's shop, lady's toiletries, dancing lessons, and chocolate sipping (see Fig. 22 in Chapter 4 and Fig. 24 in Chapter 5 and Fig. 40). One ponders whether these pictures of elegant refinement among the leisured classes are simply a stylistic reaction against the decorative baroque or a sign of aristocratic complacency. On the ceilings above the ballrooms where they danced, Gian Battista Tiepolo's figures in the clouds have bleached the color out of Venetian painting. There is no longer baroque light and shade – just blinding white, endless sky, and floating people (Fig. 42).

FURTHER READING

Architecture: D. Howard (2005); G. Zucconi (1993). *Carnival*: P. Burke (1987). *Cultural History*: O. Logan (1972); R. Messbarger (2002); E. Muir (2007); R. Oresko (1997); M. Plant (2002). *Economy:* S. Ciriacono (1983, 1988, 2001); B. Dooley (1986); J. Ferraro (2006); P. Lanaro (2006); W. McNeill (1974); B. Pullan (1968); R. Rapp (1976); D. Sella (1979, 2004); A. Zannini (1999). *Gambling:* J. Walker (1999); *Mainland Society:* M. Berengo (1956); D. Calabi and P. Lanaro Sartoro (1998); J. Ferraro (1993). *Marriage:* G. Cozzi (1976, 1981). *Material Culture:* S. Carboni (2007); G. Grevembroch (1754); R. Sarti (2001). *Music:* M. Feldman (2000, 2007); J. Glixon (2003); E. Rosand (2007). *Patrician Estate Planning:* J. C. Davis (1962, 1975). *Piracy:* A. Tenenti (1967). *Politics:* B. Dooley (1986); L. Pezzolo (2006). *Tourism:* R. C. Davis and R. Marvin (2004). *Women's Education:* P. La Balme (1984).

9

EPILOGUE: THE TIDES OF CHANGE

Once did She hold the gorgeous east in fee;
And was the safeguard of the west; the worth
Of Venice did not fall below her birth,
Venice, the eldest child of Liberty
She was a maiden City, bright and free;
No guile seduced, no force could violate
And, when she took unto herself a Mate,
She must espouse the everlasting Sea.
And what if she had seen those glories fade,
Those titles vanish, and that strength decay;
Yet shall some tribute of regret be paid
When her long life hath reached its final day;
Men are we, and must grieve when even the Shade
Of that which once was great is passed away.

William Wordsworth, 1807[1]

1. Fading Glories

When the Republic fell in 1797, it was a mere relic of its medieval past. No longer commanding maritime dominance, the wealthiest among the winged Lion's former rulers relied on rural manufacture, landed income, tourism, and inherited wealth. Venice's inferiority to the major European players on the chessboard – the Hapsburgs and the Bourbons – had relegated the government to a provincial power with little military muster. The aristocracy's luster had dimmed to a few prosperous oligarchs, the others struggling for subsistence or assuming minor bureaucratic posts. The towns and villages of the empire, ruled by entrenched local elites, looked less toward Venice to resolve their difficulties, their detachment presaging the demise of the

Figure 43. Giuseppe Borsato (1771–1849). *Napoleon Bonaparte's Arrival at Venice in 1807.* Location: Pinacoteca Ambrosiana, Milan, Italy. Photo Credit: Cameraphoto Arte,Venice/ Art Resource, NY. Image Reference: ART119874.

regional state. There was little resistance to Napoleon's armies in the spring of 1797, either on the mainland or in Venice itself. To the nearby rumble of cannon west across the lagoon, the Great Council, together with the last doge, Lodovico Manin, voted itself out in May, and Napoleon's troops soon entered Piazza San Marco. The Republic thus expired with little ado.

2. The Winged Lion under France and Austria

Napoleon replaced the aristocratic Great Council with a sixty-member Municipal Council that included former patricians, citizens who had been functionaries of the Republic, professionals, merchants, and members of the military and the church. The new administration, referred to as the Municipality, was multiethnic, including Jews, Dalmatians, and Greeks. There was also a feminist voice under the leadership of Annette Vadori, whose *Discorso sulla causa delle donne* demanded the representation of women in politics, but the French notion of fraternity did not include the female sex.

Napoleon proceeded to incinerate visual representations of aristocracy, a policy embraced by the Masons of Venice and other followers of "liberty" and "fraternity." The general began by burning the patriciate's Book of Gold, the ducal insignia, and the state Bucintoro featured in the ceremony of Venice's Marriage to the Sea. He also refashioned the identity of Baimonte Tiepolo, the former traitor of the Republic, as a symbol of democracy. Moreover, the remains of Doge Pietro Gradenigo, who ruled at the Great Council's First Closing in 1297, were removed from the church of San Cipriano in Murano and discarded. As a symbolic enactment of freedom, Napoleon expropriated to Paris the famed quadriga of bronze horses from Constantinople and the winged lion of Saint Mark atop the column in the Piazzetta. (Both were returned in 1815.) He also burned the gates of the Jewish ghetto and freed the community, erecting a Tree of Liberty. There was a range of reactions among Venetians. Among those who agreed with dismantling the former patrician regime were the saloniste Isabella Teotochi Albrizzi and the intellectual Ugo Foscolo, while the artist Giandomenico Tiepolo mourned the fall of the Republic from his villa in the countryside, penning in brown ink the scenes of degradation through the Carnivalesche figure of Pucinello.[2]

The ambitious General Bonaparte wasted no time bartering Venice for more tempting prizes. After stripping the Arsenal, he handed the city and its province over to the Austrians, who in October 1797 began the second in a series of foreign occupations rupturing political continuity on the lagoon. The Emperor Francis II resuscitated noble privilege during the eight-year Austrian interlude, engaging some of the former patriciate of Venice to serve as censors against the vestiges of democratic principles. Support of noble privilege continued when Napoleon, who became emperor of France in 1804 and six months later king of Italy, regained Venice and the Veneto at the end of 1805 (Fig. 43). He appointed his stepson Eugene de Beauharnais Viceroy of Italy and assigned Venice a French governor, who ruled together with nine advisors.

The multiple changes in regime took their toll. With Venice under Napoleon, the English confined the city's access to the Adriatic, while the Austrians set up land blockades. The interdictions made it difficult to obtain food provisions and construction materials. Venetian commerce collapsed, bankrupting the merchant community. Austrian Trieste took Venice's place as the new center of international shipping, while the Arsenal became a repair dock. Shrinking aristocratic fortunes, partly resulting from heavy taxation and forced government loans and partly from freeing property from feudal restrictions of ownership, forced the proprietors of Venetian palaces to sell to foreign buyers at low cost. They sold their entire libraries as well.

In the countryside, nobles lost half the lands of the Veneto. For the masses, economic recession increased unemployment, lowered the standard of living, and contributed to widespread poverty. Napoleon's occupation also drained Venice's artistic heritage and patrimony. Religious property was confiscated and the artwork sent to France. Parish boundaries were reconfigured and many ecclesiastical edifices were converted into depositories for grain, merchandise, and ammunition or became dumping grounds. Palaces and houses were razed to the ground to make way for new building projects.

Venice's political space was altered dramatically to satisfy Napoleon's imperial designs. The emperor set out to minimize the republican past and elevate representation of his new regime. He knocked down the monuments to former doges and gave the entrance to Piazza San Marco a neoclassical image, with a royal palace occupying the former Procuratie Nuove. He had the granary alongside the lagoon razed in 1807 and replaced it with gardens to ensure that the royal apartments enjoyed an unobstructed view. He also ordered the demolition of Jacopo Sansovino's Church of San Geminiano at the west end of the Piazza to make way for Giuseppe Maria Soli's design of a grand ballroom (Plate XV).

In addition to redefining political space, Napoleon also confiscated a great deal of sacred space, converting it for public use. The State Archives replaced the Frari convent; the Accademia delle Belle Arti, the former Scuola and Monastery of the Carità; and the city hospital, the former Confraternity of San Marco. In his efforts to modernize the city and improve public health, the emperor also commissioned a municipal cemetery at San Michele, the island across from the hospital (Plate VII, on the left behind the Church of San Giovanni e Paolo). Other innovations took place at Castello, where Napoleon engaged the architect Giannantonio Selva to design extensive gardens, now the home of the world-renowned Biennale art exposition. Originally this area had been the home of fishermen, lace-makers, threaders of glass beads, and other working-class people. Instead, a new commercial center was established between the Arsenal and the gardens along the Via Eugenia, now called Via Garibaldi, one of Venice's more popular neighborhoods. Thus Napoleon reshaped Venice, improving public sanitation and circulation as well as giving the city a little greenery, but also eradicated some of the glorious sacred and secular architecture and traditions of the past.

With the Congress of Vienna in 1814, France gave Venice to Austria for a second time. Stendhal, an habitué of Caffè Florian, witnessed the degradation firsthand and ruefully noted it in his 1818 memoirs. In the following three decades, heavy taxation in the marketplace, lack of political representation, and strict government censorship fueled the fires of rebellion to foreign rule, particularly among the bourgeoisie. In the wake of revolutionary movements throughout Europe in 1848, the Venetians Daniele Manin and Niccolò Tommaseo, together with a group of radical lawyers and intellectuals, plotted the overthrow of the Hapsburgs at Caffè Florian, while soldiers of the Austrian regime sipped coffee across the Piazza at Quadri's. Manin's temporary coalition of prosperous businessmen, many like himself successful Jews, along with unhappy Arsenal workers, succeeded in ousting the Hapsburgs and establishing a new Republic in 1848, but the experiment was short-lived. The republican rebels failed to achieve cohesion, and the principle of monarchy was once again invoked. The Austrians returned in 1849, removing Venice's jurisdictional authority over the Veneto, and they remained until their defeat in the Austro-Prussian War in 1866.

The Venetian economy underwent some improvement under the Austrians, with the installation of a tobacco industry and the expansion of glass manufacture on Murano. Both Venetians and non-Venetians prospered from these manufactures as well as trade and banking. Textiles and shipbuilding ebbed, but the market for raw products such as grain, animal hides, timber, and oil survived. In the Veneto, Venetian landowners developed modest silk-spinning and woolen industries. Venice itself, however, remained subordinate to the northeastern port city of Trieste.

By the second decade of the nineteenth century, Austrian Venice had become the ideal allegory for decline among English literati, much in the tradition of Edward Gibbon's *Fall of the Roman Empire* (1776). Lord Byron blamed the fall on Venetian hubris and tyranny (1818) while John Ruskin decried the city's physical deterioration. Native Venetians, on the other hand, devoted themselves with great zeal to preserving the Republic's glorious past. Among their important projects was cataloguing the State Archives, whose ambassadorial relations had piqued scholarly interest. Leopold Van Ranke, one of the founders of modern primary source–based history, consulted these records in 1827. The natives also established Venice's first civic museum in 1836, with Teodoro Correr's collections of arts, crafts, costumes, maps, and books. To this was added Emmanuel Cicogna's Library in 1868, and the entire patrimony was moved to the Procuratie Nuove as the Correr Museum in 1920. The enthusiasm for recovering and conserving Venice's historical past was greatly assisted by the publishing industry, which had continued to thrive despite the fall of the Republic. Between 1818 and 1852, Alvisopoli published a series of patriotic books, including Giustina Renier Michiel's history of festivals (1817–27), and Samuele Romanin set about writing his multitome *History of Venice*. Moreover, throughout this period a number of city guidebooks, some in foreign languages, emerged to assist tourists, and view painting, under the brush of Ippolito Caffi, was revived as a popular genre.

The ancient Republic proved to be a powerful cultural icon in the artistic imagination of an auspicious list of visiting celebrities during this period. In the 1840s, John Ruskin called for a genuine revival of the Gothic idiom in architecture. Giuseppe Verdi wrote an opera on the Foscari family (1844), and opera composers Rossini and Donizetti used material from Venetian songs in their compositions. Venice became part of a dream world in Charles Dickens's writings (1846). Schubert and Schuman set their lyric poems to Venetian themes, while Liszt, Chopin, and Fauré all found ways to incorporate Venice's vernacular music into their instrumental works. Thus while Venice was a vassal of the imperial Hapsburg dynasty, its years of aristocratic independence continued to be commemorated in the hearts and minds of artists and intellectuals.

As visitors increasingly flowed to the magical city on water, the Austrians improved the arteries of communication. Of signal importance, construction of a railway linking Venice with Milan in 1846 accelerated the growth of tourism and helped revitalize Venetian fortunes. In light of their commercial losses under Paris and Vienna, the Venetians shrewdly exploited the new opportunity for entrepreneurship. They developed packaged tours for British, French, and German travelers eager to flee their own cold and damp climates to embark upon literary or artistic adventures. Some tourists wandered through the city reading aloud Shakespeare, Goethe, Shelley, and Byron; others used paintbrushes to capture the changing light on palaces set atop shining mirrors. The tourist market had already acquired new energies with the gentleman's Grand Tour between 1600 and 1830, a kind of finishing school for aristocrats. But with the installation of the railway, middle-class travelers were flooding Venice in the thousands daily, and the opportunities for profit lured skilled workers away from their traditional activities to join the expanding tourism industry that needed guides and gondoliers, hostelry staff, and entertainers. To facilitate the flow of increased tourist traffic, the Austrians built two new cast-iron bridges to traverse the Grand Canal, one at the Accademia (rebuilt in 1932) linking the districts of Dorsoduro and San Marco and the other at the railway station in front of the Church of the Scalzi (rebuilt in the 1920s), linking Cannaregio and Santa Croce. To that time, Rialto alone had served as a crossing point, but the construction of two more bridges created alternative arterial routes through the city.

While visitors romanticized Venice as a city of love – the novelist George Sand with her lover Alfred de Musset sojourned at the luxurious Hotel Danieli in 1834, and Richard Wagner composed the second act of *Tristan and*

Isolde while living at the Palazzo Giustinian in 1858–9 – they also witnessed great poverty, malnutrition, and epidemic disease such as cholera. Moreover, the foundations of some of the monuments looked perilously near collapse, and the city was acquiring a shabby image. In response, Ca'd'Oro, the Fondaco dei Turchi, and the Basilica were stripped of their medieval and Renaissance forms and given a neo-Gothic overcoat, much to the dismay of purists such as John Ruskin. But Ruskin was not the first with his *Stones of Venice* (1851–3) nor the last to advocate better restoration work. Leopoldo Cicognara, an art historian from Ferrara who became president of both the Accademia delle Belle Arti (c. 1810) and the newly founded Ateneo Veneto (1812), had actively advocated the preservation of public patrimony. Moreover, the scholar Pompeo Molmenti continued the restoration cause after Ruskin. Molmenti, a graduate in law at the University of Padua, wrote a prize-winning history of private life in Venice in 1879. These were the years when the Archivio veneto and the Deputazione di Storia Patria per le Venezie were being established, and Venetians, such as the bibliographer and manuscript collector Emmanuele Cicogna (d. 1868), were working diligently to preserve Venice's history

3. Venice Joins the Young Italian Nation

Venice and the Veneto would receive their third external sovereign since the collapse of the Republic when Prussia defeated Austria in 1866 and the Veneto voted to unify with Victor Emmanuele II. The new administration set upon restructuring the city's commercial arteries and strengthening its industrial potential, making it the capital of an Italian province. This included the construction in 1871–2 of a wide walking street, now called Strada Nuova but originally the Via Vittorio Emmanuele II, to connect the Rialto market with the train station, and the Via 22 Marzo, commemorating the 1848 Revolution, between 1870 and 1875; a new aquatic route from Santa Marta to the Giudecca Canal that subordinated the commercial importance of the Grand Canal and the Rialto market; a cotton factory at Santa Marta (1833–1911); and a flour mill at Mulino Stucky on the Giudecca (1897–1920). The glass, lace, and luxury textile industries underwent revitalization during these years as well. Further, a new harbor at the Stazione Marittima revitalized Mediterranean trade, helping Venice regain its status as an important Italian port city, and the first *vaporetti*, literally little steamers, arrived in 1881 from the French Compagnie des Bateaux Omnibus de Venise, much to the chagrin of gondoliers, whose central role in the public transport business was forever upset.

The Venetians understood that culture and entertainment were essential to feeding the tourist industry. They revived the Carnival that Napoleon had suppressed in the 1880s and established the Biennale in 1895 to promote the city as a cultural center. The inaugural exhibition, attended by King Umberto I and Queen Margherita, attracted more than 200,000 visitors. It was among the first opportunities to market art to the middle class after both aristocratic and church patronage abated, and it helped develop a national consciousness as Italian artists completed with the likes of Ensor, Klimt, Renoir, Whistler, and Signac. In 1897, the Biennale acquired the modern art gallery at Ca' Pesaro, and by 1902 it began to feature local view painters and lesser known talent. Venice was among the most painted cities in the world, with Turner, Monet (Fig. 44), and Sargent coming from abroad to capture its beauty in oils, but there were a number of important local artists as well, including Ippolito Caffi, Guglielmo Ciardi, and Giacomo Favretto. The Muranese Vittorio Zecchin (1878–1947), a post-Symbolist whose work resembles that of Klimt and the Austrian Secessionists, also stood out. Eventually Venice would become an important center for modern art, notably with the Biennale of 1948, which exhibited Impressionists as well as Dix, Pechstein, Picasso, Klee, Schiele, and Magritte; the Biennale of 1973, which featured American pop art of the late sixties; and, after 1980, Peggy Guggenheim's collection, for which the Solomon R. Guggenheim Foundation funded a public museum in the late collector's former residence at the Palazzo Venier dei Leoni.

Many artists and writers witnessing late nineteenth- and early twentieth-century changes to the city's appearance longed for the nostalgic past, praising Venice's beauty but also lamenting its decadence in the Romantic idiom. Several buildings cried out for restoration. At the same time, the banks, insurance companies, and grand hotels springing up at Rialto and San Marco disrupted Venice's medieval charm. The disintegration of the thousand-year-old *campanile* in Piazza San Marco in 1902 made the aura of decay even more tangible, causing international alarm. That same year, Henry James published *The Wings of the Dove*, with a ravishingly beautiful, terminally ill woman choosing to breathe her last in Venice, city of dreams and disillusion. Venice was also the place where Thomas Mann's character Gustav Von Achenbach expired after a painful period of unrequited homosexual infatuation (1912). *Death in Venice* provided a repository of tropes for a myriad of artists and writers not only because the urban fabric was decaying in the damp climate but also because visitors chose the floating labyrinth as the place to mourn their own disappointments with life, through artistic expression and imagination. Marcel Proust's *In Search of*

Figure 44. Claude Monet (1840–1926). *Palazzo Dario,* Venice. 1908. Location: National Museum of Wales, Cardiff, Wales, Great Britain. Photo Credit: Cameraphoto Arte, Venice/ Art Resource, NY. Image Reference: ART397046.

Lost Time, written between 1909 and 1922, is a prime example of this nostalgic literature of regret.

Droves of well-heeled tourists, including Thomas Mann, took flight to the Lido, a new theater for romantic architecture, where sea resorts had become fashionable to those seeking solace. Giovanni Sardi responded to the aesthetic dreams of historicists with his Hotel Excelsior (1898 and 1908), a neo-Byzantine edifice topped with domes, turrets, and Moorish arches that harkened back to the medieval past but also recalled the grand establishments of Cairo and the Côte d'Azur. The Hotel des Bains (1905–9), on the other hand, was more sober, albeit eclectic, and introduced the celebrated thatched huts (*capanne*) to bathers seeking mini-shelters on the sand shelf. But during the first decade of the twentieth century, the Lido brought architectural innovation as well, with the Stile Liberty, Italy's Art Nouveau movement, as represented in Guido Sullam's Villa Monplaisir (1904–5). On this long coastal sand bar the romantic and historicist currents persisted into the Fascist period, as exemplified with Brenno del Giudice's eclectic Casa del Farmacista (1926–27) on the Via Sandro Gallo.

4. Venice in Peril: The Twentieth Century

If Venice lost its insularity with the construction of a railroad linking Lombardy and the Veneto, ironically it reacquired it with the development of a prosperous industrial port at Marghera beginning in 1917 and a bedroom community in Mestre in the 1920s. Marghera was the site of the new ironworks, oil refineries, and chemical industries, and during the 1930s it was also an important center of Italian armaments. The Ponte della Libertà (built between 1930 and 1933 by the architect Umberto Fantucci), a roadway from Mestre and Marghera to Venice, rendered the old city an appendage of these two large-scale suburbs that served, thereafter, as industrial and commercial junctions, respectively, as well as residential zones.

Meanwhile, little new residential building took place in the historic center. As a result, the new generations of workers employed in Venice commuted in from the suburbs, together with motoring tourists, who from 1933 were accommodated with a parking garage (designed by Eugenio Miozzi and built between 1931 and 1934) resembling a monumental city gate. The function of Venice thus changed once again, returning the city on the lagoon to insularity and to the destiny of becoming a museum site. There were some marine insurance agencies on the Zattere, but tourism was the primary source of income, with glassblowing, lace-making, manufacture of luxury textiles, and leatherwork its auxiliaries.

Venice during the Fascist period was not totally void of new working-class districts, but unlike the days of the Republic, when nobles and commoners lived alongside one another in the same parishes, workers were placed on the fringes of the historic center, at Castello, Santa Croce, and Cannaregio. Moreover, the community of Santa Elena, built in 1928 adjacent to the public gardens, was far out on the outskirts. It was difficult for commuters to get to and from these densely populated neighborhoods on the margins. The vaporetti of the early twentieth century that had made gondoliers obsolete were no longer adequate. To them were added motorboats that circled the city, eroding the foundations of the edifices along the canals. To speed up travel from the train station and the car garage to San Marco, another waterway, the Rio Nuovo, was built, further damaging the city's underside. The result of not building in the center increased the flow of commuters from the mainland, and historic Venice continued on its way to becoming a city of the elderly and visiting tourists.

This was the era of totalitarianism in Italy. Benito Mussolini and the Fascist Party had taken power in Rome on October 28, 1922, and would direct the course of the country's history for the next two decades. The period began with a program of domestic improvement, which for Venice included new building in addition to the roadway across the lagoon. Besides the new working-class districts in Venice, Fascism brought with it new public buildings between 1920 and 1940: the modernistic Heliotherapic Hospital at the Lido (1922–3); the fire station at Rio Ca' Foscari (designed by Brenno del Giudice and built between 1932 and 1934); the passenger airport at the Lido, and new pavilions for the Biennale. The Palazzo del Cinema on the Lido (designed by Luigi Quagliata and Angelo Scatttolin and built between 1936 and 1938) became the site of the International Film Festival, which began in 1932, and in the postwar period Venice's gambling houses, on the Lido for summer and at Palazzo Vendramin-Calergi in winter, attracted new sources of profit from Europe's jet set. Mussolini used the expositions at the Biennale to promote Fascist propaganda and established a string of nationalistic festivals in Venice in music (1930), film (1932), and theater (1934).

World War II brought hardship and disaster to Venice. Even though the city itself was not bombed out of respect for its monumental importance, it was heavily impacted in the Jewish quarter, first by the national racial laws of 1938, which restricted employment, teaching, learning, and performance for Jews, and then in 1943 when deportation began. Many Jews lost their lives in the Holocaust, and they are remembered and honored in Arbit Blatas Holocaust memorials (Fig. 45). Others, fortunately, managed to go underground, hidden by Venetians and other sympathetic Italians. Officially, Venice was compliant under the two-year German occupation (1943–5), but it harbored many socialists and partisans who worked in the resistance. During the war, the Venetians went hungry as food supplies were cut off, and people risked their lives dodging air bombings in order to seek food in the countryside.

Venice escaped the air bombings of war but not the cruelties of nature and human intrusion into the natural environment. Since the great floods of 1966, when waters rose 194 centimeters above the mean tide, the city on water has been an international cause célèbre because the imbalance in its ecology has threatened to bring about its ruin. In addition to the Italian government, which passed a Special Law on Venice in 1973 to stave off depopulation and inundation, some thirty philanthropic organizations from

Figure 45. *The Last Train,* by Arbit Blatas (1908–99), 1993. Monument commemorating the fiftieth anniversary of the deportation of the Jews from the Venetian Ghetto. Location: Venice, Italy. Photo Credit: J. M. Ferraro.

around the world, including UNESCO, Save Venice, and Venice in Peril, have undertaken fund-raising campaigns to restore its artwork, crumbling architecture, and cracking foundations. The city's flooding and sinking have attracted the greatest concern. The causes are many, including filling canals and redirecting tides; draining artesian water in Marghera from the bedrock underneath the lagoon to serve the oil refinery and chemical industries; deepening the canals leading into the harbors; admitting giant oil tankers, and the rise of sea levels worldwide. Further, industrial zones and banked-in fishing beds have reduced the size of the lagoon basin by half. Water and air pollution are also causes of distress. Chemical detergents destroy fish; heating systems produce smog and industrial smoke. Further, the weight of brick and marble, along with the hordes of tourists, on mudflats is sinking the city. However, thanks to the work of the academic community, technicians, and philanthropic funding organizations, much good restoration work has taken place beginning in the last three decades of the twentieth century.

5. The Eternal Allure

Venice thus has undergone sweeping changes since its beginnings. Whether one rides the train across the lagoon or motors down the causeway from Mestre, the dramatic transformations in the city's morphology are strikingly apparent (Plate XVI). With Veneto-Byzantine, Gothic, Renaissance, and

Baroque now treasured memories of the distant past, the spectator first sees a modern public housing tract at the Sacca San Girolamo (1987–90) that faintly attempts to recall the medieval Venetian tradition with its funnel-shaped chimneys. Television antennas and satellite dishes share the cityscape with pinnacles and domes. The lanterns that once lit the city and the gas lamps that replaced them in 1843 are now wired with electricity. Motor launches, vaporetti, and car ferries to the Lido transport hordes of commuters, bathers, and visitors where once aristocratic gondole or the traghetti of commoners taxied a few people at a time. A parking lot at Piazzale Roma serves as a large depository for tour buses that drop off droves of day visitors eager to enjoy the city's historical attractions. Rialto food stalls now share their space with mask and glass shops filled with wares of foreign provenance, and many other parts of the city have witnessed the disappearance of stores selling provisions to residents to make way for shops hawking souvenirs. Venice thus continues to lose permanent residents, particularly the younger generations starting new families. Some flee to the mainland because transport is more convenient and retail offerings more varied, while others simply cannot afford the real estate of a museum city. Venice is sinking, on one hand to the floods eroding its foundations, and on the other to the burdens of global tourism. Its allure, nonetheless, appears to be without limits, an invitation to reflect one last time on its eternal attraction.

Even as it has changed over the centuries, Venice, with the help of intellectuals, artists, and philanthropists, has preserved the culture from its greatest days, and everyone comes to see what has remained. If only for a few hours, it gives people the opportunity to share in Venice's historical legacy. Moreover, the aquatic environment endows Venice with a uniqueness few world cities can claim. Buildings and monuments sit upon a vast mirror, with prisms of light and color sharing the dynamic hues of sky and seasons. Domes and pinnacles, crenellations and arches are etched into waterscape. On land, the human measure of things, the labyrinth of narrow alleys and arcades promises delight to explorers wandering endless footpaths, and there are no automobiles. Byzantine, Islamic, Gothic, Renaissance, and Baroque structures offer an embarrassment of riches for the student of architecture, while interiors shelter a world patrimony of art.

The city continues to be, since the mid-nineteenth century, an important international center of scholarship. In addition to the University (est. 1829) and the nineteenth-century intellectual academies, Venice avails itself of the Giorgio Cini and Querini Stampaglia Foundations as well as the Solomon R. Guggenheim Foundation at Palazzo Venier dei Leoni (1980). Outstanding state archives at the Frari and church archival collections at the Basilica

San Marco, as well as the Correr archive and library and the Biblioteca Nazionale Marciana make Venice a subject that continues to be studied and better understood. Thanks to the Gladys Krieble and Jean Paul Delmas Foundation, begun in 1976, a host of scholars from the United States, the United Kingdom, and the Commonwealth have received funded research grants as well as subventions for the publication of scholarly monographs, while major communities of Greek and German scholars also enjoy funded institutes of study. *News on the Rialto,* a newsletter for academicians, keeps a dedicated scholarly community from around the world connected, while the American Friends of the Marciana, founded in 1997, is helping to fund the digitizing of this world-class library's important manuscript collections. Besides the endless visits from foreigners, Venice is filled with scholars, writers, artists, and expatriates from around the world who have adopted it as home or as a home away from home. Perhaps it is time to reflect on whether Venice ever just belonged to Venetians or was, at least from the first millennium, always a world city.

FURTHER READING

Architecture: P. Ginsborg (1979); D. Howard (2005); Terisio Pignatti (1971); G. Zucconi (1993). *Cultural History*: M. Plant (2002). *Tourism*: R. C. Davis and R. Marvin (2004). *Venice as Seen by Writers*: L. Byron (1905); J. Ruskin (1860).

Appendix I

APPROXIMATE POPULATION OF VENICE
DURING THE REPUBLIC

Year	Population (rounded in thousands)	Year	Population (rounded in thousands)
1200	80	1600★	150
1300	120	1630	100
1348	80	1640	120
1500★	115	1700★	140
1570	190	1764	141
1575–7	125	1790	138

Sources: ★Carlo Cipolla, *Before the Industrial Revolution. European Society and Economy, 1000–1700* (New York: Norton, 1980). All others from Fredrick Lane, *Venice: A Maritime Republic* (Baltimore: Johns Hopkins University Press, 1973), 18–19, 21, 175, 424.

Appendix II

POPULATION OF THE HISTORIC CENTER OF VENICE, 1871–2010

Year	Population (rounded in thousands)	Year	Population (rounded in thousands)
1871	129	1981	94
1901	147	2000	66
1931	164	2010	60
1951	175		

Source: http://www.commune.venezia.it. Servizi Statistica e ricerca. Serie storico della popolazione residente, p. 4055 (August 2011).

GLOSSARY

acquaroli	water bearers
Albanesi	Albanians
albergo (pl. alberghi)	an inn
androne	the main hall on the ground floor of a large palace
arengo (pl. arenghi)	twelfth-century general assembly representing Venice's six districts
armeni	Armenians
Arsenale	from the Arabic *darsiná*, a locale of manufacture. In Venice, a fortified harbor and dockyard, home to ship manufacture, the Venetian navy, and the manufacture of gunpowder
Asia	East China, Japan, Korea, and Mongolia
Asia, greater	all of Asia
Asia, Southwest	the westernmost portion of Asia; also termed West Asia
Asia, Southeast	the area south of China, east of India, west of New Guinea, and north of Australia
Auditori Novi	an appellate magistracy of itinerant judges
Auditori Vecchi	a court of appeal for both Venetian tribunals and those of the Venetian governors within the Dogado
Avogaria di Comun	tribunal of the state attorneys; guardians of constitutional law; members assigned legal cases to other judicial magistracies; kept registers of nobility and citizenship
bacaro (pl. bacari)	a tavern

bacino	the basin of water between the district of San Marco and the island of San Giorgio
bailo (pl. baili)	the Venetian ambassador-consul to Constantinople who also held judicial competencies over Venetian subjects in the city
Balla d'Oro; Barbarella	a lottery taking place on St. Barbara's day for young men's early admission to the Great Council
Barnabotto (pl. Barnabotti)	poor Venetian patricians, many of whom resided in the neighborhood of San Barnaba
bauta	a carnival mask that completely disguises the face
Beccarie	butcher stalls, with specific reference to the stalls at the Rialto market
biblioteca	library
Bucintoro Bucentaur	the Venetian state ceremonial barge of the doge
ca' (It. casa)	Venetian for house, generally referring to a palace
calle (pl. calli)	Venetian for narrow street
campana	bell
campanile	bell tower
campiello (pl. campielli)	Venetian for a small open field or square
campo (pl. campi)	Venetian for an open field or square at the center of a parish; all squares save San Marco were named *campo*
canale	refers to only three canals in Venice: the Grand Canal, that of the Giudecca, and that of Cannaregio
Candia	the Venetian term for the city of Heraklion on Crete
capitano	military governor of a subject city
capo (pl. capi)	head, of a council
chinoiseries	a French term for décor that uses Chinese imagery and artistic style
Cinque Savi alla Mercanzia	body of five magistrates, established in 1506 to oversee commerce

Cinque Savi alla Pace	body of five magistrates to oversee public safety
Clarissimo (pl. Clarissimi; f. Clarissi-ma; -me)	form of honorable address reserved for patrician men and women
Collegio	the steering committee of the Senate
Collegio del Militia da Mar	magistrates responsible for naval recruitment
commenda (pl. commende)	a business association
Compagnie della Calza Companies of the Hose	young male patrician groups, distinguished by their colorful stockings, who entertained both foreign dignitaries and the public
contrada (pl. contrade)	neighborhood
Convertite (pl. Convertiti)	an asylum for former prostitutes
Corfu	a Greek island in the Ionian Sea
corno (pl. corni)	the doge's hat
Corone (Greek: Koroni)	a town on the Greek Peloponnese
corredo (pl. corredi)	dotal goods in clothing and jewelry
cortigiana	courtesan
Council of Ten	council established in 1310 that was at times the supreme government power, composed of ten patricians as well as the doge and his six councilors; at times it also met with more, called a *Zonta*
crenellation	a wall-like barrier on the edge of a roof used to defend a building
cupola	dome
curti (It. corti)	Venetian for short, in this case referring to more recent patrician families
Derelitti	the forsaken who suffered from famine, disease, and poverty who found refuge in the Ospedaletto dei Derelitti
dogado (It. ducato)	duchy that defined the doge's reign
dogana	customs office
dogaressa (pl. dogaresse)	the wife of the doge
doge	the titular and ceremonial head of the Venetian state

Dominante, La	refers to Venice, the "dominant" center of a regional state
Esecutori alla Bestemmia	commissioners established in 1537 to regulate blasphemy, gambling, the seduction of virgins, and other moral turpitude
fabbrica (pl. fabbriche)	a manufactory
fondaco (pl. fondaci)	from the Arabic fondouk, a trading post. In Venetian *fontego/ghi*. A *casa-fondaco* was a noble palace with docks and warehouse
fondamenta (pl. fondamente)	street or quay alongside water, usually reserved for those lining the canals although some are along *rii*
forner(Pl. forneri)	baker
Frezzerie	a street named after fletchers (arrowsmiths)
Friulani	people from the Friuli region
Giovani	the Young Party within the Venetian patriciate
giudice (pl. giudici)	judge
Giustizia Nova	made up of magistrates who regulated foodstuffs, inns and taverns, and the wine trade; established in 1261
Giustizia Vecchia	made up of magistrates who oversaw ferry men, several crafts, worker wages, weights and measures, and food prices
Governatori delle Entrate	made up of officials who oversaw tax collection
Greci	Greeks
Incogniti, Accademia degli	Unknown, Academy of
latifundia	a large landed estate
Levant	the area of the eastern Mediterranean littoral between Anatolia (Turkey) and Egypt. Also termed the Eastern Mediterranean. Includes most of modern Lebanon, Syria, Jordan, Israel, and the Palestinian territories; also at times part of Turkey (which is also partly in Europe) and Iraq

Lido	a coastal off-shore bar
locanda (pl. locande)	an inn
longo (pl. longhi)	refers to long term, in this case the oldest families in the Venetian patriciate
maiolica (pl. maioliche)	Italian earthenware with colored decoration on an opaque white tin glaze
mendicante (pl. mendicanti	beggar
Mercerie	the principal shopping street of Venice, the artery connecting San Marco to the Rialto
meretrice (pl. meretrici)	prostitute
Modone (Greek: Methoni)	a village in the Peloponnese
Morea	the Peloponnese peninsula
muda (pl. mude)	a convoy of merchant galleys
niello	black metallic alloys used to fill in engraved designs on silver or other metalwork
North Africa	the northernmost region of the African continent, including Egypt, although the Sinai Peninsula is part of Southwest Asia
oculus	a circular window
ogee arch	a kind of Gothic arch. The convex curves become concave toward the arch's apex
ospedale	a refuge for travelers and those in need
otium	a Roman conception of leisure time taken with dignity
patriciate	word with Latin roots originally referring to the Roman aristocracy; used to describe the Venetian ruling class
Periclitanti	in harm's way, referring to girls in the asylum of the Zitelle Periclitanti who were in peril of losing their virginity
Petizion, Giudici di	tribunal overseeing the registration of dowries
piano nobile	the main living floor of a noble palace, usually the one above the ground floor

piazza	the term for square, which was reserved for San Marco alone
Pien Collegio	the executive committee consisting of the Signoria and the Sixteen Savii which determined the Senate agenda
Piovego (pl. pioveghi)	magistracy that oversaw canals, quays, bridges, streets, and other public works
pistore (pl. pistori)	dough maker
podestà	a Venetian governor, also called rector
pompe	pomp, ostentation, ceremonies, material display
popolo	the common people
porcellana	porcelain
portatori	carriers (of merchandise)
portego	Venetian for the central hall on the living story of a palace
Portico	an open colonnade on the side of a building
poveri vergognosi	the shameful poor
Pregadi, Pregati, Rogadi	the sixty-member thirteenth-century Senate
procurator	an advocate or defender
Procuratori di San Marco	patricians appointed for life to oversee public trusts and the finances and maintenance of the Basilica di San Marco
Procuratie	the public buildings surrounding Piazza San Marco that housed the offices of the state prosecutors
Proprio, Giudici di	tribunal that oversaw dowry restitution as well as property disputes
proto	the principal architect overseeing construction
provveditore (pl. provveditori)	a government supervisor or commissioner with a defined sphere of responsibility, such as cereals, the Mint, public construction, crafts, public revenues, customs and duties, sumptuary laws, salt revenues, and public health
Provveditori Sopra Beni Inculti	office established in 1545 that catalogued uncultivated land in the Venetian mainland
pugni	fists

Quarantia Criminal	the Council of Forty, established in 1220. The supreme appellate court; voting members of the Senate. Their three heads were part of the Signoria
ramo	a small branch of a calle
redentore	redeemer
renovation	renewal
Ricoverati, Accademia dei	an intellectual academy in Padua that discussed religious and scientific ideas
Ridotto	a gambling house in Venice, with entertainment and masquerades
rio (pl. rii)	Venetian for a small canal
rio terrà	a street that has been formed by landfill over a canal
riva	a walking bank or quayside street in front of a large expanse of water
ruga (pl. rughe)	from the French word rue, a street, usually lined with the shops of a specific item of consumption
sagomatore (var. sagomadore; pl. –dori/-tori)	oil bottlers and sellers
salizzada	a paved street
sandalo (sandalo da s'ciopo)	a small, flat-bottomed boat
Savi di Consiglio	the six patricians who were part of the Collegio; they could propose legislation
savio (pl. savi, savii)	literally, a wise person; used to name the members of specific Venetian magistrates in the Collegio, the board of trade, the tenth levied on real property, naval supplies, and the landed dominions
Scala dei Giganti	staircase of the giants at the Palazzo Ducale
Schiavone (pl. Schiavoni)	Dalmatian
scuola (pl. scuole) schola	a confraternity or guild

Sensa	the Venetian term for the Ascension. Following the Sunday of Ascension Day in May the Doge performs the ritual of wedding Venice to the sea, and the city honored the ceremonial occasion with a fifteen-day fair
Serenissima	the most serene (Republic)
sestiere (pl. sestieri)	district
Signori di Notte	lords of the night watch
Signoria	an executive council consisting of the doge, the Minor Council, and the heads of the Forty
Soccorso	institution of assistance for married women
sottoportego (pl. sottoporteghe); (It. sottoportico; pl. sottoportici)	a portion of a walkway, normally arcaded on one side, that passes beneath a building
stupro	violation of a virgin or rape
Tedesco (pl. Tedeschi; f. Tedes-ca;-che)	German
topo	a big fishing boat
traghetto	a gondola ferry
travasadori	bottlers
vadimone (pl. vadimoni)	a Venetian tribunal that guaranteed the restitution of a state-registered dowry to a widow
Zante Zakynthos	the third largest Ionian Island
Zattere	rafts referring to the quayside facing the island of the Giudecca, where once rafts were moored
zecchino	gold ducat; from the Arabic word *sikka*, meaning mint
Zitella (pl. Zitelle)	spinster
Zonta (pl. Zonte; It. Giunta-e)	Venetian for addition, in this case an addition to a group of magistrates, such as the Senate or the Ten
Zuanne, Zani (It. Giovanni)	Venetian for Giovanni, or John

NOTES

PREFACE

1 Henry James, *On Italy: Selections from Italian Hours* (London: Barrie and Jenkins, 1988), 10.

2 Rona Goffen, *Piety and Patronage in Renaissance Venice: Bellini, Titian, and the Franciscans* (New Haven: Yale University Press, 1986); Deborah Howard, *The Architectural History of Venice* (New Haven: Yale University Press, 2005), Guido Zucconi, *Venice: An Architectural Guide* (Verona: Arsenale Editrice, 2007).

CHAPTER 1. RECONSTRUCTING THE FLOATING CITY

1 Francesco Petrarch, *Epistolae seniles*, IV. 3, quoted in David Rosand, *Myths of Venice: The Figuration of a State* (Chapel Hill: University of North Carolina Press, 2001), 7.

2 *Venice: Everyman Guides* (London: Davis Campbell, 1993), 56–7; 68–9.

3 Elisabeth Crouzet-Pavan, *Venice Triumphant. The Horizons of a Myth* (Baltimore: Johns Hopkins University Press, 2002), 36–45.

4 See Deborah Howard, *Venice and the East: The Impact of the Islamic World on Venetian Architecture, 1100–1500* (New Haven: Yale University Press, 2000), 1–42, 111–32; Deborah Howard, "The Mamluks," in *Venice and the Islamic World, 828–1797*, ed. Stefano Carboni, 73–89 (New Haven: Yale University Press, 2007); Deborah Howard, "Venice as an Eastern City," in *Venice and the Islamic World*, 59–71.

5 See Howard, *Venice and the East*, 65–110.

6 Howard, *Venice and the East*, 173–88.

7 Robert Davis, *The War of the Fists: Popular Culture and Public Violence in Late Renaissance Venice* (Baltimore: Johns Hopkins University Press, 1994), 20–2.

8 See Howard, *Venice and the East*, 133–70.

9 *Venice: Everyman Guides*, 96–7.

10 Crouzet-Pavan, *Venice Triumphant*, 16.

CHAPTER 2. THE RICHES OF ASIA, EUROPE, AND NORTH AFRICA

1 See Janet L. Abu-Lughod, *Before European Hegemony: The World System, A.D. 1250–1350* (Oxford: Oxford University Press, 1989), 102.

2 Joanne M. Ferraro, "The Manufacture and Movement of Goods," in *The Renaissance World*, ed. John J. Martin (New York: Routledge, 2007), 88.

3 Antonio Fabris, *Venezia Sapore d'Oriente* (Venice: Centro internazionale della grafica di Venezia, 1990).

4 Massimo Costantini, "Le strutture dell'ospitalità," in *Storia di Venezia dalle origini alla caduta della serenissima*, Vol. V: *Il rinascimento. Società ed economia* (Rome: Istituto della enciclopedia italiana fondata da Giovanni Treccani, 1996), 881–910. Michaela Dal Borgo, archivist in the Venice State Archives, kindly permitted me to consult her unpublished study entitled, "Malvasia. Commerci e fortune di un vino dalla Grecia a Venezia. Note d' archivio attraverso i secoli."

5 Evelyn Welch, *Shopping in the Renaissance: Consumer Cultures in Italy, 1400–1600* (New Haven: Yale University Press, 2005), 235–7.

CHAPTER 3. A PRIDE OF LIONS

1 Elisabeth Crouzet-Pavan, *Venice Triumphant. The Horizons of a Myth* (Baltimore: Johns Hopkins University Press, 2002), 36–45; Luciano Pezzolo, "The Rise and Decline of a Great Power: Venice, 1250–1650," Working Paper Series, Department of Economics, Ca'Foscari University of Venice, No. 27/WP 2006 (www.dse.unive.it/pubblicazioni. 8/20/2011).

2 Holly S. Hurlburt, *The Dogaressa of Venice, 1200–1500: Wife and Icon* (New York: Palgrave Macmillan, 2006).

3 Stanley Chojnacki, "Social Identity in Renaissance Venice: The Second *Serrata*," *Renaissance Studies* 8 (1994): 341–58.

4 Stanley Chojnacki, "Identity and Ideology in Renaissance Venice: The Third Serrata," in *Venice Reconsidered: The History and Civilization of an Italian City-State,* ed. John J. Martin and Dennis Romano (Baltimore: Johns Hopkins University Press, 2000), 263–94.

5 Margaret King, *The Death of the Child Valerio Marcello* (Chicago: University of Chicago Press, 1994).

6 Stanley Chojnacki, *Women and Men in Renaissance Venice* (Baltimore: Johns Hopkins University Press, 2000), 176–7, 185–206, 227–56.

7 See Gaetano Cozzi and Michael Knapton, *Storia della repubblica di Venezia dalla Guerra di Chioggia alla riconquista della terraferma* (Turin: UTET, 1986), 8–11.

8 Gaetano Cozzi, "Authority and the Law in Renaissance Venice," in *Renaissance Venice*, ed. J. R. Hale (London: Faber and Faber, 1973), 293–345; Robert Finlay, *Politics in Renaissance Venice* (New Brunswick, NJ: Rutgers, 1981), 70–81.

9 Claudio Povolo, "Aspetti e problemi dell'amministrazione della giustizia penale nella Repubblica di Venezia. Secoli XVI–XVII," *Stato, società e giustizia nella Repubblica veneta (secoli xv–xviii),* Vol. I, ed. Gaetano Cozzi (Rome: Jouvence, 1980), 153–258.

10 Donald E. Queller, *The Venetian Patriciate: Reality versus Myth* (Urbana: University of Illinois Press, 1986), 85–112.

11 Cozzi, "Authority and the Law," 326.

12 Stanley Chojnacki, "In Search of the Venetian Patriciate: Families and Factions in the Fourteenth Century," in *Renaissance Venice,* 47–90.

13 Chojnacki, *Women and Men,* 61.

14 Alexander Cowan, *Marriage, Manners and Mobility in Early Modern Venice* (London:Ashgate Press, 2007).

15 See Gabriela Zarri, "Gender, Religious Institutions and Social Discipline," in *Gender and Society in Renaissance Italy*," ed. Judith C. Brown and Robert C. Davis (New York: Longman, 1998), 198; Anne Jacobson Schutte, *By Force and Fear: Taking and Breaking Monastic Vows in Early Modern Europe* (Chicago: University of Chicago Press, 2011), 4, 52–158.

16 Chojnacki, *Women and Men*, 95–114, 132–52.

17 Jutta Gisela Sperling, *Convents and the Body Politic in Late Renaissance Venice* (Chicago: University of Chicago Press, 1999).

18 Mary Laven, *Virgins of Venice: Broken Vows and Cloistered Lives in the Renaissance Convent* (New York: Penguin, 2002), xxiv.

CHAPTER 4. IDENTITIES AND MODES OF SOCIALIZATION

1 Anna Bellavitis, *Identité, mariage, mobilité sociale: Citoyennes et Citoyens à Venise au XVIe siècle* (Rome: École Française de Rome, 2001).

2 Frederic C. Lane, *Venice: A Maritime Republic* (Baltimore: Johns Hopkins University Press, 1973), 107–8.

3 Richard Mackenny, *Tradesmen and Traders: The World of the Guilds in Venice and Europe, c. 1250–1650* (Totowa, NJ: Barnes and Noble Books, 1987).

4 Maria Francesca Tiepolo, "Greci nella cancelleria veneziana: Giovanni Dario," in *I Greci a Venezia*, ed. Maria Francesca Tiepolo and Eurigio Tonetti (Venice: Istituto veneto di scienze, lettere ed arti, 2002), 257–314.

5 Jonathan Glixon, *Honoring God and the City: Music at the Venetian Confraternities, 1260–1807* (Oxford: Oxford University Press, 2003).

6 Dennis Romano, *Housecraft and Statecraft: Domestic Service in Renaissance Venice, 1400–1600* (Baltimore: Johns Hopkins University Press, 1996), 172.

7 Carla A. Boccato, "Aspetti della condizione feminile nel Ghetto di Venezia (Secolo XVII): I Testamenti," *Italia* 10 (1993): 105–35; Carla A. Boccato, "Testamenti di Ebrei del Ghetto di Venezia (secolo XVII)," *Archivio Veneto* 137 (1991): 119–30.

8 John Jeffries Martin, *Venice's Hidden Heretics* (Berkeley: University of California Press, 1993), 168–9.

9 Martin, *Hidden Heretics*, 158–73.

10 Robert C. Davis, *The War of the Fists: Popular Culture and Public Violence in Late Renaissance Venice* (Oxford: Oxford University Press, 1994), 20–2.

11 Bellavitis, *Identité;* Joanne M. Ferraro, *Marriage Wars in Late Renaissance Venice* (Oxford: Oxford University Press, 2001), 142–53.

12 Guido Ruggiero, *The Boundaries of Eros: Sex Crime and Sexuality in Renaissance Venice* (Oxford: Oxford University Press, 1985), 158.

13 Ruggiero, *Boundaries of Eros*, 146–68.

CHAPTER 5. MATERIAL LIFE

1 Archivio di Stato di Venezia (Hereafter ASV), *Giudici di Petizion, Inventarj, Busta* 356, No. 10, May 6, 1638, unfoliated.

2   ASV, *Giudici di Petizion, Inventarj, Busta* 337, No. 41, March 22, 1581, unfoliated.

3   ASV, *Giudici del Proprio, Vadimoni, Busta* 129, 1620, ff. 3v-4r.

4   ASV, *Giudici del Proprio, Vadimoni, Busta* 239, May 19, 1620, ff. 51v-52r.

5   ASV, *Giudici del Proprio, Vadimoni, Busta* 240, September 5, 1686, f. 176r.

6   ASV, *Giudici del Proprio, Vadimoni, Busta* 240, April 6, 1673, ff. 87v-88v.

7   ASV, *Giudici del Proprio, Vadimoni, Busta* 239, April 29,1620, ff. 34r-35r.

8   ASV, *Giudici del Proprio, Vadimoni, Busta* 239, June 11, 1645, ff. 70r-v.

9   *A Medical-Historical Dissertation by Giovanni Battista Anfossi for the Excellent Pier-Vettore Pisani, the Procurator of San Marco* (Rovigo: Gianjacopo Miazzi, 1775).

10   ASV, *Giudici di Petizion, Inventarj, Busta* 377/42, No. 6, March 31, 1674, ff. 1r-34.

11   ASV, *Giudici di Petizion, Inventarj, Busta* 463/128, No. 17, July 28, 1772, unfoliated.

12   ASV, *Giudici di Petizion, Inventarj, Busta* 459/12, No. 17, June 3, 1762, unfoliated.

13   *Venice: Città Excelentissima. Selections from the Renaissance Diaries of Marin Sanudo*, ed. Patricia H. LaBalme and Laura Sanguineti White; translated by Linda L. Carrol (Baltimore: Johns Hopkins University Press, 2008), 303–4.

14   ASV, *Giudici di Petizion, Inventarj, Busta* 337, No. 27, December 28, 1580, unfoliated.

15   ASV, *Giudici di Petizion, Inventarj, Busta* 338/3, No. 4., May 3, 1583, unfoliated.

16   ASV, *Giudici di Petizion, Inventarj, Busta* 338/3, January 1584, unfoliated.

17   ASV, *Giudici di Petizion, Inventarj, Busta* 356/21, No. 10, May 6, 1638.

CHAPTER 6. CITY OF MYTH

1   See David Rosand, *Myths of Venice: The Figuration of a State* (Chapel Hill: University of North Carolina Press, 2001).

2   Patricia Fortini Brown, *Private Lives in Renaissance Venice: Art, Architecture, and the Family* (New Haven: Yale University Press, 2004), 26–44.

3   Brown, *Private Lives*, 32–3.

4   Edward Muir, *Civic Ritual in Renaissance Venice* (Princeton, NJ: Princeton University Press, 1981), 231–50.

5   See Veronica Franco, *Poems and Selected Letters*, translated by Ann Rosalind Jones and Margaret F. Rosenthal (Chicago: University of Chicago Press, 1998); Margaret Rosenthal, *The Honest Courtesan: Veronica Franco, Citizen and Writer in Sixteenth-Century Venice* (Chicago: University of Chicago Press, 1993).

6   Jonathan Glixon, *Honoring God and the City: Music at the Venetian Confraternities, 1260–1807* (Oxford: Oxford University Press, 2003), 252–3.

CHAPTER 7. THE SERENISSIMA'S WAYWARD SUBJECTS

1   Laura J. McGough, *Gender, Sexuality and Syphilis in Early Modern Venice: The Disease that Came to Stay* (Houndmills, UK: Palgrave Macmillan, 2011), 8, 102–35.

2   John J. Martin, *Venice's Hidden Heretics* (Berkeley: University of California Press, 1993), 158–73.

3   David Chambers and Brian Pullan, eds., *Venice: A Documentary History, 1450–1630* (Oxford, UK: Blackwell, 1992), 236–7.

4   Guido Ruggiero, *Binding Passions: Tales of Magic, Marriage, and Power at the End of the Renaissance* (Oxford: Oxford University Press, 1993).

5 Sally Scully, "Marriage or a Career: Witchcraft as an Alternative in Seventeenth-Century Venice," *Journal of Social History* 28 (1995): 857–76; Joanne M. Ferraro, *Nefarious Crimes, Contested Justice: Illicit Sex and Infanticide in the Republic of Venice, 1557–1789* (Baltimore: Johns Hopkins University Press, 2008), 203.

6 Anne Schutte, *Aspiring Saints: Pretense of Holiness, Inquisition, and Gender in the Republic of Venice, 1618–1750* (Baltimore: Johns Hopkins University Press, 2001).

7 Mary Laven, *Virgins of Venice: Broken Vows and Cloistered Lives in the Renaissance Convent* (New York: Penguin, 2002), xxiv.

8 Jutta Gisela Sperling, *Convents and the Body Politic in Late Renaissance Venice* (Chicago: University of Chicago Press, 1999), 37–9; Joanne M. Ferraro, *Marriage Wars in Late Renaissance Venice* (Oxford: Oxford University Press, 2001b), 33–68.

9 See Elissa B. Weaver, *Convent Theatre in Early Modern Italy: Spiritual Fun and Learning for Women* (Cambridge: Cambridge University Press, 2002).

10 See Arcangela Tarabotti, *Paternal Tyranny*, translated by Letizia Panizza (Chicago: University of Chicago Press, 2004).

11 Ferraro, *Nefarious Crimes*, 4–7, 27–85.

12 Ferraro, *Marriage Wars*, 1–13, 38–40, 60 4, 137–8, 159–60.

13 Stanley Chojnacki, *Women and Men in Renaissance Venice* (Baltimore: Johns Hopkins University Press, 2000) 153–68.

14 Despina Vlassi, "Cause di divorzio giudicate degli arcivescovi di filadelfia secondo. I sacri canoni e le leggi della Santa Madre Chiesa Orientale," *I Greci a Venezia*, 325–40.

15 Ferraro, *Nefarious Crimes*, 3–26, 200–6.

16 Anne Jacobson Schutte, *By Force and Fear: Taking and Breaking Monastic Vows in Early Modern Europe* (Chicago: University of Chicago Press, 2011), 52–88.

17 Margaret King, *Women of the Renaissance* (Chicago: University of Chicago Press, 1991), 96.

CHAPTER 8. THE BAROQUE STAGE

1 Richard Rapp, *Industry and Economic Decline in Seventeenth Century Venice* (Cambridge, MA: Harvard University Press, 1976). An important historiographical essay for seventeenth- and eighteenth-century Venice is Brendan Doolcy, "Crisis and Survival in Eighteenth Century Italy: The Venetian Patriciate Strikes Back," *Journal of Social History* 20 (1986): 323–34.

2 Paola Lanaro, ed., *At the Center of the Old World: Trade and Manufacturing in Venice and the Venetian Mainland, 1400–1800*, Essays and Studies, Number 9 (Toronto: Centre for Reformation and Renaissance Studies, 2006). The model work for this approach is Domenico Sella, *Crisis and Continuity: The Economy of Spanish Lombardy in the Seventeenth Century* (Cambridge, MA: Harvard University Press, 1979).

3 See Salvatore Ciriacono, "Economie urbane e industria rurale nell'Italia del Cinque e Seicento. Riconversione o stagnazione?" *Rivista Storica Italiana* 113 (2001): 7–8.

4 Domenico Sella, "Industrial Raw Materials in the Import Trade of Northern and Central Italy in the 18th Century," *Journal of European Economic History* 33 (2004): 65–8.

5 Robert Davis, *Shipbuilders of the Venetian Arsenal: Workers and Workplace in the Preindustrial City* (Baltimore: Johns Hopkins University Press, 2007), 81, 227.

6 Joanne M. Ferraro, *Family and Public Life in Brescia, 1580–1650. The Foundations of Power in the Venetian State* (Cambridge: Cambridge University Press, 1993), 28–9, 37, 35–47, 61; Joanne M. Ferraro, "The Manufacture and Movement of Goods," in *The Renaissance World*, ed. J. J. Martin (New York: Routledge, 2007), 92.

7 Salvatore Ciriacono, "Protoindustria, lavoro a domicilio e sviluppo economico nelle campagne venete in epoca moderna," *Quaderni Storici* 52 (1983): 59–62; Joanne M. Ferraro, "'Making' Geographies and Polities: Representing Women in Italian Economic History," in *Structures and Subjectivities: Attending to Early Modern Women*, ed. Joan Hartman and Adele Seeff (Newark: University of Delaware Press, 2006), 75–88; Ferraro, "Manufacture and Movement of Goods," 87–100.

8 Andrea Zannini, "L'economia veneta nel Seicento: Oltre il paradima della 'crisi generale,'" *Società Italiana di Demografia Storica: La Popolazione nel Seicento. Relazione presentata al convegno di Firenze, 28–30 Novembre, 1996* (Bologna: CLUEB, 1999), 473–501.

9 Ellen Rosand, *Opera in Seventeenth-Century Venice: The Creation of a Genre* (Berkeley: University of California Press, 2007), 125–53.

10 Edward Muir, *The Culture Wars of the Late Renaissance: Skeptics, Libertines, and Opera* (Cambridge, MA: Harvard University Press, 2007), 70–107.

11 Muir, *Culture Wars*, 129.

12 Rebecca Messbarger, *The Century of Women: Representations of Women in the Eighteenth-Century Italian Public Discourse* (Toronto: University of Toronto Press, 2002).

CHAPTER 9. EPILOGUE: THE TIDES OF CHANGE

1 http://rpo.library.utoronto.ca/poem/2355.html (3/29/2011).

2 See Margaret Plant, *Venice: Fragile City, 1779–1997* (New Haven: Yale University Press, 2002), 40–1.

BIBLIOGRAPHY

ARCHIVAL SOURCES

Archivio di Stato di Venezia.
Giudici di Petizion. Inventarj.
Giudici del Proprio. Vadimoni.

MANUSCRIPTS

Anfossi, Giovanni Battista. *A Medical-Historical Dissertation by Giovanni Battista Anfossi for the Excellent Pier-Vettore Pisani, the Procurator of San Marco.* Rovigo: Gianjacopo Miazzi, 1775.

SECONDARY LITERATURE

Abu-Lughod, Janet. *Before European Hegemony: The World System, A.D. 1250 1350.* Oxford: Oxford University Press, 1989.

Allerston, Patricia Anne. "Clothing and Early Modern Venetian Society." *Continuity and Change* 15 (2000): 367–90.

——— "Wedding Finery in Sixteenth-Century Venice." In *Marriage in Italy, 1300–1600,* edited by Trevor Dean and K. J. Lowe, 25–40. Cambridge: Cambridge University Press, 1998.

Appuhn, Karl. *A Forest on the Sea: Environmental Expertise in Renaissance Venice.* Baltimore: Johns Hopkins University Press, 2009.

Arbel, Benjamin. "Jews in International Trade: The Emergence of the Levantines and the Ponentines." In *The Jews of Early Modern Venice,* edited by Robert C. Davis and Benjamin Ravid, 73–96. Baltimore: Johns Hopkins University Press, 2001.

Bellavitis, Anna. *Identité, mariage, mobilité sociale. Citoyennes et Citoyens à Venise au XVIe siècle.* Rome: École Française de Rome, 2001.

Bellavitis, Giorgio, and Giandomenico Romanelli. *Venezia. Le Città nella Storia d'Italia: Grandi Opere.* Rome: Laterza, 1985.

Berengo, Marino. *La società veneta alla fine del Settecento: Ricerche storiche.* Florence: G. C. Sansoni, 1956.

Bistort, Giulio. *Il magistrato alle pompe nella republica di Venezia: Studio storico.* Reprint of 1912 edition. Bologna: Forni Editore, 1969.

Boccato, Carla A. "Aspetti della condizione feminile nel Ghetto di Venezia (Secolo XVII): I Testamenti." *Italia* 10 (1993): 105–35.

"Testamenti di Ebrei del Ghetto di Venezia (secolo XVII)." *Archivio Veneto* 137 (1991): 119–30.

Boerio, Giuseppe. *Dizionario del dialetto veneziano.* Reprint of 1856 edition. Venice: Filippi Editore, 1973.

Bouwsma, William. *Venice and the Defense of Republican Liberty: Renaissance Values in the Age of the Counter Reformation.* Berkeley: University of California Press, 1968.

Braudel, Fernand. *Civilization and Capitalism.* 3 vols. New York: Harper and Row, 1986.

The Mediterranean and the Mediterranean World in the Age of Philip II. 2 vols. New York: Harper, 1972.

Brown, Judith, and Robert C. Davis, eds. *Gender and Society in Renaissance Italy.* London: Longman, 1998.

Brown, Patricia Fortini. *Art and Life in Renaissance Venice.* New York: Prentice Hall and Harry N. Abrams, 1997.

Private Lives in Renaissance Venice: Art, Architecture, and the Family. New Haven: Yale University Press, 2004.

Burke, Peter. *The Historical Anthropology of Early Modern Italy.* Cambridge: Cambridge University Press, 1987.

Byron, Lord. *The Works of Lord Byron: Poetry.* Vol. 5, edited by Ernest Hartley Coleridge. London: John Murray; New York: Charles Scribner's Sons, 1905.

Calabi, Donatella. "The 'City of the Jews.'" In *The Jews of Early Modern Venice,* edited by Robert C. Davis and Benjamin Ravid, 31–52. Baltimore: Johns Hopkins University Press, 2001.

"An Itinerary through the History of the Town and Its Architecture." In *Venice: An Architectural Guide,* edited by Guido Zucconi, 7–21. Verona: Arsenale Editrice, 1993.

Calabi, Donatella, and Paola Lanaro Sartoro, eds. *La città italiana e i luoghi degli stranieri, XIV–XVIII secolo.* Rome: Laterza, 1998.

Calimani, Riccardo. *The Ghetto of Venice.* Translated by Katherine Silberblatt Wolfthal. New York: M. Evans, 1987.

Carboni, Stefano. "Moments of Vision: Venice and the Islamic World, 828–1797." In *Venice and the Islamic World, 828–1797,* edited by Stefano Carboni, 13–35. New Haven: Yale University Press, 2007.

ed. *Venice and the Islamic World, 828–1797.* New Haven: Yale University Press, 2007.

Chambers, David, and Brian Pullan. *Venice: A Documentary History, 1450–1630.* Oxford: Blackwell, 1992.

Chojnacka, Monica. *Working Women of Early Modern Venice.* Baltimore: Johns Hopkins University Press, 2001.

Chojnacki, Stanley. "Daughters and Oligarchs: Gender and the Early Renaissance State." In *Gender and Society in Renaissance Italy,* edited by Judith C. Brown and Robert C. Davis, 63–86. London: Longman, 1998.

"Identity and Ideology in Renaissance Venice: The Third Serrata." In *Venice Reconsidered: The History and Civilization of an Italian City-State,* edited by John J. Martin and Dennis Romano, 263–95. Baltimore: Johns Hopkins University Press, 2000.

"Social Identity in Renaissance Venice: The Second *Serrata*." *Renaissance Studies* 8 (1994): 341–58.

Women and Men in Renaissance Venice. Baltimore: Johns Hopkins University Press, 2000.

Ciriacono, Salvatore. "Economie urbane e industria rurale nell'Italia del Cinque e Seicento. Riconversione o stagnazione?" *Rivista Storica Italiana* 113 (2001): 5–35.

"Mass Consumption Goods and Luxury Goods: The De-Industrialization of the Republic of Venice from the Sixteenth to the Eighteenth Century." In *The Rise and Decline of Urban Industries in Italy and in the Low Countries (Late Middle Ages–Early Modern Times)*, edited by Herman Van der Wee, 41–61. Leuven, Belgium: Leuven University Press, 1988.

"Protoindustria, lavoro a domicilio e sviluppo economico nelle campagne venete in epoca moderna." *Quaderni Storici* 52 (1983): 57–80.

Cohen, Sherill. *The Evolution of Women's Asylums since 1500: From Refuges for Ex-Prostitutes to Shelters for Battered Women*. New York: Oxford University Press, 1992.

Cooper, Tracy. *Palladio's Venice: Architecture and Society in a Renaissance Republic*. New Haven: Yale University Press, 2005.

Costantini, Massimo. "Le strutture dell'ospitalità." In *Storia di Venezia dalle origini alla caduta della serenissima*. Vol. V, *Il rinascimento. Società ed economia*, 881–910. Rome: Istituto della enciclopedia italiana fondata da Giovanni Treccani, 1996.

Cowan, Alexander. *Marriage, Manners and Mobility in Early Modern Venice*. London: Ashgate Press, 2007.

Cox, Virginia. "The Single Self: Feminist Thought and the Marriage Market in Early Modern Venice." *Renaissance Quarterly* 48 (1995): 513–81.

Cozzi, Gaetano. "Authority and the Law in Renaissance Venice." In *Renaissance Venice*, edited by J. R. Hale, 293–345. London: Faber and Faber, 1973.

Il doge Nicolò Contarini: Ricerche sul patriziato veneziano agli inizi del Seicento. Venice: Istituto per la Collaborazione Culturale, 1958.

"Note e documenti sulla questione del 'divorzio' a Venezia (1782–1788)." *Annali dell'Istituto storico italo-germanico in Trento* 7 (1981): 275–360.

"Padri, figli e matrimoni clandestini (metà sec. XVI–metà sec. XVIII)." *La cultura* 14 (1976): 169–212.

Repubblica di Venezia e stati Italiani. Politica e Giustizia dal secolo xvi al secolo xviii. Turin: Einaudi, 1982.

ed. *Gli ebrei a Venezia, sec. XIV–XVIII*. Milan: Comunità, 1987.

ed. *Stato, società e Giustizia nella Repubblica Veneta (xv–xviii sec.)* Rome: Jouvence, 1980.

Cozzi, Gaetano, and Michael Knapton. *Storia della repubblica di Venezia dalla Guerra di Chioggia alla riconquista della terraferma*. Turin: UTET, 1986.

Crouzet-Pavan, Elisabeth. *"Sopra le acque salse": Espaces, pouvoir et société à Venise à la fin du Moyen Age*. 2 vols. Collection de l'École Française de Rome, CLVI. Rome: Istituto Storico Italiano per il Medio Evo, 1992.

Venice Triumphant: The Horizons of a Myth. Baltimore: Johns Hopkins University Press, 2002.

Curatola, Giovanni. "Venice's Textile and Carpet Trade: The Role of Jewish Merchants." In *Venice and the Islamic World, 828–1797*, edited by Stefano Carboni, 205–11. New Haven: Yale University Press, 2007.

Dal Borgo, Michaela. "Il pesce della Serenissima." *Civiltà della Tavola* 160 (April 2005): 67–8.

Davis, James C. *The Decline of the Venetian Nobility as a Ruling Class.* Baltimore: Johns Hopkins University Press, 1962.

    A Venetian Family and Its Fortune, 1500–1900: The Donà and the Conservation of Their Wealth. Philadelphia: American Philosophical Society, 1975.

Davis, Robert C. *Shipbuilders of the Venetian Arsenal: Workers and Workplace in the Preindustrial City.* Baltimore: Johns Hopkins University Press, 2007.

    The War of the Fists: Popular Culture and Public Violence in Late Renaissance Venice. Oxford: Oxford University Press, 1994.

Davis, Robert C., and Benjamin Ravid, eds. *The Jews of Early Modern Venice.* Baltimore: Johns Hopkins University Press, 2001.

Davis, Robert C., and Garry R. Marvin. *Venice, the Tourist Maze: A Cultural Critique of the World's Most Touristed City.* Berkeley: University of California Press, 2004.

Denny, Walter B. "Oriental Carpets and Textiles in Venice." In *Venice and the Islamic World, 828–1797,* edited by Stefano Carboni, 175–91. New Haven: Yale University Press, 2007.

Derosas, Renzo. "Moralità e giustizia a Venezia nel '500–'600: Gli Esecutori contro la bestemmia." In *Stato, società e giustizia nella Repubblica Veneta (Secolo xv–xviii),* edited by Gaetano Cozzi, 431–528. Rome: Jouvence, 1980.

Dooley, Brendon. "Crisis and Survival in Eighteenth-Century Italy: The Venetian Patriciate Strikes Back." *Journal of Social History* 20 (1986): 323–34.

Dursteler, Eric. *Venetians in Constantinople: Nation, Identity, and Coexistence in the Early Modern Mediterranean.* Baltimore: Johns Hopkins University Press, 2006.

Fabris, Antonio. *Venezia Sapore d'Oriente.* Venice: Centro internazionale della grafica di Venezia, 1990.

Feldman, Martha. "Opera, Festivity, and Spectacle in 'Revolutionary' Venice: Phantasms of Time and History." In *Venice Reconsidered: The History and Civilization of an Italian City-State, 1297–1797,* edited by John Martin and Dennis Romano, 217–60. Baltimore: Johns Hopkins University Press, 2000.

    Opera and Sovereignty: Transforming Myths in Eighteenth-Century Italy. Chicago: University of Chicago Press, 2007.

Ferraro, Joanne M. "Courtship, Marriage, and Divorce in European Society." *The Encyclopedia of Social History,* Vol. 4, edited by Peter Stearns, 145–60. New York: Charles Scribner's Sons, 2001 (a).

    "Families and Clans in the Renaissance World." In *The Blackwell Companion to the Worlds of the Renaissance,* edited by Guido Ruggiero, 173–87. Oxford: Blackwell, 2002.

    Family and Public Life in Brescia, 1580–1650: The Social Foundations of the Venetian State. Cambridge: Cambridge University Press, 1993.

    "'Making' Geographies and Polities: Representing Women in Italian Economic History." In *Structures and Subjectivities: Attending to Early Modern Women,* edited by Joan Hartman and Adele Seeff, 75–88. Newark: University of Delaware Press, 2006.

    "The Manufacture and Movement of Goods." In *The Renaissance World,* edited by J. J. Martin, 87–100. New York: Routledge, 2007.

    Marriage Wars in Late Renaissance Venice. Oxford: Oxford University Press, 2001 (b).

    Nefarious Crimes, Contested Justice: Illicit Sex and Infanticide in the Republic of Venice, 1557–1789. Baltimore: Johns Hopkins University Press, 2008.

Finlay, Robert. *Politics in Renaissance Venice*. New Brunswick, N.J.: Rutgers University Press, 1981.

Fonte, Moderata. *The Worth of Women*. Edited and Translated by Virginia Cox. Chicago: University of Chicago Press, 1997.

Franco, Veronica. *Poems and Selected Letters*. Translated by Ann Rosalind Jones and Margaret F. Rosenthal. Chicago: University of Chicago Press, 1998.

Ginsborg, Paul. *Daniele Manin and the Venetian Revolution of 1848–49*. Cambridge: Cambridge University Press, 1979.

Glixon, Jonathan. *Honoring God and the City: Music at the Venetian Confraternities, 1260–1807*. Oxford: Oxford University Press, 2003.

Goffen, Rona. *Giovanni Bellini*. New Haven: Yale University Press, 1989.

  Piety and Patronage in Renaissance Venice: Bellini, Titian, and the Franciscans. New Haven: Yale University Press, 1986.

  Titian's Women. New Haven: Yale University Press, 1997

Grendler, Paul F. *The Roman Inquisition and the Printing Press, 1540–1605*. Princeton: Princeton University Press, 1977.

  Schooling in Renaissance Italy: Literacy and Learning, 1300–1600. Baltimore. Johns Hopkins University Press, 1989.

Grevembroch, G. *Gli abiti dei Veneziani di quasi ogni età con diligenza raccolti e dipinti nel secolo XVIII (1754)*. Reprint edition. Venice: Filippi Editore, 1981.

Grubb, James S. "Elite Citizens." In *Venice Reconsidered: The History and Civilization of an Italian City-State, 1297–1797*, edited by John Martin and Dennis Romano, 339–64. Baltimore: Johns Hopkins University Press, 2000.

  Firstborn of Venice: Vicenza in the Early Renaissance State. Baltimore: Johns Hopkins University Press, 1988.

  "When Myths Lose Power: Four Decades of Venetian Historiography." *Journal of Modern History* 58 (1986): 43–94.

Hacke, Daniela. *Women, Sex, and Marriage in Early Modern Venice*. London: Ashgate, 2004.

Hale, John Rigby, ed. *Renaissance Venice*. London: Faber and Faber, 1973.

Hocquet, Jean-Claude. "Venice and the Ottoman Turks." In *Venice and the Islamic World, 828–1797*, edited by Stefano Carboni, 37–51. New Haven: Yale University Press, 2007.

Horodowich, Elizabeth. *Language and Statecraft in Early Modern Venice*. Cambridge: Cambridge University Press, 2008

Horowitz, Elliot. "Processions, Piety, and Jewish Confraternities." In *The Jews of Early Modern Venice*, edited by Robert C. Davis and Benjamin Ravid, 231–48. Baltimore: Johns Hopkins University Press, 2001.

Howard, Deborah. *The Architectural History of Venice*. New Haven: Yale University Press, 2005.

  "Cultural Transfer between Venice and the Ottomans in the Fifteenth and Sixteenth Centuries." In *Cultural Exchange in Early Modern Europe*. Vol. IV, *Forging European Identities, 1400–1700*, edited by Herman Roodenburg, 138–77. Cambridge: Cambridge University Press, 2007 (a).

  "The Mamluks." In *Venice and the Islamic World, 828–1797*, edited by Stefano Carboni, 73–89. New Haven: Yale University Press, 2007 (b).

Venice and the East: The Impact of the Islamic World on Venetian Architecture, 1100–1500. New Haven: Yale University Press, 2000.

"Venice as an 'Eastern City.'" In *Venice and the Islamic World, 828–1797*, edited by Stefano Carboni, 59–71. New Haven: Yale University Press, 2007 (c).

Humphrey, Peter. *Painting in Renaissance Venice.* New Haven: Yale University Press, 1997.

Hurlburt, Holly S. *The Dogaressa of Venice, 1200–1500: Wife and Icon.* New York: Palgrave Macmillan, 2006.

Ioli-Orattini, Pier Cesare. "Jews, Crypto-Jews, and the Inquisition." In *The Jews of Early Modern Venice*, edited by Robert C. Davis and Benjamin Ravid, 97–116. Baltimore: Johns Hopkins University Press, 2001.

Jacoby, David. "Cretan Cheese. A Neglected Aspect of Medieval Venetian Trade." In *Medieval and Renaissance Venice*, edited by Ellen E. Kittell and Thomas F. Madden, 49–68. Urbana: University of Illinois Press, 1999.

James, Henry. *On Italy: Selections from Italian Hours.* London: Barrie and Jenkins, 1988.

Kertzer, David, and Marzio Barbagli, eds. *Family Life in Early Modern Times, 1500–1789.* New Haven: Yale University Press, 2001.

King, Margaret. "Caldiera and the Barbaros on Marriage and the Family: Humanist Reflections of Venetian Realities." *Journal of Medieval and Renaissance Studies* 6 (1976): 19–50.

The Death of the Child Valerio Marcello. Chicago: University of Chicago Press, 1994.

Venetian Humanism in an Age of Patrician Dominance. Princeton: Princeton University Press, 1986.

Women of the Renaissance. Chicago: University of Chicago Press, 1991.

Kittell, Ellen E., and Thomas F. Madden, eds. *Medieval and Renaissance Venice.* Urbana: University of Illinois Press, 1999.

La Balme, Patricia. "Venetian Women on Women: Three Early Modern Feminists." *Archivio veneto* 5th ser., 117 (1981): 81–109.

ed. *Beyond Their Sex: Learned Women of the European Past.* New York: New York University Press, 1984.

La Balme, Patricia, and Laura Sanguinetti, White, eds. "How to (and How Not to) Get Married in Sixteenth-Century Venice (Selections from the Diaries of Marin Sanudo)." *Renaissance Quarterly*, 52 (1999): 43–72.

Venice, Città Excelentissima: Selections from the Renaissance Diaries of Marin Sanudo. Translated by Linda Carroll. Baltimore: Johns Hopkins University Press, 2008.

Lanaro, Paola, ed. *At the Center of the Old World: Trade and Manufacturing in Venice and the Venetian Mainland, 1400–1800.* Essays and Studies. Number 9. Toronto: Centre for Reformation and Renaissance Studies, 2006.

Lane, Frederick C. *Andrea Barbarigo: Merchant of Venice, 1418–1499.* Baltimore: Johns Hopkins University Press, 1944.

Venice: A Maritime Republic. Baltimore: Johns Hopkins University Press, 1973.

Laven, Mary. *Virgins of Venice: Broken Vows and Cloistered Lives in the Renaissance Convent.* New York: Penguin, 2002.

Logan, Oliver. *Culture and Society in Venice, 1470–1790: The Renaissance and Its Heritage.* London: Batsford, 1972.

Mackenny, Richard. *Tradesmen and Traders. The World of the Guilds in Venice and Europe, c. 1250–1650.* Totowa, N.J.: Barnes and Noble Books, 1987.

Maffioli, Giuseppe. *La Cucina Veneziana.* Padua: Franco Muzzio Editore, 1982.

Mallet, Michael, and John Rigby Hale. *The Military Organization of a Renaissance State: Venice c. 1400–1617.* Cambridge: Cambridge University Press, 1984.

Maretto, Paolo. *La casa veneziana nella storia della città dall'origine all'Ottocento.* Venice: Marsilio, 1986.

Marinella, Lucrezia. *The Nobility and Excellence of Women and the Defects and Vices of Men.* Translated by Anne Dunhill. Introduction by Letizia Panizza. Chicago: University of Chicago Press, 1999.

Martin, John J. *Venice's Hidden Heretics.* Berkeley: University of California Press, 1993.
ed. *The Renaissance World.* New York: Routledge, 2007.

Martin, John J., and Dennis Romano, eds. *Venice Reconsidered: The History and Civilization of an Italian City-State.* Baltimore: Johns Hopkins University Press, 2000.

Martin, Ruth. *Witchcraft and the Inquisition in Venice, 1550–1650.* Oxford: Basil Blackwell, 1989.

Martines, Lauro. *Power and the Imagination: City-States in Renaissance Italy.* Baltimore: Johns Hopkins University Press, 1988.

McGough, Laura J. *Gender, Sexuality, and Syphilis in Early Modern Venice: The Disease that Came to Stay.* Houndmills, UK: Palgrave Macmillan, 2011.

McNeill, William. *Venice: The Hinge of Europe, 1081–1797.* Chicago: University of Chicago Press, 1974.

Messbarger, Rebecca. *The Century of Women: Representations of Women in the Eighteenth-Century Italian Public Discourse.* Toronto: University of Toronto Press, 2002.

Molà, Luca. *The Silk Industry of Renaissance Venice.* Baltimore: Johns Hopkins University Press, 2000.

Moschonas, Nikolaos. "La comunità greca di Venezia. Aspetti sociali ed economici." In *I Greci a Venezia*, edited by Maria Francesca Tiepolo and Eurigio Tonetti, 222–242. Venice: Istituto veneto di scienze, lettere ed arti, 2002.

Muir, Edward. *Civic Ritual in Renaissance Venice.* Princeton: Princeton University Press, 1981.
The Culture Wars of the Late Renaissance: Skeptics, Libertines, and Opera. Cambridge, Mass.: Harvard University Press, 2007.

O'Connell, Monique. *Men of Empire: Power and Negotiation in Venice's Maritime State.* Baltimore: Johns Hopkins University Press, 2009.

Oresko, Robert. "Culture in the Age of Baroque and Rococo." *The Oxford Illustrated History of Italy.* Edited by George Holms, 139–76. Oxford: Basil Blackwell, 1997.

Palmer, Richard. "Pharmacy in the Republic of Venice in the Sixteenth Century." In *The Medical Renaissance of the Sixteenth Century*, edited by A. Wear, R. K. French, and I. M. Lonie, 100–17. Cambridge: Cambridge University Press, 1985.

Pezzolo, Luciano. "The Rise and Decline of a Great Power: Venice, 1250–1650." Working Paper Series. Department of Economics. Ca' Foscari, University of Venice. No. 27/WP. 2006. http://www.dse.unive.it/pubblicazione (8/20/2011).

Pignatti, Terisio. *Venice: Architecture, Sculpture, Painting.* New York: Holt, Rinehart and Winston, 1971.

Plant, Margaret. *Venice: Fragile City, 1779–1997.* New Haven: Yale University Press, 2002.

Povolo, Claudio. "Aspetti e problemi dell'amministrazione della giustizia penale nella Repubblica di Venezia. Secoli XVI–XVII." In *Stato, società e giustizia nella Repubblica veneta (secoli xv–xviii)*, Vol. I, edited by Gaetano Cozzi, 153–258. Rome: Jouvence, 1980.

L'intrigo dell'onore. Poteri e istituzioni nella Repubblica di Venezia tra Cinque e Seicento. Verona: Cierri edizioni, 1997.

Il Processo Guarnieri. Buie, Capodistria, 1771. Koper: Biblioteca Annales, 1996.

Pullan, Brian. "Jewish Banks and the Monti di Pietà." In *The Jews of Early Modern Venice*, edited by Robert C. Davis and Benjamin Ravid, 53–72. Baltimore: Johns Hopkins University Press, 2001.

The Jews of Europe and the Inquisition of Venice, 1550–1670. London: I. B. Tauris, 1997.

Rich and Poor in Renaissance Venice: The Social Institutions of a Catholic State, to 1620. Cambridge, Mass.: Harvard University Press, 1971.

ed. *Crisis and Change in the Venetian Economy.* London: Methuen, 1968.

Queller, Donald E. *The Venetian Patriciate: Reality versus Myth.* Urbana: University of Illinois Press, 1986.

Rapp, Richard. *Industry and Economic Decline in Seventeenth Century Venice.* Cambridge, Mass.: Harvard University Press, 1976.

Ravid, Benjamin. "The Venetian Government and the Jews." In *The Jews of Early Modern Venice*, edited by Robert C. Davis and Benjamin Ravid, 3–30. Baltimore: Johns Hopkins University Press, 2001.

Romanin, Samuele. *Storia documentata di Venezia.* 3rd ed. 10 vols. Venice: Filippi Editore, 1972–75.

Romano, Dennis. *Housecraft and Statecraft: Domestic Service in Renaissance Venice, 1400–1600.* Baltimore: Johns Hopkins University Press, 1996.

The Likeness of Venice: A Life of Doge Francesco Foscari, 1373–1457. New Haven: Yale University Press, 2007.

Patricians and Popolani: The Social Foundations of the Venetian Renaissance State. Baltimore: Johns Hopkins University Press, 1987.

Rosand, David. *Myths of Venice: The Figuration of a State.* Chapel Hill: University of North Carolina Press, 2001.

Rosand, Ellen. *Opera in Seventeenth-Century Venice: The Creation of a Genre.* Berkeley: University of California Press, 2007.

Rosenthal, Margaret. *The Honest Courtesan: Veronica Franco, Citizen and Writer in Sixteenth-Century Venice.* Chicago: University of Chicago Press, 1993.

Rosenthal, Margaret, and Ann Rosalind Jones. *The Clothing of the Renaissance World: Europe, Asia, Africa, the Americas: Cesare Vecellio's Habiti antichi e moderni.* London: Thames and Hudson, 2008.

Ruggiero, Guido. *Binding Passions: Tales of Magic, Marriage, and Power at the End of the Renaissance.* Oxford: Oxford University Press, 1993.

The Boundaries of Eros: Sex Crime and Sexuality in Renaissance Venice. Oxford: Oxford University Press, 1985.

Machiavelli in Love: Sex, Self, and Society in the Italian Renaissance. Baltimore: Johns Hopkins University Press, 2007.

"The Strange Death of Margarita Marcellini: Male, Signs, and the Everyday World of Pre-Modern Medicine." *American Historical Review* 106 (2001): 1141–58.

Violence in Early Renaissance Venice. New Brunswick, N.J.: Rutgers University Press, 1980.

ed. *A Companion to the Worlds of the Renaissance.* Oxford: Blackwell, 2002.

Ruskin, John. *The Stones of Venice.* 3 vols. New York: J. Wiley, 1860. First published 1851–53.

Sarti, Rafaella. "The Material Conditions of Family Life." In *Family Life in Early Modern Times, 1500–1789*, edited by David Kertzer and Marzio Barbagli, 3–23. New Haven: Yale University Press, 2001.

Schutte, Anne Jacobson. *Aspiring Saints: Pretense of Holiness, Inquisition, and Gender in the Republic of Venice, 1618–1750*. Baltimore: Johns Hopkins University Press, 2001.

By Force and Fear: Taking and Breaking Monastic Vows in Early Modern Europe. Chicago: University of Chicago Press, 2011.

Scully, Sally. "Marriage or a Career: Witchcraft as an Alternative in Seventeenth-Century Venice." *Journal of Social History* 28 (1995): 857–76.

Sella, Domenico. *Crisis and Continuity: The Economy of Spanish Lombardy in the Seventeenth Century*. Cambridge, Mass.: Harvard University Press, 1979.

"Industrial Raw Materials in the Import Trade of Northern and Central Italy in the 18th Century." *Journal of European Economic History* 33 (2004): 59–70.

Sperling, Jutta Gisela. *Convents and the Body Politic in Late Renaissance Venice*. Chicago: University of Chicago Press, 1999.

Tafuri, Manfredo. *Venice and the Renaissance*. Translated by Jessica Levine. Cambridge, Mass.: MIT Press, 1989.

ed. "Renovatio urbis": Venezia nell'età di Andrea Gritti (1523–1538). Rome: Officina Edizioni, 1984.

Tarabotti, Arcangela. *Paternal Tyranny*. Translated by Letizia Panizza. Chicago: University of Chicago Press, 2004.

Tassini, Giuseppe. *Curiosità veneziane ovvero origini della denominazioni stradali di Venezia*. 8th ed. Venice: Filippi Editore, 1970.

Tenenti, Alberto. *Piracy and the Decline of Venice, 1580–1615*. Berkeley: University of California Press, 1967.

"The Sense of Space and Time in the Venetian World of the Fifteenth and Sixteenth Centuries." In *Renaissance Venice*, edited by John R. Hale, 17–46. London: Faber and Faber, 1973.

Tiepolo, Maria Francesca. "Greci nella cancelleria veneziana: Giovanni Dario." In *I Greci a Venezia*, edited by Maria Francesca Tiepolo and Eurigio Tonetti, 257–314. Venice: Istituto veneto di scienze, lettere ed arti, 2002.

Trincanato, Egli Renata. *Venezia Minore*. Milan: Edizioni del Milione, 1948.

Venice: Everyman Guides. London: Davis Campbell, 1993.

Vitali, Achille. *La Moda a Venezia attraverso i secoli. Lessico ragionato*. Venice: Filippi Editore, 1992.

Vlassi, Despina. "Cause di divorzio giudicate degli arcivescovi di filadelfia second i sacri canoni e le leggi della santa madre chiesa orientale." In *I Greci a Venezia*, edited by Maria Francesca Tiepolo and Eurigio Tonetti, 325–40. Venice: Istituto veneto di scienze, lettere ed arti, 2002.

Walker, Jonathan. "Gambling and Venetian Noblemen, c. 1500–1700." *Past and Present* 162 (1999): 28–69.

Weaver, Elissa B. *Convent Theatre in Early Modern Italy: Spiritual Fun and Learning for Women*. Cambridge: Cambridge University Press, 2002.

Welch, Evelyn. *Shopping in the Renaissance*. New Haven: Yale University Press, 2005.

Wilson, Bronwen. *The World in Venice: Print, the City, and Early Modern Identity*. Toronto: University of Toronto Press, 2005.

Zannini, Andrea. "L'economia veneta nel Seicento. Oltre il paradima della 'crisi generale.'" *Società Italiana di Demografia Storica. La Popolazione nel Seicento. Relazione presentata al convegno di Firenze, 28–30 Novembre, 1996.* Bologna: CLUEB, 1999, 473–501.

Zarri, Gabriela. "Gender, Religious Institutions, and Social Discipline: The Reform of the Regulars." In *Gender and Society in Renaissance Italy*, 193–212. London: Longman, 1998.

Zucconi, Guido, ed. *Venice: An Architectural Guide.* Verona: Arsenale Editrice, 1993.

WEBSITE

http://rpo.library.utoronto.ca/poem/2355.html

INDEX

abortion, 155, 171
academies, 190, 193, 213
Accademie. *See also* agrarian
 academies
 degli Incogniti, 189, 220
 dei Granelleschi, 191
 dei Ricoverati, 192, 223
 della Giudecca, 180
 delle Belle Arti, 204, 207
 Scienze, Lettere, ed Arti, 183
acqua alta. See floods
acquaroli, 28, 94, 217
Acre, 14–15, 30, 35, 50, 54
Adige River, 10, 43, 60
adolescence, 99
 patrician, 58
Adriatic Sea, 2, 19, 24
 colonies, 10
 and Corsairs, 177
 declining hegemony, 179
 English blockade, 203
 and Jupiter, 131
 and lagoons, 53
 littoral, 2–3, 10
 markets, 30
 migrants from, 75
 protection of, 66, 106
 Spanish threat, 177
 trade links, 11
 Venice as Queen, 132, 176
adultery, 103, 158, 168–9, 170
adulthood
 female, 59

 male, 72
 political, 56, 58–9
Aegean Sea, 10, 24, 30, 33, 41, 50, 65,
 106, 178
 markets, 30
Africa, North, 12, 28, 37, 44, 49, 68, 78,
 106, 108, 123, 130, 187, 221
Agnadello, Battle of, 62, 66, 136
agrarian academies, 183
 Brescia, 183
 Giorgiofili, 183
 Padua, 183
 Royal Agricultural Society, 183
 Udine, 183
agrarian reform, 183
agriculture, 4, 9, 41, 68, 176, 182, 186, 192
 commercial, 184, 187
Aigues-Mortes, 37
Albanesi. See Albanians
Albania, 66, 68, 76
Albanians, 11, 48, 78–9, 86, 174, 217
albergo/ghi, 48, 217
Aldine Press, 60
Aleppo, 11, 108
Alexandria, 4, 12, 16, 33, 42, 50, 106, 108,
 113–14, 156
Algarotti, Francesco, educator, 193
alum, 30, 37
Alvisopoli, publishing house, 205
Amadi family, 82
ambassadors
 education of, 58
ambassadorships, 64, 181

America
   Revolution, 180
American Friends of the Marciana, 214
Americas, 111, 187
Anabaptists, 94, 159–60
Anatolia, 38
anatomy, 125, 183
Andalusia, 186
Andreini, Isabella, actress, 168
androne. See Great Hall
Anfossi, Giovanni Battista, writer, 112
Annunciation Day, 2, 57–8, 127, 142
Antioch, 156
apéritifs, 47
Apollo, 139
apothecaries, 25, 40, 113–15, 122, 171
Apulia, 31
Aquapendente, Girolamo Fabrizio d',
      anatomist, 183
Aquileia, 2, 4
Arabs, 11, 13, 33, 41, 43, 46, 123
   Christian, 37
   medics, 45
architects
   proto, 222
   proto and *protomaestri*, 131
Archivio Veneto, 207
arengo. See assembly, general
Aretino, Pietro, writer, 155
Argos, 65
Aristotle, 153, 189
Armenia, 33, 45, 76
Armenians, 9, 37, 48, 108, 217
arrowsmiths, 9, 220
Arsenal, 12, **18**, 27, 83, 91, 99, 183–6, 203,
      204, 217
   workers, 18, 20, 36, 106, 205
artichokes, 45
artisans, 11, 50, 85, 93–5, 108–9, 159
Ascalon, 30
Ash Wednesday, 97
Asher Meshullam, banker, 90
Asia, 30, 33, **37**, 49, 108, 125, 187
   East, 34, 217
   greater, 123, 217
   Southeast, 45, 217
   Southwest, 12, 28, 130, 187, 217
Asia Minor, 46, 80, 113

assembly, general, 53, 55, 217
asylums, 165, 169, 172
Ateneo Veneto, 207
Athens, 178
   seige of, 179
Atlantic
   economies, 108, 122, 187
   states, 178
Attila the Hun, 2, 189
Auditori Novi, 67, 217
Auditori Vecchi, 217
Augsburg, 40, 80
Augustinian Order, 24
Austria, 179
Austrian rule of Venice, 203
Averroes, 183
Avogaria di Comun. *See* State Attorneys

bacaro/i. See taverns
Bach, Johann Sebastian, composer, 188
bacino, 218
Bacino San Marco, 16, 20, 195
Badoer family, 24, 52
Baghdad, 12
bailo/i, 218
bakeries, 42, 117
bakers, 9, 41, 76, 86, 108, 139, 220
Balkans, 9, 38, 80
Balla d'Oro. *See* Barbarella
balls, 135, 193, 196
Balzac, Honoré de, playwright and
      novelist, 193
banche. See Great Confraternities
Banchieri, Adriano, playwright, 168
banks, 5, 9, 20, 38, 95, 182, 208
   Pisano-Tiepolo, 181
banquets, 59, 79, 83, 95, 101, 116–17,
      121, 135
baptism, 78
Barbarella, 56, 59, 218
Barbari, Jacopo de', artist, 128
   Map of Venice, **18**
Barbarigo family, 69
Barbaro, Francesco, humanist, 172
   on marriage, 59
Barbarossa. *See* Frederick I, Holy Roman
      Emperor
Barbary Coast, 106

barbershops, 194
Barcelona, 106
barley, 41–2, 113
Barnabotti, 218, *See* patriciate: poor
    members
Baroque
    architecture, 213
    painting, 199
    period, 176
Basilica San Marco, 4, 13, 20, 32, 38, 128,
    131, 146–7, 156, 195, 207, 213
    acoustical space, 149
    Columns from Acre, **14**
    Domes, **15**
    iconography, 12
    mosaics, **13**
    musical performances, 149
    Porta di Sant'Alipio, 4, 12, 15,
        Plates I & V
    Tetrarchs, **14**
    visual language, 13
Bassano, Jacopo, painter, 131
Bassano, Leandro, painter
    Virgin in Glory & Three Avogadori, **57**
bauti. See clothing: capes
Beauharnais, Eugene de, Viceroy of Italy,
    203
Beccarie, 4042, 218, *See also* butchers and
    meat
Bedmar, Marquis of, 177
bell towers, 12, 218
    of parishes, 8
    San Marco, 2, 11, 17, 42, 139, 208
Bella, Gabriele, painter, 198
    Combat Scene on the Ponte dei Pugni, **96**
    Old Fair of the "Sensa," **188**
Bellavitis, Anna, historian, 81, 100
Bellini, Gentile, painter, 129
    Corpus Christi Procession, **76**, 129, 134
    and Islamic culture, 129
    The Miracle of the Holy Cross, 129, **130**,
        135, 144
    Procession in Piazza San Marco.
        See Corpus Christi Procession
    Saint Mark Preaching in Alexandria,
        130, **131**
    Turkish Woman, 130
Bellini, Giovanni, painter, 130

Doge Leonardo Loredan, **52**
    San Zaccaria Altarpiece, 130
Bellini, Jacopo, painter, 129
Bellotto, Bernardo, painter, 194
Bembo, Pietro, poet, 147
Ben Israel, Menasseh, scholar, 93
beret manufacture, 185
Bergamo, 61, 76
Bernadon, 154
Bernini, Gianlorenzo, sculptor, 195
Bessarion, John, Cardinal, 127
    library, 60
biblioteca, 218
Biblioteca Nazionale Marciana, 127, 214
Biennale, 204, 211
    of 1895, 208
    of 1948, 208
bills of exchange, 107
bird market, 40
bisato su l'ara. See cuisine, eel
Bishop of Philadelphia, 170
bishoprics, 71, 155–6
Black Death, 19, 75, 89
Black Sea, 3, 11, 34, 38, 41, 78
blacksmiths, 107
blasphemy, 155
Blatas, Arbit, artist, 211
    The Last Train, **212**
blockades
    Austrian, 203
    English, 203
boat
    peoples, 1
    races, 83
Boccaccio, Giovanni, writer, 163
Boccato, Carla, historian, 93
Boerio, Giuseppe, scholar, 114
Bohemia, 40
Bolognetti, Alberto, papal nuncio, 161
Bon, Bartolomeo, sculptor, 18, 132
Bon, Giovanni, sculptor, 18, 132
Bon family, 196
Bonaparte, Napoleon, king and emperor,
    203–4, 208
bonds, government, 182
Bonifacio de'Pitati, painter, 128
Book of Gold, 55, 81, 203
Book of Silver, 81

bookbindings, 109
Bordone, Paris, painter, 132
Borromeo, Charles, cardinal, 153
Borsato, Giuseppe, painter
   Napoleon Bonaparte's Arrival at Venice in 1807, **202**
Bosnian mountains, 40
botany, 125, 183
bottlers, 40, 224
Bourbons of France, 179, 201
braid, 50, 118, 198
breach-of-promise, 166
bread
   prices, 42
   varieties, 42
Brenta River, 10, 28, 196
Brescia, 47, 61, 64, 68, 76, 81, 185
   and agrarian academies, 184
Bresciano
   industry, 186
Brianza, 185
bricks, 20, 26, 186
bridge battles, 96, 144
bridges, 9, 19, 27, 96, 99, 117, 152
   Accademia, 206
   Carmine, 97
   degli Ormesini, 93
   Gesuati, 97
   Ghetto, 92
   pontoon at S.M. della Salute, 145
   pontoon at the Redentore, Giudecca, **141**
   pontoon at the Zattere, 145, 157
   Pugni, 97
   Rialto. *See* Rialto, bridge
   San Lorenzo, 135
   San Marziale, 97
   Santa Fosca, 97
   Scalzi, 206
broadcloth, 107
Bruges, 37
Bucintoro, 31, 58, 90, 203, 218
building materials, 26
bull runs, 79
Buora, Giovanni, architect, **Plate VII**
Busenello, Francesco, librettist, 189
bussolai. See sea biscuits
butchers, 38, 76

Byron, Lord George, poet, 193, 205
Byzantine architecture, 136
Byzantium, 1, 3, 11, 16, 19, 40–1, 75
   pictorial language, 12, 129
   Roman, 4

ca' (casa). See palazzi
cabinets. *See studioli*
Caffi, Ippolito, painter, 206, 208
Cairo, 11, 16, 108, 114, 209
Calle
   del Paradiso, 25, **77**
   del Pestrin, 9
   delle Beccarie, 42
calle/i, 9, 79, 99, 218
Calmo, Andrea, playwright, 168
Calvin, Jean, 94, 151, 159
campana, 218
Campania, 178
campanile/i. See bell tower(s)
campiello/i, 9, 218
Campo
   della Pescaria. *See* fish market
   delle Beccarie, 48
   San Giacomo, 48
   San Stefano, 193
campo/i, 9, 79, 99, 218
Canal of Cannaregio, 218
canale, 218
Canaletto (Giovanni Antonio Canal), painter, 194
Candelmas, 83, 95, 117
Candia, 43, 47, 65, 78, 113, 178, 218
   chancellor of, 60
   Seige of, 179
Candiano family, 51
Cannaruoli, 20, 96
Canova, Antonio, sculptor, 193
Caorle, 153
capitano. See governors of territories
capo di contrada, 82
capo/i, 218
Capponi, Neri, 147
Capuchins, 156
car ferries, 213
cardinalships, 140
Carnia, 185

Carnival, 4, 59, 88, 90, 97–8, 116, 154, 187,
    189–90, 193, 208
  music, 187
Carpaccio, Vittore, painter, 131
  The Lion of Saint Mark, **129**
Carpathian Mountains, 40
carpets, 3, 12, 90, 108, 123
  Egypt, 108
  Ottoman, 108
Carrara lords, 61
Carriera, Rosalba, painter, 198
Casa del Farmacista, Lido, 210
Casanova, Giacomo, 194
casinò. See gambling houses
Cassiodorus, 1, 137
Castellani, 20, 95–7
Catholicism
  independence from Rome, 195
  Venetian, 195
Catholic-Reformation, 151
Cebà, Ansaldo, monk, 162
celebrations
    1563 Catholic defeat of Huguenots,
      142, 151
    Conquest of Constantinople, 142
    John the Baptist's beheading, 142
    Mary Magdalene's Day, 142
    Recovery of Padua, 142
    removal of 1510 Papal Interdict, 142
    Saint Martial's Day, 142
    St. Isidore, 142
    St. Vitus Day, 143
    Triumph of Lepanto, 142, 151
    Vanquishing Genoa, 142
celibacy, 105, 155, 160, 170, 173, 190
Celts, 3
cement, 186
Cemetery of San Michele, 204, **Plate VII**
censorship, Austrian, 204
ceramics, 109, 186
cereals, 33, 42, 106, 222
Cerigo island, 178
charity, 117, 158
Charlemagne, 4
Charles I, king of England, 178
Charles V, Holy Roman Emperor, 138
chastity of women, 152

Chaucer, Geoffrey, writer, 163
cheese
  from Apuglia, 43
  from Candia, 43
  from Dalmatia, 43
chemical industries, 210
childhood
  patrician, 58
  and work, 99
children
  custody of, 170
  and proto industry, 186
chili peppers, 113
chimney pots, 25, 213
China, 33, 38, 109
China, South, 46
China Sea, 38
chinoiseries, 197, 218
chocolate, 112–13, 193, 199
  recipes, 112
choir of San Marco, 188
Chojnacki, Stanley, historian, 56, 58, 69,
    72, 169
cholera, 207
Chopin, Frederick, composer, 206
Christian era, 2, 172
Christmas, 95
Church
  Catholic, 155
Church, Catholic, 155–6, 160
churches
  Hagia Sophia, Constantinople, 12
  Holy Apostles, Constantinople, 12
  Redentore, 140, **141**, 145, 157, 195
  San Cipriano, Murano, 203
  San Francesco della Vigna, 24, 137, 140
  San Giacomo (Giacometto), 5, **7**, 38
  San Giacomo del Orio, 5
  San Giorgio Maggiore, 94, 140,
    Plate XIV
  San Giovanni Degolà, 5
  San Giovanni e Paolo, 24, **Plate VII**
  San Giovanni Elemosinario, 6, 40
  San Marcuola, 5
  San Moisè, 196
  San Pietro di Castello, 83
  San Polo, 5

churches (*cont.*)
  San Simeone Grande, 5
  San Simeone Piccolo, 196
  San Vito, 143
  Sant'Agostin, 5
  Santa Fosca, 5
  Santa Maria Assunta, Torcello, 4
  Santa Maria dei Miracoli, 82, 94, 160
  Santa Maria del Giglio, 196
  Santa Maria della Pietà. *See also* Pietà,
    Ospedale della
  Santa Maria della Salute, 141, 145, 195,
    Plate XV
  Santa Maria Formosa, 24
  Santa Maria Gloriosa dei Frari, 24, **25**
  Santa Maria Mater Dominini, 5
  Santa Marina, 142
  Santi Maria e Donato, Murano, 3–4,
    Plate II
  Santo Stefano, 24
Ciardi, Guglielmo, painter, 208
cicisbeo, 198
Cicogna, Emmanuele, scholar, 205, 207
Cicognara, Leopoldo, art historian, 207
cinnamon, 45, 112, 114
Cinque Savii alla Mercanzia, 218
Cinque Savii alla Pace, 219
cisterns, 28
citizens. *See cittadini*
citizenship, 65
cittadini, 24, 80–1, 96, 100, 118, 120,
    148, 181
  and chanceries, 60
  de intus, 81
  de intus et de extra, 81
  humanist training, *59*
  marriage alliances, 82
  marriage contracts, 104
  originari, 60, 82, 86
  per privilegio, 81
  residences, 82
  women, 81
cityscapes, 194
civic identity, 1, 57, 157
civic ritual, 31, 58
Clarissimo/a, 219
classical architecture, 135
classicism, 1–2, 123

clergy
  deviance, 163
  privilege, 156
cloth merchants, 40
clothing
  of aristocratic women, 118–20
  capes, 97
  of cittadini, 122
  cloaks, 97
  colors, 80, 117
  of courtesans, 120
  and ethnicity, 123
  gendered differences, 80
  and marital status of women, 122
  of the plague doctor, **77**
  of professions and vocations, 122
  of prostitutes, 120
  and representation, 117
  secondhand dealers, 84
  and sexual status, 80, 118
  and social class, 80, 117, 122
  used, 80, 90
  and world image, 122
cobblers, 76
codèga. See lantern bearers
Codussi, Mauro, architect, 136–7,
    Plate XII
  Ca' Loredan, **Plate XII**
coffee, 114, 182, 193, 205
coffee houses, 113, 115, 193
  Florian, 115, 193, 204–5
  Quadri's, 115, 205
cogs, 36
coinage
  debased, 123
collecting, 109, 123, 127
Collegio, 60, 67, 219, 223
  ceiling iconography, 132
  chamber, 132
Collegio dei Sette Savii, *48*
Collegio del Militia da Mar, 219
Colmenero, Antonio, professor, 112
colonialism, 32–7, 187
  and material culture, 38
Commedia dell'Arte, 97, 168, 192
commenda/e, 19, 219
commercial expansion, 51
commercial revolution, 19

Compagnie della Calza. *See* Companies of
the Hose
Compagnie des Bateaux Omnibus de
Venise, 207
Companies of the Hose, 59, 97, 116,
150, 219
Company of Divine Love, 158
compass, nautical, 33
concubines, 155, 190
condotta/e. See Jews, charters
confraternities, 27, 66, 69, 77, 81, 84, 88,
93, 95, 134, 143, 145, 150, 157, 160,
See also scuole
artistic patronage, 86
functions, 86–9
and laity, 87
loyalty to Venice, 156
and musical patronage, 150
and mythmaking, 132
savings banks, 182
Congress of Vienna, 204
Constantinople, 3, 11–12, 15, 26, 29, 38, 44,
64–5, 78, 106, 108–9, 115, 127, 129,
142, 156, 178, 203, 218
plunder, 32
sack of, 128
trade base, 34
consumption
patterns, 123
Contarini family, 24, 52, 69, 189
Contarini Niccolò, 176
Conti, Antonio, writer, 192
contrada/e, 219
convents, 73, 165
enclosure, 163
patrician women, 72
and prostitution, 161
San Giovanni Evangelista, Torcello, 72
San Lorenzo, 72
San Zaccaria, 72
Sant'Angela, 164
Convertite, 157, 219
convoys, 18, 22, 33, 37, 39, 106, 221
cooks, 46, 79, 108
Copia Sullam, Sarah, poet, 162
coppersmiths, 107
Corfu, 3132, 65, 219
Cornaro family, 37, 156

Corner, Caterina, Queen of Cypress, 136
Corner, Zorzi, 137
Corner family, 69, 140, 178
corno, 219
Corone, 65, 106, 219
corredo/i. See dowries:material goods
Correr Archives and Library, 214
Correr Museum, 179
Correr, Teodoro, 205
Corsairs, 174
cortigiana. See courtesans
Côte d'Azur, 209
cotton, 30, 35–38, 49, 108–10,
181, 184
calicò, 49
factory, 207
summer dress, 123
Council of Forty, 53, 55, 67, 82, 103,
180, 223
and Signoria, 224
Council of Pregadi, 53, 222
Council of Ten, 55, 60, 67, 70, 82, 87, 90–1,
103, 111, 132, 153, 159, 169, 177, 181,
187, 219, 224
chambers, 132
Council of Trent, 153, 157, 163, 166, 170
and marriage rites, 101
Counter-Reformation, 94, 138, 176, 188,
190, 195
iconography, 196
courtesans, 80, 98, 118, 148, 161,
187, 190
courtship, 100
Cowan, Alexander, historian, 70
Cozzi, Gaetano, historian, 67–8
Crema, 76
Cremona, 68
Cremonini, Cesare, philosopher, 152, 189
crenellations, 219
Crete, 32, 78, 89, 178, 218
ports, 65
Venetian estates, 35
Crouzet-Pavan, Elisabeth, historian, 10,
28, 53
Crusades, 19, 23, 29–33, 41–43, 45,
49, 187
booty, 22
Crypto-Jews, 92

cuisine, 41–47
  and Arabs, 46
  bigoli (coarse spaghetti), 43
  calf's liver, 44
  cod, 43
  duck, 8, 44
  dumplings, 113
  eel, 43
  eggplant, 45
  Egyptian origins, 45
  game, 8, 41, 44
  goulash, 113
  Jewish origins, 45
  Levantine, 45
  mutton stew, 44
  nervetti, 44
  panada, 46
  pevarada, 46
  polenta, 42, 111
  rice pudding, 43
  risi e bisi, 43
  salami, 43
  salted pork, 43
  saor, 44
  Saracinesca sauce, 46
  sardines, 43
  Spain, 44
  spritzers, 113
  strudel, 113
  sturgeon, 43
  sweet and sour pork, 44
  tripe, 44, 46, 48
  veal cutlets, 113
  vinegar as a preservative, 44
  wurst, 113
culture
  Arabic, 125
  Greco-Latin, 125
cupola/e, 219
curti. See patriciate: new families
Customs House. *See* Dogana
Cyprus, 11, 33, 37, 46, 65–6, 106, 114, 136,
    139, 181
  sugarcane, 46
  trade, 47

Dalmatia, 9, 31–32, 41, 43–4, 47, 49, 66, 76,
    119, 178

Dalmatians, 202, 223
  and seafaring, 86
Damascus, 11, 13, 35, 45, 50, 109, 120
Dandolo family, 53, 69
Davis, Robert, historian, 19, 95
De'Rossi, Aretafila Savini, writer, 192
decline, as literary metaphor, 205
defense
  supervision, 56
defloration, 166
Deputazione di Storia Patria per le
    Venezie, 207
Derelitti, Ospedaletto dei, 191, 219
dialect, Venetian, 191
Dickens, Charles, writer, 193, 206
diet, 41
disease, 144
districts, 8, 12, 19, 27, 53, 55, 63, 95, 206,
    224
  Cannaregio, 5, 9, 19–20, 27, 40, 49, 90,
      93, 95, 117, 137, 206, 210
  Castello, 19, 80, 95, 109, 204, 210
  Dorsoduro, 5, 19, 95, 97, 206
  Islanders, 20
  San Marco, 5, 19, 39–40, 48, 95, 206, 208
  San Polo, 19–20, 40, 95, 140
  Santa Croce, 5, 19–20, 27, 95, 196,
      206, 210
  working class, 211
Dix, Otto, painter, 208
dogado, 4, 219
Dogana, 195
dogaressa, 58, 219
  and ceremony, 58
  and guilds, 54, 58
  lineage, 58
doge, 219
  authority, 55, 142
  Byzantine model, 51
  chancery, 60
  corno (hat), 116
  councillors, 55
  food offerings, 116
  investiture, 54
  largesse, 116
  Marriage to the Sea, 31, 193, 224
  origins, 4
Doge's Palace. *See* Palazzo Ducale

doges
    Andrea Gritti, 137, 139, 146
    Bartolomeo Gradenigo, 42
    Domenico Michiel, 142
    Domenico Selvo, 45
    Francesco Foscari, 136
    Francesco Morosini, 179
    Giovanni Corner, 177
    Leonardo Loredan, **52**
    Lodovico Manin, 202
    Marino Falier, 55, 143
    Pietro Gradenigo, 54, 203
    Pietro Orseolo II, 29, 31
    Vitale II Michiel, 53
Dolfin, Zuanne, 137
Dolfin family, 140
Dominante, La, 220
Dominicans, 24
Donà family, 69
Donizetti, Gaetano, composer, 206
dough makers, 41, 222
doughnuts, 113
dowries, 104, 110
    inflation, 69, 72, 105
    legislation, 69
    material goods, 109, 219
    purpose, 104
    rules and regulations, 105
    women's contributions, 72
Drake, Francis, 187
drinking water, 27
dye, 184
    industry, 20
    plants, 33, 40, 118
    porpora, 118
    red, 35
dyers, 50

earthquakes, 157
ecclesiastical property, 156, 176, 182
Egina, 65
Egypt, 11–12, 30, 33–37, 45, 49, 65, 78, 106,
    108, 113
    sultanate, 65
Egyptians, 16, 41
embroiderers, 186
Enlightenment, 180
Ensor, James, painter, 208

entail, 73, 104, 172
entertainers, 187
episcopate, 5
Erberia, 40
Esecutori alla Bestemmia, 157–8, 165–6,
    220
ethnicity, 41, 48–49, 77, 99
Etruscans, 3
Europe, 27, 30, 34, 39, 41–42, 49, 61, 90–91,
    129, 151, 155–6, 187, 211
Europe, northern, 11, 18, 24
evangelism, 94, 159
eyewitnesses
    in legal investigations, 171

fabbrica, 220
factionalism, 19, 77, 95, 97, 100, 127,
    143, 177
    Nicolotti and Castellani, 95
    territorial boundaries, 96
fairs, 187
    Sensa, 31, 187, **188**, 193
Falier family, 24, 69
family
    behavior, 68–74
    and capital accumulation, 70
    and social organization, 103
famine, 41, 45, 103, 111, 117, 144, 182, 219
    prohibition of rich bread, 42
fans, 198
fashion, 118
    eighteenth century, 198
    French, 198
    and hierarchy, 49
Fat Thursday, Carnival, 88, 90, 116
Fauré, Gabriel, composer, 206
Favretto, Giacomo, painter, 208
feasts, 117, 144
    All Saints' Day, 95
    Ascension Day. *See* feasts, Sensa
    and confraternities, 88
    and music, 150
    La Salute, 45
    Sensa, 31, 193, 224
    St. Barbara, 56
    St. Mark, 43
    Twelve Wooden Marys, 83
Ferrari, Benedetto, entertainer, 189

Ferraro, Joanne, historian, 100, 171
 Marriage Wars, 167
finance
 supervision, 53, 56
Finlay, Robert, historian, 67
fish, 3, 5–6, 10, 34, 40–41, 43, 46, 48, 97,
 117, 212
 market, 40, 42
 varieties, 43
fishermen, 20, 40, 49, 61, 95, 117,
 185, 204
 Nicolotti, 97
fist fights (*pugni*). *See* bridge battles
Flanders, 47, 49, 76
flax, 49
floods, 211–13
Florence, 9, 119, 129, 188
flour, 40, 42, 113, 117, 165, 207
fondaco/i, 11, 21, 65, 220
 dei Tedeschi, 21, *39*, *48*, 80, *94*, **Plate VIII**
 dei Turchi, 21, *207*
 of the Seaborne Empire, 65
Fondamenta
 degli Ormesini, 9, 49
 del Ferro, 40
 del Vin, 40
fondamenta/e, 220
Fonte, Moderata, writer, 122, 168, 172
 sumptuary legislation, 122
food. *See also* cuisine
 and bridge battles, 117
 and civic ritual, 117
 consumption, 41, 115
 and feasts, 116
 geographical markers, 41
 and politics, 115
 preserved, 44
 prices, 182
 prohibitions, 116
 provisioning, 117
foods
 minor, 42
footpaths, 9
forests
 supervision, 56
forks. *See piron/i*
fortifications, 10, 21, 66, 183

Fortini Brown, Patricia, art historian,
 135, 137
Foscari family, 25, 136, 206
Foscarini, Antonio, 177
Foscolo, Ugo, writer, 203
foundations of buildings, 26
 deterioration, 212
foundling homes. *See* Pietà, La
foundry, 27, 80, 90
Fourth Lateran Council, 90
France, 44, 76, 127–8, 151, 154, 159, 183,
 193, 202, 204
 revolution, 180
Francis II, Emperor of Austria, 203
Franciscans, 24, 156
Franco, Veronica, poet, 148–9
 Family Letters to Different People, 148
Franks, 4
fraterne, 70, 72
Frederick I, Holy Roman Emperor, 13, 31
frezzeria, 115
Friulan liturgical rite, 4, 156
Friuli, 1, 9, 26, 61, 64, 119, 178
 inhabitants, 220
 wine, 47
fruits, 45
Fruttaria, 40
furatole. *See* taverns
furnishings. *See* home furnishings
furriers, 40, 79
furs, 34, 110, 118

Gabriel family, 69
Gabrieli, Andrea, composer, 86, 149
Gabrieli, Giovanni, composer, 86,
 147, 149
Galen, 183
Galilei, Galileo, mathematician, 152, 183
galleys, 106
 of convicts, 36, 66. *See* oarsmen,
 convicts
 merchant, 3, 36, 107. *See also* convoys
 passenger boats, 29
 of war, 18, 36, 66
Galuppi, Baldassare, composer, 191
gambling, 113, 157, 187, 196, 211, 220, 223
gambling houses, 113, 193

banning of women, 193
Caterina Dolfin Tron, 194
Caterina Sagredo Barbarigo, 193
Elena Venier, 193
Il Ridotto, 193, **194**, 223
Marina Sagredo Pisani, 193
San Giuliano, 194
games, 78, 83, 99, 160, 193
ball, 79
gaming houses. *See* gambling houses
gastaldi, 84
Gauls, 1, 3
gems, 108
gender, 49, 56, 80, 96, 99, 168–9,
172, 173
biases, 171
and clothing, 117
and rhetoric, 172
and social affiliation, 79
Genoa, 32, 54, 68, 83, 89, 128
Genoese, 37–37, 162
Gentile da Fabbriano, painter, 129
German occupation, 211
Germans, 9, 11, 48, 76, 79, 88, 159–60
Germany, 10, 76, 145
Gerson, Jean, theologian, 153
Ghetto, 80
Napoleonic period, 203
restricted transit, 92
Ghetto Nuovo 80, **Plates IX–X**
Ghetto Vecchio, 90–91
Giancarli, Gigi Artemio, playwright, 168
Giants' Staircase, 128, 223
Gibbon, Edward, writer, 187, 205
ginger, 46
Giorgio Cini Foundation, 213
Giorgione, painter, 131
Giornale d'Italia, 192
Giornale dei Literati d'Italia, 192
Giornale Encyclopedia, 192
Giudecca, 11, 27, 39, 94, 158, 194–5, 207,
224
Giudecca Canal, 145, 157, 207, 218
Giudice, Brenno del, architect, 210
giudici, 220
Giustiniani family, 52, 69, 189
Giustiniani, Bernardo, humanist, 2

Giustizia Nova, 53, 84, 220
Giustizia Vecchia, 44, 53, 84, 220
Gladys Krieble and Jean Paul Delmas
Foundation, 214
glass manufacture, 3–4, 9, 11, 20, 26, 31,
43, 107–8, 115, 123, 130, 184, 187, 194,
205, 207, 210
glass shops, 213
Glixon, Jonathan, musicologist, 86, 150
godparents, 78
Goethe, Johann, writer, 193
gold, 4, 12, 16, 19, 30–31, 50, 86, 106, 111,
115, 118, 121–2, 135, 137, 184, 198
Golden Books. *See* Book of Gold
Goldoni, Carlo, playwright, 97, 191–2
goldsmiths, 40, 108, 122
gondola, 8, 213
gondoliers, 78, 187, 206–7, 210
gossip, 99, 168, 171
Gothic architecture, 11, 16–18, 25,
27, 125, 129, 135–6, 140, 206,
212, 221
Goths, 16
Governatori delle Entrate, 220
government
communal, 16, 20, 24, 38, 53–5, 62, 74,
83–4
dukedom, 62, 74
La Signoria or Il Dominio, 62, 74
structure, **64**
governors of territories, 64, 218
competencies, 65
Gozzi, Carlo, playwright, 191
Gozzi, Gasparo, journalist, 192
grain, 21, 35, 40–41, 111, 122, 181,
204–5
prices, 65
provisioning, 65
trade, 183
grammar school, San Marco, 60
granary at San Marco, 204
Grand Canal, 5, 8, 12, 18–19, 23, 25,
58, 95–6, 137, 140, 145, 159, 196,
206–7, 218
artery of transport, 20
Grand Chancellor, 60
Grand Tour, 206

Great Council, 53, 56, 60, 64, 67, 69, 84,
　　152, 194, 202, 218
　chamber, 131
　dissolution, 202
　First Closing, 55, 203
　new admissions, 56, 178, 190
　restriction of membership, 54
　sale of membership, 74
　screening process, 56
　Second Closing, 56
　Third Closing, 56
Great Hall, 21, 217
Greece, 11, 58, 66, 76, 129
Greek archipelago, 178
Greek colonies of Venice, **35**
Greek language, 127
Greeks, 3, 11, 16, 37, 41, 48, 75, 78–9, 84–5,
　　108, 123, 179, 202, 220
　Diaspora, 127
Grevembroch, Giovanni, fashion writer,
　　118, 123
Grimani, Girolamo, procurator of San
　　Marco, 137
Grimani family, 140, 156, 189
Griselini, Francesco, journalist, 192
Gritti, Andrea
　Romanization of public space, 139
Gritti family, 116
Guardi, Francesco, painter
　*Feast of Maundy Thursday in
　　Venice,* **175**
Guardi, Giovanni Antonio, painter, 194
　Parlor of the Nuns at San Zaccaria, **163**
Guariento di Arpo, painter
　Coronation of the Virgin, 131
Guggenheim, Peggy, 208
guilds, 9, 53, 58, 66, 77, 81, 83, 95, 159, 184
　regulations, 84
　support of the military, 66
　women's membership, 84
Gustav III, king of Sweden, 198

haberdashers, 84
Haifa, 30, 35
hair-dos, bleached, 198
handkerchiefs, 110
Hapsburgs, 154, 179, 201, 205–6

expansion, 176
rivalry with Venice, 177
　Spanish, 138, 195
Harz Mountains, 40
hawkers, 186
Hebrew language, 93
Heintz, Joseph the Younger, painter
　Bull Hunt in Campo San Polo, **89**
　Procession on Redemption Day, **146**
hemp, 20, 49, 111, 174, 185
Henry III, king of France, 149
Heraklion, Crete. *See* Candia
heresy, 155, 158
heretics, 94
hides, 106, 205
Hindu Kush, 38
history of Venice, 152, 192
　as invention, 2, 128
Hobbes, philosopher, 180
Holocaust, 211
Holy Land, 11, 29, 187
Holy Roman Emperor, 177
Holy Roman Empire, 151, 159
home furnishings, 49, 107–11, 123
　eighteenth century, 196, **197**
honey, 35, 45–7, 114
honor, 59, 81, 83, 86, 99, 103, 121, 142, 150,
　　158, 172
　aristocratic, 73
　family, 165
　women's, 166
horses of St. Mark, **15**, 32, 203
Hotel Danieli, 206
Hotel des Bains, 209
Hotel Excelsior, 209
Howard, Deborah, architectural historian,
　　11, 16, 225
humanism
　and political ideology, 61
humanists, 2, 58, 60–61, 94, 97, 125–7,
　　136, 172
　educational program, 58
　on Venetian origins, 1
Hungarians, 16
Hungary, 34
Hurlburt, Holly, historian, 54
hydraulic engineering, 183

iconography
   Annunciation, 128
   Archangel Gabriel, 128
   of aristocratic dwellings, 135
   Justice, 16, 57, 132
   Liberty, 57
   political, 57
   Queen of Heaven, 131
   Virgin Mary, 152
   virginity, 57
illegitimacy, 166, 170
immigrants
   Jewish, 91, 161
   Portuguese, 161
immigration, 75, 106, 184
incest, 155
Incurabili, Ospedale degli, 123, 158, 191
India, 33, 38, 40, 112
Indian Ocean, 33
infanticide, 155, 171
infants
   abandonment, 171
inflation, 144
inns, 47, 53, 76, 187, 220
Inquisition
   Roman, 157
   Spanish, 91
   Venetian, 112, 148, 159–60, 189
   Venetian, and witchcraft, 161
Interdict
   of 1606–7, 140, 143, 156, 189, 195
inventories, 50, 110, 118, 123
Ionian islands, 179
Ionian Sea, 32, 178, 219
Iran, 34
Iraq, 34
iron industry, 185
ironmongers, 84
irrigation, 182
Islamic architecture, 136
Islamic artifacts, 108
Islamic cities, 11
Islamic culture, 11–12, 16, 40–1, 50, 108,
   130, 213, 225
Islamic world, 11
Isnik ware, 109
Istria, 26, 47, 76

Italian mainland, 89, 125
Italian Peninsula, 2, 19, 61, 125, 127, 154,
   166, 176
Italian regional states, 2
Italian Wars, 66

Jaffa, 30, 35
James, Henry, writer, 208
Jerusalem, 11, 13, 127
Jesuits, 156, 188, 190, 196
jewelry, 3, 69, 103, 107, 198, 219
   and sumptuary laws, 120
Jewish nations, 41
Jews, 11, 37, 41, 43, 48, 79, 86, 89, 92,
   96, 105, 108, 123, 160, 170, 202,
   205, 211
   artistic culture, 93
   and Carnival, 92
   charters, 89, 91–2
   cuisine, 45
   dialect, 93
   economic activities, 91
   expulsion from Spain, 69, 75
   and Franciscans, 91
   from Portugal, 92
   from Spain, 92
   games, 93
   hostelries, 92
   Italiani, 91
   and lending, 90
   Levantini, 91
   marked clothing, 92
   and new foods for Venice, 45
   physicians, 92
   Ponentini, 91
   Portuguese, 182
   religious practices, 93
   schole, 93, **Plate X**
   self-regulation, 92
   Spanish, 182
   synagogues, 93
   Tedeschi, 91
   women, 93
journalism, 192
justice
   administration, 53
   class bias, 173

Kant, Emmanuel, philosopher, 180
King, Margaret, historian, 58
Klee, Paul, painter, 208
Klimt, Gustav, painter, 208
Königsmarck, Otto Wilhelm, 179
Koprulu, Ahmed, Grand Vizier, 179

La Serenissima. *See* government: *La
    Signoria* or *Il Dominio*
Labia family, 178
    feasts and balls, 198
labor force, 184–5
lace, 97, 111, 118, 184, 187, 194, 198, 204,
    207, 210
lagoon, 4, 8, 12, 28, 31, 41, 43–4, 49–50, 64,
    75, 79, 95, 99, 117, 129, 177, 184, 202
    bedrock, 212
    climate, 10
    and Romans, 1
lamps, 109
    gas, 213
Lando family, 136
Lane, Fredrick, historian, 84
Lantani, Antonio, music printer, 149
lantern-bearers, 187
latifundia, 220
Latin Kingdom, 33
Latin language, 60, 127
Latins, 16
Laven, Mary, historian, 73, 163–165, 227
laws
    for the poor, 117
lawyers, 159
Le Court, Juste, sculptor, 196
lead, 184
League of Cambrai, 66, 90, 128, 139
leases, fictitious, 182
leather, 184
    workers, 107
lending, 29, 68, 73, 90–2, 160, 182
Lent, 44, 154
Lepanto, Battle of, 67, 106, 149
Levant, 11, 19, 21, 24, 33, 35, 40–41, 43, 49,
    51, 54, 68, 76, 80, 81, 113, 119, 137,
    182, 220
Library of Saint Mark's, 127, 139,
    Plate XIII. *See also* Biblioteca
    Nazionale Marciana

Lido, 3–4, 10, 29, 31, 44, 211, 213, 221,
    Plate XIV
    and Romanticism, 209
lineage
    and inheritance, 104
linen, 30, 110, 122, 185
    kerchiefs, 121
    veils, 120
Lion of Saint Mark, 4, 55, 68, 116, 128, 203
Liszt, Franz, composer, 206
loans
    forced, 22, 66, 82
locanda, 221
Locke, John, philosopher, 180
Loggetta, 139
Lombardo, Pietro, architect and sculptor,
    132, **Plate VII**
Lombards, 4
    of Venetia, 4
Lombardy, 62, 176, 178
London, 37, 225, 228
Longhena, Baldassare
    Church of Santa Maria della
    Salute, **Plate XV**
Longhena, Baldassare, architect, 141, 145, 195
longhi. *See* patriciate: old families
Longhi, Pietro, painter, 199
    Carnival Scene, **98**
    Il Ridotto, **194**
    The Pharmacist, **114**
Lords of the Nightwatch, 20, 82
Loredan, Andrea, 137
Loredan family, 69
Lotto, Lorenzo, painter, 131
Lucca, 50, 68
Luther, Martin, 94, 151, 159
Lutherans, 159
Luzzatto, Simone, scholar, 93

Mackenny, Richard, historian, 84
Maffei, Scipione, journalist, 192
magic, 155, 161
Magritte, René, painter, 208
maiolica, 109, 221
    Syrian, 109
maize, 41–42, 111, 117, 175, 182
malvasie. *See* wine, vendors
Mamluks, 11, 16, 33, 108, 225

Manelli, Francesco, entertainer, 189
Manin, Daniele, revolutionary, 205
Manin family, 178
Mann, Thomas, writer, 208–9
Mannerism, 139
Mantegna, Andrea, painter, 129
Mantua, 177
manufactures, 20, 184
  arms, 185
  Islamic, 109
  Islamic imitations, 108
  rural, 187
Marcello, Valerio, 58
Marghera
  chemical industries, 212
  oil refineries, 212
Margherita, queen of Italy, 208
Maria Theresa, Empress of Austria, 183
Marinella, Lucrezia, writer, 122, 168
marital property, 169
market, 40
markets
  fish, 38
  Rialto 97. *See also* Rialto market
  San Marco, 31, 97, 117
marriage
  age at, 102
  annulment, 167
  arranged, 170, 173
  betrothal, 104
  contracts, 104
  endogamy, 74, 104
  exogamy, 57
  failed, 157
  forced, 167
  informal arrangements, 101
  mésalliances, 100, 166
  patrician, 54, 59
  religious significance, 102
  restricted, 71, 73, 103, 170
  separation, 78, 169
  state interests, 102, 105
Mars, 128
Martin, John, historian, 94, 159
masks, 193, 213
  bauta, 218
  and gender, 97
  and social class, 97

Masonic Order, 203
masquerades, 98, 193, 223
Massari, Giorgio, architect, 196–8
material culture, 108
material life, 176
mathematics, 183
mattresses of wool, 110
Mazzetti, Carpoforo, artist, **197**
McGough, Laura, historian, 158, 165
meat
  consumption, 44
  hierarchy, 44
  turkey, 45, 113
Mecca, 37, 114
medical school, 59, 183
medicine, 122, 125
medieval period, 159, 174
Mediterranean Sea, 19, 51, 186
  markets, 30
Mehmed II, Sultan, 106
Memmo, Andrea, 183
Memo, Foscarina, 100–1
mendicant orders, 24
mendicante/i, 221
Mendicanti, Ospedale dei, 123, 191
menuti. See foods: minor
Mercerie, 9, 39, 95, 221
mercers, 94, 159, 186
merchants, 11–12, 16, 21, 24, 27, 29, 31, 37,
    39, 42, 46, 48–49, 54, 59, 66, 75, 80,
    84, 88, 91, 94, 100, 104, 108–9, 159,
    165, 174, 181, 187, 191, 202
  Armenian, 123
  entering the patriciate, 181
  Jewish, 75, 91
  Ottoman Turks, 80
Mercury, 128, 139
meretrici. See prostitution
Messbarger, Rebecca, literary scholar, 192
Messina, Antonello da, painter, 130
Mestre, 212
metallurgy, 185
metals, 37, 40
  trade, 35
metalwork, 108
  Islamic, 108
Mexico, 112
Michiel, Giustina Renier, historian, 205

Michiel family, 24, 52
midwifery, 171
    unofficial, 161
Milan, 9, 19, 68, 116, 153, 177, 206
Milanesi, 86
military resources
    financial, 66
    organization, 67
millenarians, 94, 159
    and literacy, 94
millet, 41–3, 117
Minerva, 139
mines
    supervision, 56
mining, 185
Minor Council, 53, 55
    and Signoria, 224
Mint, **7**, 93, 139, 153, 222, 224
    supervision, 56
Misserini, Giovanni Battista, 100–1
Mocenigo family, 25, 69
Modena, Leon, scholar, 93
Modone, 32, 65, 106, 221
Mohammed II, Sultan, 129
Molmenti, Pompeo, historian, 207
Moluccas, 33
monachization, 73
monastic vows, 172
Monet, Claude, painter, 208
    Palazzo Dario, **209**
moneylenders, 80
Mongols, 34, 38
    architecture, 16
Monteverdi, Claudio, composer, 149, 188
    Incoronazione di Poppea, 189
Morea, 47, 106, 178–9, 221
Morosini, Francesco, admiral and doge,
    178–9
Morosini, Paolo, humanist, 61
Morosini family, 24, 47, 52, 69
Mosque of St Athanasius, 16
motherhood
    and betrothal, 101
    and dowries, 105
    patrician, 56, 58
motor launches, 213
muda/e. See convoys

Muir, Edward, historian, 142, 144, 190
mulberries, 50, 175, 186
Mulino Stucky, 207
Municipal Council, Napoleonic
    period, 202
Murano, 1, 3, 9, 13, 20, 43, 108, 196,
    203, 205, **Plates II & VII**
music, 187
    antiphonal choirs, 147
    Baroque oratorio, 188
    Baroque revolution, 188
    basso continuo, 188
    conservatories, 191
    female ensembles, 191
    for solo voice, 188
    for the people, 150
    Franco-Flemish, 147
    madrigals, 147
    opera, 191
    opera buffa, 190
    polychoral, 147
    polyphonic, 147
    sacred, 86
    Venetian School, 147
musical instruments
    harpsichords, 149
    manufacture, 149
    organs, 149, 184
    plucked, 149, 184
    wind, 149, 184
mythmaking, 125
myths, 195
    birth of Venice, 127
    iconography, 127–42
    in opera, 189
    islanders and land peoples, 95
    and music, 149
    representation, 144
    saintly favor, 128
    Serene Republic, 95, 144, 150
    St. Mark, 126
    stability, 125, 151, 154

Nauplia, 65
navigation channels, 53
navy, 10, 42, 107, 127, 178–9, 217
Naxos, Battle of, 179

Naxos, duchy of, 106
Negroponte, 32, 65, 109, 179
neo-classicism, French, 191, 204
neo-Gothic architecture, 207
Neoplatonism, 147
Neptune, 128
Netherlands, 151
Nevers, duke of, 177
News on the Rialto, 214
Newton, Isaac, scientist, 183
Newtonianism, 193
Nicolotti, 117
    rivalries, 20
niello, 221
nobility
    and birth, 57
    consciousness, 68
Normans, 29
North Sea, 37
notaries, 24, 60, 81, 83, 93, 104, 118,
    159, 165
Nuremberg, 40, 48, 80
nuts, 33, 44, 46, 114

oarsmen
    convicts, 36
    Dalmatians, 36
    of galleys, 36, 79, 108
    of *gondole*, 8
    Greeks, 36
    from neighborhoods, 66
observatory, 183
Occagna, Gottardo, music printer, 149
oculus, 221
Oderzo, 3, 110
offal. *See* cuisine, tripe
officeholding, 68
ogee arch, 221
oil, 33, 40, 43, 47, 130, 205, 223
    refineries, 210
oligarchy, 52, 55, 67, 74, 144, 157, 180,
    181, 195
    formation, 54
Orio family, 6, 20, 38, 53
Orlando di Lasso, composer, 147
ormesin. *See* silk, varieties
orphans, 105, 118, 152

female singers, 191
Orseolo family, 31, 51
Orthodox Christians, 170
ospedale, 11, 221
Ossuna, Spanish viceroy, 177
osterie. *See* inns
otium, 221
Ottoman artifacts, 108–9
Ottoman Empire
    and Jews, 92
Ottoman Turks, 9, 36, 41, 44, 48, 60, 66,
    68, 74, 76, 78, 79, 91, 97, 106, 109, 115,
    127, 139, 142, 151, 165, 174, 178–81,
    189–90, 193, 196
    and Byzantium, 75
    war with, 74

Padua, 9, 61, 64, 76, 125, 152–54, 159,
    183, 192
    and mythmaking, 2
    University, 59
pageantry, 54, 127, 143, 146, 150, 154,
    189–90, 195
    and Venetian identity, 142
Palace of Justice, 16
palazzi
    architectural styles, 136
    Belloni-Battagia, 196
    Ca' Corner della Ca' Grande, 137, 140
    Ca' Corner-Spinelli, 136
    Ca' d'Oro, 18, 26, 135, 207,
        Plate XI
    Ca' Dolfin, 137, 140
    Ca' Farsetti, 21, **Plate III**
    Ca' Foscari, 26, **136**, 211
    Ca' Grimani, 137, **138**, 140
    Ca' Loredan, **22**
    Ca' Pesaro, 196, 208
    Ca' Rezzonico, 196–9
    Dandolo, 193
    Dario, **209**
    Ducale. *See* Palazzo Ducale
    Giustiniani, **136**
    Grassi, 196
    Labia, **199**
    ornamentation, 135
    Sagredo, **197**

palazzi (*cont.*)
  Vendramin-Calergi, formerly
    Loredan, 137, **Plate XII**
  Venier dei Leoni, 208, 213
Palazzo Ducale, 16–17, 20, 27, 38, 128, 136,
  140, **Plates IV, VI, XIII**
Palestine, 30, 65
Palladio, Andrea, architect, 140, 145,
  157, 195
  Redentore, **141**
  San Giorgio Maggiore, **Plate XIV**
  Villa Barbaro, Maser, **107**
Palma the Younger, painter, 131
papacy, 16, 140, 156–7, 176, 195
paper industry, 185
  and noble investment, 186
Parabosco, Girolamo, playwright,
  149, 168
parishes
  dell' Anconetta, 93
  della Maddalena, 93
  San Angelo Raffaele, 5
  San Barnaba, 180
  San Bartolomeo, 5, 9, 80
  San Giacomo dell' Orio, 80
  San Marcuola, 93
  San Maurizio, 140
  San Niccolò dei Mendicoli, 5, 44
  San Pietro di Castello, 5
  San Samuele, 6
  San Silvestro, 40, 47
  San Trovaso, 8, 117
  Sant'Agnese, 117
  Sant'Anna, 88
  Sant'Apostoli, 6, 88
  Santa Maria Formosa, 6, 83
  Santa Marta, 207
  and social life, 82
Parthenon, 178
Participazio family, 6, 51
pasta, dried, 43
paternity, 171
patriarch
  Aquileia, 88
  Constantinople, 127
  Venice, 4, 68, 73, 155
Patriarchal Archives, 213

Patriarchate of Venice
  tribunal, 78, 157, 167–70
patriciate, 221
  aesthetic tastes, 108
  and Aristotle, 125
  attrition, 177
  bachelors, 59, 103
  and bishoprics, 71
  consumption patterns, 135
  corruption, 67
  daughters, 56
  education. 58, *See also* humanism and
    humanists
  families, 221
  gerontocracy, 140, 153
  and humanism, 59
  intellectual development, 125
  investments, 182
  marital strategies, 71
  marriage contracts, 104
  marriage legislation, 69
  merchants, 21
  natural sons, 82
  new admissions, 181, *See* Great Council:
    new admissions
  new families, 53, 219
  nurses, 58
  officeholding, 63
  old families, 53, 177
  political consolidation, 71
  political correction, 180
  poor members, 69, 180, 182,
    See also Barnabotti
  rich and poor, 70, 121, 143
  schisms, 137, 180
  sexual behavior, 190
  social networks, 69
  sons, 57–8
  Syrian families, 54
  tutors, 58
  Young Party, 140, 152–154, 156, 176,
    195, 220
patriciate, women
  duties, 58
  enclosure, 73, 164
  fashion, 50
  kinship ties, 72

Pauline Order, 158
pawnbrokers, 91
pearls, 120
peasants, 117, 183, 185
Pechstein, Max, painter, 208
peddlers, 186
pedestrian hubs, 9
Peloponnese, 35, 66, 175, 178, 219, 221
Pepin, 4
pepper, 112, 114
    black, 45
Persia, 16, 34, 44–6
Persian Gulf, 38, 46
Persians, 16
Petizion, Giudici di, 221
Petrarch, Francesco, humanist, 1, 125, 147
Pezzolo, Luciano, historian, 53
pharmacies, 113
pharmacists, 85, 108
pharmacopeia, 33, 37, 186
philanthropy, 117, 153, 212
philosophy, 125
physicians, 81, 83, 85, 88, 90, 104, 108, 122,
    159, 165, 171
physiocrats, 182
piano nobile, 221
piazza, 222
Piazza San Marco, 12, 17, 20, 31, 41, 54,
    83, 95, 99, 115, 129, 139, 143, 145, 176,
    202, 204, 208
    Napoleonic Wing, 204, Plate XV
    political space, 143
Piazzale Roma, 213
Piazzetta della Giustizia. See Piazzetta San
    Marco
Piazzetta San Marco, 16, 132, 139, 144, 177,
    Plate XIII
Picasso, Pablo, painter, 208
pictorial tradition
    Tuscan, 129
Pien Collegio, 63, 222
Pietà, Ospedale della, 166, 171, 191
pilgrims, 29, 187
Piovego, Giudici del, 19, 53, 222
piracy, 30, 83, 93, 174, 177–9
piron/i, 45, 109
Pisani family, 156, 178

Pisani, Giorgio
    reformer, 180
Pisani, Pier-Vettore, procurator of San
    Marco, 112
Pitati, Bonifacio de', painter
    Apparition of God the Father, 126
plague, 27, 73, 75, 103, 106, 117, 122, 142,
    145, 154, 157, 166, 177–8, 186, 195
    doctor, 77
    iconography, 196
Po
    Delta, 3
    River, 10, 39, 43, 51, 60
    Valley, 61
podestà, 222, See governors of territories
Polani, Pietro, 52
Polani family, 24
police, 53, 181
political ideologies, 125
pollution, 28, 212
Polo, Marco, 28, 30
Polo brothers, 38
pompe, 222
popes
    Alexander III, 13, 31
    Clement VIII, 153
    Julius II, 62
    Paul, 206
    Paul V, 153
    Urban IV, 143
popolani, 24, 77, 150
popolo, 222
population, 19, 77, 186
    figures, 106, 182, 215–16
porcelain, 109, 121, 193, 222
pork, 44, 116
    salted, 43
Port of the Maidens, Caorle, 83
Port of Venice, 185
Porta della Carta, 16, 17, 18, 132
portatori. See porters
portego (salone), 21, 222
porters, 40, 222
portico, 222
Portugal, 44, 76
    and Jews, 91
Portuguese, 113

Post Office, **Plate VIII**
poveri vergognosi, 119, 222
Povolo, Claudio, historian, 67
Pozzo, Modesta, writer. *See* Fonte,
    Moderata
priests
    education, 155
    election of, 155
    family roles, 169
    parish, 82
primogeniture, 104, 172
printers, 76, 88, 94, 107, 146, 159
    French and Savoyard, 159
printing, 93, 112, 127, 146, 159, 184, 186
    industry, 76
Priuli, Girolamo, diarist, 74
Priuli family, 47
processions, 95, 140, 187, 190
    Corpus Christi, 134, 143
    great confraternities, 143
    June 15, 143
    La Salute, 145
    marching order, 143
    and public punishment, 144
Procuratie, 222
Procuratie Nuove, 115, 139, 204–5
procurator, 222
Procurator, Giudici del, 104, 170, 222
Procurators of Saint Mark, 118, 129, 131,
    188, 222
professions, 83
Prokofiev, Sergei, composer, 191
Proprio, Giudici del, 110, 170, 222
prostitution, 48, 76, 80, 118, 120, 157, 161,
    164, 173, 187, 190, 219
    material display, 165
    and panegyrists, 155
    and shelters, 145
    and sin, 165
    and syphilis, 155, 165
protectionism, 183–4
Protestant Reformation, 94, 151
proto-industry, 186
Proust, Marcel, writer, 193, 208
provveditore/i, 222
Provveditori
    alle Pompe, 120, 165

di Comun, 87
Sopra Beni Inculti, 222
Sopra Monasteri, 157
Pteleos, 65
public health, 204, *See also* Sanità
public prosecutor, 53
publishers, 85, 94, 159
Puccini, Giacomo, composer, 191
Puglia, 113
pugni, 222

Quarantia Criminal. *See* Council of Forty
Queller, Donald, historian, 67
Querini, Gerolamo, Patriarch of Venice, 155
Querini, Mario, 55
Querini family, 69
Querini Stampaglia Foundation, 213
Querini-Tiepolo Conspiracy, 55, 143
Querino, Angelo, 180
Quirini, Lauro, humanist, 127

Ragusans, 177
railway, 206
rain gutters, 27
raisins, 43
ramo/i, 223
rape, 32, 103, 155, 167, 224
Rapp, Richard, historian, 174
Ratisbon, 48, 80
Ravenna, 3–4
    Byzantine capital, 1
    Byzantine churches, 3
    Exarchate, 3
real estate, 21, 24, 51, 68, 73, 111,
    182, 213
reclamation of land, 182–3
redentore, 223
Regensburg, 40
regional state
    economy, 175
    formation, 61
    governance of, 62, 65, 201
    justice, 65
    manufactures, 184
    and protectionism, 65
    resources, 182
    taxation, 65

urban councils, 65
relics, 4, 12, 32, 126, 187
    of Saint Mark, 12, 128
    Saint Nicholas, 29
    Saint Roch, 145
    veneration, 144
religion
    and artisans, 94
    and heresies, 94
religious policy
    temporal independence, 152, 156
religious wars, 153
Renaissance
    architecture, 212
    classical style, 130, 136, 140, 207
    culture, 125
    discursive tradition, 192
    musical style, 149
    painting, 130
    palaces, 137
    period, 1, 150, 174
    principles of painting, 129
    Roman, 135
    and Roman ancestry, 28
    Tuscan, 137
Renoir, Auguste, painter, 208
renovatio, 223
Republic of 1848, 91, 205
Republic of Venice
    fall, 178, 202
residence patterns, 80
retailers, 186
revenues of state, 66–7, 178, 194, 222
    mainland, 67, 178
    and taxation, 66
    and war, 66
Rezzonico family, 178, 196
    feasts and balls, 198
Rialto
    bakeries, 42
    banks, 107
    bridge, 39, 128, 206
    commercial hub, 20, 23, 25, 38–40, 50
    endowed lectures, 59
    financial agencies, 38
    handicraft guilds, 83
    island, 3, 5, 39, 95, 159

market, 12, 20, 38–40, 44, 78, 99, 117,
    207, 213
    nineteenth-century development, 208
    prostitution, 165
    taverns & inns, 47–48, 160
rice, 43, 113, 175
rio, 5, 223
rio terrà, 223
ritual, 12, 54, 56, 71, 73, 88, 95, 97,
    100, 117, 143, 152, 160, 176,
    190, 224
    Marriage with the Sea, 31
    objects, 144
    penitential, 145
    sacred, 146
    Sensa, 31
riva, 223
Riva
    degli Schiavoni, 47, 49
    del Olio, 40
    del Vin, 40, 103
Rivoalto, 3–4, 51
roadway to Venice, 211
robbers, 187
Rococo style, 176
Rodriga, Daniel, Jewish consul, 92
Rogati. See Council of Pregadi
Romagna, 61
Roman Church
    pageantry, 188
Roman Empire, 1, 29
    eastern, 4
    western, 4
Romania, 29, 33, 47
Romanin, Samuele, historian, 205
Romano, Dennis, historian, 88
Romans, 1–2, 43, 127
Rome, 2, 19, 129, 135, 143, 156, 161
    ancient period, 189
    Byzantine churches, 3
    and Catholic-Reformation, 195
    collapse of, 128
    Counter-Reformation art, 195
    foundations, 2
    in iconography, 132
    model of classicism, 123, 136–7,
        139–40, 189

Rome (*cont.*)
  Mussolini, 211
  papal power, 137, 143, 152–3, 195
  and Piazza San Marco, 139
  political models, 127
  sack of, 75, 139, 159
Rore, Cipriano, composer, 147
Rosand, Ellen, musicologist, 189
Rossetti, Balthazar, 182
Rossetti, Carlo, 182
Rossini, Giacomo, composer, 206
rough play, 97
Rousseau, Jacques, philosopher, 180
Royal Gardens, 204
ruga, 223
Ruga, 9
  degli Oresi, 40
Ruggiero, Guido, historian, 103, 161
Ruskin, John, writer, 207
  Gothic revival, 206
  urban deterioration, 205
rye, 41, 117

Sacca San Girolamo, 213
sagomatore/i, 223
sailors, 43, 49, 76, 182, 185
saints, 160
  Augustine, 158
  Barbara, 56
  Demetrius, 128
  Dominic, 157
  Francis, 157
  George, 128
  Isidore, 142–43
  Justina, 142
  Lorenzo Giustiniani, 41
  Mark, 4, 128
  Nicholas, 29
  Roch, 41, 145
  Theodore, 4, 13, 20, 128
  Ursula, 88
salami, 45–46
Salieri, Antonio, composer, 191
salizzada, 223
Salizzada San Lio, 21, **23**, 25
salone (portego). See *portego (salone)*
salons, 147, 193

salt, 2, 10, 21, 34, 40–41, 46, 181, 186
  as a preservative, 43
  supervision, 55
San Giorgio, island, **Plate XIV**
sanctity, 155
Sand, George, novelist, 206
sandalo da s'ciopo, 8, 223
Sanità, 44, 113, 158, 165
Sanmicheli, Michele, architect,
     139–40
  Palazzo Grimani, **138**
Sansovino, Francesco, humanist, 2
Sansovino, Jacopo, architect, 139
  Ca' Corner della Ca' Grande, 137
  Church of San Geminiano, 204
  Giants' Staircase, Doge's Palace, 128
  Library of Saint Mark's, 132,
       Plate XIII
  Loggetta, 1537–66, 2
  Mint, **Plate XIII**
  Roman Renaissance style, 139–40
Santorio, Santorio, scientist, 183
Sanudo, Marino, diarist, 116, 121
Sanuto (Ve. Sanudo) family, 69
sapienti, 52
Sarai, 38
Sardi, Giovanni, architect, 209
Sardi, Giuseppe, architect, 196
Sargent, Paul, painter, 208
Sarpi, Paolo, Servite monk, 152, 156
  anti–Roman Church, 154
  biography, 153
  counselor of the Republic, 153
Save Venice, 212
Savii
  agli Ordini, 63
  di Consiglio, 64, 223
  di Terra Ferma, 63
  Grandi, 180
savio/ii, 223
Savoy, 76, 159
Savoyards, 177
Scala dei Giganti. *See* Giants' Staircase
Scalfarotto, Giovanni, architect, 196
Scamozzi, Vincenzo, architect, 139
  Library, **Plate XIII**
Schiavone/i, 9, 223

Schiele, Egon, painter, 208
Schola Italiana, **Plate X**
scholars
　Greek Orthodox, 80
Schubert, Franz, composer, 206
Schuman, Robert, composer, 206
Schutte, Anne, historian, 161, 172
sciences, 125, 154, 192
　Arab, 183
　and University of Padua, 183
scientists, gentlemen, 184
Scola, Giovanni, scholar, 183
Scully, Sally, historian, 161
sculpture
　Lombard, 136
　Tuscan, 136
scuola/e, 223
Scuole
　Albanesi, 27
　Carità, 27, 84, 132, 204
　Greci, 27
　of the innkeepers, 48
　Misericordia, 27, 84, 86
　San Giorgio degli Schiavoni, 27, 84, **85**
　San Giovanni Evangelista, 27, 84, 129,
　　134, 143
　San Marco, 27, 84, 132, 204, **Plate VII**
　San Rocco, 27, 84, 142, 145
　San Teodoro, 27, 84
scuole grandi, 27
scuole piccole, 27, 88
sea biscuits, 42–43
Sea of Japan, 34
Seaborne Empire
　governance of, 65
seapower
　Dutch, 174
　English, 174
　French, 174
　Hanseatic, 174
secretaries, 181
seduction, 103, 220
Selva, Giannantonio, architect, 204
Senate, 53, 55, 60, 63, 67, 70, 90, 92, 115,
　　118, 145, 153, 156–7, 177, 180, 219,
　　222, 224
　and Galileo Galilei, 183

and land reclamation, 183
and Quarantia Criminal, 223
and Redentore Church, 140
anti-Roman faction, 140
Serenissima, 224
Serlio, Sebastiano, architect, 139
servants, 78, 169
sestieri. *See* districts
sewage system, 6
sex crime, 172
sexual behavior, 103
sexuality
　regulation of, 172
　of women, 172
shields and armor, 108
shipbuilders, 18, 96
shipbuilding, 11, 18, 20, 22, 83, 99, 179,
　　184, 205
shipping
　industry, 182
　regulations, 31
ships, oceangoing, 186
shoes, high-heeled. *See zoccoli*
Sicily, 31, 106, 178, 186
Siena, 16, 68
Signac, Paul, painter, 208
Signori di Notte, 224
Signoria, 55, 63, 177, 224
　and Pien Collegio, 222
　and Quarantia Criminal, 223
Sile River, 10
silk, 38, 49
　and Anatolia, 50
　and Persian Gulf, 9
　bedcovers, 110
　berets, 122
　carpets, 108
　and China, 50
　fans, 198
　global market, 107
　home furnishings, 196
　hoods, 97
　and Iran, 50
　industry, 107, 136, 184–5, 205
　linings, 120
　origins, 49
　Ottoman influence, 109

silk (*cont.*)
   and patrician wives, 122
   and Persian Gulf, 49
   processes of manufacture, 186
   raw, 50
   ribbons, 119
   sleeves, 121
   socks, 122
   stockings, 198
   summer dress, 123
   thread, 185
   throwsters, 86
   trade, 30–4
   varieties, 49–50, 120
   wall paper, 197
   weavers, 9, 94
Silk Road, 16, 38
Silk Route. *See* Silk Road
Sinope, 65
slaves, 78
   capture, 30
   and Cornaro family, 37
   household, 78
   male, 78
   trade, 30, 34, 106
Slavs, 11, 49, 79
smuggling, 67
soap, 20, 107, 113, 184, 186
Soccorso, 158, 224
social class, 41, 48–49, 96, 115, 151, 160,
   168, 173
   and judicial process, 171
social networks, 98
socialization
   at confraternity halls, 79
   at guilds, 79
   at hospitals, 79
   modes, 77
   at the parish, 78
soda ash, 184
Soldaia, 34, 38
Soli, Giuseppe Maria, architect
   Napoleonic Ballroom, 204
Solomon
   in iconography, 16, 132
Solomon R. Guggenheim Foundation,
   208, 213

Somascan Order, 195
sorcerers, 155
sottoportego, 25, 224
souvenirs, 213
Spain, 76
   and Holy League, 106, 128
   invasions of Italy, 127
   moroccan shoes, 122
   Muslim, 43
   and syphillis, 154
   trade, 106
Spalato, 66, 92
Sparta, 34
spectacle, 99, 135, 144, 154, 176, 187,
   190, 195
spelt, 41–2, 113
Sperling, Jutta, historian, 73–4, 164,
   227, 229
spezieri. *See* apothecaries
Spice Islands, 37–38, 113
spices, 38, 40, 46–47, 108
   from Acre, 37
   and culinary revolution, 45
   inventories, 113
   jars, 109
   Levantine, 45
   and the poor, 45
   routes, 113
   sacchetti veneti, 45
   trade, 18, 29–31, 33, 68, 113
   triaca, 113
   and the wealthy, 46
   from the Yucatan, 112
Spinelli family, 136
spinners, 186
spinsters, 224
Sporades Archipelago, 65
squero, 8
Stampa, Gaspare, poet, 149
State Archives, 204–5, 213
State Attorneys, 53, 55–6, 67, 70, 103,
   171, 217
State Inquisitors, 181, 194
Stazio of Massagno, Abbondio, artist, **197**
Stazione Marittima, 207
Stendhal, 204
stick battles, 95

Stile Liberty Art Movement, 210
stockings
    Padua, 185
    Verona, 185
stonemasons, 22, 107
Strada Nuova, 207
strazzarie. See clothing, used
street names, 9
Strozzi, Giulio, composer, 189
Strozzi, Ruberto, 147
studioli, 108–9
stupro. See rape
sugar, 33, 37, 42, 47, 114, 181, 193
    Arabic origins, 46
    candy, 114
    and chocolate, 112
    and India, 46
    as a laxative, 46
    and macaroni, 46
    and Marco Polo, 38
    as a medicine, 113
    molds, 116
    refiners, 47, 107, 184
Sullam, Guido, architect, 210
Sullam, Jacob, 162
sumptuary legislation, 50, 116, 164–5, 222
    of 70, 121
    violations, 121
surgery, 183
sweet and sour, 44
Swiss cantons, 151
swordsmiths, 9, 94
Synagogue, Italian, **Plate X**
syphilis, 154, 158, 166
    in Venice, 165
Syria, 11, 33, 38, 49, 65, 106, 108–9, 181
    flower designs, 49
    and sugar, 46

tabarri. See clothing, cloaks
tableaux, 143, 156
Tabriz, 38
tailors, 84, 86, 94, 108, 159, 186
Tana, 65, 78
Tarabotti, Archangela, writer, 172
    biography, 164–5
    and enclosure, 163

Tartars, 16
taverns, 40, 47–48, 53, 76–77, 82, 84, 94, 99,
    115, 117, 139, 160, 187, 217, 220
tax farmers, 182
taxation, 55, 66, 91, 117, 123, 185
    Austrian, 203–4
    indirect, 65– 7
    revenue, 176
    of seaborne empire, 66
    supervision, 56
Tedesco/chi, 224
Tenedo, 65
Teodora, princess from
    Constantinople, 45
Teotochi Albrizzi, Isabella,
    saloniste, 203
terracotta, 186
Terranova, 41
Tessalonika, 65
textiles, 123
    and Asia, 49 50
    Dutch, 107
    English, 107
    and hierarchy, 49, 110
    Ottoman influence, 109
    as social markers, 49
    varieties, 49
theater, 187, 190
    stage scenery, 191
theaters, 189, 191
    La Fenice, 191
    Novissimo, 190
    San Cassiano, 189
    San Giovanni e Paolo, 190
    San Moisè, 190
    San Salvador, 190
Theatines, 156
Thebes, 34
thread, 185
    gold and silver, 50
tides, 3, 6, 9–10, 53, 212
Tiepolo, Baiamonte, 55, 203
Tiepolo, Domenico, painter, 198
Tiepolo, Gian Battista, painter, 199
Tiepolo, Giandomenico, painter, 203
Tiepolo, Giovanni Battista, painter,
    198, **199**

Tiepolo, Maria Francesca, archivist, 85
timber, 3, 11, 24, 30, 40, 174, 187, 205
  industry, 185
  trade, 40
Tine island, 178
Tintoretto, Jacopo Robusti, painter, 131,
    132
  Conquest of Constantinople in 1204, **30**
  Fellows of a Confraternity, **87**
  Miracles of St. Mark, 132
  Sala delle Quattro Porte, 131
Titian (Tiziano Vecellio), painter, 131
  *Portrait of a Woman Known as La
    Bella*, **119**
  Presentation of the Virgin, 132
tobacco industry, 205
tomatoes, 113
Tommaseo, Niccolò, revolutionary, 205
topo, 8, 224
tour buses, 213
tourist industry, 41, 176, 187, 191, 193, 201,
    206, 208, 210, 213
  and culture, 187
  medieval, 29
  and Venetian economy, 187
trade routes, **32–33, 36–37**
traghetto/i, 8, 213, 224
transportation by water, 8
travasadori. See bottlers
treasury, 53
Treaty of Karlowitz, 179
Trebisond, 65, 78
Trent, 151
trentaccie, 53
Trentino, 1, 76
Treviso, 61
Trieste, 179, 182, 205
  and shipping industry, 203
Trimignon, Alessandro, architect, 196
Tripoli, 108
Trojans, 1
Tron, Andrea, 180
Tron, Niccolò, textile manufacturer, 185
Tron family, 189
Troy, 61
Tunis, 106
Turchette, 9

turkey. *See* meat: turkey
Turks, 16, 40, 43
Turner, William, painter, 208
typhus, 154
tyranny
  paternal, 163
Tyre, 30

Ulm, 40
Umberto I, king of Italy, 208
underwear, 110
UNESCO, 212
University of Padua, 59, 111, 125, 147, 152,
    154, 159, 183, 207
  intellectual currents, 189
University of Venice, 213
Uskoks, 174, 176
usury, 182

vadimone/i, 105, 224
Vadori, Annette, writer, 202
Val Iperina, 185
Van Ranke, Leopold, historian, 205
vanilla beans, 113
vaporetti, 207, 213
Vecchi, Orazio, playwright, 168
Vecellio, Cesare, fashion writer, 118, 123
Vendramin family, 189
venereal disease, 158
Venetia, 2–3, 10
Venetian mainland, 43, **62–63**, 65, 68, 108,
    125, 130, 156, 176, 181, 183, 222
Veneto, 1, 10, 50, 62, 182, 185, 203, 205,
    207, 210
Veneto-Byzantine architecture, 3, 21, 24,
    27, 212
Veneto-Saracenic objects, 108
Venezia, Paolino di, Franciscan, 59
Venice
  Christian associations, 2
  city map, **7**
  cityscape, 213
  civic ideology, 73
  construction, 5
  cultural legacy, 213
  and deities of antiquity, 2
  economy, 174, 181, 186, 204, 205

a European state, 174
iconography, 131
landscape photo, 8, **Plate XVI**
morphology, 9, 212
as new Rome, 139
origins, 2, 4
relative economic decline, 184
restoration, 212
Roman associations, 2
sinking foundations, 212–13
territorial base, 2
the tourist magnet, 213
unification with Italy, 207
Venice in Peril, 212
Venier, Domenico, 149
Venier, Maffio, writer, 148
Venier family, 69
Venus
in iconography, 132
Verdi, Giuseppe, composer, 206
Verona, 10, 16, 26, 61, 68, 76, 196
Veronese, Paolo, painter, 113, 116, 131–2
    Allegory of Justice before Venice
        Enthroned, **134**
    Feast in the House of Levi, **152**
    Venice Receiving the Ducal Horn, **133**
Vesalius, 183
Via 22 Marzo, 207
Via Eugenia. See Via Garibaldi
Via Garibaldi, 204
Via Vittorio Emmanuele II. See Strada
    Nuova
Vicentine province, 180
Vicenza, 47, 61, 76, 185, 196
Victor Emmanuele II, king of Italy, 207
Vienna, 40
Villa Monplaisir, Lido, 210
villas and estates, 108, 135, 184, 196
    Barbaro, Maser, **107**
    Pisani, Strà, 198
Virgin Mary, 56, 88, 127, 145, 157, 195
    and city founding, 57
    representing Venice, 73
virginity, 57, 73, 155, 158, 173, 221
    and iconography, 190
    loss of, 166
    and political ideology, 57, 72

Vivaldi, Antonio, composer, 190–1
Volga River, 38
Voltaire, Françoise-Marie, philosopher,
    180, 192

Wagner, Richard, composer, 206
warehouses, 220, See also fondaco/i
    agricultural products, 50
    grain, 31, 42
    sea biscuits, 42
    wine, 40
wars
    Austrian Succession, 179
    Austro-Prussian, 205
    Chioggia, 83, 89
    Ferrara, 61
    Genoa, 56, 68
    of Religion, 151
    Spanish Succession, 67, 179
    Thirty Year's, 177
    World War II, 211
water
    carriers. See acquaroli
    power, 185
    supervision, 56
wax, 35, 122, 184
weavers, 50, 79, 84, 159, 186
    silk, 159
Welch, Evelyn, historian, 47
wells, 26–27, 99
wheat, 31, 37, 41–43
Whistler, James, painter, 208
Widmann family, 178
widows
    dress, 120
    pizzoccheri, 120
Willaert, Adrian, composer, 86, 146
wills, 50, 78, 93, 110, 169
wine, 43–44, 47
    barrel quality, 47, 117
    Friuli, 47
    Malvasia, 47
    sweet, 35
    trade, 33, 53, 84, 220
    varieties, 47
    vendors, 40, 47
    white, 47

witchcraft, 172
    as career option, 161
women
    "Century of Women," 192
    charismatic, 161
    and the fashion industry, 186
    and manufacture, 186
    and mining, 186
    and modesty, 120
    occupations, 76
    ornaments, 121
    patrician gift exchange, 73
    patrician inheritance
        laws, 69
    patrician widowhood, 70
    and poverty, 190
    and priests, 161
    and proto-industry, 186
    and raw silk, 50
    and salons, 192
    sexuality of, 163
    and scientific academies, 192
    and spirituality, 161
    and sumptuary legislation, 120
    and textile production, 49
wool, 35, 37, 47, 75, 110, 123

Bergamasc, 184
    coarse, 49, 123
    fulling, 185
    importation, 184
    industry, 107, 184
    Ottoman influence, 109
    summer clothing, 122
Wordsworth, William, poet, 201

Zan, Giovanni de, architect, **85**
Zannini, Andrea, historian, 186
Zante/Zakynthos, 224
Zara, 32
Zarlino, Giuseffo, composer, 147
Zattere/rafts, 145, 224
Zecchin, Vittorio, painter, 208
zecchino, 19, 224
Zen, Francesco, 137
Zeno, Apostolo, journalist, 192
Zeno, Renier, 154, 177
Ziani family, 24, 53
Zitelle Periclitanti, 158, 221
zoccoli, 50, 198
Zonta, 224
    of Council of Ten, 56, 219
    of Senate, 55, 139